CIVIL LIABILITY IN
TERRORISM-RELATED RISK

Today terrorism has become a worldwide phenomenon which does not stop at the European borders. Following the "9/11" attacks on the World Trade Center and terrorist attacks in Paris, Madrid and London, concerns have arisen in Europe about potential liability exposure for terrorism-related damage. This book tackles the problem of civil liability for damage caused by terrorist acts from several angles. The authors expertly deliver a comprehensive analysis of terrorism-related risk under international and EU law and the national tort law systems of seven representative EU Member States. They also provide a comparison of the situation in Europe with the liability environment in the US. Risk mitigation strategies are considered and critically assessed, as are alternative systems for redressing terrorism-related risks. The book concludes with a reflection on the analysis and presents possible strategies for future regulation by European lawmakers.

LUCAS BERGKAMP is a partner in Hunton & Williams LLP's Brussels office and heads the European Regulatory practice. His practice concentrates on regulatory issues, in particular environmental, health and safety, product regulation and related liability and transactional matters. He currently teaches in the Masters of European Energy and Environmental Law at KU Leuven.

MICHAEL FAURE is Professor of Comparative Private Law and Economics at Erasmus University Rotterdam, and Professor of Comparative and International Environmental Law at Maastricht University. He serves also as Academic Director of the Maastricht European Institute for Transnational Legal Research (METRO).

MONIKA HINTEREGGER is Professor of Civil Law at the Department of Civil Law, Foreign and International Private Law of the Karl Franzens University Graz, Austria. She has published abundantly on the topic of tort law and environmental liability.

NIELS PHILIPSEN is Associate Professor in Law and Economics at Maastricht University and serves as Vice-Director of the Maastricht European Institute for Transnational Legal Research (METRO).

CAMBRIDGE STUDIES IN INTERNATIONAL AND COMPARATIVE LAW

Established in 1946, this series produces high quality scholarship in the fields of public and private international law and comparative law. Although these are distinct legal sub-disciplines, developments since 1946 confirm their interrelations.

Comparative law is increasingly used as a tool in the making of law at national, regional and international levels. Private international law is now often affected by international conventions, and the issues faced by classical conflicts rules are frequently dealt with by substantive harmonisation of law under international auspices. Mixed international arbitrations, especially those involving state economic activity, raise mixed questions of public and private international law, while in many fields (such as the protection of human rights and democratic standards, investment guarantees and international criminal law) international and national systems interact. National constitutional arrangements relating to 'foreign affairs', and to the implementation of international norms, are a focus of attention.

The series welcomes works of a theoretical or interdisciplinary character, and those focusing on the new approaches to international or comparative law or conflicts of law. Studies of particular institutions or problems are equally welcome, as are translations of the best work published in other languages.

General Editors   James Crawford SC FBA *Whewell Professor of International Law, Faculty of Law, University of Cambridge*

                        John S. Bell FBA *Professor of Law, Faculty of Law, University of Cambridge*

A list of books in the series can be found at the end of this volume.

CIVIL LIABILITY IN EUROPE FOR TERRORISM-RELATED RISK

LUCAS BERGKAMP, MICHAEL FAURE,
MONIKA HINTEREGGER AND NIELS PHILIPSEN

CAMBRIDGE
UNIVERSITY PRESS

University Printing House, Cambridge CB2 8BS, United Kingdom

One Liberty Plaza, 20th Floor, New York, NY 10006, USA

477 Williamstown Road, Port Melbourne, VIC 3207, Australia

314-321, 3rd Floor, Plot 3, Splendor Forum, Jasola District Centre, New Delhi - 110025, India

79 Anson Road, #06-04/06, Singapore 079906

Cambridge University Press is part of the University of Cambridge.

It furthers the University's mission by disseminating knowledge in the pursuit of education, learning and research at the highest international levels of excellence.

www.cambridge.org
Information on this title: www.cambridge.org/9781107496552

First published 2015
First paperback edition 2018

A catalogue record for this publication is available from the British Library

Library of Congress Cataloging in Publication data
Civil liability in Europe for terrorism-related risk / Lucas Bergkamp, Michael Faure, Monika Hinteregger and Niels Philipsen.
pages   cm. – (Cambridge studies in international and comparative law)
Includes bibliographical references and index.
ISBN 978-1-107-10044-2
1. Terrorism – European Union countries.   2. Terrorism.   3. Liability (Law) – European Union countries.   4. Risk (Insurance) – European Union countries.   I. Bergkamp, Lucas, author.
II. Faure, Michael (Michael G.) author.   III. Hinteregger, Monika, author.   IV. Philipsen, Niels, 1975– author.
KJE8780.C58   2015
344.2405′325 – dc23   2015012533

ISBN 978-1-107-10044-2 Hardback
ISBN 978-1-107-49655-2 Paperback

CONTENTS

INTRODUCTION

LUCAS BERGKAMP, MICHAEL FAURE, MONIKA
HINTEREGGER AND NIELS PHILIPSEN

0.1. The problems posed by terrorism for civil liability

Terrorism raises a potential for large-scale damage. In the US, the "9/11" attacks on the World Trade Center resulted in massive property damage, thousands of cases of personal injury, pain and suffering and enormous consequential damage, including billions in lost profits.[1] Lawsuits were filed seeking compensation of damages totalling over one billion dollars. Among the parties sued in these lawsuits were not only public authorities, but also security firms and an aircraft manufacturer. The magnitude of this litigation caused concerns in the US over unlimited liability of security firms, which was believed to create disincentives for firms to develop and introduce new security technology. In response to these issues, the US Safety Act was enacted. This regime is intended to offer security companies protection against liability exposure.

Following these US developments and terrorist attacks in Paris, Madrid and London,[2] concerns have arisen in Europe about potential liability exposure for terrorism-related damage, which has been called "enterprise-threatening".[3] The group of potentially liable parties is broad and includes operators of facilities such as airports, train stations, nuclear power plants, industrial installations, governments responsible for security and private security firms. Because the US Safety Act focuses on security technology, attention has been concentrated in particular on the security industry, broadly defined to include any company that develops and implements security measures to protect against terrorism.[4] Against this background,

---

[1] www.iags.org/costof911.html; www.nytimes.com/interactive/2011/09/08/us/sept-11-reck oning/cost-graphic.html?_r=0.

[2] http://www.lefigaro.fr/international/2014/09/24/01003–20140924ARTFIG00347-la-france-a-deja-ete-la-cible-de-multiples-attaques-terroristes.php#; www.elmundo.es/documentos /2004/03/espana/atentados11m/hechos.html; www.theguardian.com/uk/july7.

[3] Bergkamp, Faure, Hinteregger and Philipsen (eds.) 2013, 291–306.

[4] There currently is no generally accepted definition of the security industry; this sector of industry, for instance, is not covered as such by the main statistical nomenclatures.

this book analyses civil liability for terrorism-related risk under international and European Union law and the laws of several representative
Member States. In addition, we compare the liability environment in
Europe to the situation in the US, which, as noted, thought it necessary to
provide for liability protection for industry through specific legislation.

Terrorism involves intentional harm aimed at creating or augmenting
fear and disrupting social life. The targets of terrorist attacks are selected
on the basis of factors such as the level of security and the ability to cause
extensive harm if security measures can be successfully circumvented.
Terrorist attacks are often conducted in response to State action (e.g.,
military intervention in another State). These factors explain why terrorism is a special category of risk that is not just a matter of private concern
for operators that may be affected by it. Liability for terrorism-related risk
poses a challenge for civil liability because it can result in large-scale catastrophic damage, the size of which can easily exceed the net asset value of a
liable corporation. As a result, in addition to liability, insurance or other

The market for security goods and services has three distinctive features: (1) it is a highly
fragmented market and divided along national or even regional boundaries; (2) it is an
institutional market, and buyers tend to be public and semi-public authorities; and (3) this
market has a strong societal dimension, as personal safety is regarded as a highly sensitive
area. The security industry provides products (e.g., detection equipment, alarm systems)
and services (e.g., guarding services), and addresses man-made and natural risks; this
book, however, covers only man-made risks, i.e. terrorism-related risk. The Commission
Action Plan for innovative and competitive Security Industry lists the following: aviation
security; maritime security; border security; critical infrastructure protection; counter-
terror intelligence (including cybersecurity and communication); crisis management/civil
protection; physical security protection; and protective clothing. In this book, only the
industry producing goods and services used for preventing mitigating damages by terrorism
and organised crime is considered as the "security industry". Thus, the security industry
can be defined to include "providers of products and services that are specifically intended
to reduce the risks of intentional damage caused by terrorism and organized crime in the
following areas: aviation security, maritime security, border security, critical infrastructure
protection, and physical security protection". The following products and services are
regarded as being provided by the security industry: scanning and detection equipment
for use with passengers and cargo (or other goods), including products for weapons and
explosives detection, chemical and biological risk detection, and radionuclide detection,
as well as services related to all of the above. The following industries are NOT part of the
security industry: defence industry, building monitoring and management industry, plant
automation and control industry, scientific automation industry, ICT industry, software,
information technologies, other providers of products and services that are not specifically
intended to reduce the risks of intentional damage caused by terrorism and organised
crime, such as providers of fences, reinforced glass, etc. Note, however, that this definition
has been used only to guide thinking generally; the analysis in this book has gone beyond
the scope of the definition.

compensation arrangements may have a role to play. Even a relatively small error, oversight or defect, as a result of which terrorists can execute their devious plans, can result in huge liability exposure. Moreover, terrorists, of course, intentionally cause harm and look for the weakest link in the chain of security (and there always is a weakest link). Operators of facilities that are exposed to terrorist attacks (e.g., airports, train stations, nuclear power plants, chemical plants, etc.) and security firms cannot necessarily limit their liability exposure by contract, in particular where contractual liability limitations have no effect vis-à-vis third parties that have suffered damage due to terrorism. Needless to say, recourse against the terrorists is almost always futile.

Civil liability does not specifically deal with terrorism-related risk. Consequently, the general liability concepts (negligence, defective product, etc.) have to be interpreted and applied to the specific case of damage caused by terrorists. The aspects that make civil liability for terrorism-related risk fairly unique may or may not influence the application of civil liability in these kinds of cases. On the one hand, the incentives created by liability will generally have a positive effect on the prevention measures undertaken by potentially liable parties. On the other hand, the question should be asked whether there is a point beyond which liability serves no further useful purpose. If there is any such point or situation, the issue arises whether some limitation of liability would be justified, in particular where other compensation mechanisms are available. Whether such a point can be identified is a function of, inter alia, the specifics of the application of civil liability to damage caused by terrorism-related risk. Attention to this issue is therefore warranted.

0.2.   Potential claimants and potentially liable parties

As the discussion above suggests, terrorism-related risk is a complex risk that is beyond the control of any individual entity. Effective combating terrorism therefore requires effective action by the government as well as by various private parties. In other words, both governments and private parties may have responsibilities and, thus, potentially also civil law duties of care in relation to terrorism-related risk. Since all citizens may become victims of terrorist attacks, there is a strong collective interest in prevention of terrorism damage and the handling of damages caused by such attacks. Given this social interest, many jurisdictions have adopted laws and policies to deal with aspects of terrorism, both in terms of prevention and compensation. Indeed, as the analysis in this book shows, the framework for dealing with terrorist risk and terrorism-related damages consists of a series of regulatory and liability programmes and mechanisms. That does not mean, however, that civil liability for damage caused by terrorism-related risk is limited by these other programmes and mechanisms; rather, they tend to supplement civil liability.

Under civil liability law, the categories of both potential claimants and potentially liable parties are wide. Potential claimants include employees, customers, consumers[5] who may have a contractual relationship with the liable party, as well as neighbours, users,[6] and other third parties, who do not have a contractual relation with the liable person. The contractual relation may make a difference since it may define the obligations of the potentially liable party and the scope of its liability for damages caused (e.g., through liability caps, standards); the issue is whether and, if so, to what extent, contracts can deviate from the extra-contractual liability regime. Where there is no contract, of course, the extra-contractual liability provisions apply to their full extent in any event. Potentially liable parties include operators of facilities, such as airports and train stations, non-security service providers operating at such facilities, such as airlines and train operators and security providers, including both service providers (e.g., guarding services) and suppliers of equipment (e.g., suppliers of detection equipment). The contractual and extra-contractual liability relations between these groups are depicted in Figure 1.

In this book, we do not address the full potential scope of liability of the State and governments. We briefly discuss Member State liability under EU law for failure to properly implement provisions of EU law. In addition, the liability of the State is covered insofar as governments or any public agencies serve as operators of facilities that may be the target of terrorist attacks, and also insofar as they may provide security services, such as guarding, subject to any special legal provisions applicable to the liability of the State.

0.3.   Structure of analysis

Accordingly, this book examines European liability laws as they relate to terrorism-related harms. An important issue is to what extent facility

---

[5] Consumers are customers, but customers are not necessarily consumers (e.g., businesses and other professional users).

[6] Users may be, but are not necessarily, customers or consumers.

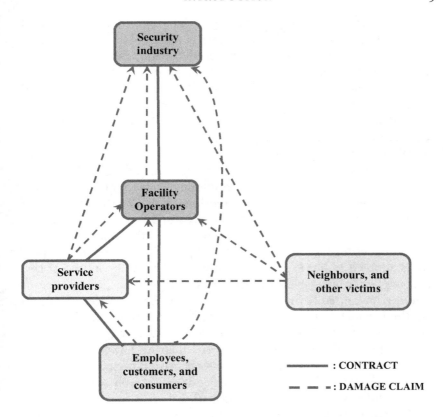

- *Security industry* includes service providers (guarding services, etc.) and product suppliers (suppliers of detection equipment, etc.).

- *Facility operators* include operators of industrial facilities and infrastructure (including airports).

- *Service providers* include airlines and train operators.

Figure 1   Potential claimants and potentially liable parties

operators and security firms, both manufacturers of security goods and providers of security services, are exposed to liability for terrorism-related damage in Europe. The focus is on both potential liability exposure and actual cases. Key questions are: What standards of liability apply? What types of damages are recoverable? Are any defences available? How are cross-border cases handled?

The book, which, to a substantial degree, is based on a study conducted by the authors,[7] has three main parts, each comprising several chapters. In Part I, the questions identified in the preceding paragraph, as well as some related questions, are analysed under the relevant international treaties and EU legislation. Chapter 1 discusses civil liability for terrorism-related risk (TRR) under international law. Some international treaties deal with issues that may be relevant to exposure to civil liability for terrorism-related risk. From a policy perspective, international treaties may suggest models for designing appropriate liability systems for such risk. This chapter reviews several international treaties, including civil aviation, nuclear liability and oil pollution conventions. For each of these regimes, we review the key substantive law provisions, including the definition of the liable persons and the covered damage, and pay specific attention to the exemptions and defences relevant to TRR. Further, this chapter also reviews issues relating to jurisdiction and procedure. A similar perspective is adopted to analyse EU legislation in Chapter 2. Under EU law, there are two liability-related instruments that could be directly relevant to terrorism-caused harm: the Environmental Liability Directive (ELD) and the Product Liability Directive (PLD). In addition, Member States could be exposed to liability under a doctrine developed by the European Court of Justice, the so-called "*Francovich*" doctrine. Likewise, secondary EU legislation may impose obligations on private parties that help to prevent terrorist attacks. If private parties do not comply with such obligations, the spectre of liability under national law arises. In Chapter 2, the EU law relevant to the liability for TRR is analysed. The Product Liability Directive and the Environmental Liability Directive are also analysed. With respect to jurisdiction and procedure, which are relevant to cross-border cases of damage caused by TRR, this chapter discusses the EU legislation regarding cross-border claims and enforcement of judgments.

Since international and EU law provide only part of the picture, Part II turns to the laws of the civil law jurisdictions of seven EU jurisdictions: England and Wales, France, Germany, The Netherlands, Poland, Spain and Sweden. General and specific liability laws, as well as relevant court cases, are analysed to determine the scope of the liability exposure of security providers and operators of facilities. A separate chapter provides a horizontal summary and comparative analysis of the various national liability regimes. As civil liability, in the final analysis, is predominantly a

---

[7] Bergkamp, Faure, Hinteregger and Philipsen (eds.) 2013, 291–306.

national law issue, this is the largest part of the book. Throughout this part, the main focus is on how key substantive topics are handled under the laws of the Member States concerned. This approach allows direct comparisons between the national regimes. National law imposes liability on one or more persons that have some relation with or responsibility for the damage that occurred. In the case of negligence, this typically is the person (or persons) that acted negligently. In the case of strict liability, the category is described in terms of status such as operator or owner. The scope of liability of these categories of liable persons is defined by a number of concepts. First, a key issue is the scope of the damage covered by particular liability regimes. Types of damage that may potentially be covered include material (physical) damage to property, personal injury (including medical expenses and disability), pain and suffering, and economic damages (lost profits). Further, except where liability is absolute (which is rare), the law provides for certain exemptions or exclusions and allows liable persons to invoke certain defences. National law imposes liability only if there is a causal relation between an event and the damage. Thus, causal concepts, including proximate cause and remoteness, are directly relevant to the scope of liability. Another key issue is how liability relates to regulation. This relation can work in two directions: regulatory compliance could protect potentially liable persons against claims and non-compliance could expose them to claims.

By way of introduction to Part II, Chapter 3 provides an overview of the various national liability regimes and of the tort law systems of analysed Member States. It furthermore surveys the bases of liability, relationship between tort liability and regulation, causation, attribution of liability, damages and available remedies and alternative compensation mechanisms. Chapter 4 then reviews specific cases that are relevant to the issue of liability for terrorism-related risk. The final chapter of this part provides a brief summary and comparison of the various national regimes with particular attention to the liability of the operator of dangerous activities, liability of security providers, liability for pure economic loss and environmental damage, and liability for damage caused by a natural disaster or an act of terror.

Part III of the book assesses the current liability regimes from legal and economic perspectives. The question is posed whether the existing laws are just and efficient. In answering this key question, this book treats liability as an instrument that pursues social goals, such as deterrence, compensation and risk-spreading. Where liability is excessive, security firms could decide to withdraw from the market or reduce the pace of innovation, which would have adverse effects on security. On the other hand, where liability is too lax, security firms may underinvest in security. Should the existing laws be amended and liability be limited? If this were done, where could potential problems arise? What solutions are available to address any such issues? The book examines liability limitations and alternatives to liability, including the US Safety Act regime, compensation funds and other mechanisms. The final chapters evaluate the security industry's liability exposure and the need for protection, as well as the potential role of the European Union in matters of terrorism-related liability, insurance and related issues.

Because this book combines international/EU and national law, and positive law and policy perspectives, it covers a large territory in an integrated fashion. The intended readership is therefore large and includes lawyers, policymakers, consultants, academics, insurers and corporate executives. It should also be useful to researchers with an interest in civil liability. Some familiarity with civil liability will be assumed, although the key concepts are generally explained in the context of terrorism-related risk.

PART I

International and EU law

1

Liability for terrorism-related risks under international law

MICHAEL FAURE, JING LIU* AND NIELS PHILIPSEN

In this chapter, we review the international law that is relevant to terrorism-related risk (TRR). We will therefore analyse different treaties concerning civil aviation, nuclear safety and environmental matters, which may have relevance both for operators and the security industry that may be confronted with TRR. We review the key substantive law provisions, including the basis of liability, the liable persons and the damage covered; and we pay explicit attention to exclusions and defences as well as to the existence of financial security and compensation mechanisms. The goal of this chapter is to analyse to what extent international treaties may have some relevance for TRR, both concerning the exposure of operators and concerning the influence on the liability of the security industry. We will also examine to what extent the features of these particular liability regimes may be interesting to consider in a possible future liability regime.

In turn, we deal with treaties related to civil aviation (1.1.), nuclear liability (1.2.), environmental liability and more particularly marine oil pollution (1.3.), and other relevant treaties (1.4.). The last section addresses the relevance of those treaties for both operators and the security industry and examines features that are of particular relevance in defining the scope and limits of liability (1.5.).

---

* Jing Liu is a postdoctoral researcher at Wuhan University China and a postdoctoral researcher in the programme on Behavioural Approaches to Contract and Tort at the Erasmus School of Law, Rotterdam (The Netherlands). She studied law at the Law School of Wuhan University and completed a doctoral dissertation on the compensation for ecological damage. She has published widely on issues of environmental damage and nuclear accidents.

1.1.   Civil aviation

In this section, two conventions will be discussed: the Rome Convention of 1952 (1.1.1.) and the Montreal Convention of 1999 (1.1.2.).

1.1.1.   *1952 Convention on Damage Caused by Foreign Aircraft to Third Parties on the Surface*

1.1.1.1.   Brief summary of the regime

The Rome Convention establishes a liability and compensation framework for damage caused by aircrafts to third parties on the surface. With the development of civil aviation, people started to realise the potential damage caused by aircrafts both to the persons and property on board and to third parties on the surface. The Convention for the Unification of Certain Rules relating to International Carriage by Air was concluded in Warsaw in 1929 and applies to damage to international carriage of persons, baggage and cargo. Damage to third parties on the surface has a different characteristic, in that usually an ex-ante contract cannot be reached between the potential injurers and victims. A separate liability regime was therefore established in 1952: the Rome Convention. This convention was later revised by the 1978 Protocol to Amend the Convention on Damage Caused by Foreign Aircraft to Third Parties on the Surface (1978 Protocol). Another attempt was made to further revise the convention and an outcome was reached in 2009: the 2009 Convention on Compensation for Damage Caused by Aircraft to Third Parties. However, this new convention has not come into force yet. Hence the analysis here focuses on the 1952 Rome Convention and its 1978 Protocol.

1.1.1.2.   Basis of liability

Strict liability is established under the 1952 Rome Convention. Article 1 requires the victim to prove only that "the damage was caused by an aircraft in flight or by any person or thing falling there from", but not the negligence of the injurer. In other words, the injurer is strictly liable, irrespective of whether a fault can be established or not. To establish liability, the convention requires that the damage is a direct consequence of the incident. If the damage is caused by "the mere fact of passage of the aircraft through the airspace in conformity with existing air traffic regulations", liability cannot be established.[1]

---

[1]   Article 1 of the 1952 Rome Convention.

1.1.1.3. Liable persons (attribution of liability)

The Rome Convention attributes liability to aircraft operators. The term "operator" is defined as "the person who was making use of the aircraft at the time the damage was caused, provided that if control of the navigation of the aircraft was retained by the person from whom the right to make use of the aircraft was derived, whether directly or indirectly, that person shall be considered the operator".[2] The registered owner can be regarded as the operator unless he proves that some other person was the operator.[3] The 1978 Protocol further clarifies the situation for State-owned aircrafts. In those cases, the person to whom the aircraft has been entrusted for operation is the liable party.[4]

With the exception of deliberate acts or omissions, Article 9 of the convention constitutes the only basis of liability for the operators. However, this convention does not expressly exclude liability of other parties and it does not prejudice the right of recourse against other parties (Article 10).

1.1.1.4. Damage covered

The Rome Convention has no provision that directly clarifies the scope of compensable damage. But when discussing the priority in awarding different types of damage, the convention mentioned several titles: loss of life, personal injury and damage to property.[5]

Liability caps are established under the Rome Convention according to the weight of the aircraft. They are defined in Table 2.[6] The Rome Convention also establishes a cap for loss of life or personal injury, which is capped at 500,000 francs per person killed or injured.[7] Liable parties will lose their right of limitation if the damage is caused by the deliberate act or omission of the operator, his servants or agents (in the course of their employment and within the scope of their authority). If a person wrongfully takes and makes use of an aircraft without the consent of the person entitled to use it, the former's liability is also unlimited.[8]

---

[2] Article 2 (2a) of the 1952 Rome Convention.
[3] Article 2(3) of the 1952 Rome Convention.
[4] Article II of the 1978 Protocol.
[5] Article 14 of the 1952 Rome Convention.
[6] Article 11(1) of the 1952 Rome Convention.
[7] Article 11(2) of the 1952 Rome Convention.
[8] Article 12 of the 1952 Rome Convention.

Table 2 *Liability caps under Rome Convention*

Aircraft weighing less than (including) 1000 kg	More than 1000 and not exceeding 6000 kg	More than 6000 and not exceeding 20,000 kg	More than 20000 and not exceeding 50,000 kg	Over 50,000 kg
500,000 francs	500,000 francs plus 4000 francs per kg over 1000 kg	2,500,000 francs plus 400 francs per kg over 6000 kg	6,000,000 francs plus 150 francs per kg over 20,000 kg	10,500,000 francs plus 100 per kg over 50,000 kg

Table 3 *Liability caps under 1978 Protocol*

Aircraft weighing 2000 kg or less	More than 2000 kg and not exceeding 6000 kg	More than 6000 kg and not exceeding 30,000 kg	More than 30,000 kg
300,000 SDRs	300,000 SDRs plus 175 SDRs per kg over 2000 kg	1,000,000 SDRs plus 62.5 SDRs per kg over 6000 kg	2,500,000 SDRs plus 65 SDRs per kg over 30,000 kg

If the total claims exceed the limit of liability, a priority rule shall apply: (1) if the claims concern only death or personal injury or concern only property damage, such claims are reduced in proportion to their respective amounts; (2) if the claims concern both types of damage, one half of the total sum distributable shall be appropriated preferentially to meet claims in respect of loss of life and personal injury; the remainder shall be distributed proportionally among all the remaining claims.[9]

The 1978 Protocol increased the liability caps as shown in Table 3.

The cap for loss of life/personal injury per person was increased to 125,000 SDRs (Special Drawing Rights).[10] The priority rule in case the liability limit is exceeded was adapted as well: it remains the same when claims concern only one type of damage; if claims concern both personal injury and property damage, a priority is given to personal injury.

[9] Article 14 of the 1952 Rome Convention.   [10] Article III of the 1978 Protocol.

Only if there is still a remainder after payment for personal injury will proportionate compensation be made to property damage.[11]

1.1.1.5.   Exclusions and defences

The Rome Convention allows a very limited defence. Article 5 states that "[a]ny person who would otherwise be liable under the provisions of this convention shall not be liable if the damage is the direct consequence of armed conflict or civil disturbance, or if such person has been deprived of the use of the aircraft by act of public authority." The usual defences, such as natural disaster or acts of terrorism, are not mentioned. Comparative negligence is established: if the damage is caused solely or partly by the victims or their servants/agents, liability can be exonerated or reduced. However, if the damage is caused by the negligence/deliberation of a servant or agent of the victim and the victim can prove that his servant or agent was acting outside the scope of his authority, liability cannot be exonerated or reduced.[12]

1.1.1.6.   Financial security and compensation mechanisms

The Rome Convention establishes a mandatory financial security system. Any Contracting Parties may require the aircraft operator to maintain insurance coverage for the liability for damage in its territory up to the liability limitation.[13] The insurer needs to be authorised to effect such insurance under the law of the State where the aircraft is registered or the State of the insurer's residence or principal place of business.[14] In addition to insurance, operators can also use other financial security mechanisms, such as a cash deposit, bank guarantee or guarantee by the Contracting State where the aircraft is registered.[15] The Rome Convention allows direct action by victims against the insurer or guarantor, if the guarantee is valid and the operator is bankrupt. However, this does not prejudice the law governing the contract of insurance/guarantee concerning the right of direct action.[16]

---

[11] Article IV of the 1978 Protocol.
[12] Article 6 of the 1952 Rome Convention.
[13] Article 15(1) of the 1952 Rome Convention.
[14] Article 15(2) of the 1952 Rome Convention.
[15] Article 15(4) of the 1952 Rome Convention.
[16] Article 16(5) of the 1952 Rome Convention.

1.1.1.7.   Relevance of the Rome Convention

Damage may be caused by the failure of alarm or security measures aimed at the prevention of a terrorist attack. According to the convention, terrorism or natural disasters cannot exonerate the operators from liability. Hence, the operator in principle remains liable. The security industry will not be held liable directly. However, recourse is still allowed under the convention. The security industry could therefore be asked to pay in accordance with applicable law in addition to the convention.

1.1.2.   *1999 Convention for the Unification of Certain Rules for International Carriage by Air*

1.1.2.1.   Brief summary of the regime

A liability regime for international carriage of persons, baggage or cargo was established in Warsaw in 1929 when commercial aviation was still in its infancy. Afterwards, a series of revisions was made from the 1950s to the 1970s. With the development of civil aviation, these instruments seemed inappropriate to address the liability and compensation issues. Under the auspices of the International Civil Aviation Organization, a new convention was concluded to modernize and consolidate the Warsaw Convention and related instruments in Montreal in 1999: the Convention for the Unification of Certain Rules for International Carriage by Air (Montreal Convention). According to its Preamble, the Montreal Convention has two aims: to ensure the protection of an equitable compensation for consumers of international carriage by air and to promote the development of international air transport operation. It applies to international carriage of persons, baggage or cargo performed by aircraft. To satisfy the requirement of "international", the places of departure and destination are either in different States Parties, or in the same State Party but the agreed stopping place is in another State.[17]

1.1.2.2.   Basis of liability

The Montreal Convention establishes three types of liability: liability for death and injury of passengers, damage to baggage and damage to cargo.

Strict liability is established for death and bodily injury of a passenger if the damage happened on board the aircraft or in the course of embarking or disembarking. In case of destruction or loss of, or damage to, baggage,

---

[17] Article 1 of the Montreal Convention.

the basis of liability depends on the checking status of the baggage. Strict liability applies for checked-in baggage. For unchecked baggage and personal items, the carrier is only liable if fault can be found for the carrier or its servants/agents.[18] Strict liability is also established for the destruction or loss of, or damage to, cargo if it was caused during the carriage by air. The period of carriage by air does not include any carriage by land, sea or inland waterway performed outside an airport.[19] The carrier is also liable for damage caused by delay in the carriage by air of passengers, baggage or cargo.[20]

1.1.2.3.   Liable persons (attribution of liability)

Articles 17–19 of the Montreal Convention impose liability on air carriers. If the carriage by air is performed by another person rather than by the contracting carrier, both the contracting carrier and actual carrier shall be held liable: the former for the whole of the carriage contemplated in the contract and the latter solely for the carriage which it performs.[21] Liability can also be addressed against the servants or agents of the contracting/actual carriers. The convention does not prejudice the right of recourse against any other person.[22]

1.1.2.4.   Damage covered

The Montreal Convention covers damage to passengers, baggage or cargo. It also applies to the delay in the carriage. Liability caps are established respectively for those types of damage.

The Carrier is liable for each passenger for death or injury of passengers up to 100,000 SDRs. For the amount in excess of 100,000 SDRs, the carrier can be exonerated from liability if it can prove that the damage was not due to the negligence or wrongful act or omission of the carrier or its servants/agents, or the damage was solely due to the negligence or other wrongful act or omission of a third party.[23]

For the damage caused by delay in the carriage of persons, the liability for each passenger is limited to 4150 SDRs (Article 22(1)). In cases of the carriage of baggage, the liability cap for destruction, loss or delay is set at 1000 SDRs per passenger, unless an ex-ante declaration allowing higher compensation exists (Article 22(2)). Similarly, for the carriage of cargo, the liability for destruction, loss or delay is limited to 17 SDRs

---

[18] Article 17 of the Montreal Convention.   [19] Article 18 of the Montreal Convention.
[20] Article 19 of the Montreal Convention.   [21] Article 40 of the Montreal Convention.
[22] Article 37 of the Montreal Convention.   [23] Article 21 of the Montreal Convention.

per kg, unless an ex-ante declaration allowing higher compensation exists (Article 22(3)).

In cases of the carriage of passengers and baggage, the carrier will lose its right to limit liability if "the damage resulted from an act or omission of the carrier, its servants or agents, done with intent to cause damage or recklessly and with knowledge that damage would probably result; provided that, in the case of such act or omission of a servant or agent, it is also proved that such servant or agent was acting within the scope of its employment".[24]

According to Article 25 of the Montreal Convention, a higher liability cap or no liability cap is also allowed if the carriage contract stipulates so.

1.1.2.5.   Exclusions and defences

The Montreal Convention in Article 20 allows for a comparative negligence defence. If "the damage was caused or contributed to by the negligence or other wrongful act or omission of the person claiming compensation, or the person from whom he or she derives his or her rights", the carrier's liability can be exonerated or reduced.

1.1.2.6.   Financial security and compensation mechanisms

A mandatory insurance framework is established under Article 50 of the Montreal Convention. States Parties shall require their carriers to maintain adequate insurance coverage for their liability.

1.1.2.7.   Relevance of the Montreal Convention

Similar to the Rome Convention, the Montreal Convention is also relevant to operators and to the security industry in case of damage caused by the failure of alarming or security measures during a terrorist attack or natural disaster. Again, terrorism and natural disasters are not valid defences and air carriers are liable parties. Recourse against security companies is allowed. Hence the security industry could be asked to pay via recourse by the carriers.

---

[24] Article 22(5) of the Montreal Convention.

1.2.   Nuclear liability

1.2.1.   Summary of the regime

In the 1960s, two international compensation regimes were established for nuclear damage: the Organisation for Economic Co-operation and Development (OECD) regime and the International Atomic Energy Agency (IAEA) regime. Under the auspices of the OECD Nuclear Energy Agency (NEA), the Convention on Third Party Liability in the Field of Nuclear Energy of 29 July 1960 (Paris Convention)[25] and the Brussels Supplementary Convention to the Paris Convention on Third Party Liability in the Field of Nuclear Energy of 31 January 1963 (Brussels Supplementary Convention) have been developed.[26] The second regime was developed under the aegis of IAEA: the Vienna Convention on Civil Liability for Nuclear Damage of 21 May 1963 (Vienna Convention).[27] Those two regimes are usually called the first generation of nuclear liability conventions.[28] On the one hand, those two regimes have made an effort in establishing international/regional regimes for nuclear liability; on the other hand, they have obvious limitations in terms of restricted geographical scope, narrow definition of nuclear damage and an insufficient amount of available compensation.[29]

Since the Paris Convention and the Brussels Convention are established under the auspices of the OECD/NEA, they are regionally confined to Western Europe, Slovenia and Turkey. The Vienna Convention's scope is worldwide. A few principles proposed in the Preliminary Report and in the Harvard Report were accepted under those two conventions.

According to the Paris Convention, the nuclear operator is liable for "damage to or loss of life of any person" and "damage to or loss of any property other than" onsite damage or property used in connection with the installations.[30]

The Chernobyl accident in 1986 triggered the intensive discussion about those limitations and later a revision process of the existing regimes was initiated. The so-called second generation of nuclear liability

---

[25] Paris Convention on Third Party Liability in the Field of Nuclear Energy, 956 UNTS 251 (Paris Convention).

[26] Convention Supplementary to the Paris Convention on Third Party Liability in the Field of Nuclear Energy, 1041 UNTS 358 (Brussels Complementary Convention).

[27] Vienna Convention on Civil Liability for Nuclear Damage, 1063 UNTS 358 (Vienna Convention).

[28] *See* Faure and Vanden Borre 2008.   [29] *See* Vanden Borre 2010, 192.

[30] Article III(a), the Paris Convention.

conventions was established thereafter. Those conventions consist of the Joint Protocol Relating to the Application of the Vienna Convention and the Paris Convention (Joint Protocol),[31] the Protocol to Amend the 1963 Vienna Convention on Civil Liability for Nuclear Damage (the Protocol to the Vienna Convention),[32] the Convention on Supplementary Compensation for Nuclear Damage (CSC),[33] the Protocol to amend the Convention on Third Party Liability in the Field of Nuclear Energy of 29 July 1960 (the Protocol to the Paris Convention)[34] and the Protocol to amend the Convention of 31 January 1963 supplementary to the Convention of 29 July 1960 on Third Party Liability in the Field of Nuclear Energy (the Protocol to the Brussels Supplementary Convention).[35]

These new conventions and protocols are designed to overcome the deficiency of the first generation of nuclear liability conventions. However, the revisions have made eight international conventions available for nuclear liability, which lead to a so-called "labyrinth of international conventions" dealing with nuclear liability issues.[36] Moreover, among the five new conventions, only two have come into force: the Joint Protocol entered into force in 1992 and the Protocol to the Vienna Convention came into force in 2003. Until now, only five countries have ratified the Protocol to the Vienna Convention (Argentina, Belarus, Latvia, Morocco and Romania) and none of them have a significant nuclear generating capacity.[37] Many large nuclear generating countries are still not members of any of those conventions, such as the US, Canada, Japan, China, South Korea, Russia, South Africa and Switzerland.

---

[31] Joint Protocol relating to the Application of the Vienna Convention and the Paris Convention, 42 Nuc. L. Bull. 56 (1988) (Joint Protocol).

[32] Vienna Convention as Amended by the Protocol of 12 September 1997 to Amend the Vienna Convention on Civil Liability for Nuclear Damage (the Protocol to Vienna Convention).

[33] Convention on Supplementary Compensation for Nuclear Damage (CSC).

[34] Paris Convention on Third Party Liability in the Field of Nuclear Energy as amended by the Additional Protocol of 28 January 1964 and by the Protocol of 16 November 1982, and by the Protocol of 12 February 2004 (the Protocol to the Vienna Convention).

[35] Convention Supplementary to the Paris Convention on Third Party Liability in the Field of Nuclear Energy (as Amended by the Additional Protocol of 28 January 1964 and by the Protocol of 16 November 1982, and by the Protocol of 12 February 2004) (the Protocol to the Brussels Supplementary Convention).

[36] For the patchy and complicated approach under international nuclear liability conventions, see D.E.J. Currie 2008.

[37] Of these five countries, only Argentina and Romania have nuclear capacity. The net nuclear power generating capacity of Argentina is 935 MWe and that of Romania is 1300 MWe in 2009. See Schwartz 2009.

1.2.2. Basis of liability

A system of absolute liability is established under the Paris Convention.[38] According to the Paris Convention, the operator is liable for damage caused by a nuclear incident in a nuclear installation or involving nuclear substances coming from such installations.[39] To prove the fault of nuclear operators is no longer necessary to establish liability. Liability established under the Paris Convention is quite stringent since many classical exonerations, such as force majeure, Acts of Gods or intervening acts of third persons under general tort law, are no longer applicable.[40] The available exonerations are an act of armed conflict, hostilities, civil war and insurrection. The operator is not liable for damage caused via a grave natural disaster of an exceptional character unless the legislation of the Contracting Party in whose territory his nuclear installation is situated provides to the contrary.[41] Similar stipulations about absolute liability and exonerations can also be found under the Vienna Convention.[42] However, under the Vienna Convention, there is an additional possibility for operators to be relieved of their liability: the competent court can, according to the applicable law, relieve the operator wholly or partly from his obligation if the operator can prove that the damage resulted from gross negligence or an act or the omission of the victims.[43]

The conventions of the second generation have not changed the principle that strict liability is imposed on the operator of a nuclear power plant. However, an important change took place as far as the available defences for the operator are concerned: natural disasters are no longer an applicable defence.[44]

1.2.3. Liable persons

Under the Paris Convention, liability is channelled to operators. No one else is liable for the damage caused by a nuclear incident.[45] The "operator" is defined as "the person designated or recognized by the competent public authority as the operator of that installation".[46] These provisions

---

[38] The expose des motifs of the Paris Convention, point 14.
[39] Article III(a), the Paris Convention.
[40] The expose des motifs of the Paris Convention, point 48.
[41] Article IX, the Paris Convention.   [42] Articles I(1)(k), IV(1)(3), the Vienna Convention.
[43] Article IV(2), the Vienna Convention.
[44] See Article IX, The Protocol to the Paris Convention; Article IV(3), The Protocol to the Vienna Convention.
[45] Article VI(a)(b), the Paris Convention.   [46] Article I(a)(vi), the Paris Convention.

can hold other parties engaged in nuclear activities liable since the Paris Convention is the only legal basis for a claim against a nuclear operator in case of the identified incidents.[47] This concentration of liability is based on two reasons: to avoid the complicated legal procedures to identify the liable parties and to allow a concentration of insurance capacity.[48] Under the Paris Convention, the operators in principle do not have a right of recourse against the other parties. This is because it is argued that allowing recourse will make it necessary for suppliers to seek insurance coverage and will lead to costly duplication of insurance.[49] However, recourse is possible if the damage results from an act or omission done with intent to cause damage or if and to the extent provided by contract.[50] The Vienna Convention has similar provisions.[51]

Again, this principle of channelling liability exclusively to the nuclear operator can also be found in the second generation nuclear liability conventions as well as in the convention on the liability of operators of nuclear ships. The latter convention even explicitly holds "except as otherwise provided in this convention no person other than the operator shall be liable for such damage".[52]

This channelling of liability has some relevance for operators in the nuclear security industry. It means, effectively, that only the operator of a nuclear power plant will be held liable for a nuclear incident and that hence the security industry can in principle – without stipulation of recourse – not be held liable for the damage caused as a result of a nuclear accident, even if the nuclear accident would hypothetically have been caused by negligence on the side of the security industry.

1.2.4.   Damage covered

Under both the Paris Convention and the Vienna Convention, the operator's liability is limited both in amount and in time. The Paris Convention sets the maximum liability of the operator at 15 million SDRs, but allows the Contracting Party to establish by legislation a greater or lesser amount considering the capacity of insurance and financial security. The Contracting Party can also require a lower amount according to the nature of the installation. The lower amount should be no less

---

[47] Article VI(c)(ii), the Paris Convention.
[48] The expose des motifs of the Paris Convention, point 15.
[49] Ibid., point 18.   [50] Article VI(f), the Paris Convention.
[51] Articles II(5) and X, the Vienna Convention.
[52] Limited rights of recourse are allowed under Article II(6) of the Convention on the Liability of Operators of Nuclear Ships.

than 5 million SDRs.[53] The Paris Convention introduces a cap on liability, taking into account the difficulties of operators to seek financial security.[54] The flexible expression allows the Contracting Parties to set the limit higher than that set in the Paris Convention. For example, in Sweden the limit on liability is set at 300 million SDRs according to the Nuclear Liability Act (SFS 1968:45).[55] Germany even adopted a system with unlimited liability.[56] Under the Vienna Convention, the cap of liability should be no less than US \$5 million.[57] The statute of limitations under both the Paris Convention and the Vienna Convention is set at ten years from the date of the nuclear accident. They both allow the extension of the extinction periods by Contracting Parties if the operator is covered by insurance or other financial security.[58]

The liability limitation has, however, been changed under the second generation nuclear conventions. The Protocol to the Paris Convention increases the limit for nuclear operators to be no less than 700 million euro. The Contracting Party can reduce the liability to be no less than 70 million euro for an incident originating from a nuclear installation, or to be no less than 80 million euro for the carriage of nuclear substances according to the reduced risks.[59] The convention even allows the adoption of unlimited liability by the Contracting Parties, as long as the financial security required is no less than the amount mentioned above.[60]

1.2.5. Exclusions and defences

This issue has in fact already been dealt with when we discussed the scope of liability above (see 1.2.2.). Summarising, already under the first generation conventions, more particularly under the Paris Convention, classic

---

[53] Article VII(b), the Paris Convention.
[54] The expose des motifs of the Paris Convention, point 43.
[55] OECD: Nuclear Legislation in OECD Countries, Regulatory and Institutional Framework for Nuclear Activities: Sweden, 13, available at: www.oecd-nea.org/law/legislation/sweden .pdf.
[56] *Gesetz über die friedliche Verwendung der Kernenergie und den Schutz gegen ihre Gefahren (Atomgesetz – AtG) vom 23. Dezember 1959, Neufassung vom 15. Juli 1985, letzte Änderung vom 31. Juli 2011* (Act on the peaceful utilisation of nuclear energy and the protection against its hazards (Atomic Energy Act) of 23 December 1959, as amended and promulgated on 15 July 1985, last amendment of 31 July 2011), § 31.
[57] Article V, the Vienna Convention.
[58] Article VIII, the Paris Convention; Article VI(1), the Vienna Convention.
[59] Article VII(a)(b), the Protocol to the Paris Convention.
[60] Article X(b), the Protocol to the Paris Convention.

exonerations such as force majeure or the intervention of a third person were no longer available, but the operator was not liable for damage caused by a grave natural disaster of an exceptional character. However, that exception was also eliminated under the second generation international conventions: natural disasters are no longer an applicable defence.[61]

1.2.6. Financial security and compensation mechanisms

It is important for the international regimes on nuclear liability to seek financial security coverage for the operator's liability. Both conventions require the operator to have and maintain insurance or other financial security up to the cap of its liability.[62] Insurance is the most popularly used instrument for an operator to cover its liability. In fact, the cap on liability is usually set as the maximum available amount from the insurance market. Since insurance is available per installation for a fixed period rather than in respect of a single incident, the potential resources available for compensation may be reduced after the first incident. Under these conditions, the Contracting Parties may need to intervene.[63] It is for the Contracting Parties to decide the nature, form and extent of the compensation according to applicable national law.[64]

The liability limits established under the Paris Convention and the Vienna Convention are quite low compared to the potential catastrophic damage that a nuclear incident can cause. The liability is limited to promote the development of the peaceful use of nuclear capability. To provide the potential victims better protection, the Brussels Complementary Convention was established under the auspices of the NEA in 1963. Under the Brussels Complementary Convention, two additional layers of compensation are added in terms of public funds. Therefore, the total amount of money available for compensation is increased to 300 million SDR and a third layer compensation system is established: first, the operator is liable up to an amount of at least 5 million SDRs via its financial security; between this amount and 175 million SDR, the Installation State needs to

---

[61] Article IX, The Protocol to the Paris Convention; Article IV(3), The Protocol to the Vienna Convention.
[62] Article X, the Paris Convention; Article VII, the Vienna Convention.
[63] The expose des motifs of the Paris Convention, point 49.
[64] Article XI, the Paris Convention; Article VIII, the Vienna Convention.

make public funds available; for the amount between 175 and 300 million SDR, compensation is made out of public funds by all Contracting Parties according to a specific formula.[65] The Installation State can escape its obligation under the second layer by setting the liability limit at no less than 175 million SDRs. In that case the whole amount up to 175 million SDR needs to be made available by liable operators.

This system of a three-tier compensation has also been changed under the second generation nuclear liability conventions. Not only has the amount of the limitation of liability been increased,[66] but the available public funds were increased as well. From the maximum amount of operators' liability set by the Protocol to the Paris Convention up to 1200 million euro, the Installation State needs to pay in terms of public funds. Public funds need to be made available by all Contracting Parties according to a set formula of compensation between the amounts of 1200 million euro and 1500 million euro.[67] Thus the available resources for compensation in case of a nuclear accident are increased significantly: from 300 million SDRs (approximately 327 million euro) to 1500 million euro.

The compensation capacity also increased under the IAEA regime. The Protocol to the Vienna Convention increases the liability limitation to no less than 300 million SDRs, or no less than 150 million SDRs, provided the Installation State will make public funds available to cover the amount between the set limitation to 300 million SDRs.[68] Thus the revision has introduced a second layer of compensation. Though the amount is also significantly increased, it is modest compared to the possible significant damage and it is set at just the same level as the original Paris Convention and the Brussels Supplementary Convention. The CSC Convention also provides two tiers of compensation: a first 300 million SDRs is paid by public funds from the Installation State and another 300 million SDRs from the collective funds from the Contracting Parties.[69]

The amount of compensation under the Paris and Brussels Conventions is summarised in Table 4. Note, however, that the Convention on Supplementary Compensation has not entered into force yet. Hence, the "old" amounts from the first column still apply.

---

[65] Article III(a)(b), the Brussels Complementary Convention.   [66] See 1.2.4.
[67] Article III(b), the Protocol to the Brussels Complementary Convention.
[68] Article V(1), the Protocol to the Vienna Convention.
[69] Articles III(1) and IV(1), the CSC Convention.

Table 4 *Coverage caps before and after the 2004 amendments (in million €)*

	Paris (1960) and Brussels (1963) Conventions (caps for France, 1968 law as amended)	Amending Protocols of the Paris and Brussels Conventions (2004)
Operator's liability cap	91	700
State intervention	140	500
Contracting Parties' coverage	150	300
Total	381	1500

1.2.7.   Jurisdictional and procedural issues

There are several procedural issues with respect to the nuclear liability conventions.

A first question that arises relates to the geographical scope of the conventions. The Paris Convention does not apply to "nuclear incidents occurring in the territory of non-Contracting States or to damage suffered in such territory unless otherwise provided by the legislation of the Contracting Party in whose territory the nuclear installation of the operator liable is situated".[70] The geographical scope of the Vienna Convention is less clear. Some argue that since the convention itself is silent on its geographical scope, the Vienna Convention on the Law of Treaties will apply. The convention applies to damage occurring in the territory of a State Party, on board aircraft registered in that State and on ships flying its flag.[71] Others deduce from the article about the competent court[72] that the geographical scope depends on the competent court, and thus damage resulting from non-Vienna States could be covered by the Vienna Convention.[73]

The second generation nuclear liability conventions and more particularly the Joint Protocol has broadened the scope of application of the conventions. Under this Joint Protocol the operator of a nuclear installation situated in the territory of a party to one convention shall be liable for the nuclear damage suffered in the territory of a party to either the Paris Convention or the Vienna Convention. The Protocols are also designed to be

---

[70] Article II, the Paris Convention.   [71] Lamm 2006.
[72] Article VIII, the Vienna Convention.   [73] Blanchard 2000.

attractive by broadening the applicable geographical scope. The Protocol to the Vienna Convention applies to nuclear damage wherever suffered, with a permitted exclusion if a non-Contracting Party has nuclear installations but does not offer reciprocal benefits.[74] The Protocol to the Paris Convention also covers damage suffered in some non-Contracting Parties which satisfy some specific requirements.[75]

A second jurisdictional aspect is that both the Paris Convention and the Vienna Convention have an "exclusive jurisdiction" clause: the jurisdiction lies only with the courts of the Contracting Party within whose territory the nuclear incident occurred. If the nuclear accident happens outside the Contracting Party's territory or the place cannot be determined, the jurisdiction lies with the courts of the Installation State of the liable operator.[76] Since nuclear damage may have a transboundary effect, the exclusive jurisdiction can ensure that the cap of liability is not exceeded and that a fair distribution of compensation takes place, if the claims lead to insoluble problems.[77]

A third jurisdictional aspect relates to the statute of limitations. Since the health impact of nuclear radiation may not manifest itself for decades, the revised conventions also extend the statute of limitation for claims for personal injury and death. Those kinds of claims need to be brought within thirty years from the date of the accident.[78]

1.2.8. *Relevance of the nuclear liability conventions*

Nuclear installations could of course be the target of terrorist activities. A consequence of the channelling of liability to the operator, discussed above, is that only the operator of the nuclear installation is held liable under the nuclear liability conventions discussed in this section. This hence excludes in principle the liability of the security industry. They cannot, at least on the basis of the nuclear liability conventions, be held liable for damage resulting from a nuclear accident.[79]

---

[74] Article I A, the Protocol to the Vienna Convention.
[75] Article II(a), the Protocol to the Paris Convention.
[76] Article VIII, the Paris Convention; Article XI, the Vienna Convention.
[77] The expose des motifs of the Paris Convention, point 54.
[78] Article VIII(a)(i), the Protocol to the Paris Convention; Article VI (1)(a)(i), the Protocol to the Vienna Convention.
[79] Another issue is whether they still could be liable under the national laws of Member States. That topic will be discussed in the various chapters of Part II.

1.3.   Marine oil pollution

1.3.1.   Brief summary of the regime

The international oil pollution compensation system consists of two important conventions that are somewhat interrelated. The two regimes are introduced briefly here: the first is composed of the International Convention on Civil Liability for Oil Pollution Damage (the CLC)[80] and the second is the International Convention on the Establishment of an International Fund for Compensation for Oil Pollution Damage (the Fund Convention).[81] Those two conventions are important early conventions on oil pollution liability and apply to ships carrying oil in bulk as cargo.[82]

The international liability regime for oil pollution started to develop in the 1960s. The Torrey Canyon oil spill awakened the broad public awareness of the oil pollution risks. Before the coming into being of the international conventions, some voluntary scheme was adopted: the Tanker Owners Voluntary Agreement concerning Liability for Oil Pollution (the TOVALOP),[83] under which fault liability with a reversal of the burden of proof is imposed on the tanker owner or the bareboat charter. The TOVALOP is complemented by another voluntary agreement by the oil industry: the Contract Regarding an Interim Supplement to Tanker Liability for Oil Pollution (the CRISTAL). The CRISTAL established a fund to cover oil pollution damage in addition to the TOVALOP with the contributions from oil industry.

Shortly after the adoption of the voluntary agreement, an international convention was reached under the auspices of the International Maritime Organization (IMO). In 1969 the CLC was passed, together with a Resolution on the Establishment of an International Compensation Fund for Oil Pollution Damage. This resulted in the adoption of the 1971 Fund Convention.

Two years after the adoption of the 1969 CLC, the 1971 Fund Convention was passed. The 1971 Fund Convention has two aims: to provide

---

[80]   The original CLC was adopted in 1969, and it was revised in 1992 (hereinafter the "1969 CLC" and the "1992 CLC"). The 1969 CLC, 973 UNTS 3, RMC I. 7.30, II 7, 30; the 1992 CLC, Misc 36 (1994), Cm 2657, RMC I, 7.51, ii. 7.51.

[81]   The original Fund Convention was adopted in 1971, and it was revised in 1992 (hereinafter the 1971 Fund Convention and the 1992 Fund Convention). The 1971 Fund Convention, 1110 UNTS 57, Cmnd 5061, the 1992 Fund Convention, RMC I.7.111, II.1.7.111, Misc 37 (1994), Cm 2658.

[82]   The 1992 CLC, Article I 1; the 1992 Fund Convention Article I 2.

[83]   TOVALOP 1969.

compensation when the protection available from the 1969 CLC is inadequate and to relieve ship-owners from additional financial burden.[84]

1.3.2. Basis of liability

Strict liability is adopted in the 1969 convention. Hot debates took place during the negotiation of the convention on whom the liability should rest. Under the influence of the international regimes for nuclear liability, no doubts have been expressed on the reasonability of the channelling of liability. The debates focused on whether it should be the ship-owner or the oil industry that bears the liability.[85] In the end, a compromise was made: liability under the CLC fell on the shoulders of the ship-owner. As a price, the oil industry also needed to contribute to the compensation through a compensation fund. At the conference to pass the 1969 CLC, it was agreed that an international compensation fund would be established in the near future. Liability under the CLC is strict.

1.3.3. Liable persons

As far as the creation of the 1969 CLC and the 1971 Fund Convention is concerned, it is clear that the 1969 CLC created a channelling of liability to the tanker owner. The ship-owner is defined as "the person or persons registered as the owner of the ship or, in the absence of registration, the person or persons owning the ship".[86] The 1969 CLC pre-empts other legislations: no other claims are eligible other than those under the convention. It shows explicitly that no claims are made against the servants or agents of the owner.[87] Scholars deduce from the explicit list that claims against other parties, for example, the cargo owner and the operator, are still possible according to applicable national laws.[88] Recourse against a third party is allowed under the 1969 CLC.[89]

In 1992, two protocols were adopted to revise the original conventions. The 1992 CLC broadened the scope of persons that can be protected from the liability and this hence strengthens the effect of channelling.

According to the 1992 CLC, not only servants or agents of the owner but also some other parties, such as the pilot or any other person who is not a member of the crew and performs services for the ship, any

---

[84] The 1971 Fund Convention, Article 2(1).   [85] Wang 2007.
[86] The 1969 CLC, Article I 3.   [87] Ibid., Article III 4.   [88] Verheij 2007.
[89] The 1969 CLC, Article III, 5.

charterer, any person performing salvage with the consent of the owner or on the instructions of a competent public authority, any person taking preventive measures and their agents or servants, are also exonerated from oil pollution liability.

As we also mentioned with respect to the nuclear liability conventions,[90] the channelling of liability constitutes a major advantage for the security industry. To the extent that the security industry would (of course indirectly) be involved in marine oil pollution damage falling under the scope of the CLC (although it seems hard to imagine such a case), the security industry is protected by the channelling of liability: only the tanker owner can be held liable on the basis of the CLC, thus excluding liability of other parties including the security industry that may have contributed to the marine oil pollution.

1.3.4.   Damage covered

The liability established under the 1969 CLC was capped at 210 million francs or 2000 francs for each ton of the ship's tonnage. The amount is higher than that under the 1957 Convention on the Limitation of Ship-owners' Liability, but still far from covering the whole potential damage that can be caused by oil pollution. The ship-owners' right of limitation cannot be used if the incident occurred as a result of his actual fault or privity.[91]

Several serious oil spills that happened after the adoption of the original CLC and the Fund Convention – for example, the Amoco Cadiz in 1978 and the Tanio in 1980 – triggered the revisions to the original conventions. The first protocols to revise the conventions were reached in 1984. Since the US did not ratify the protocols, they could not come into force. Nevertheless, the changes in the 1984 protocols are largely incorporated in the 1992 protocols.

In 1992, two protocols were adopted to revise the original conventions: the 1992 CLC and the 1992 Fund Convention. This 1992 CLC increased the limit of liability to 4.51 million SDRs or 89.77 million SDRs, depending on the size of the ships. As a compromise to the increase of the liability limit, the criteria for when the ship-owners lose their right to limit liability are further constricted: damage should result from their wilful misconduct.[92]

---

[90] See *supra* 1.2.3.   [91] The 1969 CLC, Article V 2.   [92] The 1992 CLC, Article V 1, 2.

1.3.5. Exclusions and defences

As far as the marine pollution liability convention is concerned, one should make a distinction between, on the one hand, exclusions that could exclude the strict liability of the tanker owner and, on the other hand, exclusions that would lead the ship-owner to lose his right of limitation. In the latter case, the exclusion would hence not be a defence but, to the contrary, a reason to enlarge the scope of liability of the tanker owner.

Liability is excluded, according to Article 3 of the CLC, if the owner proves that the damage:

(a) resulted from an act of war, hostilities, civil war, insurrection or a natural phenomenon of an exceptional, inevitable and irresistible character, or
(b) was wholly caused by an act or omission done with intent to cause damage by a third party, or
(c) was wholly caused by the negligence or other wrongful act of any government or other authority responsible for the maintenance of lights or other navigational aids in the exercise of that function.

Article 3(3) moreover holds that if the owner proves that the pollution damage resulted wholly or partially either from an act or omission done with intent to cause damage by the person who suffered the damage or from the negligence of that person, the owner may be exonerated wholly or partially from his liability to such person.

As far as the limitation of liability is concerned, Article 5(2) of the CLC provides that the owner shall not be entitled to limit his liability under the convention if it is proved that the pollution damage resulted from his personal act or omission, committed with the intent to cause such damage or recklessly and without knowledge that such damage would probably result.

1.3.6. Financial security and compensation mechanism

The 1969 CLC requires the owner of a ship registered in a Contracting State and carrying more than 2000 tons of oil in bulk as cargo to maintain insurance or other financial security up to his limits of liability. In addition to insurance, the financial security can also be in the form of bank guarantee or a certificate delivered by an international compensation fund.[93] This requirement remains in the 1992 CLC.[94] Similar provisions can also be found in the Bunker Convention.[95] Though both regimes allow insurance and other instruments to be used to cover the liability, the most popular instruments are insurance, especially Protection and Indemnity Policies (P&I Policies).

In addition to the financial security provided to back up the (limited) liability of the tanker owner, additional funds are provided via the Fund Convention. This Fund Convention has, however, gone through various evolutions that have to be sketched now.

The 1971 Fund Convention plays two roles: to compensate the victims and to indemnify the ship-owners. It complements the compensation from the 1969 CLC under these situations if: no liability can be established under the 1969 CLC, and if owners and their financial guarantors are financially incapable of compensation and the damage exceeds the owners' liability. To encourage preventive measures, the costs raised from the voluntary activities of the owners are also treated as pollution damage.[96] The Fund has no obligation to pay if it can prove that the damage resulted from an act of war, hostilities, civil war or insurrection, or oil from a warship or a State-owned/operated ship or if the claimant cannot prove that damage resulted from a ship-related incident. Contributory negligence can also be used as a defence for the fund.[97]

The compensation available from the 1971 Fund is not unlimited: the total sum of the amount from the 1969 CLC and the 1971 Fund Convention is capped at 450 million francs. The Fund is financed by big oil importers in Contracting States. The eligible importers need to make initial contributions as the working capital of the fund and the annual contributions to cover the administrative expenses and claims.[98] The calculation of contributions is based on a fixed sum for each ton of contributing oil received.[99] The Contracting State has the obligation to ensure that the eligible contributing importers appear on a list and to communicate it to the Fund.[100] The Contracting State can also declare that it assumes the obligation that lies on the importers within its territory to make contributions.[101]

---

[93] The 1969 CLC, Article VII 1.   [94] The 1992 CLC, Article VII.
[95] International Convention on Civil Liability for Bunker Oil Pollution Damage (BUNKER) 23 March 2001, Article VII.
[96] The 1971 Fund Convention, Article 4(1).   [97] Ibid., Article 4(2)(3).
[98] Chao 1996.   [99] The 1971 Fund Convention, Articles 11(1), 12(2).
[100] Ibid., Article 15(1).   [101] Ibid., Article 14(1).

The original CLC and Fund Convention proved to be insufficient to cover the potential catastrophic oil pollution damage. In 1992 a new compensation fund was established. The 1992 Fund Convention removed the function of the Fund to alleviate the burden of liability of ship-owners. Therefore, the only function of the 1992 Fund is to provide additional protection to the victims of oil pollution. The conditions of the application of the 1992 Fund to compensate victims are the same as those of the 1971 Fund.[102] The available compensation from the 1992 CLC and the 1992 Fund Convention is increased to 203 million SDRs.[103]

The 1992 Fund Convention came into force in 1996, when the 1971 Fund Convention was still in force. The co-existence of the two funds was problematic since that diluted the capacity of each fund to provide sufficient compensation. In 2000, a Protocol was passed to allow for an early winding up of the 1971 Fund. According to this Protocol, the 1971 Fund ceases to be in force when the number of Contracting States falls below 25, or the total quantity of contributing oil falls below 100 million tons, whichever is earlier. The 1971 Fund ceased to be in force on 24 May 2002. But it still continues in compensating for damage from incidents before that day.[104] As of January 2012, the 1992 Fund Convention has 105 Member States.

Although the limitation of compensation under the 1992 Fund Convention was increased considerably, shortly after its adoption the amount was dwarfed again by yet other catastrophic oil pollution case.[105] Under this background, a Supplementary Fund was established in a 2003 Protocol.[106] The Supplementary Fund provides an additional layer of compensation for oil pollution victims under the 1992 CLC and the 1992 Fund Convention. In other words, a condition for the payment from the Supplementary Fund is that the victim is entitled to compensation under the 1992 CLC and the 1992 Fund Convention, and is unable to obtain full and adequate compensation from them.[107] The Supplementary Fund Convention increases the aggregated amount of compensation up to 750 million SDRs.[108]

---

[102] The 1992 Fund Convention, Article IV 1.   [103] Ibid., Article IV 4.
[104] www.iopcfund.org/intro.htm.
[105] The Nakhodka accident near Japan in 1997 and the Erika disaster in France in 1999 are two examples.
[106] Protocol of 2003 to the International Convention on the Establishment of an International Fund for Compensation for Oil Pollution Damage, 1992 (The Supplementary Fund Protocol), RMC II. 7.115.
[107] The Supplementary Fund Convention, Article IV 1.   [108] Ibid., Article IV 2.

1.3.7.   Jurisdictional and procedural issues

There are several procedural issues mentioned in the CLC which are worth mentioning. A first point is that Article 2 clearly provides that the convention exclusively applies to pollution damage caused

- in the territory, including the territorial sea of a Contracting State and
- in the exclusive economic zone of a Contracting State, established in accordance with international law or otherwise in a zone not extending more than 200 nautical miles.

Pollution damage that falls outside of this territory and would for example be caused in high seas would hence not fall within the scope of the CLC.

According to Article 9 of the convention, where an accident has caused pollution damage in the territory, including the territorial sea or exclusive economic zone of one or more Contracting States or preventive measures have been taken to prevent or minimise pollution damage in such territory, actions for compensation may only be brought in the courts of any such Contracting State or States. Reasonable notice of any such action shall be given to the defendant and each Contracting State shall ensure that its courts possess the necessary jurisdiction to entertain such actions for compensation.[109] Moreover, Article 10 provides that any judgment given by a court with jurisdiction in accordance with Article 9 which is enforceable in the State of origin where it is no longer subject to ordinary forms or review shall be recognised in any Contracting State except:

- where the judgment was obtained by fraud; or
- where the defendant was not given reasonable notice and fair opportunity to present his case.

Article 8 moreover provides that the rights of compensation under the CLC shall be extinguished unless an action is brought within three years from the date when the damage occurred. However, in no case shall an action be brought after six years from the date of the incident which caused the damage. Where the incident consists of a series of occurrences the six-year period shall run from the date of the first occurrence.

1.3.8.   Relevance of the marine oil pollution conventions

Whereas we indicated that the nuclear liability conventions may have some relevance for TRR, given the fact that nuclear installations may be targeted

---

[109]   Article IX(2) of the CLC.

by terrorism and the security industry moreover may have taken measures aiming at the prevention of TRR, terrorism is (although it can obviously never be totally excluded) much less likely with respect to objects falling under marine oil pollution conventions covered in this section. Again, as a result of the exclusive channelling of liability, it will be the tanker owner who is liable in case a marine pollution incident would be caused by terrorism, leading to damage falling under the scope of the marine oil pollution conventions. Since the liability is in principle exclusively channelled to the tanker owner, this excludes the possibility of holding the security industry liable on the basis of the marine pollution conventions discussed in this section.

1.4.   Other relevant treaties

In this section, the following treaties are discussed: the 2010 International Convention on Liability and Compensation for Damage in Connection with the Carriage of Hazardous and Noxious Substances by Sea (1.4.1.), the 2003 Protocol on Civil Liability and Compensation for Damage Caused by the Transboundary Effects of Industrial Accidents on Transboundary Waters (1.4.2.) and the 1971 United Nations Convention on International Liability for Damage Caused by Space Objects (1.4.3.).

1.4.1.   2010 International Convention on Liability and Compensation for Damage in Connection with the Carriage of Hazardous and Noxious Substances by Sea

1.4.1.1.   Brief summary of the regime

The carriage of hazardous and noxious substances (HNS)[110] might lead to accidents and endanger human health as well as environmental and

---

[110] According to Article 1 of the HNS Convention, these substances are: oil, noxious liquid substance, defined in Regulation 1.10 of Annex II to the International Convention for the Prevention of Pollution from Ships, 1973, as modified by the Protocol of 1978 relating thereto, as amended, and those substances and mixtures provisionally categorised as falling in pollution category X, Y or Z in accordance with Regulation 6.3 of the said Annex II; dangerous liquid substances carried in bulk listed in Chapter 17 of the International Code for the Construction and Equipment of Ships Carrying Dangerous Chemicals in Bulk, as amended, and the dangerous products for which the preliminary suitable conditions for the carriage have been prescribed by the Administration and port administrations involved in accordance with paragraph 1.1.6 of the Code; (iv) dangerous, hazardous and harmful substances, materials and articles in packaged form covered by the International Maritime Dangerous Goods Code, as amended; liquefied gases; liquid substances carried in bulk with a flashpoint not exceeding 60°C; solid bulk materials

economic interests. The CLC has established a liability regime which governs compensation for oil pollution damage.[111] Nevertheless, many accidents involve the carriage of hazardous substances other than the substance that is governed by the CLC Convention, i.e. oil. The International Convention on Liability and Compensation for Damage in connection with the Carriage of Hazardous and Noxious Substances by Sea (hereafter the HNS Convention)[112] has been concluded for addressing liability and compensation issues concerning damage resulting from the carriage of such substances.

Personal injuries, environmental damage, economic losses and the costs of preventive measures which resulted from the carriage of hazardous and noxious substance by vessels are governed by the HNS Convention.[113] The type of damage which is governed by the HNS Convention varies according to the place of an accident. According to Article 3, the scope of application of this Convention is divided into four sections: (1) in the territory of a State Party, all damage is governed by the HNS Convention, (2) in the exclusive economic zone of a State Party, only environmental damage is governed by the Convention, (3) on board a ship registered in a State Party or, in the case of an unregistered ship, on board a ship entitled to fly the flag of a State Party, all damage is governed by the HNS Convention other than environmental damage which has been caused by the substances carried by the ship, and (4) preventive measures are governed by the Convention everywhere they have been taken.

Furthermore, the Convention excludes from its scope damage that is subject to the jurisdiction of the CLC Convention and damage caused by specific radioactive materials. Furthermore, the Convention shall not apply to warships, naval auxiliary or other ships owned or operated by a State and used only on Government non-commercial service. It does not apply to the extent that its provisions are incompatible with legal rules on workers' compensation or social security schemes.[114] The HNS Convention imposes a strict liability regime on the owner of the ship.

---

possessing chemical hazards covered by the International Maritime Solid Bulk Cargoes Code.

[111] As has been discussed in detail in 1.3. *supra.*

[112] The International Convention on Liability and Compensation for Damage in Connection with the Carriage of Hazardous and Noxious Substances by Sea (HNS Convention) was adopted on 3 May 1996 but did not enter into force until 2010; that entry into force was in fact superseded by the 2010 Protocol which was adopted on 30 April 2010; but which has not entered into force.

[113] Article 1 of the HNS Convention.   [114] Article 4 of the HNS Convention.

However, the owner is required to maintain compulsory insurance or similar financial security up to the limitation of liability. The owner will enjoy the limitation of liability up to certain amounts articulated in the HNS Convention but only if he complies with the conditions of the HNS Convention.[115]

The HNS Fund has been established in order to support a limitation of liability of the owner. If the amount of damage exceeds the financial cap or no liability for the damage arises under chapter 2 of the HNS Convention (on "liability of the owner"), or when the owner is financially incapable to fully compensate the victims, the HNS Fund will pay compensation under specific regulations which are articulated in the Convention.[116] The HNS Fund has both a general account for all types of substances and a separate account for specific substances such as oil, liquefied natural gas (LNG) and liquefied petroleum gases (LPG). The HNS Fund has been supported by initial and annual contributions of the "receiver" in the State Party. For each type of substance that has a separate account or a general account, specific total quantities of imported substances have been specified by the Convention. In case the total quantities of the substance exceed the amounts which are clarified in the convention, the receiver shall pay a contribution.[117] The amount of the contributions and other related regulations are determined by the HNS Fund on a yearly basis.

1.4.1.2.   Basis of liability

The nature of the carriage of substances under the application of the HNS Convention is dangerous and has a high probability of accidents. Therefore, according to tort law he who carries on a dangerous activity is liable for the harm imposed by the activity. The HNS Convention establishes a strict liability regime. According to Article 7 of the HNS Convention, the owner of the ship shall be liable for damage caused by any hazardous or noxious substance during the carriage by ship.

Although it is mostly the ship-owner who can influence the accident risk, some other risks cannot be controlled by him. According to Article 7 of the HNS Convention, the owner will not be held liable if the damage was wholly caused by the negligence or other wrongful act of any government or other authority responsible for the maintenance of lights or other navigational aids; or if the shipper or any other responsible person did

---

[115] Article 9 of the HNS Convention.
[116] Chapter 3 of the HNS Convention.
[117] Articles 16, 17, 18 and 19 of the HNS Convention.

not furnish adequate information concerning the hazardous and noxious nature of the substances carried by the ship. In addition, if the damage was caused by the intentional act or omission of a third party, the owner will be excluded from liability. Other persons involved, such as the members of the crew and even any person taking preventive measures, will not be held liable unless the damage resulted from their personal act or omission, committed with the intent to cause such damage, or recklessly and with knowledge about the possible risks.[118]

1.4.1.3.   Liable persons

Since most ship accidents are caused by human error,[119] the owner of the ship will be held prima facie liable. The causes of the accident can be related to a defect in the ship or cargo or to environmental conditions.[120] The ship-owner according to Article 1 is defined as "the person or persons registered as the owner of the ship or, in the absence of registration, the person or persons owning the ship". However, in the case of a ship owned by a State and operated by a company which in that State is registered as the ship's operator, "owner" shall mean such company. By establishing a strict liability rule, the registered owner or the actual owner of the ship is presumed to be the party which is best capable of preventing accidents.

However, the owner of the ship might be excluded from liability if the owner can prove that the accident was caused by other persons or by force majeure,[121] such as an act of war, hostilities, civil war, insurrection or a natural phenomenon of an exceptional, inevitable and irresistible character. Moreover, if it has been proved that the damage was wholly caused by the act or omission of a third party, the owner will not be held liable. However, it seems that if the damage was (only) partly caused by a third party, the owner would not enjoy an exclusion of liability. A similar condition is articulated for the damage resulting in a wrongful act of authorities responsible for the maintenance of navigational aids, including governments. Since the nature of the substance which is carried by the ship has a great impact on the occurrence and prevention of accidents, information about the type of substances plays an important role in preventing accidents and minimising the costs thereof.

Yet, if the shipper or any other person who is responsible for providing information concerning the hazardous nature of substances fails to do so, the owner will not be held liable for the damage. In cases that the owner

---

[118] Ibid.   [119] Toffoli et al. 2005.   [120] Gluver and Olsen 1998.
[121] Article 7 of the HNS Convention.

and his servants know or reasonably ought to have known of the hazardous and noxious nature of the substances shipped, they will be held liable, but if this is not the case, it is the responsibility of the shipper or any other person concerned to inform them. However, the methods for notifying such information or details about the extent of the hazardousness of those substances are not clarified in the HNS Convention.

No claim for compensation for damage may be made under the HNS Convention against members of the crew, agents or servants of the owner, or against charterers, persons performing salvage operations, and persons taking preventive measures,[122] unless the damage resulted from intent or recklessness by these persons. If two or more ships carrying noxious or hazardous substances are involved in an accident, each ship-owner will be held separately liable for the damage caused.[123] However, the owners will be held jointly and severally liable for damage that is not reasonably separable.[124] If damage resulting from a ship carrying HNS is not separable from other factors, all damage is deemed to result from that ship. This is only different if the pollution damage is subject to the Convention on Civil Lability for Oil Pollution Damage 1969 or if the damage is caused by radioactive material as defined in the International Maritime Dangerous Goods Code or in the International Maritime Solid Bulk Cargoes Code.[125]

1.4.1.4. Limitation of liability

There are two arrangements for the limitation of liability under the HNS Convention. A first tier is allocated to the liability of the ship-owner and a second tier provided by the compensation duty of the HNS Fund. The ship-owner is entitled to limit his liability depending on the tonnage of the ship and the form of the transported substances (bulk HNS or packaged HNS), according to a calculation scheme provided in Article 9 of the Convention. If the amount of the damage exceeds the liability cap of the owner, the HNS Fund will step in.

For damage that has been caused by a ship carrying bulk HNS, up to 2000 units of tonnage, 10 million units of account shall be paid by the owner. When the ship's tonnage exceeds this number, the following

---

[122] The term "preventive measures" here refers to "any reasonable measures taken by any person after an incident has occurred to prevent or minimize damage"; see Article 1(7) of the HNS Convention.

[123] Article 8 of the HNS Convention.   [124] Ibid.

[125] Articles 1 and 4 of the HNS Convention.

amounts shall in addition be paid by the owner: for each unit of tonnage from 2001 to 50,000 units of tonnage, 1500 units of account; for each unit of tonnage in excess of 50,000 units of tonnage, 360 units of account.[126] Furthermore, the maximum total amount of compensation for each accident is 100 million units. For damage caused by packaged HNS, a similar baseline of tonnage of the ship has been defined. Nevertheless the amounts of compensation in case of a ship carrying packaged HNS are higher than those for ships carrying bulk HNS; the total aggregate amount for a packaged HNS ship is 115 million units of account per incident.[127] When damage is caused by both bulk HNS and packaged HNS, or where it is not possible to determine whether the damage originating from that ship has been caused by bulk HNS or by packaged HNS, the (higher) packaged form limitations will be applied.

The establishment of a liability cap allows the insurability of such damage and consequently a better compensation of victims. However, a limitation of liability may reduce the incentives of the ship-owner to invest in the prevention of accidents if the damage "resulted from the personal act or omission of the owner, committed with the intent to cause such damage, or recklessly and with knowledge that such damage would probably result".[128] Nevertheless, in the absence of regulation which requires due care from the owner, a "moral hazard" risk might still emerge, since the aforementioned Article only encompasses intentionally or recklessly committed acts or omissions.

Furthermore, the owner shall establish a fund under Article 9(3) of the HNS Convention in order to benefit from the limitation of liability. This fund shall be constituted by a deposited total amount of compensation (based on the tonnage and form of carriage) or providing a financial guarantee acceptable under the regulation of the State Party in which the fund is constituted. After constitution of the fund all claims shall be brought before this fund and none of the assets of the owner, other than the fund, shall be arrested.[129]

---

[126] Article 9(1)(a) of the HNS Convention.

[127] According to Article 9(1)(b) of the convention, where the damage has been caused by packaged HNS, 11.5 million units of account for a ship not exceeding 2000 units of tonnage; and for a ship with a tonnage in excess thereof, the following amount in addition to that: for each unit of tonnage from 2001 to 50,000 units of tonnage, 1725 units of account; for each unit of tonnage in excess of 50,000 units of tonnage, 414 units of account.

[128] Article 9(2) of the HNS Convention.   [129] Article 10 of the HNS Convention.

The second tier of compensation is assigned to the HNS Fund. The HNS Fund has been established for compensating damage under the HNS Convention for three purposes: first, when the total admissible claims exceed the ship-owner's liability; second, when the owner or the insurer are not financially capable to cover the claims for compensation for damage in the first tier; and third, when the owner has not been held liable under the HNS Convention.[130] Nonetheless, the Fund will not pay any compensation if the damage was caused by an act of war, etc., or by HNS discharged from a government-owned non-commercial ship, or if the claimants cannot prove the causal link between damage and an incident involving HNS ships. In addition, similar to the liability of the owner, for damage resulting from an act or omission done with intent to cause damage by the person who suffered the damage or from the negligence of that person, the HNS Fund may be exonerated from its obligation to pay compensation to such person.[131]

The HNS Fund's duty to compensate is also limited. If the aggregate amount of the damage exceeds the ship-owner's liability, the compensation will be paid up to 250 million units for any specific accident.[132] In some cases, where no liability is attached to the ship-owner, the aggregate amount of compensation is 250 million units of account. Thus, the maximum total amount to be paid under the HNS Convention for compensation of damage is 250 million units. If the damage is much higher than the payable compensation by the Fund, the amount of payment will be divided between claimants with an equal proportion of their admissible claims, other than claims in respect of death or personal injury which have priority over other claims up to two-thirds of the total amount. Moreover, compensation in accordance with this HNS Convention might be paid even if the owner has not constituted a fund, by the Assembly of the HNS Fund.[133]

In sum, there is a two-tier system of liability (caps) under the HNS Convention: the first tier concerns the ship-owner's liability and the second tier concerns the HNS Fund. Since the amount of compensation due by the HNS Fund also has a limit, any damage can only be compensated

---

[130] Article 14(1) of the HNS Convention.

[131] According to Article 14, if the HNS Fund proves that such damage resulted from an intended act of the victim, it may be exonerated from its obligation to pay compensation to such person although not for preventive measures.

[132] Article 14(5) of the HNS Convention.   [133] Article 14(7) of the HNS Convention.

up to that amount. Hence, there is still a possibility that damage which falls under the HNS Convention is not fully compensated.

1.4.1.5.   Financial security and compensation mechanism

According to Article 12 of the HNS Convention, the owner of a ship carrying HNS is required to take insurance or to maintain other acceptable financial securities to cover sums fixed by applying the limits of liability. However, the State of the ship's registry or any relevant State Party should issue a certificate attesting that insurance or other financial security is in force in accordance with the provisions of the HNS Convention.

The liability of the owner has been limited under the HNS Convention. For this purpose, a specific mechanism has been set up by the HNS Convention for compensation of the damage. As stated above (see 1.4.1.4.), if the ship-owner enjoys a limitation of liability, the owner shall constitute a fund for the total sum representing the limit of liability before the competent court or other competent authorities of any one of the States Parties whether that action against the owner has been brought or not.[134] Any claim against the owner can only be exercised before this fund.[135] The aforementioned fund might be established either by depositing the sum or by providing a financial guarantee, according to the applicable law of the court or other competent authority.

All the claims shall be brought before the established fund. If the owner or any other person has paid compensation for damage before establishment of the fund, he will be subrogating the rights of the claimant which has been compensated by him. Given the compulsory insurance under the HNS Convention, the insurer or other person providing financial security is entitled to constitute a fund in accordance with the regulation of the HNS Convention, even if the owner is not entitled to a limitation of liability.[136] This will reduce the administrative cost of the compensation.

1.4.1.6.   Jurisdictional issues

Claimants can take legal action in a court in the respective State Party having jurisdiction over the damage. The competent court will have exclusive jurisdiction to consider all matters relating to damage and compensation. According to Article 38(1) of the HNS Convention, where an accident

---

[134] Article 9(3) of the HNS Convention.   [135] Article 10 of the HNS Convention.
[136] Article 9(11) of the HNS Convention.

has caused damage in the territory of a State Party, or preventive measures have been taken to prevent or minimise damage in such territory, actions for compensation may be brought only in the courts of this State. Since, according to Article 3 of the HNS Convention, contamination of the environment caused in the exclusive economic zone of a State Party has been included in the scope of the application of the HNS Convention, if such damage is caused in the exclusive economic zone of a State Party, that respective State Party has jurisdiction over the case.[137]

Generally the action against the HNS Fund for compensation shall follow before a court having jurisdiction in respect of actions against the owner or the owner's insurer. In case the ship-owner is exempted from liability, a legal action against the HNS Fund must be brought in a court which would have been competent if the ship-owner had been liable. When the owner has not been identified yet, the action will be brought against the Fund only in State Parties where the damage occurred.[138] Therefore, the mechanism of compensation under the HNS Convention has been based on the establishment of the fund, primarily according to the regulation of the competent court and by the owner or insurer. This procedure shall be validated by the respective State Party. Nonetheless, if the amount of damage exceeds the liability of the owner or if any other reasons which shift the liability for compensating damage to the HNS Fund are present, the competent court shall determine the compensation by the HNS Fund. Thus, actions against the HNS Fund can only be brought before the competent court and through litigation in the tort system.

1.4.1.7.   Conclusions

It can be concluded that the HNS Convention covers damage which results from ships carrying HNS. With respect to compensation of damage caused by such substances, priority is given to personal injury and the cost of preventive measures. The owner of the ship is held strictly liable but can be entitled to a liability limit; members of the crew are exempted from liability, except for cases of intent or reckless actions. The strict liability regime has been complemented by compulsory insurance up to the amount of the liability cap. Moreover, in case the operator cannot be held liable for all damages or is financially unable to compensate all damages, compensation for damage in connection with the carriage of

---

[137]   Articles 3(b) and 38 of the HNS Convention.
[138]   Article 39 of the HNS Convention.

HNS by sea will be provided by the HNS Fund, which is established as a second-tier compensation regime. Thus, the damage can be compensated either through insurance or through the HNS Fund mechanism.

1.4.2.   2003 Protocol on Civil Liability and Compensation for Damage Caused by the Transboundary Effects of Industrial Accidents on Transboundary Waters

1.4.2.1.   Brief summary of the regime

Under the auspices of the United Nations Economic Commission for Europe (UNECE), five environmental treaties have been negotiated, all of which are now in force.[139] With respect to compensation for transboundary damage and recalling the relevant provisions of the Convention on the Protection and Use of Transboundary Watercourses and International Lakes and the Convention on the Transboundary Effects of Industrial Accidents (1992),[140] the Civil Liability Protocol[141] was adopted on 21 May 2003. However, this Protocol is not yet in force.[142] According to Article 1 of the Civil Liability Protocol, its objective is "to provide for a comprehensive regime for civil liability and for adequate and prompt compensation for damage caused by the transboundary effects of industrial accidents on transboundary waters".

Various problems may arise in case of transboundary damage. For example, the affected State might not have been informed about the adverse environmental impact of certain activities. Also, even after being aware of this adverse impact, affected States may face obstacles to start litigation against polluting States. Also, there is no harmonised definition of the concept of "environmental damage". The aforementioned conventions include some provisions on damage definition, prevention of damage and cooperation among respective States in the context of transboundary pollution, while provisions on liability for and

---

[139] For more information see: www.unece.org/env/welcome.html.

[140] In particular Article 7 of the former and Article 13 of the latter.

[141] Its full name is Protocol on Civil Liability and Compensation for Damage Caused by the Transboundary Effects of Industrial Accidents on Transboundary Waters to the 1992 Convention on the Protection and Use of Transboundary Watercourses and International Lakes and to the 1992 Convention on the Transboundary Effects of Industrial Accidents. The protocol is not in force yet.

[142] http://treaties.un.org/pages/ViewDetails.aspx?src=TREATY&mtdsg_no=XXVII-16&chapter=27&lang=en#1. The Protocol was signed by 24 Parties in 2003, but only one (Hungary, on 25 June 2004) made the step to "ratification, acceptance, approval or accession".

compensation of transboundary damage are laid down in the Civil Liability Protocol.

The Parties to the Protocol have accepted the polluter-pays principle as a basis for the liability regime, taking into account that this principle is generally accepted in international environmental law.[143] Based on the polluter-pays principle, operators are strictly liable for the damage caused by industrial accidents (Article 4(1)).[144] Furthermore, a fault-based liability might apply to other persons such as servants or agents of the operator, if they cause or contribute to damage by their "wrongful, intentional, reckless or negligent acts or omissions" (Article 5). Following an accident, the operator shall take all reasonable measures for mitigation of damage according to the applicable domestic law and other relevant provisions of the conventions. The liability of operators is financially limited, based on the types of substances and their quantities (Article 9 and Annex 2). The Protocol contains a provision on financial security (Article 11).

1.4.2.2. Basis of liability

The Protocol applies to damage caused by the transboundary effects of an industrial accident on transboundary waters and only to damage suffered in a country other than that where the industrial accident has occurred.[145] With that in mind, Article 4 of the Protocol imposes strict liability on operators for damage caused by an industrial accident.

The operator can escape liability if he or she can prove that the accident resulted from "an act of armed conflict, hostilities, civil war or insurrection", or if it is "the result of a natural phenomenon of exceptional, inevitable, unforeseeable and irresistible character". Furthermore, no liability shall be attached to the operator if the damage is "[w]holly the result of compliance with a compulsory measure of a public authority of the Party where the industrial accident has occurred" or is "wholly the result of the wrongful intentional conduct of a third party".[146] The exclusion from liability according to the abovementioned reasons would be granted only if the operator has been taking appropriate safety measures according to the applicable law.[147]

---

[143] See the preamble to the Civil Liability Protocol.
[144] Industrial hazardous activities are listed in the Annex of the Convention on the Transboundary Effects of Industrial Accidents.
[145] Article 3 of the Civil Liability Protocol.   [146] Article 4(2) of the Civil Liability Protocol.
[147] Ibid.

Moreover, without prejudice to the strict liability regime, a fault-based liability might be imposed on persons who have caused or contributed to the accident by their wrongful, intentional, reckless or negligent acts or omissions.[148] Hence, strict liability will be imposed on operators to the extent that damage has not been caused by the wrongful act of other persons. In other words, the operator and the operator's agents or servants are identified as separate persons in the Protocol. When also taking into account the right of recourse defined in Article 7 of the Protocol and the fault-based liability for other parties than the operator in Article 5, one could argue that the basis of liability is not only strict liability, but strict liability and negligence as complementary regimes.

1.4.2.3.   Liable persons

The concept of "operator" has been defined in Article 1(e) of the 1992 Convention on the Transboundary Effects of Industrial Accidents as "any natural or legal person, including public authorities, in charge of an activity, e.g., supervising, planning to carry out or carrying out an activity". There is no separate definition of this concept in the Civil Liability Protocol, but it can be deduced that operators can be private entities as well as State-owned companies.[149]

In cases that two or more operators are involved in one accident, the claimant has the right to seek full compensation for the damage from any or all of the operators liable. If one of the operators proves that only part of the damage was caused by an industrial accident within its responsibility, that operator would be held liable only to the extent of his or her responsibility (Article 4(4)). Furthermore, the person liable may be entitled to a right of recourse against any other person also liable under the Protocol, e.g., pursuant to the law of the competent court or based on contractual arrangements.[150]

1.4.2.4.   Limitation of liability

The Protocol includes financial limits on the amount of compensation. This limitation of liability may allow insurability of such damage, especially when taking into account the provisions on financial security which are also defined in Annex II of the Protocol (respectively 2.5, 10 and 10

---

[148] Article 5 of the Civil Liability Protocol.
[149] Article 11 of the Protocol explicitly considers also the financial security of State-owned operators.
[150] For details see Article 7 of the Civil Liability Protocol.

million units of account; see further below). However, damage exceeding the amount of financial liability is not compensated via the provisions of the Civil Liability Protocol. Even if the damage resulted from a personal act or omission by the operator, he or she can enjoy limitation of liability.

1.4.2.5. Financial security and compensation mechanism

Operators shall ensure that they have financial security covering at least the minimum limits specified in Annex II of the Protocol: 2.5 million units of account for Category A hazardous activities and 10 million units of account both for Categories B and C.[151] The type of financial security has not been prescribed; Article 11 in that respect refers to "insurance, bonds or other financial guarantees including financial mechanisms providing compensation in the event of insolvency".[152]

1.4.2.6. Conclusions

The Civil Liability Protocol, which is not yet in force, establishes a strict liability regime for operators with respect to compensation for damage caused by the transboundary effects of industrial accidents on transboundary waters. This regime is complemented by a financial limitation of liability which, inter alia, may facilitate the insurability of such damage. However, the minimum amount of financial security prescribed by the Protocol is only a quarter of the amount of the liability cap. A claimant can directly bring action against the insurer, unless a State explicitly opts out of this regime.

It might be concluded that the aim of the Protocol is to establish a liability regime which to some extent governs transboundary water industrial accidents. According to the UNECE website, the Protocol "will give individuals affected by the transboundary impact of industrial accidents on international watercourses (e.g., fishermen or operators of downstream waterworks) a legal claim for adequate and prompt compensation". Also, it "fills one of the major gaps in international environmental legislation and solves the problem of uncompensated damage in neighbouring countries".[153] Nevertheless, since the adoption of the Protocol on 21 May

---

[151] For a definition of the categories, see Annex I and II of the Protocol or section 1.4.2.4. *supra.*

[152] Article 11(1) of the Civil Liability Protocol.

[153] www.unece.org/env/civil-liability/welcome.html. More potential benefits of the Protocol are listed there, including its expected effects on prevention of accidents.

2003 only Hungary has ratified it and all other State Parties have not.[154] One reason might be the scope of the Protocol, which includes a wide range of industries. Another reason might be uncertainty concerning the effectiveness and practical usefulness of the Protocol (with its wide range of exclusions and possibilities to opt out of certain clauses).

1.4.3.   *1971 United Nations Convention on International Liability for Damage Caused by Space Objects*

1.4.3.1.   Brief summary of the regime

Elaborating on Article 7 of the 1967 UN Outer Space Treaty,[155] the 1971 Convention on International Liability for Damage Caused by Space Objects (Liability Convention) provides that a launching State shall be absolutely liable to pay compensation for damage caused by its space objects on the surface of the earth or to aircraft. Furthermore, a launching State shall be liable for damage due to its faults in space. The convention also provides for procedures for the settlement of claims for damages. Agreement on the Liability Convention was reached in the General Assembly in 1971 and the convention entered into force in September 1972.

1.4.3.2.   Basis of liability

The convention imposes *absolute liability*, which refers to a liability system without any defence or exclusion. Article 2 states that "[a] launching State shall be absolutely liable to pay compensation for damage caused by its space object on the surface of the Earth or to aircraft in flight".

The convention in Article 3 also introduces a negligence-based liability, by imposing liability on a launching State for damage due to its faults in space: "In the event of damage being caused elsewhere than on the surface of the Earth to a space object of one launching State or to persons

---

[154] For more information, see: https:////treaties.un.org/Pages/ViewDetails.aspx?src= TREATY&mtdsg_no=XXVII-16&chapter=27&lang=en.

[155] Treaty on Principles Governing the Activities of States in the Exploration and Use of Outer Space, including the Moon and Other Celestial Bodies, adopted on 27 January 1967. Article 7 reads as follows: "Each State Party to the Treaty that launches or procures the launching of an object into outer space, including the Moon and other celestial bodies, and each State Party from whose territory or facility an object is launched, is internationally liable for damage to another State Party to the Treaty or to its natural or juridical persons by such object or its component parts on the Earth, in air space or in outer space, including the Moon and other celestial bodies."

or property on board such a space object by a space object of another launching State, the latter shall be liable only if the damage is due to its fault or the fault of persons for whom it is responsible."

1.4.3.3.   Liable persons

The Liability Convention refers to the concept of "launching States". According to Article 1 of the convention, this term means: "(i) A State which launches or procures the launching of a space object; (ii) A State from whose territory or facility a space object is launched." The term "launching" also includes attempted launching.[156]

In Article 4 a system of joint and several liability is introduced with respect to all damage being caused elsewhere than on the surface of the earth to a space object of one launching State or to persons or property on board such a space object by a space object of another launching State and of damage thereby being caused to a *third* State or to its natural or juridical persons. In such case the first two States shall be jointly and severally liable to the third State.[157] The burden of compensation per State depends on the extent to which each of the States were at fault (i.e. a system of proportional liability). If the extent of the fault cannot be established, the States will have to share the burden of compensation equally.

Joint and several liability is also imposed whenever two or more States *jointly launch* a space object and thereby cause damage (Article 5). The participating States in a joint launching may conclude agreements regarding the apportioning of liability among themselves, as long as this does not limit the right of the State where the damage occurs to be compensated.

1.4.3.4.   Damage covered

In the preamble to the convention, the need is recognised to ensure prompt payment of a full and equitable measure of compensation to victims of damage caused by space objects. The term "damage" is defined in Article 1 of the convention and refers to "loss of life, personal injury or other impairment of health; or loss of or damage to property of States or of persons, natural or juridical, or property of international intergovernmental organizations".[158] Hence, damages seem to relate to property damage and personal injury.

---

[156] Liability Convention, Article 1(b) and (c).
[157] See furthermore Article 4(1).   [158] Liability Convention, Article 1(a).

Article 12 adds to this that the amount of the compensation

> shall be determined in accordance with international law and the principles of justice and equity, in order to provide such reparation in respect of the damage as will restore the person, natural or juridical, State or international organization on whose behalf the claim is presented to the condition which would have existed if the damage had not occurred.

1.4.3.5.   Exclusions and defences

There are no exclusions or defences. Article 6(1) of the convention states that exoneration from absolute liability can only be granted if a launching State establishes that the damage "has resulted wholly or partially from gross negligence or from an act or omission done with intent to cause damage on the part of a claimant State or of natural or juridical persons it represents".

1.4.3.6.   Conclusions

The concept of absolute liability without any defence or exclusion for damage caused by space objects on the surface of the earth or to aircraft in flight is very interesting. However, to our knowledge the convention has never been applied. Also, the convention does not include any provisions on financial security or insurance.

Another striking aspect of this convention is the fact that liability is attributed to the State and not to operators. It has been indicated in the legal literature that this is the only treaty where States are held directly liable.[159]

1.5.   Conclusions

In this chapter, we analysed the extent to which operators could be held liable on the basis of (national legislation implementing) international treaties dealing with civil aviation, nuclear liability and environmental liability. The question was equally asked to what extent those international treaties could give rise to liability of the security industry. In this respect, seven specific liability regimes were analysed. We will first provide a brief comparison of those liability regimes (1.5.1.); subsequently, we will examine to what extent those liability regimes can be applied to operators or to the security industry (1.5.2.). Finally, we will briefly address the

---

[159] See e.g., Sands and Peel 2012.

question of whether some lessons could be drawn from the study of those international treaties if a future liability regime for the (European) security industry were to be shaped (1.5.3.).

1.5.1.   Comparing liability regimes

The seven liability regimes addressed in this chapter can be categorised into three groups. The first group of conventions relates to civil aviation, more particularly the Rome Convention on "damage caused by foreign aircrafts to third parties on the surface" and the Montreal Convention on "international carriage by air". The second set of conventions deals broadly with nuclear liability. After the discussion of these nuclear liability conventions we presented the international conventions dealing with civil liability for and compensation of damage caused by oil pollution, more particularly the Civil Liability Convention for Oil Pollution Damage (CLC) and the International Convention on the Establishment of an International Fund for Compensation for Oil Pollution Damage (Fund Convention). The third set of conventions deals with other relevant treaties, whereby we selected those treaties that also have provisions on liability: the International Convention on Liability and Compensation for Damage in Connection with the Carriage of Hazardous and Noxious Substances by Sea (HNS Convention), the Protocol on Civil Liability and Compensation for Damage Caused by the Transboundary Effects of Industrial Accidents on Transboundary Waters (Civil Liability Protocol) and finally the UN Convention on International Liability for Damage Caused by Space Objects (also referred to as the 1971 Liability Convention).

The main features of the liability regimes in these seven conventions are summarised in Table 5.

1.5.2.   Relevance of the international treaties for TRR

The conventions discussed above are relevant in the sense that they often channel liability to particular operators. In some cases this constitutes an exclusive channelling. This is for example the case in the CLC, which in principle channels liability exclusively to the ship-owner. Hence, the liability of others is excluded. The same seems to be the case in the HNS Convention which equally channels liability to the ship-owner. Also in cases where involvement of the security industry may be more likely, such

Table 5 *Scheme 1: comparison of liability regimes in international treaties*

Criterion	Rome	Montreal	Nuclear	Oil	HNS	Protocol	Space
Basis	SL[160]	SL	absolute	SL	SL	SL	absolute
Liable persons	operator; liability of others not excluded	air carrier, but liability of others possible as well	operator	ship-owner	ship-owner	operator	launching State
Damage	cap	cap	cap	cap	cap	cap	–
Defences not natural disasters/ terrorism	armed conflict; not terrorism/ natural disaster	armed conflict; not terrorism/ natural disaster	armed conflict and civil war; not natural disaster	war; exceptional natural disasters	war; exceptional natural disasters	war; exceptional natural disasters no defences	no defences
Financial security	mandatory security	mandatory security	mandatory security	mandatory security	mandatory security	mandatory security (limited)	–
Additional funding			State intervention	fund	fund		

[160] "SL" means strict liability.

as in the nuclear area, there is a strong reliance on channelling to the operator of the nuclear power plant. Exceptions to this channelling are quite difficult and would only occur if for example there is an agreement between the operator of the nuclear power plant and the third party (presumably the security industry). However, it is unlikely that the security industry would voluntarily accept liability in case of a nuclear accident. In that sense it can be held, as was mentioned above, that exclusive channelling to (for example) the operator of a nuclear power plant or a ship-owner (like in the case of the CLC and HNS Convention) in fact shields the security industry from liability. Furthermore, in the case of the Convention on International Liability for Damage Caused by Space Objects, liability is attributed to the "Launching States".

In some cases the channelling is not exclusive and other parties can still be held liable. This is, for example, the case in the Montreal Convention on International Carriage by Air. However, the persons who could be held liable are also addressed in a limited manner in the convention, for example indicating that liability would be possible against other agents of the contracting or actual carrier. A similar provision can be found in the Rome Convention where channelling is also not exclusive. Moreover, both conventions still have the possibility of a right of recourse against other liable parties.

It is, however, important to note that defences in international conventions are relatively limited. For example in the case of the Rome and Montreal Conventions terrorism or natural disasters do not constitute a ground of excuse or justification. This in a way is (again) reassuring for the security industry since it means that the exclusive channelled (strict) liability will still apply to the designated operators in the international conventions, again limiting the likelihood that on the basis of those conventions one would call on the liability of the security industry. That would in fact only be possible in case of recourse, and then only in those conventions that allow for such a recourse.

Summarising, the study of these liability regimes in the international treaties do not create a specific liability regime for the security industry; on the contrary, it seems that the exclusive channelling to others rather provides a shield from liability for the security industry. However, the channelling of liability has as a consequence that it will primarily be the operators who are liable. Moreover, we equally indicated that usually terrorism is not a ground for excluding the liability of operators. The conclusion of this study of the international treaties is therefore that operators will largely be held liable for TRR; not the security industry.

1.5.3. Policy relevance

We can now address the question of whether the seven conventions that
we have studied in more detail in this chapter provide interesting features
that could be taken into account for a potential (European) liability regime
for the security industry. A first interesting feature, when looking at the
table that summarised the liability regimes, is that all treaties we examined
are based on strict liability. This is to some extent not surprising since
all treaties apply to so-called hazardous activities and strict liability often
applies to ultra-hazardous activities.

Another important feature already mentioned was the channelling of
liability to the operator. Especially when discussing the international conventions with respect to nuclear liability and marine oil pollution liability,
we argued that an exclusive channelling of liability can undoubtedly be
considered as beneficial to the security industry. After all, when only the
operator (e.g., of a nuclear power plant) is indicated as liable person this
automatically removes the threat of liability from the security industry.
However, one should be careful of implying from the mere fact that many
international conventions use this channelling of liability, that it would
therefore also be a useful or interesting device for a potential liability
regime for the security industry. Such channelling of liability is highly
criticised in the literature. The main problem is that when liability is
exclusively channelled to one liable operator, this automatically excludes
liability of all others who also could have contributed to the accident risk.
If one believes that liability rules also provide incentives for prevention
(as is argued, e.g., in law and economics literature) that may not be a
desirable effect. Indeed, channelling may remove the incentives for prevention for persons other than the single operator to whom the liability
risk is channelled.

Similar arguments apply with respect to another feature that was apparent in six out of the seven international conventions discussed above, that
liability is always limited. Indeed, most international conventions apparently pay an important price for the strict liability of the operator, i.e.
a financial cap is put on the liability of the operator. But again, literature with respect to the nuclear and marine pollution conventions was
very critical with respect to the financial cap on liability. The criticism
is directed on the one hand to the fact that the operator will only have
incentives to prevent an accident to the amount of the limited liability.
A financial cap could hence reduce the incentives for prevention. On the
other hand, to the extent that the actual damage could be substantially
larger than the capped liability, victims would remain uncompensated.

This leads to a third type of criticism, that a financial cap on liability de facto allows operators to externalise harm to society. From an economic perspective a financial cap in fact constitutes a subsidy to industry, which may be problematic.

Similar criticisms were also formulated with respect to yet another interesting feature in both the nuclear liability and marine oil pollution conventions, that additional funding is provided. In the case of the nuclear conventions this additional funding is provided by the installation State (the so-called second layer) or by all signatory States (the so-called third layer). This State intervention is heavily criticised in the literature, arguing that public funds are used to compensate victims, subsidising once more the nuclear industry. That effect is not present in case of the marine pollution conventions. The International Oil Pollution Compensation Fund is financed through contributions by oil receivers and the same is the case for the HNS Fund which is equally financed by industry. Given the criticisms on those devices this could constitute an important lesson for a future liability regime for the EU security industry: the literature addressing nuclear liability and the liability for marine-oil pollution strongly doubts the usefulness of a financial cap on liability, and criticises exclusive channelling and the provision of additional funding through the public purse.

One additional important feature is apparent in six out of the seven international treaties we discussed, that the operators that are held exclusively liable according to the conventions also need to show mandatory insurance. The overview of the conventions in this chapter shows that, apparently, at the international level the introduction of a duty to provide financial security in order to be able to meet the strict liability from the conventions seems to be the state of the art and could be considered as "best practice". The liability regimes discussed in this chapter moreover nicely show that at the policy level a broad set of options can be provided to operators to provide proof of their solvency. This should hence not necessarily be limited to insurance. For example, the Rome Convention and the Civil Liability Protocol refer to a variety of financial security mechanisms such as cash deposits, bank guarantees and guarantees by the Contracting State. These are interesting examples if one were to consider the introduction of a duty to provide financial security to cover the liability.

Liability for terrorism-related risk under EU law

LUCAS BERGKAMP AND NICOLAS HERBATSCHEK[*]

2.1. Introduction

Although no EU-wide regime on third-party liability for terrorist acts exists, there is EU law that is relevant to terrorism-related risk (TRR), including EU legislation and some judgments of the European courts. This chapter analyses these EU laws. It discusses the EU law that is relevant to civil liability exposure of both Member States and private parties. In addition, it analyses the potential effects of EU regulation that itself does not set forth any liability rules, but may contain requirements and obligations that may indirectly affect liability exposure in positive or negative ways. As a supranational legal regime, EU law also sets forth rules that are relevant to cross-border civil liability litigation, which deserve some attention.

For the most part, the analysis of relevant EU legislation focuses on legal provisions, not European court judgments. As a general rule, case law has not played a significant role in the interpretation of this EU legislation, but there are a few cases under the EU's liability legislation that may be relevant to the liability exposure for terrorism-related risk. These cases are highlighted. Reasons as to why case law of the European courts in these domains is, by and large, not pertinent to the issues central to our analysis include the lack of litigiousness in Europe (see 8.1.) and the fact that EU legislation is implemented through the laws of the Member States and proceedings are brought before the national courts, with the European

---

[*] Nicolas Herbatschek is an Associate in the law firm of Hunton & Williams LLP, Brussels. He has broad experience in counselling multinational companies on regulatory and liability issues. In addition to European law, he advises on national environmental and health and safety regulations and managing related risks, including general civil, product and environmental liability. Mr Herbatschek holds graduate degrees in law from the University of Virginia, where he was a Fulbright scholar and a University of Virginia School of Law scholar, and the Université Catholique de Louvain, Belgium.

courts getting involved only if the national courts believe that EU law issues arise. An analysis of the national case law is provided in Chapter 3, which deals with the law of the Member States.

The first section of this chapter discusses the *Francovich* doctrine. This doctrine creates, at EU level, liability of Member States for failure to implement EU law. The focus is on its relevance to terrorism-related risk. The second section considers the EU's policies in relation to terrorism and specifically the legislation regarding the compensation of crime victims. In the third section, the discussion shifts to two legal instruments that would appear to be directly relevant to the liability exposure in relation to terrorism-related risk, i.e. the Environmental Liability Directive and the Product Liability Directive. The fourth section considers secondary EU law that regulates activities and products, and its potential effects on the exposure of governments and private parties to liability for terrorism-related risk. In this section, a few European directives and regulations that are relevant to activities involving risk and security products are reviewed, and some general comments are made about the effect of such laws on liability exposure. In the fifth section, EU secondary legislation relevant to cross-border damage and claims is discussed, including the recognition and enforcement of judgments in civil and commercial matters (the "Brussels I Regulation") and the law applicable to non-contractual obligations (the "Rome II Regulation").

2.2. Member State liability for terrorism-related risk under the *Francovich* doctrine

The debate on liability for damage caused by terrorism typically revolves around liability of private parties and insurance coverage, while little attention is devoted to the liability of Member States. Member States may be liable for damages caused by a serious breach of an obligation to implement a provision of EU law. As discussed below, existing EU secondary legislation imposes obligations on private parties to take measures to protect potential victims from TRR. If a Member State fails to implement such an obligation, under certain conditions, that State may be liable to a citizen whose rights were not adequately protected. This is the essence of the *Francovich* doctrine.

In *Francovich* v. *Italy*, the European Court of Justice held that Member States, if the conditions discussed below are met, are liable to make reparation to private individuals whose Community law rights were infringed due to the State's failure to take all measures necessary to achieve the results prescribed by a directive.[1] This right to compensation is based on two grounds. First, the Court argued that "the full effectiveness of Community rules would be impaired and the protection of the rights which they grant would be weakened if individuals were unable to obtain redress when their rights are infringed by a breach of Community law for which a Member State can be held responsible."[2] Second, the Member State's obligation to compensate this loss is inherent in Article 5 of the EEC Treaty (now, Article 4(3), Treaty on European Union), which obliges a Member State to take all appropriate measures to ensure fulfilment of their obligations under EU law, including, according to the Court, the duty to undo the consequences of a breach of EU law.[3] To take one of the regimes discussed in this chapter as an example, the failure of a State to oblige an operator to take preventive or restorative measures under the Environmental Liability Directive, would likely give rise to *Francovich* liability, as a result of which this State would have to pay compensation to a private individual whose rights have been infringed as a consequence of its inaction.

The *Francovich* doctrine was further developed in a series of subsequent judgments of the Court. In *Brasserie du Pêcheur*, the Court deliberated on whether State liability can arise not as a result of a failure to implement an EU directive, but rather due to the enactment of domestic legislation that infringes EU law. Drawing upon an analogy with the State liability doctrine under public international law, the Court held that if an organ of the State breaches EU law, the State may be held liable for the damages suffered by individuals as a result of this breach. Therefore, if an organ of the State breaches its EU law obligations, individuals can invoke State liability.[4] The Court found, however, that not every breach of EU law is sufficient to trigger liability. Rather, the breach must be "sufficiently serious",[5] such that a Member State "in the exercise of its rule-making powers, manifestly and gravely disregards the limits on those powers".[6] The organ of the State must have committed "manifest and grave disregard", rather

---

[1] Joined Cases C-6/90 and C-9/90 *Francovich* v. *Italy* [1991] ECR I-5357.
[2] Ibid., para 33.   [3] Ibid., paras 33–6.
[4] Joined Case C-46/93 and C-48/93 *Brasserie du Pêcheur* v. *Federal Republic of Germany* and *The Queen* v. *Secretary of State for Transport* [1996] ECR I-1147, para 42.
[5] Case C-5/71 *Aktien-Zuckerfabrik Schöppenstedt* v. *Council* [1971] ECR 975.
[6] Joined Cases C-178/94, C-179/94, C-188/94, C-189/94 and C-190/94 *Erich Dillenkofer* v. *Federal Republic of Germany* [1996] ECR I-04845.

than merely having erred, since "the exercise of the legislative function must not be hindered by the prospect of actions for damages whenever the general interest . . . requires legislative measures to be adopted which may adversely affect individual interests."[7] There is no need to demonstrate that the State was at fault, however, so *Francovich* liability is strict.[8] If the Member States were left very little or no discretion with regard to implementation and application of particular EU legislation, then the mere infringement of EU law may be enough to constitute a breach.[9] The notion of a breach of an EU law provision implies that a State cannot be found liable for simply interpreting EU legislation divergently, insofar as this interpretation does not conflict with the text of the law.[10] Moreover, the Court has rejected the argument that State liability applies only to provisions that are not directly effective, because "it is all the more so in the event of infringement of a right directly conferred by a Community provision upon which individuals are entitled to rely before the national courts."[11]

2.3.   EU laws and policies regarding terrorism

This section takes a look at the EU's laws and policies specifically directed at the fight against terrorism. We first review the EU counter-terrorism policy and then analyse the legislation on the compensation of victims of violent crime, including terrorism.

2.3.1.   EU policy on combating terrorism

Following 9/11, in 2002, the EU Council adopted Framework Decision 2002/475/JHA, which provides a common definition of terrorist and

---

[7] Joined Case C-46/93and C-48/93 *Brasserie du Pêcheur* v. *Federal Republic of Germany* and *The Queen* v. *Secretary of State for Transport* [1996] ECR I-1147, para 45.

[8] Joined Case C-46/93and C-48/93 *Brasserie du Pêcheur* v. *Federal Republic of Germany* and *The Queen* v. *Secretary of State for Transport* [1996] ECR I-1147, para 94–96; Joined Cases C-178/94, C-179/94, C-188/94, C-189/94 and C-190/94 *Erich Dillenkofer* v. *Federal Republic of Germany* [1996] ECR I-04845, para 28.

[9] Case C-5/94 *The Queen* v. *Ministry of Agriculture, Fisheries and Food,* ex parte Hedley Lomas (Ireland) Ltd. [1996] ECR I-2553.

[10] Case C-392/93 *The Queen* v. *H.M. Treasury,* ex p. British Telecommunications [1996] ECR I-1631.

[11] Joined Case C-46/93 and C-48/93 *Brasserie du Pêcheur* v. *Federal Republic of Germany* and *The Queen* v. *Secretary of State for Transport* [1996] ECR I-1147, para 18–23.

terrorist-linked offences.[12] Although all operational work is performed by EU States' law enforcement and intelligence authorities, the EU's commitment is to combat terrorism globally, while respecting human rights, so as to make Europe safer. As the Council recognised, the Member States have primary responsibility in this area. To support the Member States, EU policy pursues four objectives: prevention, protection, pursuit and response.[13] To achieve prevention of terrorism, the EU intends to prevent radicalisation and recruitment of terrorists by identifying the methods, propaganda and the instruments used by terrorists.[14] The EU plays a role in coordinating the Member States' activities in these areas and facilitates the sharing of information and determining best practices.[15] The protection policy is aimed at reducing the vulnerability of targets to attack and limiting the resulting impact of attack. Collective action for border security, transport and other cross-border infrastructures are the key protection instruments.[16] With respect to increasing transport security, Member States must examine the weak spots of transport systems and enhance the security of roads, trains, airports and seaports by implementing agreed common standards.[17] A European programme for critical infrastructure protection is to be developed and implemented. Member States must also cooperate to combat chemical, biological, radiological and nuclear materials (CBRN).[18]

The third part of the EU's counter-terrorism policy involves the pursuit of terrorists across borders. This policy is aimed at (1) cutting off access to attack materials (arms, explosives, etc.), disrupting terrorist networks and recruitment agents, and tackling the misuse of non-profit associations,[19] (2) eliminating sources of terrorist financing by carrying out inquiries, freezing assets and impeding money transfers,[20] and (3) interfering with the planning of terrorist activities by impeding the communication and dissemination of terrorists' technical knowledge, especially via the Internet.[21] Member States must work together directly and through Europol and Eurojust; the European arrest warrant and

[12] Council Framework Decision 2002/475/JHA of 13 June 2002 on combating terrorism [2002] OJ L 164/3.
[13] Council of the European Union, "The European Union Counter-Terrorism Strategy", Brussels, 30 November 2005, 14469/4/08 (rev 4).
[14] Council Framework Decision 2002/475/JHA, Articles 6 and 7.
[15] Council Framework Decision 2002/475/JHA, Article 8.
[16] Ibid., Articles 15–18.   [17] Ibid., Article 21.   [18] Ibid., Article 20.
[19] Ibid., Article 28 et seq.   [20] Ibid., Article 29.   [21] Ibid., Article 28.

the European evidence warrant are legal instruments intended to assist them in their efforts. A Financial Action Task Force (FATF), of which the Commission is a member, provides recommendations, some of which are implemented by European legislation.

Acknowledging that the terrorist threat cannot be reduced to zero, the EU has also developed a response strategy. The Member States have primary responsibility to deal with terrorist attacks when they occur and may often rely on the response systems that have been developed to address natural or technological disasters and on the European civil protection mechanisms.[22] If a terrorist attack occurs, Member States must exchange information and share resources in a spirit of solidarity. Member States must also ensure that appropriate assistance and compensation is made available to the victims of terrorism and their families.[23] The EU's strategy is complemented by a detailed action plan listing all relevant measures to be taken under the four pillars of this strategy.[24]

It has been argued that the EU's role in counter-terrorism policy is paradoxical. Member State governments agree in principle that cooperation at the EU level is a good thing because of the cross-border nature of the terrorist threat, but to protect their national sovereignty they are reluctant to give the EU the necessary powers (such as investigation and prosecution) and resources (such as spies and money) it would need to be truly effective.[25] Even stronger, the question has also been asked whether the EU's counter-terrorism policy is a "paper tiger".[26] To enhance the fight against terrorism, in 2008, the Council adopted Framework Decision 2008/919/JHA,[27] which amended the Framework Decision on Combating Terrorism of 2002 to require that Member States make public provocation, recruitment and training for terrorism official crimes. A Commission report of September 2014 shows that questions remain as to the full compliance of the implementing measures in some Member States.[28]

---

[22] Ibid., Articles 32–34.   [23] Ibid., Article 36.

[24] Council of the European Union, "Implementation of the Strategy and Action Plan to Combat Terrorism", Brussels, 20 May 2007, 9666/07 (Add 1).

[25] Keohane 2005.   [26] Bures 2011.

[27] Council Framework Decision 2008/919/JHA of 28 November 2008 amending Framework Decision 2002/475/JHA on combating terrorism, OJ L 330/21.

[28] European Commission, "Report from the Commission to the European Parliament and the Council on the Implementation of Council Framework Decision 2008/919/JHA of 28 November 2008 amending Framework Decision 2002/475/JHA on combating terrorism", COM(2014) 554 final.

In the context of liability for terrorism-related risk, the EU counter-terrorism policy is relevant chiefly because it defines Member States' responsibilities and obligations. In doing so, the EU counter-terrorism policy could be deemed to create a potential set of duties of care for Member States, the breach of which may trigger liability on their part if breach of such obligations causes damage. Whether or not it would trigger liability, of course, is a function of national law. Liability for breach of the Member State's responsibility for ensuring appropriate compensation would be a special case; if the claim prevails, it would mean that the judiciary would ensure that such compensation is awarded and either itself determine the amount or order the executive to do so. Note, however, that the EU also adopted a specific directive requiring compensation for victims of violent crime, including terrorism.

2.3.2. Directive 2004/80/EC relating to compensation to crime victims

2.3.2.1. Brief summary of the regime

Directive 2004/80/EC relating to compensation to crime victims[29] (the "Compensation Directive") was adopted pursuant to the Council's 2004 Declaration on Combating Terrorism.[30] It requires that Member States operate a compensation scheme for victims of violent intentional crime committed in their territory. This scheme is available to victims, regardless of their country of residence.[31] The amount paid out to victims must be fair and appropriate.[32] To facilitate compensation in cross-border cases, victims are entitled to ask for assistance from the authority of the Member State in which they reside.[33]

Although the Compensation Directive does not relate to civil procedure, it may affect third-party liability exposure. Terrorism involves intentional violent crime covered by the Compensation Directive. Thus, where terrorist attacks strike, injured citizens will likely have claims pursuant to the directive. Any compensation they are granted under these schemes will likely reduce the amounts that they could claim in civil litigation. In common law, the deduction of amounts recovered through other means from compensation payable under civil liability law is known as the "collateral source" rule.

---

[29] Council Directive (EC) 80/2004 relating to compensation to crime victims [2004] OJ L 261/2.
[30] Compensation Directive, Articles 1–2.
[31] Ibid., Article 12.　　[32] Ibid., Article 12.　　[33] Ibid., Articles 1–6.

2.3.2.2.   Implications for liability for terrorism-related risk

The Compensation Directive significantly improves the compensation of crime victims, including the victims of acts of terrorism. Because of the ease with which compensation can be claimed under the Directive, victims of acts of terrorism might favour this compensation regime rather than suing any party involved, such as a facility operator or security provider, in particular if the amounts of compensation available under the Compensation Directive are equivalent to what could be obtained in civil litigation (assuming the collateral source rule applies). Given that Member States have an affirmative obligation under EU law to provide compensation, failure to do so will likely result in exposure to liability.

The specific rules and modalities for compensation, including the total amount of compensation, may vary from one Member State to another. Of interest to facility operators and security providers, the Compensation Directive does not set forth a subrogation mechanism that would allow a Member State to claim reimbursement from a party liable for the harm. The availability of any subrogation right should be assessed under the applicable law, as determined under the Brussels I Regulation (see above).

2.4.   EU legislation relevant to liability for terrorism-related risk

2.4.1.   Environmental Liability Directive

2.4.1.1.   Brief summary of the regime

With the Environmental Liability Directive (hereafter "Directive" or "ELD"), the EU established a framework for environmental liability based on the "polluter pays" principle aimed at prevention and remediation of environmental damage.[34] The Directive covers water pollution, damage to protected habitats and species and land contamination.[35] Under the ELD, the liable party is the "operator", i.e. the natural or legal person that carries out an occupational activity. Based on the "polluter pays" principle, the Directive imposes strict liability on operators of risky or potentially risky occupational activities listed in an annex to the Directive. Fault liability applies to operators of non-listed activities, but this

---

[34] Council Directive 2004/35/EC concerning Environmental Liability with regard to the Prevention and Remedying of Environmental Damage [2004], OJ L 143/56, Article 1 (ELD). For a commentary, see Bergkamp and Goldsmith (eds.) 2013.

[35] ELD, Article 2.

liability is limited to damage to protected habitats and species. Operators are required to take the necessary preventive action in case of an "imminent threat" of environmental damage. They are also obliged to remedy environmental damage once it has occurred. In specific cases where the operator fails to act or is not identifiable, the competent authority of the Member State involved may carry out the necessary preventive or remedial measures. Remediation measures must lead to the remediation of the damaged resources (nature, water, soil) to or towards the "baseline condition". If restoration in kind of natural resources is not possible or only partly possible, equivalent resources must be created at another location.

As the ELD involves minimum harmonisation, Member States may enact more stringent provisions in relation to the prevention and remedying of environmental damage.[36] ELD liability cannot be limited or excluded by contract.

2.4.1.2. *Exclusions and defences*

The ELD provides for exclusions from its scope (e.g., for nuclear installations and oil pollution damage covered by international treaties) and gives operators several defences against liability. Article 8(3) stipulates that the operator shall not be required to bear the costs of preventive or remedial actions, if it can prove that the damage was caused by third-party intervention or resulted from compliance with a compulsory order (Article 8(3)).

The defence for damage caused by a third party could be relevant to damage caused by terrorism, since terrorists are third parties in relation to this defence. Under the draft version of the ELD, this defence was subject to the additional condition that the third party intentionally caused the damage, but the final wording of Article 8(3) does not impose this condition. It does impose the condition, however, that "appropriate safety measures" were in place.

The ELD does not define the term "third party". In any event, persons, both natural persons and legal entities that are not related to the operator and access the operator's site without authorisation are covered by this term. This includes terrorists and other criminals. Employees, on the other hand, are likely not third parties and, thus, if an employee acting outside the scope of his authority causes environmental damage, the company cannot invoke the defence. In some cases, however, employees

---

[36] Ibid., Preamble No. 29 and Article 16.

could qualify as third parties, such as where an employee causes a bomb to explode at the facility over the weekend. If the operator has a contract or business relation with the putative third party, the defence may or may not be available. A maintenance service provider that performs services solely for one company (i.e. as it were, an employee) may not be considered a third party. The "polluter pays" principle suggests that the concept of third party should not be interpreted restrictively: if the third party under contract with the operator causes environmental damage, there is no reason to reject the defence and treat the operator as the polluter. Note, too, that even if the operator cannot invoke the defence, it may still have a claim against the third party that actually caused the damage under contract or civil law.

The condition that appropriate safety measures must be in place for the defence to be available raises the issue of how far the requisite safety measures should go. The operator should in any event implement the safety measures required by law, regulations and the permits for the facility. Whether he should go beyond this minimum needs to be analysed on a case-by-case basis. If the safety measures required by law are onerous and aimed at establishing a high level of safety, there would appear to be no reason to raise that level further for purposes of the defence. Industry standards and best practice may also play a role in this assessment. The potential for terrorist acts to cause damage, on the other hand, is not an independent factor in determining the safety measures required for the defence to apply. Thus, if an operator failed to take reasonable ("appropriate") safety measures (e.g., it did not fence its site), it cannot invoke this defence.

Relevant third-party acts include negligent and intentional acts, as well as any other acts. In all of these cases, there is a third-party damage-causing act and, if appropriate safety measures were in place, the operator is not exposed to liability under the ELD. This is an equitable result, because, like the environment, the operator is also a victim of the terrorists; it is free of blame and the damage-causing event should be considered beyond his control.

In addition to the defences of Article 8(3), the Directive allows for a permit defence and a state-of-the-art defence. Article 8(4) of the ELD states that

> Member States may allow the operator not to bear the cost of remedial actions if he demonstrates that he was not at fault or negligent and that the environmental damage was caused by an emission or event expressly

authorised by and fully in accordance with the conditions of, an authorisation conferred by or given under applicable national laws and regulations which implement the legislative measures adopted by the Community specified in Annex III, as applied at the date of the emission or event.[37]

Hence, if national law so provides, the permit defence would be available to the operators of dangerous occupational activities listed in Annex III to the Directive.[38] The state-of-the-art defence is also at the option of the Member States. If this defence is available, an operator is not liable where his activity was not considered to cause harm according to the state of scientific and technical knowledge at the time of the damage-causing activity. Specifically, the ELD stipulates in Article 8(4)(b) that "where an emission or activity or any manner of using a product causes damage and the operator demonstrates that scientific and technical knowledge at the time when the emission was released or the activity took place did not consider it likely that such damage would occur, Member States may allow the operator not to bear the restoration costs."[39] Note that the ELD requires that the operator demonstrates that it complied with the permit, or that the risk was unknown at the time of the accident and the objective state of scientific and technical knowledge did not enable the operator to detect the risk.[40] The permit defence and the state-of-the-art defence could be relevant defences in relation to TRR. If, for instance, environmental damage was caused by an industrial facility that was attacked by terrorists, the operator would not be liable if it can show permit compliance. Likewise, if a terrorism-related risk was not detectable at the time of the incident (e.g., liquid explosives ingested by a suicide terrorist that can be detonated remotely), the operator might escape liability.

2.4.1.3.   Causation

Pursuant to Article 6(1) of the ELD, the operator is required to take the necessary remedial measures if damage has been caused by its activity. This obligation thus turns on the question of whether there is a causal relationship between the operator's activity and the damage. The ELD is, by and large, silent on causation. It does not specify whether the burden of proof of the existence of a causal relationship lies with the operator or with the authorities. In accordance with the general rule, which places the

---

[37] Ibid., Article 8(4).   [38] Wenneras 2004.
[39] ELD, Article 8(4).   [40] Ibid., Articles 8(3) and 8(4).

burden of proof on the plaintiff, the authorities should prove causation; if a defendant invokes a defence, however, the burden of proof shifts to it. An indication that the ELD follows the general rule is that Article 8(3) and (4) concerning the permit and the state-of-the-art defences, respectively, put the burden of proof explicitly on the operator,[41] which could be interpreted to suggest that in all other cases, the authorities must provide proof.

In the *Augusta* cases, the European Court of Justice has confirmed that the authorities bear the burden of proof with respect to causation and that the use of causal presumptions is subject to serious restrictions.[42] Specifically, the Court found that plausible evidence capable of justifying the presumption is required in each case (e.g., the facility is located close to demonstrated pollution and there is a correlation between this pollution and the substances used by the operator). In the case of multi-party causation, the Member States are free to impose either joint and several liability, or allocate liability on the basis of some formula. Accordingly, Article 9 of the ELD states that if more than one operator causes environmental damage, the cost of remedying that damage is allocated among the operators in accordance with the law of the Member State concerned, in particular with respect to "the apportionment of liability between the producer and the user of a product".[43]

2.4.1.4.   Environmental Liability Directive's implications for terrorism-related risk

The ELD regime applies to operators of facilities that may be the target of terrorist attacks (such as chemical plants) and security providers. If, however, the activities concerned are not covered by the pertinent annex of the ELD,[44] the operator is exposed only to fault (as opposed to strict) liability and only for damage to protected habitats and species. Airports and train stations, for instance, are not likely to be covered by the annex and are thus subject to the fault liability regime. Chemical plants and power plants, on the other hand, are likely to be subject to strict liability;

---

[41] Cf. Wagner 2005.

[42] C-378/08, *Raffinerie Mediterranee (ERG) SpA, et al.* v. *Ministero dello Sviluppo Economico et al.* [2010] ECR I-01919, and Joined Cases C-379/08, *Raffinerie Mediterranee (ERG) SpA, Polimeri Europa SpA and Syndial SpA* v. *Ministero dello Sviluppo Economico et al.* and C-380/08, *ENI SpA* v. *Ministero Ambiente e Tutela del Territorio e del Mare et al.* [2010] ECR I-02007. For further discussion, see Bergkamp 2010.

[43] ELD Article 9.   [44] Annex III, ELD.

nuclear power plants benefit from an exception, if they are covered by the nuclear regimes listed in another annex to the ELD.[45]

A key issue with respect to damage caused by terrorism is whether the operator can invoke the defence of Article 8(3) of the ELD. If this defence applies, the operator will not be exposed to financial liability and, by implication, from all liability under the ELD. For the defence to apply, the operator must demonstrate that "appropriate safety measures" were in place. Since the ELD does not further define this term, what safety measures were "appropriate" has to be determined on a case-by-case basis. In determining appropriate safety measures in a specific case, relevant criteria may include (1) the hazards and risks generally associated with the activity, (2) the chance that the activity might be the target of a terrorist attack and any specific information available to the operator of an impending attack, (3) the costs of the safety measures already taken and the costs of additional measures that could have prevented the attack, and (4) whether the terrorist attack would have been prevented had the measures deemed appropriate been taken. The last factor, of course, has to do with the causal link: if appropriate measures would not have prevented the attack and thus the damage would have ensued despite appropriate safety measures, the damage was not caused by the lack of safety measures and, thus, if the defence is unavailable, the issue arises whether there is a causal link between the operation of the activity and the damage; under a counter-factual causal test ("but for" the failure to take appropriate safety measures, the damage had not occurred), no causation would be found.

Another difficult issue arises where damage has been caused by an activity at a site due to malperformance of an independent contractor that provided security services to the site. For instance, a guard employed by a security firm provides services at a chemical plant pursuant to a contract with the plant's operator and fails to properly check a visitor, who then commits an attack on the site's installations causing massive water pollution, soil contamination and natural resource damage. In this case, the issue is whether the security activity can be regarded as the activity that caused the damage. If so, the operator of that activity (i.e., the security firm) could be liable, but given that this activity is not subject to strict liability, the operator would only be exposed to fault liability for damage caused to protected habitats and species. If, on the other hand, the relevant activity is deemed to be a chemical plant, the plant's operator

---

[45] Annex V, ELD.

would be strictly liable for all environmental damages (water, land and natural resources).

2.4.2.   Product Liability Directive

2.4.2.1.   Brief summary of the regime

The Product Liability Directive[46] (hereafter "Directive" or "PLD"), as amended by Directive 1999/34,[47] harmonises the laws of the Member States on product liability. It imposes liability on manufacturers for certain kinds of damages caused by defective products. The term "product" is defined as "all movables even if incorporated into another movable or into an immovable".[48] This definition is broad and covers security products, i.e. any products used for security purposes, such as guns, bulletproof vests, detection equipment, etc. It does not cover services, even if they are provided in connection with products, such as security service providers using detection equipment for purposes of detecting explosives at an airport.[49]

The scope of damages to which liability attaches, however, is limited. The producer of a defective product is liable for death, personal injury and damage to private goods caused by the defect. Economic damage, such as lost profits, or damage to commercial property is not covered. Note, however, that the PLD covers damage suffered by both consumers and non-consumers that are natural persons. Liability under the PLD does not require fault on the part of the producer; the mere existence of a defect is sufficient. Liability is not absolute and the PLD sets forth certain defences, including the so-called "development risk" and "compliance" defences. Further, PLD liability cannot be limited or excluded by contract.

2.4.2.2.   The concept of defect

Under the PLD, the concept of "defect" is indirectly defined. Article 6 of the PLD provides that "[a] product is defective when it does not provide

---

[46] Council Directive 85/374/EEC on the approximation of the laws, regulations and administrative provisions of the Member States concerning liability for defective products [1985] OJ L 210/29 (Product Liability Directive, PLD).

[47] Council Directive (EC) 99/34 amending Council Directive 85/374/EEC on the approximation of the laws, regulations and administrative provisions of the Member States concerning liability for defective products [1999] OJ L 141/20.

[48] PLD, Article 2.

[49] Cf. Case C-495/10 *Centre hospitalier universitaire de Besançon* v. *Thomas Dutrueux* [2011] ECR I-00000.

the safety which a person is entitled to expect, taking all circumstances into account." Thus, the test is not necessarily a consumer expectation test; bystanders may also have a safety expectation. The relevant circumstances that determine the safety expectations include "(a) the presentation of the product; (b) the use to which it could reasonably be expected that the product would be put; and (c) the time when the product was put into circulation." The first of the factors relates to representations made with respect to the product and its performance, the instructions provided with the products and any warning and other relevant information. The second factor deals with foreseeable use, which is also affected by the information provided with the product and basically excludes any misuse (with the possible exception of foreseeable misuse) from being considered reasonably foreseeable use. The third factor implies that defect is a relative term: "[a] product shall not be considered defective for the sole reason that a better product is subsequently put into circulation."[50] Thus, detection equipment that is unable to detect certain types of explosives (e.g. semtex) is not defective because equipment that can detect such explosives has subsequently become available. Note that this provision does not state the opposite, i.e. that such equipment should be considered defective if it is placed on the market after semtex-detection equipment has become available. There will likely be substantial differences between the types of equipment, notably with respect to price. Users may have good reasons, including costs, to choose lower performance equipment over high performance equipment and their choice, of course, cannot be held against the producer, except if the equipment came with a warning or other informational defect (see below).

Three types of defects can be distinguished: manufacturing defects, design defects and informational (or "warning") defects.[51] Security products can be defective under all three of these categories. Detection equipment can be defective because a problem occurs during assembly, as a result of which the equipment deviates from the manufacturer's specifications. It can be defective because the operating instructions are inadequate. These two types of defects are relatively straightforward. The concept of design defect, however, is the most problematic, because design relates not only to technical possibilities but also to costs. In other words, design may involve trade-offs between performance and costs; cheap, low performance equipment, however, is not necessarily defective, even if

[50] PLD, Article 6.2.   [51] Lovells 2003.

high performance equipment is available. Whether there is a design defect may also relate to the information provided with the product; if that is so, the question arises whether design defect should be an independent category.

Where a non-security product is implicated in a terrorist attack, the issue might arise whether the non-security product should have incorporated a certain specific feature. For instance, if a car exploded due to a terrorist lighting the gas tank, the question is whether the tank should have had a lock. Could the absence of a lock be regarded as a design defect that would render the whole car defective? In other words, do reasonable safety expectations include an expectation that the gas tank is outfitted with a lock? To answer this question, the three non-exhaustive factors of the defect test listed above should be considered; all three (i.e. (1) the presentation of the product, (2) the use to which it could reasonably be expected that the product would be put, and (3) the time when the product was put into circulation) might all be relevant in this regards. If the conclusion is that the gas tank should have been outfitted with a lock to be non-defective based on design grounds, a further issue arises – the reason for the expectation of a lock. A lock may be regarded as necessary to prevent theft of gas, but not to prevent a terrorist from lighting it up. In such cases, the issues arises whether the absence of a lock makes the car defective in relation to terrorism-related damage and if so, whether there is a causal link between the defect and the damage.

2.4.2.3. *Exclusions and defences*

Liability under the PLD is not "absolute". The PLD provides several defences and grounds for exoneration. The producer is not liable if he proves:

(a) that he did not put the product into circulation; or
(b) that, having regard to the circumstances, it is probable that the defect which caused the damage did not exist at the time when the product was put into circulation by him or that this defect came into being afterwards; or
(c) that the product was neither manufactured by him for sale or any form of distribution for economic purpose nor manufactured or distributed by him in the course of his business; or
(d) that the defect is due to compliance of the product with mandatory regulations issued by the public authorities; or

(e) that the state of scientific and technical knowledge at the time when he put the product into circulation was not such as to enable the existence of the defect to be discovered; or

(f) in the case of a manufacturer of a component, that the defect is attributable to the design of the product in which the component has been fitted or to the instructions given by the manufacturer of the product.[52]

The defence under (e) is known as the "development risk" defence. Member States are not required to provide for the development risk defence in their national law and they are explicitly authorised by the PLD not to do so.[53] The producer may also be partly or totally exonerated from liability if he shows that the damage is caused both by a defect in its product and the fault of the injured person or any other person under his responsibility.[54]

In the context of terrorism-related risk, all of these defences may be relevant, depending on the facts of the case. Interesting issues arise with respect to the compliance defence, the defence that the defect did not exist at the time when the product was put into circulation and the "development risk" defence. The compliance defence is available if a security product (say, detection equipment) is defective due to prescriptions of mandatory regulations. If the applicable regulations prescribe only performance objectives (i.e. ends, not means), it is highly unlikely that a defect could be due to the regulations.

The producer bears the burden of proof with respect to the defence that the defect did not exist when the product was put into circulation. Of course, this proof typically cannot be full and comprehensive, and reason has to be applied. If, for instance, a product has been in use for a long time without any problems of the sort that now result in a defect, the producer's burden of proof is fairly light; a general showing of a sound quality control system might suffice and at that point the burden of proof would shift to the other party who would have to provide information showing that the defect was inherent to the product when it was put into circulation.

---

[52] PLD, Article 7.

[53] Ibid., Article 15(1). All Member States have done so, except Finland and Luxembourg. Certain products are also excluded from this defence in France (human blood and derivatives) and Germany (medicinal products and GMOs).

[54] PLD, Article 8(2).

The "development risk" or "state-of-the-art" defence is available only if the most advanced objective state of scientific and technical knowledge did not enable the producer to detect the defect.[55] It is not sufficient to prove that there was no known method of detection within the industry. In the security industry, relevant knowledge may reside with the industry, but also with the public authorities or universities and research institutions. Such knowledge, however, may for security reasons not be publicly available, or not be available to all security products providers. This may pose a problem if a claim made in connection with a terrorist attack alleges that the design of the detection equipment involved should have enabled a particular risk to be detected (e.g., an airport security detection system should have detected thin layers of a new type of explosive hidden in books) and the technology that allowed the "defect" to be cured was proprietary and not generally available. In such cases, the producer can avail itself of the defence if it shows that it could not detect the "defect" using all knowledge and technology available to it. The PLD does not treat as defective a security product that could not detect a risk (e.g., a particular method used by terrorists to hide explosives) that was unknowable and undetectable at the time the product was put into circulation, because users cannot expect the impossible. If the defect is known but undetectable, application of the development risk defence raises issues. In the UK, a court ruled that a supplier of blood contaminated by a known infectious agent was liable for the ensuing damage, even though this agent was undetectable.[56] A Dutch court adopted a different position in a similar case involving the HIV virus, which could not be detected in the particular blood product that was contaminated.[57] Similar issues may arise with respect to risks that are known in general and detectable in specific cases, but that cannot be eliminated. Such products may not be defective and, if they are, the development risk defence is irrelevant.

---

[55] "The defense cannot be satisfied simply because the standard precautions in the interested industrial sector had been complied with ... the producer of a defective product must prove that the objective state of scientific and technical knowledge, including the most advanced level of such knowledge, at the time when the product in question was put into circulation was not such as to enable the existence of the defect to be discovered." See Case C-300/95 *Commission* v. *United Kingdom* [1997] ECR I-02649, paras 25 and 29. For a detailed discussion of the development risks defence and its impact on innovation, see Fondazione Rosselli 2004.

[56] *A & Others* v. *National Blood Authority* [2001] 3 All ER 289 (QBD).

[57] *Hartman* v. *Stichting Sanquin Bloedvoorziening* [1999] NJ 621 (Rb Amsterdam).

2.4.2.4.   Causation

For a producer to be liable, the defective product must have caused the damage for which compensation is claimed. The PLD does not provide any rules regarding causation. This issue is left to the Member States, as the PLD requires only that the damage was "caused by" the defective product. It has been generally recognised that a defective product can "cause" damage actively (i.e. by transmitting a virus in the case of contaminated blood), but also passively (i.e. by not providing a benefit that should have been provided, e.g., a bulletproof vest with holes in it). Thus, a security product can be found to have "caused" damage if it failed to detect a risk.

Under national law, the causation rules applicable to civil liability generally will often apply. Some sort of "*conditio sine qua non*" test may have to be met and serves a minimal causal requirement. A further test may involve whether the damage was foreseeable or whether the defective product was the proximate cause of the damage. It should be remembered, however, that the kind of damages that are covered by the PLD are limited and include only personal injury, death and damage to personal property; as to these types of damages, there may well be a tendency not to be overly demanding in construing causation.

2.4.2.5.   Product Liability Directive's implications
for terrorism-related risk

At the EU level, the PLD regime is one of the few liability regimes. It establishes a civil liability mechanism that is relevant to all products, including both non-security products (such as cars) and security products (e.g., airport screening equipment), but not security services. It imposes no-fault liability on producers for defective products. A product is defective if it does not meet the safety expectations of the public at large. A producer may be able to avail itself of one of several defences, including the "state-of-the-art" defence.

The PLD may create specific challenges in the case of terrorism-related damages. Some security products are intended to protect against risks intentionally created by terrorists, who are trying to circumvent or "outsmart" security systems in an attempt to cause massive damages. With respect to both security and non-security products, the concept of design defect may raise issues. For instance, the design of a security product could be deemed defective if it did not protect against a specific risk, but if the risk is not detectable, the producer may be able to invoke the "development risk" defence. Whether a security product's design is defective is a function of the applicable safety expectations. Security product providers are not in a position to influence the safety expectations of the public-at-large, however, because they have limited access to the public and because information on the limitations of security products cannot be freely communicated for security reasons. Thus, in the specific case of the security industry, the objectives of the PLD, i.e. ensuring that products meet expectations, may not be realisable. Likewise, the development risk defence against known but undetectable risks may not be available in all jurisdictions. In theory, as discussed above, similar issues could arise with respect to non-security products, but in practice this may be less likely.

In short, in the case of security products, the PLD channels risks to the producers of such products, but these producers do not necessarily have effective options to address such risks. National product liability laws may be able to address these issues by construing their PLD-transposing legislation creatively, in particular in relation to the concept of defect. Of course, there are also ways in which these issues could be addressed at the EU level. For instance, the PLD could be amended to provide that security products complying with European or national standards are presumed to be non-defective. Such a rule would resolve many issues over the putative defectiveness of security products. In the absence of evidence that there are problems in practice, proposals for any amendments would likely be regarded as premature.

2.4.3.   Regulations and effects on liability

There are many EU laws that directly or indirectly pursue safety or security objectives. Directive 89/686 on personal protective equipment,[58] for instance, sets forth safety requirements for personal protective equipment ("PPE"), which are intended to ensure the health protection and safety of users. Harmonised European standards have been developed to facilitate proof of conformity with the general safety requirements. Compliance with these standards confers a presumption of conformity of the PPE with the Directive's safety requirements. Another example of EU law aimed at protecting safety is Directive 2012/18 on the control of major-accident

---

[58] Council Directive 89/686/EEC of 21 December 1989 on the approximation of the laws of the Member States relating to personal protective equipment [1989] OJ L 399/18.

hazards involving dangerous substances (the "Seseo Directive").[59] It
applies to establishments where dangerous substances are used or stored
in large quantities, mainly in the chemicals, petrochemicals, storage and
metal-refining sectors. Under the Seveso Directive, operators of covered facilities are required to prepare and implement a "major-accident
prevention policy" (MAPP) setting out the operator's overall approach,
including appropriate safety management systems, for controlling major-
accident hazards.[60] This MAPP must be designed to ensure a high level of
protection of human health and the environment and be proportionate
to the major-accident hazards; if national law so requires, it must be filed
with the national authorities. In addition, operators of some facilities
must prepare a safety report that should set forth details of the facility, the
dangerous substances present, possible major-accident scenarios and risk
analysis, prevention and intervention measures, etc.[61] The safety report
must be made available to any person who so requests.[62] Member States
must prohibit the operation of any storage facility, if the measures taken
by the operator for the prevention and mitigation of major accidents are
seriously deficient. These two examples can be supplemented with many
others.

EU legislation imposing safety or security requirements may affect
exposure to third-party liability for terrorism-related risk. This legislation does not impose any liability rules, but potentially affects civil liability
exposure in opposite ways: it can expand or decrease liability exposure. On
the one hand, it can expand liability exposure in at least two ways. First, it
increases the applicable standards by requiring that measures be taken so
that products and activities present no risks or only the minimum risks
compatible with the product's use or the activity's purpose. With more
stringent standards the risk of non-compliance increases, which, in turn,
may increase the liability risk. Second, it may require disclosure of information (such as safety-related information) on the basis of which claims
could be asserted. For instance, safety information disclosed by operators may give potential claimants facts to support their claims. In many
jurisdictions, non-compliance with regulatory requirements may constitute breach of obligation or negligence per se, which may trigger liability
exposure.[63] At the very least, non-compliance with regulations constitutes

---

[59] Directive 2012/18/EU of the European Parliament and of the Council of 4 July 2012 on
the control of major-accident hazards involving dangerous substances, amending and
subsequently repealing Council Directive 96/82/[2012] OJ L 197/1.
[60] Seveso Directive, Article 8.5.   [61] Ibid., Article 10.   [62] Ibid., Article. 14.2.b.
[63] For the situation in the seven jurisdictions analysed in the comparative study, see 3.2.

a factor that may be taken into account in determining whether an operator is negligent. Both of these effects may be relevant to terrorism-related risk. If, for instance, a chemical facility fails to adopt the organisational and risk mitigation measures required by the Seveso Directive and, as a result thereof, terrorists gain access to the site and can cause an explosion, such non-compliance may be regarded as "negligence per se" or at least a strong indication that the operator was negligent. Likewise, the data on the facility, the substances present and the risk management measures, which must be disclosed, may be used by plaintiffs to argue, for example, that the risk management measures were inadequate given the properties and volumes of the substances present.

On the other hand, compliance with the regulations could potentially limit effective liability exposure in two ways. First, if regulations impose effective preventive measures that companies would not otherwise take, compliance may, as a matter of fact, reduce the risk of any incidents. For instance, companies may be required by regulations to adopt measures to avoid unsafe products being placed on the market, or, if they are placed on the market, to mitigate any adverse consequences. Second, an activity or product that complies with the applicable regulatory requirements may be regarded as not being conducted negligently, not "defective" under the PLD, or otherwise not meeting the test for a liability rule to be applicable. Any such determination is likely to be made on a case-by-case basis, as liability laws rarely provide that compliance with the regulatory standards precludes civil liability; there is an exception, however, for regulations that do not permit any variation from the regulatory regime, which are effectively mandatory orders in the sense of the PLD.

As discussed in 2.2. above, failure to implement EU law could also result in liability of Member States. If, for instance, a Member State "manifestly and gravely disregards" its obligations to implement the Seveso Directive and consequently a terrorist attack ensues, that State may be exposed to liability. Since the substantive provisions of the Seveso Directive leave the Member States very little discretion with regard to implementation, the mere infringement of EU law may well be enough to constitute a sufficiently serious breach that triggers liability.

2.4.4. EU legislation regarding cross-border claims

In this section, we discuss two EU regulations that deal with aspects of cross-border claims and litigation: the Brussels I Regulation and the Rome II Regulation. These regulations are intended to make it easier for plaintiffs to pursue claims against defendants outside their own Member

State or otherwise related to international or cross-border events. In addition to these regulations, there are also EU law instruments addressing issues such as the service of judicial and extra-judicial documents,[64] the taking of evidence,[65] and mediation,[66] which are not discussed in this section.

2.4.4.1.   Regulation 44/2001 on the jurisdiction and the recognition and enforcement of judgments in civil and commercial matters

This section reviews the rules applicable to choice of jurisdiction in case of multi-jurisdictional litigation.

2.4.4.1.1.   Brief summary of the regime   Regulation 44/2001[67] ("Brussels I Regulation") sets rules for adjudicatory jurisdiction in civil and commercial matters and the recognition and enforcement of judgments. In other words, it addresses the question of which courts, or, more accurately, the courts of which Member States, have jurisdiction in civil and commercial matters. Parties may agree on the competent jurisdiction, unless the Brussels I Regulation grants exclusive jurisdiction to the courts of a particular Member State (e.g., cases related to rights *in rem* in immovable property) or otherwise limits the freedom to choose the applicable law (e.g., in relation to consumer or insurance contracts).[68]

In the absence of a contract, the default rule is that the courts of the Member State where the defendant is domiciled have jurisdiction,[69] unless the Brussels I Regulation gives special jurisdiction to the courts of another Member State. In contractual matters, the seller of a product, including a security product, may also be sued in the Member State where the product was or should have been delivered, and a provider of services, including security services, may also be sued in the Member State where the services were or should have been provided.[70] In extra-contractual matters, the

---

[64] Regulation (EC) 1393/2007 on the service in the Member States of judicial and extrajudicial documents in civil of commercial matters (service of documents), and repealing Council Regulation (EC) 1348/2000, OJ 2007, No. L324, 10 December 2007, 79.

[65] Council Regulation (EC) 1206/2001 on cooperation between the courts of the Member States in the taking of evidence in civil or commercial matters, OJ 2001, No. L174, 27 June 2001, 1.

[66] Directive 2008/52/EC on certain aspects of mediation in civil and commercial matters, OJ 2008, No. L136, 24 May 2008, 3.

[67] Council Regulation (EC) 44/2001 on the jurisdiction and the recognition and enforcement of judgments in civil and commercial matters, OJ 2001, No. L12, 16 January 2001, 1.

[68] Brussels I Regulation, Article 23.   [69] Ibid., Article 2.   [70] Ibid., Article 5(1).

plaintiff may also file legal proceedings in the courts of the country where the harmful event occurred,[71] or the court that hears criminal proceedings relating to the events that give rise to the civil claims, if such a court has jurisdiction for civil proceedings.[72] This rule could apply in the case of terrorism, if terrorist attacks result in criminal proceedings.[73] Insurers may be sued in the Member State of their domicile, in the Member State where the plaintiff is domiciled (if it is a policy holder, the insured or a beneficiary), or, with respect to liability insurance, in the Member State where the harmful event occurred.[74] In application of the principle of *lis pendens*, all courts, except the court first seized, must suspend proceedings and decline jurisdiction if the court first seized declares itself competent.[75] A similar rule is optional if the various legal proceedings cover related, albeit not identical, actions.

If there are multiple defendants in a particular case, one of whom is a facility operator or security provider, the operator or security provider could be sued in any Member State where any one of the co-defendants are domiciled, if the claims are closely connected.[76] In the case of third-party proceedings, an operator or security company may also be sued in the court seized of the original proceedings, unless these proceedings were instituted solely with the object of moving the case to another jurisdiction.[77] A judgment from one Member State's court must be recognised in all other Member States, with limited exceptions, such as in the case of judgments manifestly contrary to public policy.[78] It may also be enforced in other Member States, provided that it has been declared enforceable by a court of that Member State after an assessment that the application for enforceability meets certain formal requirements.[79]

2.4.4.1.2. Conclusions The Brussels I Regulation harmonises rules that determine the jurisdiction competent for civil and commercial matters. It is thus applicable to claims against the security industry instituted by victims of terrorism or customers of security services. The Brussels I Regulation allows parties to select a governing law that is either in favour of or disadvantageous to the security company involved. It also facilitates cross-border litigation which, indirectly, expands liability exposure.

---

[71] Ibid., Article 5(3). For further reading, see Magnus and Mankowski 2007, 202 et seq.
[72] Brussels I Regulation, Article. 5(4).
[73] For further reading, see Magnus and Mankowski 2007, 202 et seq.
[74] Brussels I Regulation, Articles 8–14.   [75] Ibid., Article 27.
[76] Ibid., Article 6(1).   [77] Ibid., Article 6(2).   [78] Ibid., Articles 33–37.
[79] Ibid., Articles 38–52.

A clear regime for establishing the selection of jurisdiction and how to recognise and enforce judgments saves time and transaction costs. The Brussels I Regulation also decreases the risk for the security industry to be sued in various countries for the same event of terrorism, since rules on tort and contractual claims as well as on *lis pendens* favour a single forum for the same event. The place where the damage occurred can, however, sometimes be completely unpredictable in the case of a terrorist act involving means of transportation (e.g., an aeroplane), which may make it difficult for the security industry to determine in advance which law will apply.

2.4.4.2.   Regulation 864/2007 on the law applicable to non-contractual obligations

2.4.4.2.1.   Brief summary of the regime   Regulation 864/2007[80] (the "Rome II Regulation") establishes rules to resolve conflicts of laws in relation to non-contractual obligations in civil and commercial matters, such as damages caused by tort or *culpa in contrahendo*.[81] In the absence of choice of law by the parties,[82] the Rome II Regulation provides default rules.[83]

The specific rules for product liability designate as the applicable law, in order of priority, (1) the law of the country where the victim had his or her habitual residence when the damage occurred, if the product was marketed in that country; (2) the law of the country of acquisition, if the product was marketed in that country; or (3) the law of the country in which the damage occurred, if the product was marketed in that country. If the defendant could not reasonably foresee the marketing of its product, or similar products, in that country, the applicable law must be the law of the country in which that defendant is habitually resident. These rules are set aside, however, and a different law will apply, if the law of that country has a "manifestly closer connection" to the tort.[84]

The law applicable to cases involving environmental damage is the law of the country in which the damage occurred, unless the plaintiff chooses the law of the country in which the event occurred. In other tort cases, the applicable law will be the law of the country in which the damage occurred,

---

[80] Regulation (EC) 864/2007 of the European Parliament and of the Council of 11 July 2007 on the law applicable to non-contractual obligations (Rome II), OJ 2007, No. L199, 31 July 2007, 40 (Rome II Regulation).
[81] Rome II Regulation, Article 2(1).   [82] Ibid., Article 14.   [83] Ibid., Articles 4–12.
[84] Ibid., Article 5(2).

unless both plaintiffs and defendants have their habitual residence in the same country at the time the damage occurred or another country has a "manifestly closer connection" to the tort, in which case the law of that country applies.[85]

The Rome II Regulation provides that the law selected based on these rules must be applied even if it is not the law of a Member State.[86] Consequently, at least in theory, the liability of operators and security providers may be determined by the laws of any country in the world. In addition to the applicable law, the Rome II Regulation regulates the burden of proof and presumptions, which are to be determined based on the law governing contractual obligations.[87] If there are multiple liable persons and one of them satisfies the claim in whole or in part, the Rome II Regulation provides that the law governing the payer's right to claim recourse from the other debtors is the same as the law governing the payer's obligation towards the creditor.[88] A similar rule applies to contractual obligations under the Rome I Regulation. This provision would thus, arguably, apply to a situation where a creditor has a contractual claim against a debtor (e.g., an airline) as well as a claim based on tort law against another person (e.g., a provider of security products or services). If a third person has a duty to satisfy the creditor, the law applicable to that obligation will also govern whether and to what extent the third person is subrogated in the rights of the creditors against the debtors.[89] The Rome II Regulation also grants a direct right of recourse to the victim against the insurer if this is provided by either the law applicable to the non-contractual obligation or the law applicable to the insurance contract.[90]

2.4.4.2.2.   Conclusions   The Rome II Regulation harmonises the rules applicable to conflicts of law in non-contractual matters. It is thus applicable to claims from victims against operators or security providers. Note that it does not apply to potential *Francovich* liability of a Member State, or, more generally, to Member State liability for acts and omissions in the exercise of governmental authority (*acta iure imperii*).[91] The Rome II Regulation allows parties to select a governing law that is either in favour of or disadvantageous to the operator or security provider involved. It also facilitates cross-border litigation which, indirectly, may expand the industry's liability exposure as a matter of fact. On the other hand, a clear

---

[85] Ibid., Article 4(2) and (3).
[86] Ibid., Article 3.   [87] Ibid., Article 22(1).   [88] Ibid., Article 20.
[89] Ibid., Article 19.   [90] Ibid., Article 18.   [91] Ibid., Article 1(1).

regime for establishing the applicable law can save time and transaction costs.

Similar to the Brussels I Regulation, the place where the damage occurred can be completely unpredictable in the case of a terrorist act involving means of transportation (e.g., an aeroplane), which may make it difficult for operators and security providers to determine in advance which law will apply. A further complication arises from the somewhat diverging rules applicable to tort and product liability, if, for example, the victim sues both the manufacturer of explosives detection equipment under product liability law and a service provider under general civil liability or tort law.

2.5. Conclusions

This chapter provided an analysis of secondary EU legislation relevant to the liability exposure of private parties and Member States for terrorism-related risk. As discussed, Member States may be liable under the *Francovich* doctrine if they act or fail to act in violation of EU law and, as a result, increase the chances of a terrorist attack. For the substantive liability of private parties, the two EU liability instruments discussed in 2.3., above, namely, the Environmental Liability Directive and the Product Liability Directive, are of particular relevance. In this concluding section, we compare these two liability regimes and then discuss the indirect effect of EU regulatory regimes on civil liability for terrorism-related risk.

2.5.1. Liability regimes

Of the EU regulatory regimes discussed in this chapter, only two are truly liability programmes, the Environmental Liability Directive (ELD) and the Product Liability Directive (PLD). The main features of these two regimes are summarised in Table 6.[92]

2.5.2. Regulatory regimes

Aside from the ELD and PLD, the EU legislation discussed in this chapter does not set forth any liability rules. Nonetheless, this legislation may affect liability exposure indirectly or as a matter of fact. The focus was on

---

[92] Not all aspects of these liability regimes are addressed, since the regimes did not have any provisions regarding evidence and proof, and jurisdictional and procedural issues.

Table 6 *Comparison of ELD and PLD liability regimes*

Features of regime	ELD	PLD
Liable persons	Operator	Producers and importers
Damage covered	Environmental damage; no financial cap	Personal injury and damage to private goods; cap at option of Member State
Exclusions	Permit compliance defence and state-of-the-art defence at option of Member State	Development risk defence, but can be excluded at option of Member State
Causation	Determined by national law of Member State	Determined by national law of Member State
Financial security	At option of Member State and mandatory in some Member States	Not mandatory, but often used in practice

legislation that imposes regulatory requirements on operators and security providers aimed at increasing safety and security, which are relevant to terrorism-related risk. The purpose of the analysis provided in this chapter was to determine the potential effects of these regimes on the liability exposure of operators.

With regard to liability exposure of private parties, these regulatory regimes are double-edged swords. On the one hand, these regulatory regimes can lead to an expansion of liability exposure. This is particularly the case where the applicable standards are very stringent and exceed the standards otherwise required under general domestic law, which may increase the chance of non-compliance. Indeed, these regulatory regimes establish detailed safety standards and impose information disclosure obligations which allow plaintiffs to assess whether a product is safe. Moreover, liability exposure may also be triggered as a result of non-compliance with regulatory standards which may constitute negligence per se under national law. On the other hand, compliance with a regulatory regime can also lead to the limitation of liability exposure. This could be the case if the regulation provides incentives for compliance, thus limiting the risk of non-compliance and hence also limiting liability exposure. Moreover, while compliance with regulatory standards does not preclude exposure to civil liability, it may be a relevant factor when evaluating the degree of liability of the operator, since an activity or a product that meets the regulatory requirements may be regarded as "safe", or, in the PLD's terms, not "defective".

2.5.3. Relevance for the security industry

This final section addresses the extent to which the various regimes examined in this chapter are applicable to the operation of activities that could be targeted by terrorists and to the provision of security services aimed at combating terrorism or organised crime. While it is true that any type of legislation could potentially be considered relevant to industrial activities or the security industry, in many cases the link is somewhat tenuous. There are two truly EU liability regimes, however, that contribute, to some extent, to liability exposure for terrorism-related risk. Under the PLD regime, as discussed, security products could be deemed defective if they do not provide the security that the public may expect in the particular case. In the absence of case law, it remains to be seen how the public's expectations with respect to security will be construed. The PLD, however, covers only personal injury and private property intended for private use or consumption, to the exclusion liability for (1) moral pain and suffering, (2) damage to property for solely professional use and (3) pure economic loss. The optional liability cap and the state-of-the-art defence may further limit the liability of a security provider. This defence is important to security providers, because there continue to be developments in both techniques and tactics used by terrorist and the technology to combat terrorism (and only a few Member States have chosen to exclude its application). Although the EU regulations concerning jurisdiction and recognition and enforcement of judgments facilitate cross-border litigation, their net effect on the actual liability exposure of private parties is likely small.

PART II

Liability for terrorism-related risk under Member State law

This Part addresses the current liability situation for terrorism-related risk according to the national tort law systems of seven jurisdictions of EU Member States: England and Wales, France, Germany, The Netherlands, Poland, Spain and Sweden. The jurisdictions constitute a good mix of common law and civil law systems, and include representatives of the major legal families, namely common law, Germanic, Romanic and Nordic law. With the addition of Poland, one major jurisdiction of the new democracies of Eastern and Central Europe is also represented.

This Part starts with a description of the liability rules of these seven jurisdictions for the operators of dangerous activities and the liability situation for enterprises which provide services or products for the operation of dangerous activities. The bases for this survey are the case studies in Chapter 4 and the findings of the national reports provided for the "Study evaluating the status quo and the legal implications of third-party liability for the European Security Industry"[1] commissioned by the European Commission which can be found in Annex 3 of the study under http://ec.europa.eu/enterprise/policies/security/files/final-report-tpl-11-10-2013_en.pdf. The national tort law experts who wrote the national reports for the study are

- **Claire McIvor** (University of Birmingham) for England and Wales;
- **Florence G'sell** (Université de Lorraine) for France;
- **Peter Rott** (University of Copenhagen) for Germany;
- **Siewert Lindenbergh** and **Willem van Boom** (Erasmus University Rotterdam) for the Netherlands;
- **Ewa Baginska** (Nicolaus Copernicus University Torun) for Poland;
- **Pedro del Olmo** (University Carlos III of Madrid) for Spain; and
- **Philip Mielnicki** and **Marten Schultz** (Stockholm University) for Sweden.

[1] Ref. Ares (2013) 3320480 – 23/10/2013.

In Chapter 4, the same national tort law experts analyse five fictional cases. These cases explore the liability risks for (1) the operators of dangerous activities, such as chemical plants or aeroplanes, (2) the renderer of services or provider of products to the operation of dangerous activities, and (3) failures of security providers to protect public infrastructure undertakings, or the public as such, in general and in case of a terrorist attack. In these cases a special focus is put on possible catastrophic incidents in order to find out whether enterprises must face existence-threatening liability risks when disaster strikes. Case 1, "Defective emergency stop button", shows the application of the national rules concerning fault-based liability and liability for products (products liability or any other applicable strict liability). It describes the types of damage that are compensable (personal injury, property damage, pure economic loss) under these rules and explores the consequences of breach of technical standards or regulations for the liability of the producer of a technical device. Case 2, "Defective safety programmable logic controller", explores the liability for the rendition of security services with a special emphasis on the liability consequences of natural disasters and the attribution of liability in case of multiple tortfeasors. Case 3, "Public service (infrastructure) undertaking", examines the liability of the security provider in case of a terrorist attack against a public service (infrastructure) undertaking and the recourse option of the public service undertaking against the security provider. Case 4, "Border control", explores the liability of the security provider, be it a security consultant or the provider of security equipment, to the public authority and analyses the recourse option of the public authority against the security provider. Case 5, "Aeroplane-crash", describes the liability situation of the security provider in case of an aeroplane accident and the recourse option of the air carrier against the security provider.

Chapter 5 describes, based on the findings of these case studies, the liability situation of the operators of dangerous activities and of enterprises which render services or products to such operations. The results of this study are then summarised in 5.5.

Civil liability systems of seven EU Member States

MONIKA HINTEREGGER

3.1.   Bases of liability

3.1.1.   Fault-based liability

3.1.1.1.   Legal basis

All seven jurisdictions provide for a sort of fault based-liability. The preconditions for the attribution of liability are rather similar, but not identical. In the common law jurisdiction of England and Wales the most important head of liability is the tort of negligence, the tort most similar to the concept of fault-based liability in civil law. In the civil law countries fault-based liability is regulated in the civil codes. In Germany the basic provision is § 823 BGB (*Bürgerliches Gesetzbuch*) which provides for two heads of liability. According to § 823(1) BGB, a person is liable who, intentionally or negligently, unlawfully injures the life, body, health, freedom, property or another right of another person. Under § 823(2) BGB liability is provided for the intentional or negligent breach of a statutory duty. In the Netherlands fault-based liability is defined in Article 6:162 BW (*Burgerlijk Wetboek*). In France, Poland and Spain the civil code provides for a general clause on fault liability.[2] In Sweden it is a general rule, established by case law and legal doctrine, that liability requires fault. Since 1972 this rule is explicitly laid out in the Swedish Tort Liability Act (*Skadeståndslag*).

   If contractual and non-contractual claims are available, the claimant is free to choose either cause of action. The only exception is France, where the claimant who can rely on contractual liability is not allowed to invoke extra-contractual liability (*principe de non cumul*).

---

[2] Articles 1382 et seq. French Civil code (*Code civil*); Article 415 of the Polish civil code (*Kodeks cywilny*); Article 1902 of the Spanish civil code (*Código civil*). In Spain, when damage was caused by a criminal act, liability is regulated by the criminal code (*Código penal*) which provides for comparable rules.

3.1.1.2.   Duty of care and unlawfulness

The tort of negligence in England and Wales is comprised of four elements: actionable damage, duty of care, breach of duty and causation.
For cases where it is not apparent that the defendant owed a duty of care
to the claimant, courts developed the "*Caparo* test".[3] According to this
test, a duty of care exists if the following requirements are met: foreseeability, proximity and, as a broad-policy consideration, the requirements
of fairness, justice and reasonableness. This test is applied when the existence of a duty of care is not apparent, for instance when the negligence
claim relates to omissions, psychiatric harm or pure economic loss. For
the provision of financial services a duty of care to third parties will generally only be established if the conditions of the "*Hedley Byrne* test"[4]
are met which requires, on the one hand, that the defendant voluntarily
assumed responsibility to protect the financial interests of the claimant
and, on the other hand, that the claimant reasonably relied on this act.
Moreover, under English tort law there is no general duty to prevent damage to another. A duty to rescue is only recognised if there is some kind
of special relationship of close proximity between the defendant and the
claimant. Special duty of care obligations are imposed on manufacturers,
designers, installers and repairers of products and on occupiers, who are
obliged to take reasonable care to ensure that their product or property
does not cause foreseeable physical injuries to another.

In the civil law countries, an action under fault-based liability must
meet four requirements: actionable damage, unlawfulness, fault and causation. With respect to the criterion of unlawfulness, there is a basic
difference between the Romanistic countries and the other jurisdictions.
In the two Romanistic countries that are analysed in this study, France
and Spain, the criterion of unlawfulness is not regarded as a separate
requirement but is absorbed by the criterion of fault. Fault is thus an
unlawful conduct that violates an obligation or a duty imposed by law or
custom, or a general standard of behaviour. In Germany and the Netherlands the behaviour of a tortfeasor is regarded as unlawful if it infringes
a protected subjective right of another (life, property, personality right,
etc.) or if it violates a statutory duty. In the latter case it is necessary
that the damage and the person who claims for the damage are within
the protective scope of the infringed rule. Whether this is the case must

---

[3] Established in *Caparo Industries Plc* v. *Dickman* [1990] 2 AC 605.
[4] *Hedley Byrne Co Ltd* v. *Heller & Partners Ltd* [1964] AC 465 and *Henderson* v. *Merrett
Syndicates Ltd* [1995] 2 AC 145.

be determined through interpretation of the rule. Dutch law recognises a further, more general category, the "*maatschappelijke betamelijkheid*", according to which a behaviour which contravenes an agreed standard in society can be deemed unlawful.

3.1.1.3.   Breach of duty of care and fault

While the criterion of unlawfulness relates to the assessment of the act of the tortfeasor, the prerequisite of fault deals with the blameworthiness of the concrete actor. The assessment of fault in the civil law countries meets the English concept of the "reasonable person". In English law this standard results from the assessment of several factors including the magnitude of the risk, the gravity of the harm, the cost of precautions and the social utility of the defendant's conduct. The assessment of fault follows rather an objective (France) or predominantly objective standard (England and Wales, Germany, the Netherlands). In all of these jurisdictions specialists and professionals must meet a higher standard according to their special knowledge and abilities.

3.1.1.4.   Contributory negligence

In all of the analysed jurisdictions, contributory negligence of the claimant is a defence.[5] For personal injury claims in Sweden this defence, however, only applies if the behaviour of the claimant amounts to gross negligence or if he acted with intent. In all jurisdictions contributory negligence leads to a reduction of damages.

3.1.1.5.   Vicarious liability

All jurisdictions provide for vicarious liability, but the concepts are quite different.[6] In England and Wales vicarious liability covers not only employers who are liable for the misdemeanour of their employees in the course of their employment, but also relationships that are merely "akin to employment", like the position of a priest in a church (see *The Catholic Child Welfare Society* v. *Various Claimants*[7]). As reaffirmed by *Lister* v. *Hesley Hall*,[8] vicarious liability includes intentional wrongdoing and takes a rather broad view of what constitutes the required "close connection" between the behaviour of the employee and the employer.

---

[5] England and Wales: Law Reform (Contributory Negligence) Act 1945; France: Article 1386–13 *Code civil*; Germany: § 254 BGB; Netherlands: Article 6:101 BW; Poland: Article 362 *Kodeks cywilny*; Spain: Article 1103 *Código civil*; Sweden: Tort Liability Act Chapter 6 section 1.

[6] See Chapter 4, Case 2 Question c.   [7] [2012] UKSC 56.   [8] [2001] UKHL 22.

In case of loaned employees, even dual vicarious liability can be applied. The employer is entitled to bring an indemnity claim against the employee, but there is a tradition for such claims not to be enforced. The victim can also directly sue the employee.

Vicarious liability also applies in French law provided that the employee acted within the course of the employment and the limits of his tasks. In this case the employee cannot be sued personally. Recourse by the employer against the employee is possible, but restricted to cases of gross negligence. Swedish law also provides for vicarious liability of the employer, but does not usually allow the employer to take recourse against the employee or the third party to sue the employee for damages.

In the Netherlands Article 6:170 BW provides for vicarious liability for employers for the tortious acts committed by their employees. This extends not only to formal labour contracts, but also to other comparable relationships provided that there is a certain hierarchy between the principal and the agent. The employee can be directly sued by the victim, but the employer bears the full burden of liability unless the employee acted intentionally or with gross and wilful negligence (Article 6:170(3) BW).

Article 430 of the Polish Civil code has an equally broad concept of vicarious liability for employers and comparable persons. The employee cannot be directly sued by the victim, unless the employee acted with intent or the employer is insolvent or under-insured, or the damage was not inflicted in the course of the employment (Article 120 Labour Code). In labour relations the recourse is limited to the equivalent of three months' earnings of the employee unless the employee acted with intent.

In Germany vicarious liability in non-contractual relationships is more restricted. According to § 831 BGB, the principal is liable for harm to third parties that is caused by an agent who is subjected to the principal's authority. The agent must act unlawfully, albeit not necessarily with fault. The principal is exonerated if he proves that he exercised reasonable care when selecting the agent or managing the activity, or if the damage would have occurred even if this care had been exercised.

Spanish law, however, does not provide for vicarious liability in the strict sense. Employees can be directly sued by the victim under fault-based liability. According to Article 1903 *Código civil*, employers are liable for damage caused by their employees for their own fault which however is presumed by law (*culpa in eligendo* and *vigilando*). Employers' liability only applies to entrepreneurs and requires that the damage is caused by an employee in the course of the employment. Whether the employee must act negligently or not is still disputed by legal doctrine. Recourse against the employee who has acted with fault is possible, but very uncommon. As Spanish law requires a hierarchical relationship between the principal and the agent, the principal is not responsible for the tortious act of an independent contractor unless the principal himself committed fault (*culpa in eligendo* or *vigilando*) or violated non-delegable duties.

The same rule applies under Polish law where liability for the independent contractor requires fault on behalf of the principal (Article 429 *Kodeks cywilny*). The principal can be exonerated from liability if he proves either that he was not negligent in choosing the contractor (*culpa in eligendo*) or that he entrusted the performance of the activity to a professional, be it a person, enterprise or other institution.

In the Netherlands Article 6:171 BW extends vicarious liability to cover the independent contractor if the contractor's activity was actually, or at least in the perception of third parties, part of the client's business. Germany and Sweden do not accept vicarious liability for the independent contractor in extra-contractual liability.

3.1.1.6.   Burden of proof

In principle the burden for the proof of fault lies with the claimant in all of the jurisdictions. In England and Wales there is no exception to this rule. Under certain conditions, however, the doctrine of *res ipsa loquitur* may be applied by which the breach of a duty of care is inferred from the fact that the thing that caused the damage was under the sole control of the defendant or his agent, and that the accident is such that it would not normally happen in the absence of negligence. In many civil law countries (Germany, the Netherlands, Poland) a comparable instrument to lighten the burden of proof is concept of the prima facie evidence which plays an important role in medical malpractice cases.

For certain fields of liability or under certain conditions, the burden of proof is shifted to the defendant. In Germany special rules apply for the burden of proof concerning vicarious liability in non-contractual relationships under § 831 BGB and in product-liability cases. If the claimant can establish that the product is defective and that the defect caused the damage, the producer must show that he was not at fault. In the Netherlands Article 150 of the Dutch Code of Civil Procedure allows the court to reverse the burden of proof if this is stipulated by a special statute or if it is seen to be reasonable and fair. Polish law provides for a presumption of fault in cases of vicarious liability concerning liability for the independent contractor, minors and incapable persons. In France fault is assumed if a certain duty is imposed by a statute or by the courts. The defendant then can only escape liability in cases of force majeure or if he can show a ground of justification (e.g., self-defence). In Spain the courts are ready to infer the defendant's fault from the fact that damage occurred or to attribute the burden of proof to the defendant based on the "theory of risk" according to which the burden of proof lies with the person who profited from the introduction of a risk.

The required standard of proof varies in the jurisdictions analysed. The lowest standard of proof applies in England and Wales and the Netherlands, where the relevant standard of proof is the balance of probabilities. German, Spanish and Swedish law require that facts are established with high probability, while in Poland the required level of probability is close to certainty (beyond reasonable doubt). French law does not deal with the notion of "standard of proof" as such, but merely requires that fault must be established as provided by Articles 1315 and 1353 *Code civil.*

3.1.2.   Product liability

In all of the jurisdictions analysed, product liability is regulated according to the Product Liability Directive,[9] although national courts still apply specific national product liability rules derived from fault-based liability (England and Wales, France, Germany, the Netherlands). Although the national laws implementing the Product Liability Directive[10] follow the rules of the directive very closely, some deviations gave rise to infringement proceeding before the European Court of Justice (ECJ). A prominent example is the English implementation of the "development risks" defence of Article 7(e) of the Directive[11] which prompted the European

---

[9]   Council Directive (EEC) 374/85 on the approximation of the laws, regulations and administrative provisions of the Member States concerning liability for defective products [1985] OJ L210/29 as amended by Directive (EC) 34/99 of the European Parliament and of the Council [1999] OJ L141/20.

[10]   France: law no. 98–389 19 May 1998 which inserted the new section IV "*de la responsabilité du fait des produits défectueux*" (*Code civil*, Article 1386–1 to 1386–18) into the *Code civil;* Germany: *Produkthaftungsgesetz;* Sweden: *Produktansvarslag* (1992:18); UK: Consumer Protection Act 1987; Poland: Article 449[1]–449[10] civil code; Spain: *Ley* 23/1994 of 6 July 1994 "*de Responsabilidad Civil por los daños causados por productos defectuosos*" (LRPD) as revised by Royal Legislative Decree 1/2007 of 16 November 2007 "*por el que se aprueba el texto refundido de la Ley General para la Defensa de los Consumidores y Usuarios y otras leyes complementarias*" (TRLDCU).

[11]   Section 4(1)(e) Consumer Protection Act 1987.

Commission to bring an infringement action against the UK according to Article 258 TFEU (ex-Article 226 TEC). The ECJ admitted that there are some inconsistencies in the wording of the two provisions but nevertheless dismissed the application because it did not doubt that the courts in the UK would interpret section 4(1)(e) Consumer Protection Act 1987 in the light of the wording and the purpose of the Directive.[12] With respect to France, which was already condemned in 1993 by the ECJ for not implementing the Directive,[13] the issues brought before the ECJ by the Commission were the inaccurate implementation of the liability of the supplier,[14] the broad definition of recoverable damage, which also included property damage for the professional user of a product,[15] and the non-implementation of the 500 euro threshold for damage to property.[16]

In Poland the notion of the importer and the definition of the absolute prescription period deviate slightly from the rules of the Directive. According to Spanish law, the supplier who markets a product despite having knowledge of a defect is liable to a third party as if he were the producer, from whom nonetheless, after having paid damages to the victim, he may seek recovery. In Spanish law the "reasonable" period provided by Article 3 § 3 of the Directive for the supplier to identify the producer is three months. Slight deviations from the Directive also exist with respect to the prescription period.

All of the analysed countries allow for the development risk defence as provided by Article 7(e) of the Directive, except for certain products (France: products derived from the human body; Germany: pharmaceuticals; Spain: medicines, food or foodstuffs for human consumption) and, except for Spain, include the recovery of non-pecuniary damages. Germany and Spain provide for liability caps in case of death or personal injury (Germany: 85 million euro; Spain: 63,106,270.96 euro).

---

[12] Case C-300/95 *Commission of the European Communities* v. *United Kingdom* [1997] ECR I-2649.

[13] Case C-293/91 *Commission of the European Communities* v. *French Republic* [1993] ECR I-1.

[14] Case C-52/00 *Commission of the European Communities* v. *French Republic* [2002] ECR I-3827; Case C-177/04 *Commission of the European Communities* v. *French Republic* [2006] ECR I-2461.

[15] Case C-285/08 *Moteurs Leroy Somer* v. *Dalkia France and Ace Europe* [2009] ECR I-4733.

[16] Case C-52/00 *Commission of the European Communities* v. *French Republic* [2002] ECR I-3827; Case C-183/00 *María Victoria Gonzáles Sánches* v. *Medicina Asturiana SA* [2002] ECR I-3901.

3.1.3.   Special liability regimes

3.1.3.1.   General instruments increasing liability exposure for dangerous activities

English law has no general strict liability regime for dangerous activities. With respect to damage caused by polluting interference the torts of public and private nuisance are applicable which do not require fault. While public nuisance provides for recovery for personal injuries and property damage as well as pure economic loss, private nuisance requires interference with a proprietary interest in land and covers only property damage. Moreover, the rule in *Rylands* v. *Fletcher*,[17] a sub-category of private nuisance, establishes a form of semi-strict liability governing property damage caused by the escape of dangerous things.

In France a very comprehensive and in practice very important no-fault liability is provided by Article 1384(1) *Code civil*, according to which the custodian of a thing is responsible for the harm caused by the thing ("*responsabilité du fait des choses*"). The thing need not be dangerous. According to Article 1384(2) *Code civil*, an exception applies to the custodian of the thing, be it land or chattels, for damage to the neighbourhood caused by fire. In this case the victim has to prove fault on behalf of the custodian. Special rules amounting to strict liability apply for damage caused to the neighbourhood ("*troubles de voisinage*"). Under this theory, the claimant must only prove an excessive level of the disturbance. The fact that the disturbance was abnormal can be induced from the excessive quality of the interference but also from the violation of regulation. Permissible objections include only fault of the victim and force majeure, which requires that the damage was caused by facts that came from outside and were of an unforeseeable and irresistible character. However, Article L 112–16 of the Code of Construction and Housing may restrict from a cause of action any plaintiff who only subsequently moved into the vicinity of an existing plant under certain conditions.

German law does not provide for a general rule of no-fault liability for dangerous activities. There is, however, a number of statutory strict liability rules for specific activities,[18] and under certain conditions courts

---

[17] [1866] LR 1 Ex 265.

[18] Including aeroplanes, genetically modified organisms, nuclear installations, medical products (pharmaceuticals) and environmental harm as outlined below. Further examples are the strict liability of car drivers and car owners under the Road Traffic Act (*Straßenverkehrsgesetz*; StVG) and of train operators, operators of energy, gas and liquid pipes under the Liability Act (*Haftpflichtgesetz*, HPflG).

are inclined to reverse the burden of proof for fault when damage is caused by a dangerous activity.

In the Netherlands dangerous activities can elicit the reversal of proof concerning causation ("*omkeringsregel*"). For the professional use or possession of dangerous substances, the Dutch Civil code provides a special strict liability regime that covers damage to persons and property, but not pure economic loss (Articles 6:175 BW et seq.). With respect to this head of liability a broad range of defences apply.[19] Strict liability is further provided for defective objects (movables: Article 6:173 BW; immovables: Article 6:174 BW).

Polish law provides for several strict liability statutes for certain objects and dangerous activities (see below). According to Article 435 of the Polish Civil code, the person who runs an undertaking set into motion by natural forces (steam, gas, electricity, liquid fuel etc.) is liable for any damage to persons and property caused through the operation of the enterprise or business. The operator is not liable in cases of force majeure, or if he proves that the damage was caused exclusively through the fault of the injured party or of a third party for whom he is not responsible. A special no-fault liability applies to the organiser of a mass event (Article 5 of the Act on Mass Events of 20 March 2009).[20]

In Spain courts have started to impose strict liability on the operator of abnormally dangerous goods or activities, although this is not explicitly provided by law. Moreover, courts tend to tighten fault-based liability under Article 1902 *Código civil* by reversing the burden of proof for the proof of fault.

Swedish law provides for a series of strict liability rules for dangerous activities covering the risks of aeroplanes, nuclear installations, railways and electricity providers as well as the causation of environmental harm or damage caused by oil spills from a sea vessel.[21] Outside these statutes, however, courts are rather reluctant to hold tortfeasors strictly liable. A particular feature of Swedish law is the existence of alternative no-fault

---

[19] Article 6:178 BW: armed conflict, civil war, revolt, riots, insurgence or mutiny; natural event of an exceptional, unavoidable and irresistible nature; the damage is solely caused by following an order or regulation of the government or intentionally caused by a third party or is the result of a nuisance, pollution or any other consequence for which no liability would have existed on the basis of the general principles of tort law if the defendant had caused it intentionally.

[20] *Dziennik Ustaw* (Journal of Laws, Dz. U.) 2009, no. 62, at 504, as amended.

[21] For the explanation of some of these strict liability statutes see below.

compensation schemes with respect to injuries of patients or workers and harm caused by pharmaceutical products.

3.1.3.2.   Special third-party liability regimes

3.1.3.2.1.   Aeroplanes   In Europe liability of the air carrier for damage caused to passengers is regulated by Regulation 889/02,[22] which is based on the Warsaw Convention of 12 October 1929[23] as amended by the Montreal Convention of 28 May 1999.[24] According to the Warsaw–Montreal regime, the air carrier is obliged to compensate passengers for death and bodily injury for up to 113,100 special drawing rights (SDR) subject only to the defence of contributory fault of the victim (Articles 20 and 21 Montreal Convention). For damage exceeding this cap the air carrier is liable according to fault-based liability with presumption of fault. The air carrier is exonerated if he proves that the damage was not due to the negligence or other wrongful act or omission of the carrier or its servants or agents, or that the damage was solely due to the negligence or other wrongful act or omission of a third party (Article 21(2) Montreal Convention). With respect to baggage and cargo, special rules and liability caps apply (Article 17 et seq. Montreal Convention). Regulation 889/02 extends these rules to all flights, whether domestic or international, operated by Community air carriers, and provides some rules favourable to the harmed passenger (advance payments in the event of bodily injury, jurisdiction of the courts of the passenger's principal place of residence, increase of liability limits in the event of delay and damage to baggage). Minimum insurance requirements for air carriers and aircraft operators in respect of passengers, baggage, cargo and third parties, for both commercial and private flights, are provided by Regulation 785/04 on insurance requirements for air carriers and aircraft operators (as amended by Regulations 1137/08 and 285/10).[25] The objective of this Regulation is to establish minimum insurance requirements for air carriers and aircraft operators

---

[22] Regulation (EC) 889/02 of the European Parliament and of the Council amending Council Regulation (EC) 2027/97 on air carrier liability in the event of accidents [2002] OJ L140/2.

[23] Convention for the Unification of Certain Rules Relating to International Carriage by Air (Warsaw, 12 October 1929).

[24] Convention for the Unification of Certain Rules for International Carriage by Air (Montreal, 28 May 1999; (2001) OJ L194/39).

[25] Regulation (EC) 785/04 of the European Parliament and of the Council on insurance requirements for air carriers and aircraft operators [2004] OJ L138/1; Regulation (EC) 1137/08 of the European Parliament and of the Council adapting a number of instruments subject to the procedure laid down in Article 251 of the Treaty to Council Decision 1999/468/EC, with regard to the regulatory procedure with scrutiny [2008] OJ L311/1; Commission Regulation (EU) 285/10 amending Regulation (EC) No 785/2004 of the

in respect of passengers, baggage, cargo and third parties to cover the risks associated with aviation-specific liability (including acts of war, terrorism, hijacking, acts of sabotage, unlawful seizure of aircraft and civil commotion).

Damage to persons other than passengers is regulated by the national laws. Of all the countries that are analysed in this comparison only Spain is a party to the 1952 Rome Convention.

Most countries provide for special strict liability rules for aeroplane accidents. In England and Wales, aircraft owners are strictly liable for all material loss to third parties (section 76(2) of the Civil Aviation Act 1982). Liability is unlimited in amount and only subject to a defence of contributory negligence. In France strict liability is provided by the Code of Transports. German law also provides for comprehensive strict liability for damage caused by aeroplanes. According to § 33 LuftVG,[26] the owner of the aeroplane is strictly liable for damage to the life, physical integrity or health of a person or to property caused by an accident. This strict liability obligation applies to any third party who uses the aeroplane without the consent and knowledge of the owner (§ 33 para 2 sent 1 LuftVG). The rules on contributory fault, joint and several liability and heads of damages are in line with the general rules of the BGB (§§ 34 et seq. LuftVG). Liability is capped according to the weight of the aeroplane. In Poland strict liability for the operator of an aircraft is provided by a special statute.[27] As the law refers to liability based on Article 435 of the Polish Civil code, the operator is not liable in cases of force majeure, or if he proves that the damage was caused exclusively through the fault of the injured party or of a third party for whom he is not responsible. In Spain third-party liability for the operator of an aeroplane is regulated by the Act of Aeronautical Navigation (LNA).[28] This Act provides for strict liability connected with compulsory insurance and liability caps. According to Article 121 LNA, the airline or operator is additionally liable under fault-based liability if the employee acted with intent or gross negligence. In Sweden, the Act on Liability for Damage caused in the Course of Aviation from 1922[29] provides for non-contractual strict liability of the owner of the aircraft

---

European Parliament and of the Council on insurance requirements for air carriers and aircraft operators [2010] OJ L87/19.

[26] Air Traffic Act (*Luftverkehrsgesetz*) of 1 August 1922, *Reichsgesetzblatt* (Imperial Law Gazette; RGBl) 1922 I, 681, recast in *Bundesgesetzblatt* (Federal Law Gazette; BGBl) 2007 I, 698, and last amended in 2012, BGBl 2012 I, 1032.

[27] Articles 206–207 Aviation Law, Act of 3 July 2002, Dz. U. 2012, at 933 as amended.

[28] 21 June 1960.

[29] *Lagen* (1922:382) "*angående ansvarighet för skada i följd av luftfart*".

regarding personal injuries and property damage on the ground. Dutch law does not provide for special liability rules for the victims of aeroplane accidents. Third parties who are victims of an aeroplane accident must thus rely on the general tort law system.

3.1.3.2.2.   Genetically modified organisms (GMOs)

Of all countries analysed, only Germany[30] and Poland[31] provide for specific strict liability statutes covering liability for GMOs.[32] French law only provides for public law obligations[33] which, however, can lead to compensation obligations under civil law.

England and Wales, the Netherlands and Sweden have no special liability rules for GMOs. In the Netherlands it is still unclear whether the strict liability for dangerous substances (Article 6:175 BW) applies to damage caused by GMOs.

3.1.3.2.3.   Nuclear installations

In all countries analysed, third-party liability for nuclear installations is determined by the International Convention on Nuclear Third-Party Liability.[34] Germany, France, the Netherlands, Spain, Sweden and the United Kingdom belong to the Paris and Brussels Conventions on Nuclear Third Party Liability. The Paris Convention[35] provides for the elaboration and harmonisation of third-party liability and insurance against nuclear risks. The 1963 Brussels Supplementary Convention, which is only open for members of the Paris Convention, supplements the Paris Convention by providing for additional compensation out of public funds. On 12 February 2004 the Member States of the Paris Convention signed a new Protocol to the Paris Convention[36] and a new Protocol[37] to the 1963 Brussels Supplementary

---

[30] *Gesetz zur Regelung der Gentechnik* of 16 December 1993, BGBl 1993 I, 2066.

[31] Law of 22 June 2001 on Genetically Modified Organisms, Dz. U. 2007, no. 36, item 233.

[32] For a comprehensive description and analysis of these regimes and for liability for genetically modified organisms in other countries see Koch 2010.

[33] OGM 10–25 June 2008.   [34] See under 1.2.

[35] Convention on Third Party Liability in the Field of Nuclear Energy (Paris, 29 July 1960), as amended by the Additional Protocol of 28 January 1964 and by the Protocol of 16 November 1982.

[36] Protocol to amend the Convention on Third Party Liability in the Field of Nuclear Energy of 29 July 1960, as amended by the Additional Protocol of 28 January 1964 and by the Protocol of 16 November 1982.

[37] Protocol to amend the Convention of 31 January 1963 Supplementary to the Paris Convention of 29 July 1960 on Third Party Liability in the Field of Nuclear Energy, as amended by the Additional Protocol of 28 January 1964 and by the Protocol of 16 November 1982.

Convention.[38] Both new Protocols form an integral part of the relevant convention, but are not yet in force.[39]

Poland belongs to the 1963 Vienna Convention[40] and the 1997 Protocol to the Vienna Convention.[41] The Paris and the Vienna Convention are linked together by the 1988 Joint Protocol[42], which mutually extends the benefits of one convention to the members of the other convention. Four of the countries analysed (Germany, the Netherlands, Poland and Sweden) belong to the Joint Protocol, while three countries (France, Spain and the United Kingdom) do not.

All nuclear liability conventions provide for non-fault liability for damage caused by a nuclear incident. Liability is concentrated on the operator of a nuclear installation ("legal channelling"). Liability of the operator covers nuclear incidents in a nuclear installation or involving nuclear substances coming from such an installation and also under certain conditions, nuclear incidents occurring during the carriage of nuclear substances. The concept of legal channelling ensures that claims for the compensation of nuclear damage may only be directed against the operator of a nuclear installation and not against any other person, such as suppliers, carriers, contractors or other third parties. Such persons are not liable at all, neither under the specific nuclear liability regime established by the convention nor according to other liability provisions provided by national tort law, such as product liability[43] or fault-based liability.[44] In order to ensure that the risk is in any case allocated to the operator, Article 6(f) of the 1960 Paris Convention even limits the operator's right

---

[38] Convention of 31 January 1963 Supplementary to the Paris Convention of 29 July 1960 on Third Party Liability in the Field of Nuclear Energy, as amended by the Additional Protocol of 28 January 1964 and by the Protocol of 16 November 1982.

[39] Hinteregger and Kissich 2004.

[40] Vienna Convention on Civil Liability for Nuclear Damage (Vienna, 21 May 1963; IAEA INFCIRC/500).

[41] Protocol to Amend the Vienna Convention on Civil Liability for Nuclear Damage of 12 September 1997, IAEA INFCIRC/566 (1997 Vienna Convention).

[42] Joint Protocol Relating to the Application of the Vienna Convention and the Paris Convention of 21 September 1988, IAEA INFCIRC/402.

[43] See also Article 14 of the Council Directive (EEC) 374/85 on the approximation of the laws, regulations and administrative provisions of the Member States concerning liability for defective products [1985] OJ L201/29, amended by the Directive (EC) 34/99 of the European Parliament and of the Council [1999] OJ L141/20.

[44] There are only two exceptions: according to Article 6(c)(i) of the Paris Convention, the convention does not prevent (1) liability of an individual who intentionally caused damage by a nuclear incident, and (2) liability of a person duly authorised to operate a reactor comprised in a means of transport, if the operator's liability is excluded by the convention.

to recourse. Recourse is only available if an individual person (but not a legal entity) has intentionally caused the damage, or if the right to recourse is expressly provided by contract. The second goal of legal channelling is to restrict the operator's liability. This means that the operator's liability is exclusively regulated by the convention and the national laws implementing it.

The operator is obliged to provide for financial security (principle of congruence of liability and coverage). In order to exclude forum shopping, jurisdiction only lies with the courts of the Member State in whose territory the nuclear incident occurred, or, if the nuclear incident occurs outside the territory of the State, or, if the place of the nuclear incident cannot be determined with certainty, with the courts of the Member State in whose territory the nuclear installation of the liable operator is situated ("exclusive jurisdiction"). Applicable law, both substantive and procedural, which is not specifically governed by the convention, is the law of the competent court (*lex fori*). The nature, form and extent of the compensation, as well as distribution matters, are regulated by national law. The Paris Convention and the national laws implementing it must be applied without any discrimination based upon nationality, domicile or residence in order to ensure equal treatment of victims (principle of non-discrimination). Judgments that are enforceable under the jurisdiction of the competent court must be recognised and enforced in all the other Member States. Compensation, insurance and reinsurance premiums, including interests and costs, must be freely transferable between the contracting countries.

Liability is limited in amount and time. Article 7(b) of the 1960 Paris Convention provides that the maximum liability of the operator with regard to damage caused by a nuclear incident is 15 million Special Drawing Rights (SDR) of the International Monetary Fund (approximately 18.2 million euro). In order to cover this liability, the operator is obliged to have and to maintain insurance or other financial security for this amount. Member States, taking into account the operator's possibilities of obtaining coverage, are allowed to provide for a lower or higher liability cap by legislation, or – despite the principle of congruence of liability and coverage – even unlimited liability.[45] With regard to less dangerous nuclear installations and substances, the liability cap may also be reduced. The minimum amount of liability and coverage is 5 million SDR (approximately 6.1 million euro). The 2004 PC-Protocol increases liability sums

---

[45] See Pelzer 1982, 51; Pelzer 1988, 97.

substantially. It establishes a minimum amount of 700 million euro (Article I(H) 2004 PC-Protocol). This minimum liability cap of 700 million euro cannot be reduced according to the capacity of the insurance market, as was provided by Article 7(b)(i) of the 1960 Paris Convention. Thus, Member States are only allowed to deviate from this amount by establishing a higher liability cap or unlimited liability by national legislation. Signatory States of the 2004 PC-Protocol may establish a lower liability cap of at least 70 million euro for less dangerous nuclear installations and at least 80 million euro for the carriage of nuclear substances (Article I(H) 2004 PC-Protocol). Interests and costs are not considered to be compensation for the purposes of the convention. Thus, if they are awarded by a court, they must be paid by the liable operator in addition to the compensation sum (Article I(H) 2004 PC-Protocol).

The operator of a nuclear installation has only very few defences available. According to Article 9 of the 1960 Paris Convention, the operator is not liable for harm caused by a nuclear incident directly due to an act of armed conflict, hostilities, civil war or insurrection. If the damage is caused by a natural disaster of an exceptional character, the 1960 Paris Convention allows for a defence, unless provided otherwise by national legislation. The 2004 PC-Protocol eliminates this exoneration (Article I(J)). Thus the operator of a nuclear installation will also be liable for damage directly caused by a natural disaster, be it of an exceptional character or not. The 2004 PC-Protocol, however, allows national law to provide for a defence of contributory negligence in case of gross negligence or the intentional actions of the person suffering the damage (Article I(G) 2004 PC-Protocol).

In England and Wales the Paris and Brussels Conventions were implemented by the Nuclear Installations Act 1965 which provides for a liability cap of £140 million per nuclear incident. In April 2012 the UK government announced its intention to implement the 2004 Protocols to the Paris and the Brussels Convention, which will increase the existing operator liability limit of £140 million per incident to 1200 million euro.[46]

France already increased the operator liability to the level of the 2004 Protocols, which is 700 million euro per nuclear incident by Law of 13 June 2006 (which amended Law no. 68–943 of 30 October 1968). This amendment also introduced the defence of gross negligence of the victim.

---

[46] Department of Energy and Climate Change, "Compensating victims of nuclear accidents", 24 January 2011, www.gov.uk/government/consultations/compensating-victims-of-nuclear-accidents (accessed 25 August 2014).

The liability caps for "reduced risk installations" (as defined by decree no. 91–335 of 12 April 1991) and for the transport of nuclear materials, if the transport is covered by the Paris Convention, specifically 70 million euro and 80 million euro respectively, are also in line with the 2004 Protocols. If the transport is not covered by the Paris Convention, the liability cap is increased to 1.2 billion euro. Compensation provided by the State according to the Brussels Convention is 1.5 billion euro. In the event that loss for personal injury exceeds this amount, further compensation will be provided by special decree. Special rules apply for the liability for damage caused by nuclear ships, implementing the Brussels Convention of 25 May 1962[47] (Law no. 65–956 of 12 November 1965 modified by the Laws nos. 68–1045 of 29 November 1968 and 88–1093 of 1 December 1988).

In Germany, the Nuclear Power Act (*Atomgesetz*)[48] declared the Paris Convention directly applicable. It, however, provides for several deviations from the convention, most importantly for unlimited liability of the operator. Limitations only apply with respect to damage in another country with limitations (reciprocity) and in exceptional cases such as natural disasters or war where there is a cap of 2.5 billion euro.

In the Netherlands, the Paris–Brussels regime is implemented by the Nuclear Accidents Liability Act ("*Wet aansprakelijkheid kernongevallen*"), which provides from 1 January 2013 onwards a cap of 1.2 billion euro. In Spain, the liability cap is 700 euro as provided by the Act on Civil Liability for Nuclear Damage of 28 May 2011,[49] and in Sweden, where the actual liability cap is set at 300 million SDR,[50] the new act on nuclear liability[51] which is not yet in force will provide for unlimited liability with the obligation for coverage by insurance for up to 1.2 billion euro.

In Poland, where the obligations derived from the Vienna Convention were implemented by Title 12 (Articles 100–108) of the Polish Atomic Law[52], the liability cap is set at 300 million SDR. If claims exceed the limit, a special fund must be created. In addition, the State covers the compensation for damage to persons above the sum guaranteed in the insurance policy.

---

[47] Brussels Convention on the Liability of Operators of Nuclear Ships (Brussels, 25 May 1962).

[48] "*Gesetz über die friedliche Nutzung der Kernenergie und den Schutz gegen ihre Gefahren*" of 23 December 1959, recast in BGBl 1985 I, 1565, as amended BGBl 2012 I, 212.

[49] Law 12/2011, 27 May, "*sobre responsabilidad civil por daños nucleares o producidos por materiales radiactivos*".

[50] *Atomansvarighetslagen* (1968:45).   [51] *Lag* (2010:950).

[52] Act of 29 November 2000, consolidated text Dz. U. 2012, at 264.

3.1.3.2.4. Medical products (pharmaceuticals) The only country which provides for a special strict liability regime for medical products is Germany. According to the German Pharmaceuticals Act (*Arzneimittelgesetz*, AMG) the producer of a medical product that is intended for human use is strictly liable for damage caused by the product. The development risk defence does not apply. Liability is capped and there is obligatory financial coverage. Claims on the basis of fault-based liability and product liability remain unaffected (§ 91 AMG).

In France professionals in the health sector are under an obligation to secure the health products they use (see Law no. 2002–203 of 4 March 2002). The Netherlands, Poland and Spain do not provide for specific liability rules for medical products. In all of these countries the liability for pharmaceuticals is regulated by product liability law with the peculiarity that in France the development risk does not apply for medicinal products derived from the human body and in Spain to medicines in general. In Sweden injuries caused by pharmaceuticals are covered by a no-fault insurance scheme set up by the pharmaceutical industry.

3.1.3.2.5. Environmental harm Directive 35/04 on environmental liability with regard to the prevention and remedying of environmental damage[53] which harmonised the rules on the prevention and restoration of site contamination and on loss of biodiversity in the European Union has not interfered with national tort law remedies for the compensation of environmental harm. The picture of liability for environmental harm is thus heterogeneous in the countries analysed. Environmental damage underlies the rules of general tort law including nuisance law and general strict liability regimes, such as Article 1384(1) of the French *Code civil* (liability of the custodian of a thing) or Article 435 of the Polish Civil code which, according to Article 324 Environmental Protection Law of 27 April 2001,[54] does not require that the installation is run with the use of natural forces if the installation is dangerous. In Spain, environmental harm is covered by Article 1908 *Código civil* which provides for strict liability for harm to persons and property caused by toxic fumes.

Specific and comprehensive strict liability regimes for environmental harm are provided in Germany and Sweden. The German Environmental Liability Act 1990 (UmwHG) imposes strict liability on the operator

---

[53] Directive (EC) 35/04 of the European Parliament and of the Council on environmental liability with regard to the prevention and remedying of environmental damage [2004] OJ L143/56.

[54] Dz. U. 2001, no. 62, at 627 as amended.

of certain dangerous installations exhaustively listed in Annex 1 to the UmwHG. An exclusion applies in the case of force majeure (§ 4 UmwHG); § 6 UmwHG provides for a rebuttable presumption of causation. Liability is limited in amount to a maximum of 85 million euro per environmental impact incident and liability for negligible property damage is excluded. The Act does not cover damage to the environment if it does not constitute property damage or personal injury. A special strict liability rule is provided for damage to water, including ground water (§ 89(2) Water Management Law).[55] In Sweden, Chapter 32 of the Environmental Code provides for strict liability for the owner, or the keeper of land, concerning personal injury, property damage and substantial pure economic loss. With respect to this cause of liability, the burden for the proof of causality is reduced from high probability as required by general tort law to the balance of probabilities. Compulsory environmental clean-up insurance for hazardous activities, originally provided in the Environmental Code, was abolished in 2010. English law has no comprehensive regime of liability in respect of environmental harm. A special cause of action for harm caused by controlled waste is provided by the Environmental Protection Act 1990.[56] French law provides for a special insurance compensation mechanism in case of damage which is declared a technological disaster by the administrative authority.[57]

3.2.   Relationship between tort liability and regulation

3.2.1.   Relationship between tort liability and regulation in general

The relationship of tort liability with regulation is rather complex. Compliance with regulation does not affect strict liability obligations or, as a general rule which has its exceptions, liability according to neighbourhood liability (nuisance). It has, however, important relevance for the application of fault-based liability in civil law systems and the tort of negligence in common law.

In all of the jurisdictions, public law standards are used by courts to determine the required standard of care.[58] They can also be an important

---

[55] *Wasserhaushaltsgesetz*, BGBl 2009 I, 2585.

[56] Section 73(6) of the Environmental Protection Act 1990: liability for the breach of statutory duty of section 34(1) Environmental Protection Act 1990.

[57] Law no. 2003–699 from 30 July 2003.

[58] This also applies to technical standards provided by national or international Standardisation Committees, such as the International Standardisation Organisation (ISO) or the

source for establishing a legal duty to act in order to prevent the occurrence of damage. Courts, however, use these standards only as an indication of what the required standard in general is and do not feel bound by it for the individual case. It is a general rule that compliance with public law standards does not exempt the defendant from tort liability.[59] Courts will always assess the required duty of care according to the individual circumstances of the case. Private law standards thus can surpass the standards set by public law. An exception only applies in those special circumstances when the harm is caused because of compliance with mandatory regulations issued by the public authorities, as is, for instance, provided by Article 7(d) Product Liability Directive or Article 8(3)(b) Environmental Liability Directive.

Failure to comply with regulation, however, is in all jurisdictions a strong indication that the defendant breached the required standard of care (common law) or acted unlawfully or with fault (civil law). Statutory rules may also serve as rules with a protective scope (*Schutzgesetz*). Whether this is the case is a matter of construction. According to the theory of the protective scope of the rule (*Schutzzwecklehre*), which is accepted in many civil law jurisdictions, the breach of certain regulatory duties that aim to protect the concrete victim affects tort liability in two ways. On the one hand, it establishes unlawfulness and on the other hand it concretises the scope of liability with respect to the group of persons protected by the rule and the type of compensable damages. In English law the breach of a statutory duty constitutes a distinctive tort in its own right and allows the award of damages to the person injured by the breach if he belongs to the group protected by the statute.

3.2.2.   Specific regulations affecting liability risks of security providers

Some activities of security enterprises are covered by more general legislation concerning the use of security devices, like weapons or monitoring devices, or rules regarding the safety of software.

Several countries (France, the Netherlands, Poland and Sweden) provide for special rules concerning the licensing of security enterprises and the supervision of their activities which establish quality requirements and rules concerning the competence and training of the employees. These

---

European Committee for Standardisation (CEN) or, as the French reporter indicates, even to internal company regulations or professional codes of ethics.

[59] See the answers to Case 1, Question e in Chapter 4.

rules are enforced by public agencies. Special rules apply with respect to airport security.[60]

3.3.   Causation

3.3.1.   Standard burden of proof regarding causation

In principle, the burden of proof for causation falls on the claimant. In English and Dutch law, the required standard of proof for the proof of causation is the balance of probabilities. In Sweden, the required standard is very high (certainty beyond reasonable doubt), but in complex cases of causation courts are inclined to apply a somewhat lower burden of proof ("clearly more probable" than any other explanation). The Spanish reporter did not relate to any degree of probability but rather stressed that the Spanish courts require that the facts are established to the conviction of the court. In medical liability and other fields of technological complexity, reasonable probability may already suffice to prove causation in Spanish law. The same seems to apply in France where the courts, however, are more easily inclined to assume causation in complex cases where causation is difficult to establish. In Germany, the standard is a very high level of probability. This is nowadays also the level required by the Polish courts which used to require a very high level of probability close to certainty (beyond reasonable doubt). In Poland, this relaxation is mainly applied in complex causation scenarios involving personal injury, but not for claims for lost profits. With respect to public authority liability, liability for animals and personal liability of minors or incompetent persons, the level is even lowered to the balance of probabilities which, according to scholarly opinions, should also be the standard in cases of nuclear liability.

3.3.2.   Instruments to lighten the burden of proof regarding causation

Causation is usually established with the so-called "but for" test, according to which causation is not established unless it is shown that the damage would not have occurred without the factor in question. In England and Wales, the connection must be proved according to the balance of probability standard. In France the theories of "direct link" or "adequate causation" are sometimes invoked as well.

---

[60] Regulation (EC) 300/08 of the European Parliament and of the Council on common rules in the field of civil aviation security [2008] OJ L97/72 as amended by Commission Regulation (EU) 18/10 [2010] OJ L7/3.

In all countries analysed, courts have some discretion with respect to the establishment of causation. In complex situations, especially in medical liability cases, or in cases involving multiple causes, various strategies are applied to lighten the burden of proof for the claimant. These strategies are rather diverse and range from the classical prima facie evidence (Germany) or *res ipsa loquitur* (England and Wales, the Netherlands, Poland) to more sophisticated strategies in order to cope with only statistical evidence like the attribution of damages according to the loss of a chance (France, Netherlands), or proportional liability (the Netherlands), or the English "doubles the risk" test, where the claimant can establish causation by showing that the defendant's breach doubled the original statistical risk. Some jurisdictions also provide for presumptions of causation. In the Netherlands, courts may reverse the burden of proof if this is seen as reasonable and fair (Article 150 Code of Civil Procedure). In France presumptions of causation are applied with respect to certain diseases (HIV, hepatitis C, DES-litigation) and in Poland, in pollution cases.

3.4. Attribution of liability

If the separate and independent acts of two or several tortfeasors cause separate injuries or divisible harm, the liability of each defendant is limited to the extent of his contribution to the overall harm. All jurisdictions provide for **joint and several liability** if two or more tortfeasors cause harm to the victim as part of a joint venture. The same applies if the tortfeasors act independently and separately and the harm is indivisible. As a consequence, each tortfeasor can be sued by the victim for the entire sum of compensation. In the civil law systems this is explicitly provided in most of the civil codes. In France it was established by case law and in Spain this rule is explicitly provided only in special liability statutes and the criminal code but generally recognised by case law and scholarship.

The tortfeasor who compensated the victim then has a right of **recourse** against the other contributors. The decisive criteria for the assessment of the shares of the contributors differ in the various countries. In Germany the general rule of the BGB (§ 426 BGB) is apportionment per capita, while in products and pharmaceutical liability, apportionment is conducted according to the particular circumstances of the individual case. In the Netherlands, the apportionment is the result of a more comprehensive assessment which includes fault, the individual circumstances of the case and equity. English and Polish law also refer to the circumstances of the case, in particular to the fault of each contributor and the degree to which the latter contributed to the occurrence of the damage. In Swedish law, the damages must be apportioned according to what is reasonable, but the main factor is the seriousness of fault of each contributor.

If the liability was incurred **without fault**, it is split in equal shares in most countries. In some jurisdictions (England and Wales, Poland and Sweden) it is held that in case of concurrence of fault-based liability and strict liability, the contributor who was at fault has to bear the whole damage.

3.5.   Damages and available remedies

3.5.1.   Types of compensable damages

It is generally accepted in all of the jurisdictions that tort liability covers personal injury, property damage and consequential financial loss. This includes damages for pain and suffering. This now also applies to German law which did not provide for damages for pain and suffering in strict liability statutes in the past, but eliminated this restriction in 2002.[61] Compensation for other types of non-pecuniary loss is often restricted to certain specific cases (e.g., Germany, the Netherlands, Poland).

The compensability of pure economic loss is more disputed. In England and Wales pure economic loss is only recoverable under exceptional circumstances. The same applies in Germany, where pure economic loss is not covered by the general tort law provision of § 823(1) BGB, but only by § 826 BGB for the intentional infliction of damage in a manner contrary to public policy and by § 823(2) BGB on breach of a statutory duty. That statutory duty, however, must have the purpose of protecting the victim's patrimony independently from physical injury or damage to property. In Sweden, pure economic loss is only compensable if the loss was caused by a criminal act (Chapter 2 Section 2 Tort Liability Act) and, according to case law, if there is a relationship of reliance between the tortfeasor and the claimant. Moreover, some strict tort liability statutes[62] offer special protection for pure economic loss.

French, Dutch, Polish and Spanish law follow the principle of full compensation and do not distinguish pure economic loss as a separate head of damage in general tort law. Compensation includes non-pecuniary and

---

[61] BGBl 2002 I, 2634.
[62] Chapter 32 of the Environmental Code and Section 7(3) of the new Nuclear Liability Act.

pure economic loss. The most comprehensive view is taken by French law which follows the principle of full compensation including non-pecuniary and pure economic loss. These countries restrict the compensability of pure economic loss, however, through considerations of causality and attribution of the loss. French and Spanish law require a sufficiently direct causal link between the tortious behaviour and the damage. For liability for breach of contract, Article 1150 of the French *Code civil* requires that the loss was foreseeable when the contract was concluded. In Poland such a limiting effect is brought about by the concept of adequate causation established by Article 361 § 1 of the Polish Civil code. This limit is excluded when the breach was particularly serious, which is the case when the tortfeasor acted with intent or with gross negligence. In the Netherlands Article 6:98 BW provides that damage shall be attributed according to the nature of the damage and the nature of the liability. Foreseeability, although not expressly mentioned, also plays an important role. Courts thus have a considerable margin of discretion in the attribution of damage to the tortfeasor, which is exercised differently for the different types of damage.

In English and German tort law, **environmental harm**[63] is not a recognised head of damage. It is only compensable if it constitutes property damage or personal injury. But the costs for clean-up and prevention of environmental damage are recoverable as pecuniary loss under general tort law provided that the claimant can show a sufficient legal interest in the measure. This is at any rate the case with the owner of the polluted property. The same applies in the Netherlands who go one step further and grant legal standing also to associations or foundations with vested interests in environmental matters. The same principles apply in Poland, but, in addition, Polish law allows certain institutions (State Treasury, local authorities or ecological organisations) to sue for compensation for harm to the environment under the Environmental Protection Law (Articles 322 et seq.) and the Law on GMOs (Article 57 subsection 2). In Sweden, the Environmental Code provides for strict liability for personal injuries, property damage and pure economic loss caused by emissions or disturbances from an activity on a nearby property including environmental clean-up. The most comprehensive recognition of environmental damage is provided by French law, where it has become a special head of damage in tort law. Environmental damage is addressed in several environmental regulations and was explicitly recognised as head of damage

---

[63] For liability under Dir 35/04 on environmental liability with regard to the prevention and remedying of environmental damage see Part I, 2.4.1.

by the French Supreme Court (*Cour de cassation*).[64] It covers property damage, pure economic loss, remedial action including the cost of remedial action and even non-pecuniary damage. In case of pure ecological damage (e.g., loss of biodiversity), special interest groups (nature protection associations) may be entitled to claim damages.

3.5.2.   *Exclusion of heads of damage by contractual agreement*

In all of the analysed countries, except in France, tort law liability can be limited by contractual stipulation. This contractual freedom is, however, limited by various rules concerning special heads of liability which prohibit the contractual limitation or exclusion of liability as is for instance provided by Article 12 of the Product Liability Directive. For general tort law, due to **Dir 13/93 on unfair terms in consumer contracts,**[65] it is common standard in all the countries that in B to C (business to consumer) relationships, fault-based liability for personal injury cannot be excluded or limited by standard terms.[66] In most countries this rule is extended to B to B (business to business) relationships, as such terms do not pass the required reasonableness test (e.g., Germany, the Netherlands, Poland). In the same context, English law does not distinguish between consumer and business contracts and, according to Article 2 of the Unfair Contract Terms Act 1977, declares contractual clauses that exclude liability for death or personal injury resulting from negligence void. Clauses excluding liability for any other loss or damage resulting from negligence are subject to a test of reasonableness and are void, if unreasonable. As regards exclusion clauses in relation to liability for breach of contract, a test of reasonableness will also apply if one of the parties is dealing as a consumer or if the contract is conducted using written standard terms of business.

In Germany, any exclusion or limitation of liability for damage to property arising from a grossly negligent breach of duty is ineffective. In the Netherlands and Spain, such clauses are subject to a test of reasonableness. Although exclusion or contractual limitation of liability is in principle allowed in contracts in B to B relationships, such exclusions can be tested under general fairness rules including the assessment of such factors as the relative bargaining powers, the degree of fault and the extent and nature of the losses incurred.

---

[64] Crim. 25 September 2012, no. 10–82.938, D. 2012. 2711.
[65] Council Directive (EEC) 13/93 on unfair terms in consumer contracts [1993] OJ L95/29.
[66] Council Directive 13/93, Article 3(3) Annex 1(a).

3.5.3.   Special instruments for mitigating the liability of the tortfeasor

No country provides for a **liability cap** for fault-based liability. In Germany and Spain liability caps are quite usual in strict liability statutes. In the Netherlands, liability caps can be provided by the executive according to Article 6:110 BW, but so far no limitations have been introduced. For particular providers of services (pilots, air traffic controllers) and certain public authorities (Bank of the Netherlands, Financial Markets Authority), liability is restricted to intentional, grossly negligent or wilfully reckless behaviour. In France and Poland, liability caps are mainly provided in fields of liability that are regulated by international conventions (e.g., nuclear liability) and for hotel keepers (Article 849 § 1 Polish Civil code; Article 1953 al. 3 and Article 1954 al. 2 French *Code civil*). In France liability caps are also provided for transportation and by certain compensation schemes (workers compensation, natural disasters, etc.). In Sweden, the special alternative compensation schemes for patients or pharmaceuticals are subject to caps. In tort liability, Swedish law does not accept liability caps and will in future even provide for unlimited liability in nuclear liability law.

Reduction clauses are not a common instrument for mitigating the liability of the tortfeasor. Of all analysed countries, only the Netherlands (Article 6:109 BW) and Poland (Article 440 CC) have such explicit rules, but in both countries this instrument has not yet been widely used. According to Article 440 of the Polish Civil code, the reduction clause can be applied only to physical persons. It allows only the reduction and not the total exclusion of damages and is not applied in cases of intentional fault, gross negligence or personal injury or where the person liable has liability insurance cover. In Spain, Article 1103 CC allows courts to mitigate damage arising from negligence on a case-by-case basis. Compensation for personal injuries and death is often awarded according to a tariff system developed for road traffic accidents that is now under revision.

3.6.   Alternative compensation mechanisms

3.6.1.   Alternative compensation schemes

The picture concerning alternative compensation mechanisms is heterogeneous. All of the countries provide for compulsory liability insurance in certain areas (motor vehicles, aeroplanes, nuclear installations etc.). In Poland, security companies that provide for security services directed at the guarding of human life and property at airports are obliged to take out liability insurance.[67] According to the regulation issued by the Ministry of Finance on 4 October 2012,[68] the insurance does not cover inter alia war risks, hostilities and acts of terror. All damages are covered and the insurer may not limit its liability. The minimum guarantee sum for the period of coverage of maximum twelve months is set at 5000 SDR per 1000 passengers serviced or 5000 SDR per 100,000 kg of cargo or post serviced in the previous year, whichever sum is higher. If the company carries out its services on more than one airport, the minimum guarantee sum must be the higher sum that applies to a given airport.

All countries have special rules concerning the coverage of personal injury by social security which are, however, very different, and all countries have compensation funds for specific areas, e.g., for crime victims (Germany, France, Spain, Sweden and the UK),[69] natural disasters (France), technological disasters (France), patient and pharmaceutical injuries (Sweden), or vaccine damage (UK) and workers' injuries (Sweden).

3.6.2.   Compensation schemes for victims of terrorism

Special compensation schemes for victims of terrorism are provided in France, Spain and the UK.[70] The British compensation scheme was introduced in 2012 and covers victims of overseas and domestic terrorism[71] who cannot obtain compensation from other sources. Payments are calculated by reference to a tariff system similar to the one used for the Criminal Injuries Compensation Scheme, with a maximum individual payment of £ 500,000.

In France, the law of 9 September 1986[72] created a Compensation Fund for the Victims of Acts of Terrorism (FGTI) which is funded by a tax on property insurance contracts. This fund compensates only personal injuries. For property damage, compensation must be provided by the insurers. Following the terrorist attacks of 11 September 2001, insurers refused to continue to cover some of these risks and they are now shared between insurers, reinsurers and the State.

---

[67] Article 22a of the Law of 22 August 1997 Dz. U. 2005, no. 145 item 1221 as amended.
[68] Dz. U. 2012, item 1123.   [69] Koch 2010, 263.
[70] For an explanation of the new terrorism insurance schemes see Part III.
[71] The Stationery Office, "The Victims of Overseas Terrorism Compensation Scheme 2012" (Gov.uk, 27 November 2012).
[72] C. assur., Article L. 126–1 and L. 422–1 sqq. as amended by Law no. 86–1020 of 9 September 1986.

In Spain, the 2011 Act of Recognition and Comprehensive Protection of Victims of Terrorism[73] provides subsidies to victims in case of death, personal injury[74] and kidnapping caused by terrorists. It also provides contributions for damage caused to cars, industrial or commercial establishments and to the headquarters of political parties and trade unions. The French and the Spanish act provide for subrogation.

3.6.3. *Special rules on case management*

All of the national legal systems analysed provide for special rules on case management. The approaches towards collective redress, however, vary a lot. Traditional mechanisms of joining of actions, like joinder of parties, can be observed in all national legal systems. The legal solutions concerning further collective redress mechanisms are rather unique and can thus hardly be compared. In the last few years, a trend towards the introduction of new collective redress mechanisms can be observed in various Member States. New mechanisms have been created recently in Germany (a group action for capital market law claims and a skimming-off procedure for unfair competition law cases),[75] in the Netherlands (a collective settlement procedure)[76] and in Poland (group action for claims of consumer protection, claims based on product liability and claims based on tort law)[77]. Group actions are also available in the UK,[78] Spain[79] and Sweden[80]. Nevertheless, none of the national legal systems analysed provides for a US-style class action.

---

[73] *Ley 29/2011, 22 September "de Reconocimiento y Protección Integral a las Víctimas del Terrorismo"*.

[74] Annex I of the LRPIVT contains the following amounts for different kinds of injuries with permanent effect: death 250,000.00 euro; severe disability 500,000.00 euro; absolute permanent disability 180,000.00 euro; total permanent disability 100,000.00 euro; partial permanent disability 75,000.00 euro.

[75] Capital Market Model Claims Act (*Kapitalanleger-Musterverfahrensgesetz* [KapMuG] and § 10 of the Unfair Competition Act (UWG).

[76] Dutch Collective Settlement of Mass Damage Act (*Wet Collectieve Afwikkeling Massaschade* [WCAM]).

[77] The Act of 17 December 2009 on Pursuing Claims in Group Proceedings, Dz. U. 2010, no. 7, item 44.

[78] Part 19 of the Civil Procedure Rules 1998.   [79] 2000 Act of Civil Procedure.

[80] Class Action Act 2002 (*lag* (2002:599) *om grupprättegång*).

4

Case studies*

4.1.   Case 1 – Defective emergency stop button

Company X operates a steel plant. A year ago it bought a heavy stamping machine from Company A. While operating the machine, worker B sees that C, who is part of a group of visitors on a plant tour, is getting too close to the machine. B pushes the pilot trigger to stop the machine. The pilot trigger was built into the machine by A in order to allow the sudden stop of the machine by cutting the electricity supply. Due to a manufacturing defect, the button fails to function and C gets injured.

Question a: *Is A liable for C's injury? Please describe all heads of liability that are applicable.*

England and Wales

A could be sued by C for damages for personal injury in both negligence and under the Consumer Protection Act 1987 (CPA). Arguably, the ineffective safety feature makes the machine itself defective and potentially dangerous. In negligence, it would be easy for C to satisfy the *Caparo* test for duty of care.[1] Whether or not A is in breach of its duty will depend on the nature of the defect. If the defect was one that would probably not have been prevented, foreseen or discovered by a reasonable manufacturer in the circumstances, then the defendant will not be liable. In terms of causation, it would be easy for the claimant to demonstrate that the harm would not have occurred if the machine had powered down as expected. There should not be any obstacles to C invoking the strict liability regime under the CPA 1987. The issue of defectiveness seems straightforward and A is clearly a relevant producer.

---

* Cases: Monika Hinteregger; England and Wales: Claire McIvor; France: Florence G'sell; Germany: Peter Rott; Netherlands: Siewert Lindenbergh and Willem van Boom; Poland: Ewa Baginska; Spain: Pedro del Olmo; Sweden: Philip Mielnicki and Marten Schultz.
[1] Established in *Caparo Industries Plc v. Dickman* [1990] 2 AC 605.

France

A is liable as the manufacturer of this defective machine on the basis of Law no. 98–389 of 19 May 1998 (Article 1386–1 ff *Code civil*). The various conditions of liability are fulfilled here. The machine in question is indeed a product since it is a chattel. This machine is defective because it does not offer the safety that can reasonably be expected since the safety button did not work. Because of this defect, the machine did not stop which in turn led to the accident. C is a private person who has suffered injury for which he can get full compensation.

Germany

A would be liable under general tort law (§ 823 para 1 BGB), breach of a statutory duty (§ 823 para 2 BGB with § 230 of the Criminal Code (*Strafgesetzbuch*; StGB)) and § 1 ProdHaftG. As required by § 823 para 1 BGB in its special interpretation by the courts in product liability cases, A is liable for damage caused by defective products. The stamping machine was obviously defective since the pilot trigger did not function,[2] and this failure caused physical injury to C. A would have to prove that they did not act negligently, which is extremely difficult in practice, and the case gives no indication of any excuse for the manufacturing defect.

Due to the injury, C can claim for restoration of his health (§ 249 para 1 BGB) or the amount of money that is necessary for this (§ 249 para 2 BGB). In practice, of course, C would normally be covered by health insurance and not pay for medical treatment. In that case, however, the claim would pass by law to the insurance provider (§ 116 Social Code X, *Sozialgesetzbuch* X) which could take recourse to A. Moreover, C can claim damages for pain and suffering (§ 253 BGB). The same applies to liability under § 1 ProdHaftG.[3] However, liability is strict here and A would have no possibility to avoid liability by proving that it did not act negligently. § 8 sent 2 ProdHaftG also provides for damages for pain and suffering. In contrast, in order to establish liability under § 823 para 2 BGB due to the breach of the statutory duty of § 230 StGB not to injure a person negligently, it would be for C to prove A's negligence.

---

[2] On the malfunction of an automated pilot trigger see OLG Hamm, 5 October 1995 (1996) NJW-Entscheidungsdienst – Versicherungs-/Haftungsrecht (NJWE–VHR) 22.

[3] For a case of failing airbag software see BGH, 16 June 2009, (2009) NJW 2952 – airbag.

The Netherlands

A is liable under the EU Product Liability Directive's terms in his capacity as manufacturer of the defective product (the machine and the safety emergency stop button) for the personal injury of C (presuming A manufactured the machine). These EU provisions were transposed into Dutch law (Article 6:185 BW). A is also liable under the common fault-based liability conditions, if C can prove wrongfulness and imputability. Here, C would need to substantiate his claim by asserting that the defective nature was caused by some form of negligence of A.

Poland

A is liable to C and the claims should be brought under the product liability regime (Article 449[1]ff Civil Code). Personal injury is fully reparable, and a list of heads of damage eligible for compensation can be drawn on from Articles 444–446 Civil Code. In the case of bodily injury or a disturbance of health, the redress of damage covers all resulting costs (Article 444 para 1 Civil Code). This term covers all necessary and suitable expenses causally linked to the injury, e.g., cost of treatment, special diet, etc. Pursuant to Article 444 para 2 Civil Code, if a victim completely or partially loses his ability to work or if his needs have increased or his future prospects have been diminished, he may demand an appropriate annuity from the person obliged to redress the damage. Any of the above conditions, whether alone or concurrent with others, constitutes a sufficient ground for the claim. However, according to case law, an annuity based on the loss of earning capacity or on the loss of future prospects may not be awarded to a minor. The victim may furthermore claim non-pecuniary loss stemming from the bodily injury (Article 445 para 1 Civil Code).

Spain

A is liable under Article 137 TRLDCU, i.e., under the Spanish system of liability for defective products. The stamping machine is a defective product because it is not a safe product and fails to perform as it was designed.[4] It is not clear whether we are dealing with a manufacturing defect or with a defect in design. In any case, defectiveness is clear.[5] In

---

[4] See Salvador and Ramos 2008, 139, for an application of the so-called malfunction doctrine. A similar idea is conveyed in Azparren 2011, 1196.

[5] The Spanish Act on liability for defective products does not use that distinction. It only makes a brief mention of the manufacturing defect in Article 137.2 TRLDCU (cf Article 11

this case, it also seems easy to prove the defect, the damage caused and the causal link between them (Article 139 TRLDCU).[6] As the dangerous features of the machine mean it does not work properly, the defect in this case affects both the safety of the product and its contractual conformity.[7]

Also, A is liable to X under the general rules of contractual liability.[8] The personal injuries suffered by the victim would probably be litigated under non-contractual liability rules, even if the victim was the machine-owner and a party to the sales contract.[9] If the victim was one of X's employees, the case would probably be considered a working accident and would be litigated accordingly in the social jurisdiction.[10]

Sweden

The injury falls outside the statutory and traditional notion of product liability between a consumer of a defective product and its producer. However, defective products that constitute a particular danger to persons and property give rise to special security duties on the part of the producer, which may not be transferred to another party.[11] Furthermore, personal injuries give rise to special protection despite the fact that C has no direct or indirect contractual relationship with A.[12] Strict liability may thus be at hand.

Question b: *Is A liable to C if C has, by his own fault, contributed to the damage?*

TRLDCU, implementing Directive 2001/95/EC). On the contrary, that distinction is well known among legal writers. Amongst many others see J Solé Feliu, *El concepto de defecto del producto en la responsabilidad civil del fabricante* (Tirant lo Blanch 1997) 569.

[6] Parra Lucán 2008.

[7] Martín-Casals and Solé Feliu 2008, 631. The case law also uses the same idea, as can be seen in STS 3 October 1991and STS 31 July 1997 (RJ 5617).

[8] Díez-Picazo 2008, 771.   [9] Díez-Picazo 2011, 216.

[10] Parra Lucán 2011, 309, who quotes B. Rodríguez Sanz de Galdeano, *Responsabilidades de los fabricantes en materia de prevención de riesgos laborales* (Lex Nova, 2005) and *La obligación de seguridad del fabricante de productos de trabajo y sus implicaciones en materia de responsabilidad civil y seguridad social* (2006) 2 *Indret* 5. In the Spanish experience with asbestos litigation, the most common outcome was to sue the employer under labour law. See Malo 2007, 119. Legal writers are involved in controversies about the question of whether these cases should be litigated under the social jurisdiction or not. See STS (1st Chamber) 15 January 2008 (RJ 1394). See Martín-Casals and Solé Feliu 2010 and Yzquierdo 2008.

[11] Cf NJA 1986, 712.

[12] Cf NJA 1989, 389 (strict liability in relation to teacher eating salmonella-contaminated food at the school's canteen).

England and Wales

A would be able to argue that C has been contributorily negligent under the Law Reform (Contributory Negligence) Act 1945 and if successful, his liability would be reduced proportionately.

France

Article 1386–13 *Code civil* provides that the fault of the victim is a defence. It allows the defendant to be partially or totally exempted. It is up to the judge to assess the extent of this exemption according to the circumstances. One can assume that the exemption will be total if the fault of the victim was irresistible and unpredictable, i.e., if it has the characteristics of a force majeure. When the exemption is only partial, the apportionment is at the discretion of the trial court which, in principle, takes into account the seriousness of the offence committed by the victim.

Germany

Contributory fault does not exclude liability but will be set against the damage to be paid. This general rule of § 254 BGB is either referred to or repeated in all relevant pieces of strict liability legislation, including § 6 para 1 ProdHaftG. The exact shares of liability would be determined by the court in accordance with the contributions of the parties involved.[13]

The Netherlands

If C was contributorily negligent, A would still be liable but a proportionate reduction of damages in view of the contributory fault would be in order. See Article 6:101 BW and the outline of that provision rendered above.

Poland

A is still liable. In the products liability regime, contribution by the victim's own fault will not absolve the producer. It may, however, be the reason for reducing the damages pursuant to Article 362 Civil Code.

---

[13] See, for example, LG Dusseldorf, 30 November 2005, (2006) NJW-RR 1033 – floor husking machine.

Spain

Under the defective products liability system provided by TRLDCU, the contribution of the victim to his own damage would lead to a smaller damages award.[14] The solution would be similar under the contractual or non-contractual liability system, as was explained in answer to Question a) (see Articles 1103 CC and 104 CP).

Sweden

Reduction of damages for personal injuries due to contributory fault requires gross negligence on the part of the injured person (Tort Liability Act ch 6 s 1).

Question c: *Would it make any difference if C had suffered property damage instead of personal injury?*

England and Wales

No, it would not make any difference.

France

If C's damage is related to private property or goods designed for private use or consumption, compensation is possible under the provisions of the law. However, compensation is granted only for damage of at least 500 euro.

Germany

Liability under § 823 paras 1 and 2 BGB would be the same as under Question b. Also, A would be liable to C under § 1 ProdHaftG but the threshold of 500 euro would apply (§ 11 ProdHaftG).

The Netherlands

No, this would not make any difference.

---

[14] Article 145 TRLDCU states so very clearly.

Poland

As regards damage to property, damages shall not cover the destruction of the product itself or the profits which the injured party might have achieved in relation to its use (not applicable to C's claims) – see Article 449^7 para 1 Civil Code. However, in the strict liability regime, C may not claim property damage from A, should any have been sustained (destroyed clothes, glasses, etc.), unless: it exceeds the amount of 500 euro; it concerns items ordinarily intended for personal use; the injured party has used it mainly in such a manner (Article 449^2 Civil Code). In that case, he has to bring his claim for property damage under the fault regime (Articles 415 and 449^{10} Civil Code).

Spain

Not in this case. The TRLDCU can be the legal basis for a claim for personal injuries or death and also for property damage if it does not encompass those two kinds of damage. It may be underscored that, on the contrary, only Article 1902 permits a claim for non-pecuniary damage regardless of any other kind of damage (*daño moral*). In the Spanish legal tradition, moral harm is normally acknowledged but the transposition of Directive 85/374/EEC in Spain introduced a limit to the damage, which has been criticised by legal writers.[15]

Sweden

Since general principles of tort law apply and not statutory product liability, one may put into question of whether strict liability also protects the property interest of C. C's claim could be barred based on the principle that such liability does not fall within the protective scope of A's liability. Instead, C's claim could be barred here, since it is a third-party loss (i.e., a separate consequential harm to another person's harm), which as a general rule is not compensable.

Question d: *Because of the incident, company X cannot operate the stamping machine for fourteen days. Accordingly, company X cannot fulfil the contract*

---

[15] See the criticisms in Parra Lucán 2011, 48; Gómez Pomar 2008, 668–669. For their part and in an isolated opinion, M Martín-Casals and J Solé Feliu, "¿Refundir o legislar?" (2008) 92 Revista de Derecho Privado (RDP) 379, 98–99 believe that things have changed in the text of TRLDCU. See some criticism of this opinion in M Pasquau, "Daños causados por productos" in M Rebollo Puig and M Izquierdo Carrasco (eds), *La defensa de los consumidores y usuarios* (Iustel 2011) 1838.

with Y in time. X has to pay Y 200,000 euro for breach of contract. Due to X's failure to fulfil the contract, Y has to renounce a profitable contract and suffers 50,000 euro loss of profits. Is A liable to X and Y for their losses?

England and Wales

Since these losses would be classified as purely financial, it would not be recoverable in either negligence or under the CPA 1987. The special rules governing pure economic loss in negligence would not apply to these facts.

France

Company X suffers from a loss that is the result of the malfunction of the machine supplied by A. A will therefore be liable for breach of contract. Under the law of sale, A must compensate the loss sustained by X due to its non-compliance with its obligation to deliver non-defective goods that are in conformity with the contractual stipulations.

There is no contractual relationship between A and Y that would justify damages for breach of contract. The question is whether A could be tortiously liable. The *Cour de cassation* recognises that selling a defective product is a fault. However, the causal link between such a fault and the damage suffered by Y seems too remote to justify A's liability.

Germany

X's claim would be a contractual claim. Under the sales contract (§ 433 BGB), the seller is obliged to deliver the purchased good. If that good is defective and the buyer suffers damage, including economic loss, the seller is liable for breach of contract under § 280 para 1 BGB. Liability requires negligence though; however, the burden of proof for not having acted negligently lies on the seller (§ 280 para 1 sent 2 BGB). There would be no claim under the ProdHaftG since no other product has been damaged. Pure economic loss cannot be recovered under the ProdHaftG. The same applies to tort law liability under § 823 para 1 BGB. § 823 para 1 BGB requires the violation of the life, body, health, freedom, property or another right of another person. Pure economic loss is not covered by this tort.

A would not be liable to Y. Tort law does not apply to the situation since the general provision of tort law, § 823 para 1 BGB, requires the death or injury of a person, damage to property or another violation of a special interest. In contrast, it does not cover pure economic loss. In principle, third parties could enjoy the protection of the contract between A and X, under the concept of a "contract with protective effect on third parties" (*Vertrag mit Schutzwirkung für Dritte*).[16] This concept, however, has certain requirements that are not met here, including the proximity between the contracting partner (X) and the third person (Y) and the foreseeability of that relationship on A's part.

The Netherlands

This depends on the relationship between A and X. Assuming their relationship is a contract of sales and assuming that the defectiveness of the button amounts to non-conformity of the item sold under the contract (Article 7:17 BW), A would in principle be liable for consequential losses stemming from non-performance of the contract. Whether the damage can reasonably be considered the consequence of the non-performance for the operation of Article 6:98 BW depends on the circumstances of the particular case. For instance, it may be relevant to know whether A was in fact negligent in performing the contract or whether the defect could not easily have been discovered by A.

Poland

A is liable for X's loss. In general, both the actual loss of assets and the enhancement of liabilities are to be regarded as damage in Polish law. However, when the loss takes the latter form it causes certain problems. As regards future liabilities owed to third parties, the law focuses on liabilities such as those arising from breach of contract with third parties, when originally the breach committed by the plaintiff was triggered by the defendant's tortious act. Such a breach can give grounds for the third party's claim for full compensation or for liquidated damages. Once the damages are paid, the situation is quite clear because the scope of the plaintiff's loss can be determined with sufficient certainty. However, if the third party's claims have not been satisfied, there are doctrinal controversies as to the determination of the moment when the damage

---

[16] Established case law, see for example BGH, 7 November 1960, 33 BGHZ 247.

arises. There are certain arguments for allowing recourse to be claimed (against A) as soon as X's claims against Y accrue or, even further in time, when they are adjudicated. X could demand payment to the hands of Y.[17] Such a solution would be applicable only to a pecuniary performance and not to the situation where the creditor (Y) demands specific performance from X.

This view is, however, not generally supported by legal scholarship. Most authors and courts adhere to the opinion that until the debt (claim) is paid, the plaintiff's alleged loss (i.e., his enhanced liabilities) is pure speculation (the third party might in fact receive nothing in satisfaction of his claims). The theory behind this argument is enshrined in the principle *ne quis ex damno suo lucrum faciat*.[18] Nevertheless, a resolution of the Supreme Court of 10 July 2008, III CZP 62/08 may suggest a change in this approach.[19] The court adhered to the view that the third parties' accrued claims against the injured were a compensable element of *damnum emergens*. In consequence, once X repairs the losses suffered by Y, his claim for contribution against A materialises and accrues.

A claim between A and Y would be recognised in Polish law. First, Article 361 para 2 Civil Code establishes the principle of full compensation. In the absence of contrary provisions of a contract or law, redressing of the damage includes losses that the victim incurred (*damnum emergens*) and lost profits (*lucrum cessans*). Second, the establishment of pecuniary damage is based on the theory of difference: damage is the difference between what the victim would have had at his disposal with respect to the values affected by the damage if the event that caused the damage had not occurred, and what he actually has at his disposal in consequence of this event. However, the loss of expected profits is usually more difficult to evaluate in light of the adequate causation requirement because a hypothetical situation must be taken into consideration. The plaintiff must show that the loss of profits has actually been brought about. Subjective expectations and hopes of the plaintiff will not meet this requirement. Gaining *lucrum cessans* must be objectively feasible and real. Hence, X has to establish that he lost a profit which was to be obtained with certainty or at least with a high degree of probability. It seems that in the case scenario, the requirements for the claim are met.

---

[17] See Dybowski 1981, 288; Kaliński 2008, 276 ff.
[18] See Szpunar 1998, 118, 119.   [19] OSNC 7–8/2009, item 106.

Spain

Under the Spanish rules on contractual liability, X can claim damages from A and these include the 200,000 euro paid for breach of contract (Articles 1106 and 1107 CC).[20]

A is not liable to Y for the 50,000 euro loss of profits. Article 129.1 TRLDCU clearly states that only personal and – with some exclusions – property damage may be compensated under the strict liability for defective products. As already stated, the 50,000 euro may be claimed by Y from A on a contractual basis.[21]

Sweden

This liability should be decided under the law of sales of goods. The malfunctioning button has rather abruptly limited (or stopped) the use of the machine. Thus, it is questionable that product damage to other property is at hand.[22] Instead, the pure economic loss should be decided under the rules of the Sales of Goods Act[23] (ss 40 and 67). Indirect losses such as contractual damages to another contracting party are compensable if negligence or a guarantee is at hand.

On the same basis, loss of profits from a contract with another party are indirect losses recoverable if negligence is at hand. There is very little room under the Sales of Goods Act to interpret an implied guarantee, even for key characteristics of the bought product.

Question e: *Would it make any difference whether or not the emergency stop button complies with a national standard provided by a legal provision (law or regulation) or the EN-standard issued by the European Committee for Standardization?*

England and Wales

It might make a difference to the assessment of breach for negligence purposes and to the assessment of defectiveness under the CPA 1987. But

---

[20] Morales Moreno 2010, 61; Soler 1998, 156 ff. See also, Carrasco 1989, 680; Llamas Pombo 2010, 1218.

[21] It should be highlighted that in Spanish law, as in other French inspired civil codes, there is an action which allows the claim of a creditor against his debtor's debtor (*debitor debitoris*), if the first debtor was insolvent. This action is called "*acción subrogatoria*" and is contained in Article 1111 CC. See more about this in Sirvent 1997.

[22] See NJA 1996, 68 (concerning the scope of a functional notion of property damage).

[23] Köplag (1990:931).

the mere fact of compliance in itself would not automatically render the product defective.

France

The question here is whether or not the product provides the security that can be legitimately expected. However, the fact that the manufacturer followed the rules of art or existing standards is insufficient to exclude liability. The same solution applies if the producer obtained an authorisation to market the product from a State authority.[24] Compliance with these standards is only a minimum requirement, but does not exempt the producer from taking extra precautions to ensure the safety of users. The *Cour de cassation* has, for example, ruled that compliance with administrative regulation cannot exonerate the manufacturer.[25]

If it can be established that the emergency stop button does not comply with a standardisation rule, the defective nature of the product will be much easier to establish and A's fault will also be easier to prove.

Germany

It would make no difference under the product liability law of the Prod-HaftG, as only the compliance with a mandatory legal norm triggers the defence of § 1 para 2 no 4 ProdHaftG. In contrast, it could make a difference under general tort law. Compliance with an industrial norm has often been used by the court to establish the lack of foreseeability of damage and therefore to deny the breach of a duty. There have been exceptions, though, where courts have disregarded technical standards where they did not reflect the necessary standard of care. For example, in the ice hockey case, a spectator was injured by a puck that flew over the board. Although the height of the board was in compliance with the relevant German standard, the *Bundesgerichtshof* regarded this norm as generally too low. The court held that "they [the technical norms] do not always determine the ultimate care that can be expected in a particular case and do not discharge the judge from his duty to take account of the safety interests of potential victims himself."[26]

If it can be proved that the emergency stop button is not in line with the relevant technical norm, most courts recognise a strong presumption

---

[24] Article 1386–10 *Code civil.*   [25] Cass civ (1) 27 January 1998, Bull civ I, no 33.
[26] BGH, 29 November 1983, (1984) NJW 801 – ice hockey.

of negligence.[27] Thus, under normal circumstances, courts would find A liable under § 823 para 1 BGB unless A can show that the technical solution chosen is equivalent to the technical standard and actually safe. There is no difference under the product liability regime of the *Produkthaftungsgesetz*.

The Netherlands

Non-compliance with "soft law" standards may be relevant and indicative for assessing non-conformity of the machine with the reasonable expectations of the buyer under the contract. If the EN-standard is "hard law" in the sense that the machine should comply with the standard in order to comply with administrative regulations, then non-compliance will probably result in non-conformity without further requirements and will make the seller liable in contract for non-performance.

Poland

Under the product liability regime, if the product conformed to the compulsory technical standard set by an appropriate State agency as mandatory law, the manufacturer may use this as a defence against strict liability (Article 449³ para 2 Civil Code). The interpretation of this exonerating ground is very narrow. The mandatory regulations have to embrace the exact quality of the product that can be causally linked with the damage. In other words, the producer may not escape liability by saying that the product complied with binding regulations as such. Polish legal scholarship takes the view that compliance with safety standards is not decisive in respect of the establishment of the producer's liability, as that liability is based on risk.[28] It follows that the plaintiff could question the level of the legal standards by trying to prove them to be too old or not to meet the

---

[27] BGH, 1 March 1988, (1988) NJW 2667 – playground; BGH, 4 April 1989, (1989) NJW-RR 921 – scaffolding; BGH, 12 November 1996, (1997) NJW 582 – fire water pond; BGH, 27 April 1999, (1999) NJW 2593 – scaffolding; BGH, 4 December 2001, (2002) NJW-RR 525 – water pipe; *Bayerisches Oberstes Landesgericht* (BayObLG), 4 January 1996, (1996) NJW-RR 657 – stair rail; OLG Celle, 8 August 2001, (2002) NJOZ 270 – staircase; OLG Dusseldorf, 22 April 1994, (1994) NJW-RR 1310 – scaffolding; OLG Cologne, 17 April 1991, (1992) Neue Zeitschrift für Verkehrsrecht (NZV) 364 – traffic light; OLG Cologne, 7 April 1997, (1998) NJW-RR 1634 – ski binding; OLG Rostock, 15 September 2003, (2004) NJW-RR 825 – storm damage; OLG Stuttgart, 12 March 1999, (2000) NJW-RR 752 – scaffolding; LG Frankfurt aM, 12 September 1997, (1999) NJW-RR 904 – slide.

[28] See Jagielska and G Żmij, 2007, 224 ff.

ordinary consumer expectation test and, consequently, base his claims on fault (Article 415 in conjunction with Article 449[10] Civil Code).[29]

Non-compliance with technical norms makes no difference for the regime of strict liability as the lack of safety of the product is measured according to the consumer expectation test. For the concurrent fault-based liability, a proof of wrongfulness will suffice to establish liability pursuant to Article 415 Civil Code. This will make a difference only with respect to claiming compensation for property damage not covered by the strict product liability regime as well as for contractual claims of X against A.

Spain

If the emergency stop button does not comply with the EN-standard issued by the European Committee for Standardisation or with a national standard provided by a legal provision, that would suffice to prove that A has been negligent. It is true that these standards may have been set to protect the workers in the plant and not the occasional visitor, but this would probably not be thoroughly explored by a Spanish court in this case, due to the importance of the defect.[30]

The fact that the emergency stop button does comply with those standards, both the compulsory and the voluntary ones, would be a good point of departure for the defendant trying to exonerate himself from liability by application of Article 140.1.b TRLDCU, i.e., by trying to prove that the defect appeared after the product was put into circulation.

Sweden

Not as regards C's right to extra-contractual damages on a non-statutory basis. As regards X, that might prompt the conclusion that A was not negligent, but not per se.

4.2. Case 2 – Defective safety programmable logic controller

Computer firm A developed a special computer program for company B which runs a chemical plant. The computer program should ensure that in

---

[29] See Łętowska 2002, 123.
[30] See del Olmo 2007, 260 for more information about how these standards are established in legal provisions. In case law, STS 17 July (RJ 4571). For an explanation of the protective scope of the rule, Pantaleón 1993, 1987 and Martín-Casals and Solé Feliu 2010, 2050.

case of an emergency, the production process is ramped down in a controlled manner. On Monday 7 June, a heavy earthquake shakes the region where the plant is situated. Due to a programming defect, the production process is shut down immediately and as a consequence, dangerous chemicals escape from the plant into the surroundings.

The local fire brigade C takes emergency measures to remove the chemicals from the water and to stop the chemicals from leaking into the nearby river. The costs of these relief measures for C amount to 30,000 euro. For fear of pollution of the groundwater, the local water supplier D employs tank wagons for the water supply of the local community for four weeks after the incident at the cost of 70,000 euro. On the adjoining land, the chemicals leak into the groundwater. Neighbour E who uses the well on his land for the supply of drinking water suffers health damage. The removal of the chemicals from the well costs neighbour E 50,000 euro.

Question a: *Are A or B, or both of them, liable for these costs? If B is liable, can B take recourse against A?*

England and Wales

There is no legal basis on which A could be held civilly liable for the financial costs incurred by C (fire brigade) or D (water supplier). It is possible that B, as operator of the activity resulting in the chemical escape, could be held liable towards C and D in public nuisance. This would involve, among other things, proving that the incident had affected a significant number of people in the area. C and D could easily show that they had suffered specific damage over and above that sustained by everyone else who had been the general class of victims. A would be potentially liable in negligence to E for his personal injuries, damage to his property and consequential financial costs involved in removing the chemicals. B is potentially liable to E for the same losses on the basis of the rule in *Rylands* v. *Fletcher*: the accumulation of chemicals would be a non-natural use of land, there is an escape, the chemicals are likely to be classified as dangerous and the harm is arguably not too remote. For the purposes of *Rylands* v. *Fletcher* liability, the escape does not have to be reasonably foreseeable. If B was held liable, he would be able to seek contribution from A under the Civil Liability (Contribution) Act 1978.

France

The Law of 2008 cannot be applied to losses that have been incurred by private individuals. The general rules of civil liability will apply in such a case. Here it is the liability for the action of things based on Article 1384 al. 1 *Code civil* or the "theory of nuisance" that will apply. B will have to compensate for all these costs. The only defence that would be possible for B would be to establish that the earthquake was a case of force majeure which was the sole cause of the pollution.

B can take recourse against A on the basis of breach of contract. The question here is to determine whether A should be liable for all the amounts that B will pay since, under French law, only foreseeable losses are compensable in case of breach of contract. Article 1150 *Code civil* provides that the debtor is liable only for losses that were foreseen or that could have been foreseen when the contract was formed. This limit is excluded when the breach was particularly serious, i.e., in case of *faute dolosive* ("intentional breach") or *faute lourde* ("severe breach or gross negligence"). Article 1150 *Code civil* is not interpreted as referring to the foreseeability of the amount of the loss but to the predictability of the nature of the loss.[31] This foreseeability is assessed by lower judges by determining the consequences of the breach that could be reasonably foreseen by a bonus *pater familias*. The characteristics of the contract in question must obviously be taken into account. For example, the owner of a luxury hotel should normally suspect that customers are in possession of valuables or large sums of money.[32] Judges deny compensation for certain losses that appear unpredictable given the circumstances, for example the nature of the contract or the prior relationship between the parties. For example, the buyer of a machine who receives a machine damaged in transport will not be compensated for the savings that he intended to make with this new machine because such savings were not predictable for the transporter.[33] If a train is delayed, passengers can obtain reimbursement of their ticket or of the ticket of the connecting train they had to take, but they cannot be compensated for the loss of a day of vacation.[34]

In this case, the pollution of the river appears to be sufficiently predictable for A. Nevertheless, another condition must be taken into account in this case. Article 1151 *Code civil* provides that the causal link between the breach and the loss must not be too indirect. In this case, it could be argued that the causal link between the programming defect and the pollution is not sufficiently direct to retain A's liability for the whole damage.

---

[31] Cass com 4 March 1965, JCP G 1965, II, 14219, note R Rodière.
[32] Cass civ (1) 5 February 1957 D 1957, 232 (hotel) Cass civ (1) 3 June 1998, JCP G 1999, II, 10010, note N Rzepecki (tour operator).
[33] Cass com 6 January 1970 Bull civ IV, no 6; *Revue Trimestrielle de Droit commercial* (RTD com) 1972, 772, obs P Hémard.
[34] CA Paris, 31 March 1994, Gaz Pal 1994, 1, 407.

It would probably be decided that A is partially liable for the final losses, since other factors contributed to the accident.

For the same reason, one might ask if A could be directly liable for the victims' loss on the basis of Article 1382 *Code civil*. Since other factors, such as the earthquake, contributed to the occurrence of the pollution, A's liability would probably be reduced to a small share of the total loss.

Germany

Under established German court practice, the claims of the fire brigade C could come under *negotiorum gestio* (*Geschäftsführung ohne Auftrag*, § 677 BGB). The prerequisites of this claim are that the fire brigade (as the agent) acts on behalf of A and B (as the principals) without their consent. In the context of fires, the courts have for a long time accepted that the fire brigade not only acts on its own behalf (fulfilling its professional duties)[35] but also on behalf of those who would suffer damage and those who are liable for the damage.[36] This case law has always been criticised in academic writing but has been sustained until now.[37] It has been applied, among others, to principals that came under strict liability regimes, such as a railway company under the regime of the *Haftpflichtgesetz*.[38] The same rules apply to the local water supplier D.

It should be noted though that there have been additional complications due to the fact that the public fire brigades[39] act upon a public law mandate and that the laws of the States (*Länder*), which are competent for regulating the public fire brigades, vary in terms of who should bear the costs of firefighting. Under some State laws firefighting is free of charge, which has triggered the question of whether this only applies to the owner of the burning property or also to the party who would incur liability. Recently, courts have interpreted these provisions restrictively in the sense that a claim under § 677 BGB is not excluded by such State laws.[40] In any case, situations that are covered by strict liability under

---

[35] See BGH, 10 April 1969, (1969) NJW 1205; BGH, 24 October 1974, (1975) *Juristenzeitung* (JZ) 533; BGH, 15 December 1975, (1976) NJW 748.

[36] See BGH, 20 June 1963, (1963) NJW 1825; BGH, 4 December 1975, (1976) NJW 619.

[37] See, for example, Thole 2010, 1243, 1243 ff.

[38] See BGH, 20 June 1963, (1963) NJW 1825.

[39] Not all fire brigades are public fire brigades, though.

[40] See, for example, BGH, 28 June 2011, (2011) *Neue Zeitschrift für Verwaltungsrecht – Rechtsprechungsreport* (NVwZ-RR) 925; OLG Brandenburg, 4 November 2010, (2011) NJW-RR 962. For an overview of the problems see Franßen and Blatt 2012, 1031.

environmental legislation are usually not covered by the free-of-charge duties of fire brigades.[41] Moreover, the *Länder* have enacted legislation under which the municipalities can claim compensation for firefighting on the basis of public law,[42] which shall not be considered hereinafter.

In essence, the fire brigade C and the local water supplier D have a claim for compensation of their expenses under §§ 677 and 670 BGB if A and B are liable for the damage.

B would, in principle, be liable for damages under the *Umwelthaftungs-gesetz*. Chemical plants are listed in nos. 45 ff of the annex to the UmwHG and are therefore within the scope of the strict liability regime of § 1 UmwHG. However, the UmwHG only applies to damage to persons and property and does not cover ecological damage such as the pollution of the groundwater. Groundwater is nobody's property. The same applies to potential liability under § 823 para 1 BGB.

Ecological damage is dealt with by the *Umweltschadensgesetz* (Environmental Damage Act; UmwSchadG) that has implemented Directive 2004/35/EC. Under § 5 UmwSchadG B would be required to avoid the pollution and under § 6 UmwSchadG to clean it up. However, the UmwSchadG is regarded as forming part of public law,[43] and it is not meant to give rise to a damages claim. The situation would, however, be covered by § 89 para 2 *Wasserhaushaltsgesetz*. Under this provision, if substances (unintentionally) leak into the water from a facility that is intended to, among other things, produce, store or transport those substances, the operator of that facility is liable for the damage caused. The predecessor of § 89 para 2 WHG – § 22 para 2 WHG until 2010 – has been used by the courts as another damage claim in the context of *negotiorum gestio*.[44] § 89 para 2 sent 3 WHG provides for an exemption in case of force majeure.

Force majeure has been defined by the BGH as an external incident caused by natural forces or by third-party acts that cannot be foreseen and that cannot be avoided with reasonable cost and with utmost care, and that also must not be accepted due to its frequent occurrence.[45] An earthquake can be one such incident of force majeure.[46] It should, however, be noted that the possibility of an earthquake needs to be considered when designing the security concept of a facility. Thus, the mere

---

[41] See Günther and Borbe 2012, 1197, 1197 ff.   [42] See Günther and Borbe, ibid.
[43] See Ruffert 2010, 1177, 1178.   [44] See BGH, 22 July 1999, (1999) NJW 3633.
[45] BGH, 23 October 1952, 7 BGHZ 338.
[46] See LG Saarbrücken, 25 January 1966, (1967) VersR 385.

realisation of that possibility cannot as such be regarded as force majeure. Only an earthquake of unexpected strength would come under this description.

In contrast, A cannot possibly be liable under § 89 para 2 WHG as he is not operating a facility in the terms of § 89 para 2 WHG. He could potentially be liable under the ProdHaftG or § 823 para 1 BGB but both do not cover ecological damage. Thus, A cannot be liable for the pollution of the groundwater and therefore the fire brigade cannot have acted as his agent in the terms of § 677 BGB.

The local water supplier D has not suffered property damage either, but merely economic loss. Thus, first of all, A is not liable for D's damage under § 89 para 2 WHG, product liability law or § 823 para 1 BGB. The same applies to B since none of the liability rules in question cover economic loss. The only possible claim for compensation would again be § 677 BGB. The argument could be that D ensures that the leakage does not lead to personal damage and therefore prevents damage claims of the customers against A and B. However, this would require D to act as an agent for A and B rather than fulfilling D's own obligations towards its customers. The latter seems to be the case since D is obviously obliged under the supply relationship – which is a sales contract in the terms of § 433 BGB – to supply safe drinking water. Thus, D is not acting on behalf of A and B but in its own interest.

In contrast, E suffered health damage and damage to his property, the well. Thus, § 1 UmwHG and § 823 para 1 BGB can apply as far as B is concerned. Indeed, B could be liable under the strict liability regime of § 1 UmwHG. Again, it would seem that the exemption for cases of force majeure, § 4 UmwHG, is not applicable. Neither would compliance with planning permission help since that only defeats the presumption of causation of § 6 UmwHG but not the strict liability where causation can be proven.

Liability under § 823 para 1 BGB would require negligence, whereby negligence of A cannot be attributed to B. B could be negligent if it had made a poor choice of software supplier, or if it should have made a test run, which the facts of the case say nothing about.

As far as A is concerned, the question is whether defective software comes under the regimes of the ProdHaftG or § 823 paras 1 and 2 BGB. The controversial issue of the treatment of intellectual goods in physical form under the ProdHaftG has been discussed in German academia. Case law is still not available. Most likely, intellectual goods that are not in physical form do not come under the product liability regime of § 2 ProdHaftG

since § 2 ProdHaftG requires a movable good.[47] In contrast, physical goods
are included, according to the wording of § 2 ProdHaftG, even if their
main purpose is to make an intellectual good visible; and the majority
of academic authors consider the ProdHaftG to be generally applicable
to software.[48] Some academics have proposed restricting the notion of
physical goods in such a way that false information (i.e., the intellectual
good within the physical good) should not trigger product liability.[49]
Others have suggested merely not applying the ProdHaftG where, in
fact, a service is rendered rather than a good produced. With regard to
software, a common distinction is made between standard software, which
is treated as a good, while individually produced software is considered to
be a service.[50] According to this latter opinion, the software developed by
A would not come under the ProdHaftG. Otherwise, he could be regarded
as producer of a part product.[51]

In any case, A would be liable under § 823 para 1 BGB, a provision
that does not distinguish between tangible and intangible goods and
therefore clearly applies to damages to health and property caused by
failing software.[52] Failing software suffers from a design defect.[53] Clearly
there is a causal link between A's software and the leaking of the chemicals,
and A also acted negligently. Finally, A could be liable under § 823 para 2
BGB with § 3 *Produktsicherheitsgesetz* (Product Safety Act; ProdSG),[54]
which requires producers to put only safe products into circulation. The
question is again whether or not software is a product in the terms of
§ 2 no 22 ProdSG, where products are defined as "goods, substances or
preparations which have been manufactured in a production process".
This has been discussed controversially in academic writing, and some
authors have argued in favour of a broad notion of products that would
cover software.[55]

B's recourse against A could be based on two different grounds: on the
internal recourse between two tortfeasors that are jointly and severally

---

[47] See, for example, Spindler and Klöhn 2003, 410. In contrast, Taeger 1996, 257, 261 argues
that software is always incorporated in a physical product.
[48] See Wagner 2009, no 13; Spindler 2008, fn 28 at 8.   [49] See Foerste 1991, 1433, 1438.
[50] See Meier and Wehlau 1990, 95, 95 ff; Wagner, 2009, no 14.
[51] See Meyer and Harland 2007, 689, 694.
[52] See also Spindler 2004, 3145, 3146 who mentions incidents due to the failure of software
in chemicals plants, hospitals or flights security.
[53] See Meyer and Harland 2007, 693; Taeger 1996, 268.
[54] BGBl 2011 I, 2178, corrected in BGBl 2012 I, 131.
[55] See, for example, Runte and Potinecke 2004, 725, 725 ff; Spindler 2004, 3148; Zscherpe
and Lutz 2005, 499, 499 ff.

liable, or on the contract for works and services, § 631 BGB. To what extent recourse can be based on the contract obviously depends on the contract terms and the liability regime that the parties have agreed on. It should be noted, though, that German unfair contract terms law applies to business-to-business contracts. Thus, an unfair risk distribution in the contract may be invalid under § 307 BGB.[56]

The Netherlands

The case does not mention any negligent acts or omissions on the part of A or B. Note that if it was proved that A or B was in fact negligent, then the scope of their liability would be widened considerably. If there is no wrongful behaviour involved, the question is whether there is strict liability involved. Liability of A and/or B vis-à-vis C (fire brigade clean-up and mitigation of further damage): B is the professional operator of a dangerous substance (Article 6:175 BW; see above 4.1, question c). Although this is strictly speaking not property damage or consequential loss, the expenses for alternative supply of water do seem to fall within the scope of the strict liability for risks materialising from such dangerous substances. Article 6:184 BW includes reasonable cost of avoidance or mitigation of death, personal injury, property damage and consequential losses as compensable harm under Article 6:175 BW – irrespective of who took the measures. Strict liability for dangerous substances is subject to defences listed in Article 6:178 BW. If the damage was the result of a natural event of an exceptional, unavoidable and irresistible nature, then the liability lapses. The case states, however, that it was not the earthquake but the defect that caused the damage. Thus, one assumes that the mechanism was supposed to have worked even under the stress of extreme forces of nature. Hence, subject to the limitations set by Article 6:98 BW, B is strictly liable vis-à-vis C. Note, however, that there is an important obstruction which may bar any claim for compensation. If the fire brigade was the public fire department, then public law considerations may bar any claim in tort.[57]

A is the software manufacturer. It is unclear whether the CJEU would decide that tailor-made software is a product under the terms of the

---

[56] Meyer and Harland 2007, 692 suggest that the software supplier should at least be partly liable if he was contractually obliged to perform quality control.

[57] See HR 11 December 1992, NJ 1994, no 639.

European Product Liability Directive. If it did decide so, this would open up the possibility for consumers to claim private property losses and personal injury. The case, however, mostly refers to professional damage and therefore we will leave the Product Liability Directive out of the discussion. That said, there is little foundation available for holding A liable unless it is proved by the claimant that A was negligent and that he could have foreseen that damage would occur. Then a claim on the basis of Article 6:162 BW may succeed. However, it is important to stress that in the absence of strict liability, the mere fact that the software was defective does not constitute an imputable wrongful act on the part of A. One would need to substantiate what A did wrong rather than assert that the software was defective. The relationship between A and B is probably governed by their IT contract. Since the software seems to be tailor-made, it is unlikely that this will be categorised as a sales contract.[58] Hence, the rules on services contracts (*opdracht*) will apply. If the contract does not stipulate anything in particular with reference to the distribution of (liability) risks between A and B, the apportionment of liability between them is decided by the standard laid down in Article 6:102 BW. All relevant circumstances would have to be weighed, such as whether A was negligent. If so, it seems likely that A will be ordered to bear the brunt of the damage.Liability of A and/or B vis-à-vis D (alternative supply of water): B is the professional operator of a dangerous substance (Article 6:175 BW). Although strictly speaking this case does not involve property damage or consequential loss, the expenses for alternative supply of water do seem to fall within the scope of the strict liability for risks materialising from such dangerous substances. Article 6:184 BW includes reasonable cost of avoidance or mitigation of death, personal injury, property damage and consequential losses as compensable harm under Article 6:175 BW. Subject to the limitations set out by Article 6:98 BW, B is strictly liable vis-à-vis D. As far as A is concerned as well as the relationship between A and B, refer to the answer above. Liability of A and/or B vis-à-vis E (health damage by consuming contaminated water; clean-up costs): B is the professional operator of a dangerous substance (Article 6:175 BW). Health damage and prevention of such damage fall within the scope of the strict liability for risks materialising from such dangerous substances (see also Article 6:184 BW). Subject to the limitations set out by Article 6:98 BW, B is strictly liable vis-à-vis E.

---

[58] According to Dutch law, the sale of standard software is considered to be a sales contract even though software is not a tangible object.

Poland

Company A was employed to develop a program that would prevent exactly the risk that was realised, i.e., the risk of shutting down the production process immediately instead of in a controlled manner, and the following risk of the damaging consequences of such an immediate shutdown. The programming defect is thus the source of damage that coincides with the earthquake, but the earthquake is not to be seen as a legal cause of the damage, although from the viewpoint of company A, it would prima facie appear to be a force majeure.

Both the running of the production process and an emergency event such as the heavy earthquake are conditions *sine quibus non* of the damage, but what we examine here is the impact of the failure of the computer program to work correctly in the case of any emergency. If the failure is due to the defect discovered in the programming, then we cannot consider a heavy earthquake to be force majeure, since it is in fact a prerequisite of the computer program safeguards to start operating.

In general, company B is strictly liable for damage pursuant to Article 435 Civil Code as it is an enterprise that employs natural forces in its operation and creates a higher risk of damage. Force majeure may exonerate the enterprise if it is an exclusive cause of the damage. A heavy earthquake is undoubtedly a category of force majeure. But the question is whether it absolves B from liability.

Legal authorities vary as to who carries the burden of proof of force majeure and causation in cases based on Article 435 Civil Code. According to some authors, it is sufficient that the plaintiff proves the causal link in fact (*conditio sine qua non*) between the operation of the enterprise and the damage.[59] Another distinguished professor of law is of the opinion that there is a presumption of a causal connection between the activity of an enterprise and the damage, which can be rebutted by the proof of an exonerating fact.[60] The dominant view is that an event fulfilling the conditions of force majeure exempts the defendant from strict liability and at the same time breaks the causal link between his activity (the operation of the enterprise) and the damage sustained.[61] The courts agree with this approach, but they emphasise that any one of the three possible exonerating facts must be the exclusive cause of the damage in order to

[59] See Safjan 2005, 1233; Dybowski 1981, 270.
[60] See Lewaszkiewicz-Petrykowska 1967, 130.
[61] See Nesterowicz 1988, 428. Compare Dubis 2008, 770.

deny the liability.[62] Hence, no other causes, whether attributable or not to any person (such as a defect in the security program) that would pass the test of adequate causation may exist in a given situation.

In the light of the above, we should add that company B is not able to raise the exclusive fault of A's computer program to exclude its liability, either. A is not a person for whom B is not liable (a second exonerating ground) and the defect is not an exclusive fault that led to the damage.

Typically, as soon as it is established that the alleged damage is linked to the operation of the defendant's enterprise (B) and B submits evidence of the exonerating fact, the courts will also require evidence from him that no other causes within the defendant's sphere exist (or if any come into play – that they are not in the normal causal connection with the damage).[63]

Hence, under Polish law, Company B will be liable for the costs of the relief measures borne by C (30,000 euro), for the preventive cost of the water supply to the local community borne by the local water supplier D (70,000 euro), as well as the costs for the removal of the chemicals from neighbour E's well, 50,000 euro. All elements are either preventive costs that are permitted under the relevant environmental law and Article 439 Civil Code (with respect to C's and D's costs) or are adequate consequences of the tort (with respect to E's losses).

As to D's claims, Article 18 PREP allows the landholder to demand indemnity if the preventive or remedial measures that were carried out on his land caused him (individual) damage. In accordance with Article 323 EPL, anyone who is exposed to the risk of damage, or who incurred damage through another's illegal influence on the environment, may demand from the person liable that he restores the lawful state and takes preventive measures, such as installing safety appliances or machines. Where the preventive action is impossible or unreasonably difficult, the claimant may demand that the actor abstains from the infringement.

The relationship between Article 323 EPL and the "law of neighbours" in the Civil Code is debatable. The opinion that the EPL broadens the remedies available in the Civil Code quite rightly prevails.[64] Conversely, the nature of liability in the law of neighbours is not clear either. Pursuant

---

[62] SN judgment of 27 July 1973, II CR 233/73, OSPiKA 1974/ 9, at 190, cmt A Rembieliński, SN judgment of 28 November 2007, V CSK 282/07, OSNC-ZD 2/2008 item 54.

[63] SN 28 November 2007, V CSK 282/07, OSNC-ZD 2008/2, at 54.

[64] See Skoczylas 2003, 68.

to the dominant view in the legal writings, the liability is delictual.[65] An *actio negatoria* (Article 222 para 2 Civil Code) and a claim to abstain from infringement on the basis of Article 144 Civil Code may be brought against any person who infringes upon the environment. According to Article 144 Civil Code, the owner of real estate should, in exercising his rights, refrain from activities which would disturb the utilisation of neighbouring real property above an average degree, based on the socio-economic purpose of the real property and local conditions. This claim belongs to owners and persons enjoying other proprietary rights. An activity that would disturb the neighbouring land beyond the acceptable local standards is illegal; thus, it creates a claim for damages based on the general rules.

As regards claims by C and D, B is under duty to cover remedial costs. Based on Article 326 EPL, the person who has repaired the damage to the environment has a right of indemnity against the actor who caused it; however, it is limited to the reasonable expenses incurred in the restoration of the previous state.

As regards E's claims, B's liability extends to all damage that is inadequate-causal relation (Article 361 para 2 Civil Code). Both the damage to E's health and the pollution of groundwater on the adjoining land is such reparable damage.

According to Article 363 para 1 Civil Code:

> [the] damage shall be redressed according to the choice of the injured person, either by the restitution of the previous condition or by the payment of an appropriate sum of money. However, if the restoration of the previous condition were impossible or if it resulted for the person obliged in excessive difficulties or costs, the claim of the injured person shall be limited to a performance in money.

Hence, the victim has a choice between claiming restoration in kind and payment of damages. The Supreme Court held, for example, that the principle of full reparation requires that the victim is granted the claim for restoration of access to drinking water on the property where he lives, which is to be realised by the construction of a new well if the existing well cannot be used because it has been polluted by the tortfeasor.[66] In this judgment the court emphasises that damages are to restore the victim to the position he would have been in if the wrong complained of had not

---

[65] See Katner 1982, 130; Maśniak 2003, 99 ff.
[66] SN judgment of 29 November 1982, I CR 377/82, OSNC 9/1983, at 134.

been committed. The court looks at the whole situation of a victim. The tortfeasor may not impose the pecuniary form of compensation on the victim.

Company B has the right of recourse against company A as the latter caused damage due to the improper performance of the contract for services. It is a full recourse claim. In Polish law the debtor is liable according to Article 361 Civil Code (which applies to claims brought both *ex delicto* and *ex contractu*). Polish law does not make any distinction between foreseeable and unforeseeable damage. The damage must be in an adequate causal relationship. Naturally, the contractual limitation of the scope of indemnity (i.e., limitations in the contract between A and B) will apply as long as they concern property damage and are not invalid under general contract rules.

Company A's liability towards third parties is fault-based; hence it is more difficult to pursue A in court. However, if A was sued successfully, then both A and B will still answer for the same damage as multiple tortfeasors. In order to determine all the persons who should be allocated joint and several liability, it is critical that the law imposes tort liability on all of them, whether as a direct tortfeasor (here: A) or through vicarious liability (here: B).

Article 444 paras 2 and 3 Civil Code is a general principle dealing with the right to contribution and indemnity of the parties jointly and severally liable in tort, whatever the basis in law of the wrongdoers' liability (negligence, strict liability or equity principle). The right to contribution envisaged in Article 441 para 3 (of the person liable regardless of fault) materialises only when the wrongdoer's fault was a sole cause of the damage.[67]

The difference between paras 2 and 3 is blurred. Besides the circumstances mentioned in s 2 of Article 441 Civil Code (that is, fault and the degree of contribution to the occurrence of damage), the extent of the contribution claims is also determined by other circumstances related to the commission of a tort, such as the motives of the tortfeasors, the actual participation in the infliction of the damage and the benefits received for the tort. The findings of the court ruling in a lawsuit brought by the victim are not binding on the court hearing the claims for contribution brought by the obligors who performed.[68]

---

[67] SN judgment of 16 October 1958, 3 CR 81/58, OSPIKA 1/1960, at 6.
[68] SN judgment of 30 April 1957, 3 CR 340/56, OSPIKA 4/1958, at 98.

Spain

Is B liable?

Under the Spanish rules on liability for environmental damage contained in LRM, B's liability is excluded because of the occurrence of an act of God (Article 3.4 LRM).[69] Were it not the case, B would be held liable according to the general rules of LRM: B is a factory clearly included in the strict liability regime provided by LRM (cf Annex III, numbers 1 and 8) and the damage has been caused to the water (Article 2 LRM).[70] If B was liable, the situation could be described as follows:

(1) The cost of the relief measures taken by C could be claimed from B (Articles 17 and 19 LRM). Here it can be seen that the Spanish transposition of the Directive grants a broader protection than the one provided by the European text. Those costs, once B has been held liable for them, could be claimed from A through the regular contractual actions derived from the flawed software. Even if the accident had not been caused by an extraordinary earthquake, B would not be liable for the cost of the water supply incurred by D. The reason is that this cost is not an environmental cost.

(2) In principle, the damage sustained by E is excluded from the LRM regime (Article 5) and remitted to the general rules of the Civil Code.[71] Nevertheless, the costs incurred by E in the removal of the chemicals from the well could be included in the LRM if we consider the well as a private asset with environmental relevance. In this case, E would have the option of choosing between the general rules of the Civil Code and the civil jurisdiction or the LRM rules. These rules would allow E to make the public administration take measures against B in order to make him repair the damaged environment and pay damages (Article 41 LRM).[72] Damage to E's health is not included under the LRM, but in the general rules of the Civil Code (Article 5 LRM).[73] Articles 1902 and 1908 CC contain the main part of those general rules applicable in this case study. Both of them permit claiming damages for personal

---

[69] This outcome is clearly established in Spanish law, as can be seen in Ruda 2008, 374 or Orteu Berrocal 2008, 165, 192.
[70] See Orteu Berrocal 2008, 175 and 180.   [71] Among many others see Carrasco 2008, 158.
[72] See Álvarez Lata 2008, 59 for more information. See STS 11 October 1994 (RJ 7478) for a point of view of causation in a case of a contaminated well.
[73] Likewise, individuals cannot act on pure environmental damage, as can be seen in STS 31 May 2007 (RJ 3431), with a note by Ruda 2007, 153.

injuries and for property damage.[74] Traditionally, they have been interpreted in case law as imposing strict liability for environmental damage or, at least, as based on a rebuttable presumption of fault.[75] Nevertheless, it is not probable that a claim based on Article 1902 CC (or Article 1908 CC) would be successful in this case study, because of the extraordinary strength of the earthquake.

Is A liable?

It is not easy to say whether or not the facts in this case study would allow the imposition of liability upon A. Although it would be a more feasible line of action to sue B for those who have the possibility to do so, D and E could sue A under the general rules of the Civil Code.[76] Again, the strength of the earthquake would be a considerable hurdle to overcome. The claim against A might be a good choice if we consider that the earthquake exonerates B from liability but not A because the software would have worked incorrectly even in the event of an earthquake of normal strength.[77]

It is even more difficult to say whether or not a claim based upon the software as a defective service would be successful in Spanish law. There is no case law on cases of this kind and it is unclear whether or not the rules on consumers' and users' protection contained in TRLDCU are intended to protect a bystander or not.[78] The defectiveness would not be a problem, as the software would also have malfunctioned if the earthquake had been of normal strength.

---

[74] In STS 16 January 1989 (RJ 101) there is a good example of how these two provisions of the Civil Code permit making good of both personal injuries and property damage.

[75] To confirm this and for case law citations, see Santos Morón 2003, 3027; Carrasco 2008, 152 and Álvarez Lata 2008, 100.

[76] For a favourable point of view of a preventive damages award, see Ruda 2008, 378 and M Martín-Casals 2011, 15.

[77] See Martín-Casals 2011, 37 for an up-to-date version of the problems of uncertain causality in our legal system.

[78] Also Pasquau 2011, 1843 is of the opinion that currently the case law does not allow clear answers in this field. To see the controversy over the situation of bystanders in this area, Parra Lucán 2011, 248–249 holds that the TRLDCU, following the 1984 LGDCU, does not protect a bystander. On the contrary, Pertíñez 2011, 1826 thinks that the TRLDCU might have introduced bystander protection into the Spanish legal system, because the Government was authorised by the legislative delegation to make things clearer while writing the text of the TRLDCU. See the doubts on this subject among the legal writers before the TRLDCU was passed in Bercovitz, "Artículos 25–29" Bercovitz and Salas (eds. 1992, 715 (cf 684 for additional information on the said doubts).

Sweden

To begin with, C's loss (and for the same indirect reasons, D's loss in relation to A and B) are not compensable losses based on a very special principle which limits the scope of the right to seek redress under tort law for public authorities. Certain public services in society are part of the State's general responsibility to keep systems in function. For that, tort law does offer protection.[79] For example, if a road traffic accident results in costs for emergency rescue as well as costs for the road traffic authority to clean up the road in order to maintain the functioning of traffic on the road, those costs are not recoverable for the State under tort law and should therefore not be recoverable for another. However, the State (and public authorities) still has other protection for harm to property, such as costs to restore a bridge damaged by a road traffic accident. Both C's and D's costs are of the former non-compensable nature.

B is liable to E based on environmental strict liability (Environmental Code, ch 32 s 3) for pollution of ground waters and the consequential personal injury. Swedish tort law does not accept general limitation on strict liability regimes due to third-party interventions or force majeure.[80] These limitations are traditionally only introduced as a direct consequence of international conventions, such as in the field concerning nuclear installations. Otherwise, strict liability is limited to the "typical risk" of the dangerous activity at hand. A natural catastrophe would thus not result in exculpation for B. The State's right to environmental clean-up costs (ch 10) is, however, excluded in cases of exceptional natural disasters (s 19).

A's possible liability lies elsewhere. A's breach of contract in relation to B cannot be invoked by E to make a direct claim against A. Instead, a non-contractual duty for A to protect E's property rights has to be established.[81] It is questionable if that can be established here, and if not, A's possible negligence falls outside the protective scope vis-à-vis E. Instead, it could be deemed a non-compensable third-party loss, i.e., A caused B damage to property which consequentially caused E's property damage.

Question b: *The computer program was especially designed for the prevention of pollution damage in case of natural disasters. The earthquake of*

---

[79] NJA 2011, 331.   [80] Hellner and Radetzki 2010, 177, 341.
[81] Cf 2001 p 711; NJA 2007, 758; NJA 2009, 16.

7 June, however, was of an exceptional strength. Is A liable for the damage described in the case?

England and Wales

The only basis on which A could seek to avoid liability in this respect would be to argue that the earthquake constituted an intervening act of God capable of negating the legal causation element of negligence. But it is unlikely to succeed for two reasons. First, since the faulty program was specifically designed as a safety device for emergency situations, it would be difficult for A to argue that the earthquake, however strong, was a wholly unforeseeable event. Second, it was the malfunctioning program rather than the earthquake that directly caused the escape of chemicals. If it could be established that, in the event of the program operating correctly to shut down the plant, the harm to E would still have occurred as a result solely of the earthquake, then A will avoid liability on the grounds that there is no factual connection between his breach and E's actionable damage.[82]

France

The question at stake is to determine whether this event can be considered as a case of force majeure that would exclude A's liability. The definition of "force majeure" is traditionally based on three characteristics: unpredictability, irresistibility and exteriority. The *Cour de cassation* recently reformulated the definition of force majeure by focusing only on the two conditions of unpredictability and irresistibility. The criterion of exteriority now seems, if not abandoned, at least secondary.[83]

Lower judges have discretion to assess the existence or absence of the conditions of a case of force majeure. Yet the *Cour de cassation* reviews the characterisation of the facts made by lower judges. A storm[84] or an earthquake[85] are the kinds of events usually considered to constitute force

---

[82] *Barnett v. Chelsea and Kensington Hospital Management Committee* [1969] 1 QB 428.

[83] Cass ass plén 14 April 2006, no. 04–18.902 , no. 02–11.168, Bull Ass plén nos. 5 and 6; JCP 2006. 10087, note P. Grosser; RTD civ 2006. 775, obs P. Jourdain; D 2006, 1577, note P. Jourdain.

[84] Cass civ (2) 5 January 1994, no. 92–13.853, Bull civ II, no. 13. Cass civ (3) 11 May 1994, no. 92–16.201, Bull civ III, no 94.

[85] CA Paris, 5 December 2005, Gaz Pal 2006, Somm 2640.

majeure. But it is still necessary that these events have characteristics of unpredictability and irresistibility. For example, it was held that there was no force majeure in the case of a cyclone that caused the collapse of a crane on a building because such a collapse was not unpredictable (since it had been announced by weather forecasts) nor compelling (since it would have been possible to disassemble the crane).[86] Therefore, if it is possible to prove that the strength of this earthquake was unpredictable and irresistible, A will not be responsible.

Germany

Since A is not liable under § 1 UmwHaftG or § 89 para 2 WHG, the exception of force majeure does not apply. However, under § 823 para 1 BGB he also only has to take precautions to avoid foreseeable damage. If the earthquake of 7 June was such as could not be expected, A was not required to take such an exceptional strength into consideration when producing the program. He may still have acted negligently in that it did not work at all but there would be no connection between his negligence and the damage as the damage would have occurred anyway.

The Netherlands

The aim for which the program was designed may be relevant in assessing negligence on the part of A. If, however, the program was not defective but merely incapable of withstanding the extreme circumstances, no imputable wrongfulness will be established. If the programme was defective, the defect was caused by negligence of A and damage could have been prevented if A had been more cautious in designing the programme, then a claim on the basis of Article 6:162 BW may succeed within the confines of Article 6:98 BW.

Poland

The same analysis as in question a: if the force majeure was of such strength that it switched off the whole operation then exoneration might come into question, but the case scenario underlines the defect of the computer program, so the strength of the earthquake is irrelevant.

---

[86] Cass civ (2) 18 March 1998, no. 95–22.014 , Bull civ II, no. 97, RTDciv 1999, 113, obs P. Jourdain. Cass civ (2) 18 March 1998, no. 95–22.014 , Bull civ II, no. 97, RTDciv. 1999. 113, obs P. Jourdain.

Spain

There is no clear answer to this question in the Spanish law of non-contractual liability. It is possible to say that the defective software would have malfunctioned even in case of a weaker earthquake and therefore A is not exonerated from (the whole?) liability for the act of God. On the other hand, it is easier to say that in any case the regular contractual remedies are available to B.

Sweden

Following the argument above, one could perhaps argue that A has a special "safety obligation" towards third parties due to the dangerous nature of A's program. Nevertheless, it is questionable if A owes E that duty.

Question c: *The flaw of the program was caused by the carelessness of the programmer F who is employed by A. Are A, F or both of them liable for the harm as described in the case? If A or F are liable, can they take recourse against the other party?*

England and Wales

A would be vicariously liable for F's negligence. Technically, A is entitled to bring an indemnity claim against F, but there is a tradition for such claims not to be enforced.[87] It would be possible for E to sue F instead of A. In this situation, F could request that A be joined to the proceedings as a co-defendant. But otherwise, he would have no recourse against A.

France

The *Cour de cassation* has ruled that an employee shall not be personally liable when he acts within the limits of his tasks.[88] However, the employee is personally liable and the employer is exonerated from liability when

---

[87] Giliker explains that there is, in effect, a "gentleman's agreement" within the insurance sector for employer liability insurers not to pursue indemnity claims in the absence of collusion or wilful misconduct: Giliker 2010, 32 f.

[88] Cass ass plén, 25 February 2000, *Costedoat*, Bull no. 2, p 3, BICC, no. 512, 1, concl M. Kessous, rapp Mme Ponroy; RJDA 2000, 395, obs J.P. Dorly; D 2000, 673, note P. Brun; JCP 2000 G II, 10 295, note M. Billiau; JCP G 2000, I, 241, no 5, obs G. Viney; Resp civ et assur 2000, chron no. 11, obs H. Groutel, RTDC 2000, 582, obs P. Jourdain.

the employee has acted outside his mandate, without permission, for purposes unrelated to his tasks.[89] In addition, if the employee's intentional misconduct corresponds to a criminal offence he is personally liable for it: in such case, the victim can obtain compensation from both the employer and the employee.[90] In this case, since F acted within the limits of his mandate and did not commit any criminal offence, F is not directly liable for the harm. Nevertheless, A is vicariously liable because F's acts were accomplished within the framework of his functions (Article 1384 al. 5 *Code civil*).[91]

If A has compensated the victims, recourse is possible against F. Originally the employer had a right of recourse against the employee based on subrogation for the full amount granted to the victim. However, this right of action has not been widely used. Indeed, most of the time it is the employer's insurer who pays the compensation to the victim. However, the Code of insurance (Article L 121–12 para 3 Code assurance) prohibits the employer's insurer from taking direct action against the employee, unless the employee committed an intentional fault (malice, malveillance). However, if the employee is personally insured for his own civil liability (which is unusual), the employer's insurer is free to act against the employee's insurer for any kind of fault. This state of the law has been altered since the *Cour de cassation* decided that the employee shall not be personally liable when he acts within the limits of his tasks.[92] In such case, the employer's recourse cannot be based on subrogation, since the victim had no action against the employee who acted within the limits of his mandate.[93] Subrogation is possible only in circumstances where the employee exceeded the limits of his tasks. In all other cases, the employer's recourse must be based on the labour contract and comply with labour law rules. Under labour law, the employer has a right of recourse against the employee only if the employee acted with gross negligence (*faute lourde*).[94] The recourse action must be brought before labour courts (the *Conseil des Prud'hommes*).

---

[89] Cass ass plén, 10 June 1977, Bull no. 3, 5; Cass ass plén, 17 June 1983, Bull no. 8, 11; Cass ass plén, 15 November 1985, Bull no. 9, 12; Cass ass plén, 19 May 1988, Bull no. 5, 7.

[90] Cass ass plén, 14 December 2001, Cousin, Bull no. 487, D 2002, 1230, note J. Julien.

[91] Cass ass plén, 25 February 2000, *Costedoat* (see fn 179).

[92] Cass ass plén, 25 February 2000, *Costedoat*, (see fn 179 above).

[93] Cass civ (2), 20 December 2007, no. 07–13.403, Bull civ II, no. 274; Resp civ et assur 2008, no. 50, note H. Groutel; D 2008, 648, obs D. Sommer and P. Nicoletis.

[94] Cass soc, 16 January 2007, no. 06–40.954, Resp civ et assur 2007, no. 109; Cass soc, 25 October 2005, Bull civ V, no. 299.

Germany

Generally speaking, in their internal relationship with their employers, employees are not liable for each type of negligent conduct. According to the established case law of the *Bundesarbeitsgericht* (Federal Labour Court; BAG), the general line is that employees are fully liable for intentional and grossly negligent conduct, while they are not liable at all for slight negligence. In the case of medium negligence, the damage will be shared. However, it all depends on the circumstances of the individual case and the risk of the activity, as well as the existence of insurance coverage.[95] In the case at hand, it would seem that the huge risk connected with the software would speak for at best very limited liability of F in his internal relationship with A. Thus, if A had to pay damages, it could recover nothing or not much from F. If F had to pay damages, he could claim relief from A under the employment contract.

The Netherlands

It seems most likely that A and F would be jointly and severally liable, although usually the focus would be on A. F is liable for his own negligent act (Article 6:162 BW) and A is vicariously liable (Article 6:170 BW). Between A and F, the damage is apportioned in such a way that the employer bears the full burden of liability unless F acted intentionally or with gross and wilful negligence (Article 6:170 (3) BW).

Poland

In order to determine all the persons who should be allocated joint and several liability, it is critical that the law imposes tort liability on them, whether as a direct tortfeasor or through vicarious liability. If damage was the result of acts or omissions of an employee, the employer is vicariously liable for a "subordinate" in accordance with Article 430 Civil Code. This liability is based on risk, but the fault of the employee is the condition of liability. Article 441 para 1 Civil Code lays down a general rule of joint and several liability in all cases where more than one person is liable for the damage arising from a tort. In reality, however, an employer is the only party that bears civil liability for the loss inflicted by an employed person

---

[95] See, for example, BAG, 27 September 1994, (1994) Neue Zeitschrift für Arbeitsrecht (NZA) 1083; BAG, 28 October 2010, (2011) NJW 1096.

who commits negligence. Pursuant to the provisions of the Labour Code (*kodeks pracy* of 1974), if an employee causes damage to a third party while performing his duties, the employer is solely obliged to redress the damage (Article 120 para 1). This provision means that the victim cannot file his claims in court against the employee (F), but exclusively against the employer (A), who is obliged to redress the damage in accordance with the provisions of the Civil Code.

According to case law, the above rule contained in Article 120 of the Labour Code abrogates the direct liability of an employee unless one of the following three exceptions applies: (1) the damage was caused by an intentional fault, (2) the employer is insolvent or under-insured, or (3) the damage was not inflicted in the course of employment, but "on the occasion" of employment.

Within the labour relations, recourse is limited to the equivalent of three months' earnings of an employee unless the latter inflicted the damage intentionally, in which case the employer, after having paid the damages, may claim full recourse.

Spain

Under the LRM regime, the only person liable is operator B.[96] Under the Civil Code rules, the victim could always sue both the employee and the employer together or separately and a joint strict liability regime (*in solidum*) would be applicable. Once A has paid the awards, it could take recourse against F (Article 1904 CC). It should be highlighted that these actions are not very commonly pursued in our legal system.[97]

Sweden

If A is liable, that company is also liable for its employees under the rules of vicarious liability. The employee is protected from personal liability as well as claims of recourse from his employer.

Question d: *Due to the incident, the nearby factory G is not able to fulfil its contracts and suffers a loss of 40,000 euro. Are A, B or F liable for this loss?*

---

[96] The concept of operator can be found in Guerrero Zaplana 2010, 62.
[97] Domenech Pascual 2008, 5.

England and Wales

Neither A nor F would be liable in negligence for this pure economic loss. If a significant number of people were affected by the incident, it is possible that G could sue B for public nuisance, in which case its pure economic loss would be recoverable.

France

The only grounds that G could rely on in order to be compensated are B's strict liability on the basis of Article 1384 al. 1 *Code civil* or of the "theory of nuisance". But it is also necessary to establish that there is a sufficiently direct causal link between G's breach of contract and the pollution of the water. For example, if the plant had to stop working because of the pollution, then there is a direct causal link that justifies B's liability.

Germany

None of them would be liable for the loss as none of the relevant torts covers pure economic loss.

The Netherlands

The answer to this question depends heavily on the circumstances of the case, including the extent of the fault of the parties involved. The restrictions of Article 6:98 BW apply. That said, at first glance it seems unlikely that B is liable under the strict liability of Article 6:175 BW since the damage suffered by G would not be categorised as death, personal injury, property damage or consequential loss. Whether F is liable depends on the nature of the tort committed and other circumstances. Note that the first question is whether F committed a tort vis-à-vis G. This depends, inter alia, on Article 6:163 BW. The test is whether F should have acted otherwise than he did in view of the interests of G – were these interests foreseeable for F? Were they not too remotely removed from the first tier of injured parties? Then, there is the limitation set out by Article 6:98 BW which needs to be overcome. Thus, we cannot answer with certainty whether F is liable. If he is, then A is vicariously liable (Article 6:170 BW).

Poland

B is liable to G and A is liable in recourse to B. The analysis of the claim for frustrated contracts is the same as above in Case 4.1 Question d.

Spain

The Spanish legal system does not exclude liability for purely economic loss as such. Therefore, it is possible for G to sue B successfully. If G does so, the final outcome would depend on the certain character of the damage and the assessment of the causal link by the judge.[98]

Sweden

B is strictly liable to G for pure economic loss resulting from the contamination or other disturbances G's factory may suffer from the spill. The nature of the loss may raise issues of adequate causation. A is not liable to G for the same reasons as in the case of E.

Question e: *Assume that the cause of the incident is not an earthquake but instead a terrorist attack. The damage amounts to 2.5 billion euro. Would there be a difference if the cause of the incident was an act of organised crime?*

England and Wales

Assuming that the chemical escape would not have occurred if the program had operated properly, then it will not make any difference that the incident was triggered by a terrorist attack. If the nature of the attack was such that it would probably have caused the chemical leak even in the event of the program working properly to shut down the plant, then again, A or F should be able to avoid liability in negligence on the basis of lack of factual causation.

France

There are arrangements for compensating the consequences of terrorism in French law through a compensation fund. But compensation is granted

---

[98] Martín-Casals and Ribot 2004-a, *passim.*

through the fund only for injuries, not for property damage. Here, the act of terrorism will probably be considered a case of force majeure that allows B to be exonerated from liability since this event "absorbs" the causality of pollution. A's liability towards B will probably also be excluded.

Germany

In terms of the liability of B under § 89 para 2 WHG, a terrorist attack would come under the exception of force majeure if it was beyond reasonable expectations and prevention. As far as A's liability is concerned it would seem to depend on the effects of that terrorist attack. If it only had the effect of a "normal" earthquake so that the software would have ramped down production in a controlled manner if it had not been defective, A would still be liable under § 823 para 1 BGB. In contrast, if the effects were graver than an earthquake of the kind that was anticipated and in light of which the preventive software was designed, A would not be liable since even functioning software would not have prevented the damage.

The Netherlands

Terrorist attacks would be considered intentional wrongdoing. If A was under a contractual duty to design software that was supposed to resist such attacks, then there may be wrongful negligence of A involved. The strict liability for dangerous substances does not apply if the damage was intentionally caused by a third party (Article 6:178 BW). This exonerates B from liability. Whether organised crime counts as intentional wrongdoing, depends on the motives for causing the damage.

Poland

The same analysis under Article 435 Civil Code: the jurisprudence emphasises that the fault of a third party, which exonerates from the strict liability, is to be understood as applying when the fault is the exclusive cause of the damage. Moreover, the third party must be identified.

Spain

Article 14 LRM excludes the operator's liability when, despite adequate safety measures being adopted, the environmental damage was caused by a third-party alien to the operator's organisation. Under the Civil Code, a terrorist attack would play the same role played by the act of God in Case 4.2. and therefore the same results already described may be obtained.[99]

Remember that the LRPIVT – and the monetary subsidies it establishes for victims of terrorism – would be applicable. On the other hand, the role that the so-called Consortium for Insurance Compensation would play should be underscored.[100]

Sweden

The strict liability discussed above, under the Environmental Code ch 32, is not in general subject to exceptions due to third-party interventions (*novus actus interveniens*) or force majeure.[101] But terrorism may fall too far outside the scope of the so-called "typical risk" that environmental strict liability is based upon and therefore exclude liability.

4.3. Case 3 – Public service (infrastructure) undertaking

Company A is in charge of the operation of the security of the waterworks of city B. It provides manned guards to prevent unauthorised access to the plant and also operates the alarm systems of the plant. On 2 October, terrorist C enters the plant and contaminates the water with radioactive material which is extremely poisonous (Polonium-210). Company A could have prevented terrorist C from entering the premises but failed to do so due to negligence. The consequences of the terrorist attack are disastrous (100 people are killed,

---

[99] Martín-Casals and Ribot 2004-b, 97–98.

[100] This Consortium (*Consorcio de Compensación de Seguros*) is a public corporate body created by the Ministry of Economy. Its organisation and functions are currently covered in RDL 7/2004, 29 October, passing the Revised Text of the Statute of the Consortium for Insurance Compensation (*Estatuto Legal del Consorcio de Compensación de Seguros*, ECCS). Damage caused by terrorism is included in the extraordinary risks that the Consortium covers, pursuant to Article 6.1.b of its Statute. On this, see Martín-Casals and Ribot 2004-b, 90–92.

[101] Cf Environmental Code ch 10 on the State's right to compensation for clean-up costs, which *is* subject to a liability exemption with regard to natural disasters and acts of war or similar. Terrorism is not necessarily encompassed here as is the case for the new Nuclear Liability and Compensation Act (*Lag* (2010:950) *om ansvar och ersättning vid radiologiska olyckor*), where the acts of war or similar exemption is not specified. This ambiguity can be traced back to international agreements.

4500 suffer from radiation sickness, the drinking water and the water supply system are contaminated). The total damage amounts to 25 billion euro.

Question a: *Is city B liable to the injured inhabitants (damage to person and property damage)? Can city B take recourse against A?*

England and Wales

B would not be automatically liable to the injured inhabitants. B could only be liable for proven negligence. Evidence that B had failed to maintain or to implement an adequate security system would be required. An isolated act of carelessness on the part of an independent contractor would not suffice.

France

In principle, it is up to the State to compensate the loss caused by a lack of protection against acts of terrorism.[102] However, it should be highlighted that since 1986 (Law no. 86–1020 of 9 September 1986) compensation for injuries caused by terrorist acts (Articles L 126–1 and L 422–1 ff *C assur*) is granted by the Guarantee Fund for Victims of Terrorist Acts and other Offenses (FGTI). This fund only compensates injuries resulting from an act of terrorism. This means that the State may be liable for other losses. For its part, the municipality can be liable only for deficiencies that relate to the missions performed by municipal police and mentioned in sections of Article L 2212–2 of the *Code général des collectivités territoriales*. This article provides that "the municipal police is to maintain good order, safety, security and public healthiness" and specifically mentions the prevention of pollution among the police's missions.[103]

---

[102] CE 22 October 1975, *Sté Saada père et fils et Cts Saada*, Gaz Pal 1976, 1, 63, note F. Moderne; 28 May 1984, *Sté française de production*, Recueil des arrêts du Conseil d'Etat (Rec CE), 736, D 1986, IR 22, obs F. Moderne and P. Bon; Dr adm 1984, no. 334; CE sect 27 April 1987, *Cts Yener et Cts Erez*, Rec CE 151, D 1988, somm 53, obs F. Moderne and P. Bon, *Revue Française de Droit Administratif* (RFDA) 1987 636, concl C. Vigouroux, RD publ 1988, 902, AJDA 1987 487 and 450, chron M. Azibert and M. de Boisdeffre, Dr adm 1987, no. 378.

[103] Article L 2212–2 *Code général des collectivités territoriales*: "*La police municipale a pour objet d'assurer le bon ordre, la sûreté, la sécurité et la salubrité publiques. Elle comprend notamment . . . 5 Le soin de prévenir, par des précautions convenables, et de faire cesser, par la distribution des secours nécessaires, les accidents et les fléaux calamiteux ainsi que les pollutions de toute nature, tels que les incendies, les inondations, les ruptures de digues, les*

It seems that, in this case, it is the municipality which may be liable. In the eyes of the French administrative courts, such liability requires the proof of gross negligence (*faute lourde*), especially in case of protection against terrorism.[104] Gross negligence[105] is characterised by reference to the nature of the obligation breached by the wrongdoer. In most cases, this obligation is considered as "essential". Gross negligence may also correspond to an inexcusable behaviour, especially when the police did not prevent the occurrence of damage which it was able to prevent. Gross negligence can, besides, correspond to an evident fault whose characters appear indisputable. Finally, gross negligence may be characterised by the seriousness of its consequences: the intensity of the harm suffered by the victim reveals the existence of such a fault.

Furthermore, it was judged that the State is liable for the errors committed by private agents contractually linked to the administration for the execution of policy measures.[106] This solution should be the same, a fortiori, for the city's liability.

Under these conditions, the responsibility of city B is possible if it is found that the misconduct is serious enough to justify liability. But such liability will only compensate the losses that are not compensated by the FGTI, i.e., economic loss and property damage. However, one could wonder whether FGTI could have recourse against the city since Article L 422–1 al. 3 *C assur* provides that the FGTI "is subrogated to the rights possessed by the victim against the person responsible for the damage". However, such recourse seems to be possible only against private persons; since the FGTI is a public organisation that is funded by a tax on insurance contracts, an action of the fund against the State would probably make no sense.

Finally, if B is liable for the consequences of A's negligence, B will have a right of recourse against A on the basis of breach of contract.

éboulements de terre ou de rochers, les avalanches ou autres accidents naturels, les maladies épidémiques ou contagieuses, les épizooties, de pourvoir d'urgence à toutes les mesures d'assistance et de secours et, s'il y a lieu, de provoquer l'intervention de l'administration supérieure." See also Book 5 Title 1 *Code de la Sécurité Intérieure.*

[104] CE 29 October 1948, *de Santis et Sté Cachou Gallus*, Rec CE 401; 27 April 1979, *Sté Le Profil*, RecCE 170, D 1980.60, note J.-F. Couzinet (robbery); CE 17 October 1948, Ritz, Rec CE 396 (manslaughter); CE 22 October 1975, Bergon, Rec CE 521, RD publ 1976, 397 (sabotage).

[105] Vandermeeren 2005.

[106] CE 10 October 2011, *Min Alimentation, Agriculture et Pêche*, req no 337062, AJDA 2011.1985, obs Grand.

Germany

Under normal circumstances, city B would have a water supply contract with all those who use their water; in particular since water is still supplied by local monopolists. The supply of water is treated as a sales contract in terms of § 433 BGB.[107] It would include the contractual obligation to supply water that is not detrimental to health. Under the normal contract law rules, breach of the contract would lead to liability under § 280 para 1 BGB unless the supplier can demonstrate that he has not acted negligently. However, water supply comes under the special regime of the *Verordnung über Allgemeine Bedingungen für die Versorgung mit Wasser* (AVBWasserV). § 6 AVBWasserV states liability rules that are identical to § 280 para 1 BGB when it comes to damage to persons and property but limit liability in case of pure economic loss. Negligence of a third party that the supplier makes use of is treated as his own negligence: § 278 BGB. Making use of a third party not only includes the making use of during performance but also the making use of a third party to protect the contracting party's interests.[108] Thus, city B is liable towards its customers for A's negligence. Liability would include damage to persons and property damage.

City B would also be liable under the Product Liability Act. Water is a product in the terms of § 2 ProdHaftG.[109] It may also be assumed that city B is the producer since water normally undergoes some treatment by the waterworks.[110] No exception applies, in particular the product has not been made defective after it has been put into circulation[111] but before. However, the cap of 85 million euro (§ 10 ProdHaftG) and also the threshold of 500 euro concerning property damage apply.

In general tort law, the courts have applied the special burden of proof rules of product liability law to contaminated water.[112] Thus, city B would be liable unless they can prove that they did not act negligently themselves in organising the water supply (§ 823 para 1 BGB) and that they selected and supervised A well (§ 831 BGB). If they cannot prove that, liability would be unlimited in amount, unlike under the Product Liability Act.

B's recourse against A could be based on two different grounds: on the internal recourse between two tortfeasors that are jointly and severally

---

[107] BGH, 4 October 1972, (1972) NJW 2300.
[108] See, for example, BGH, 11 July 1995, (1995) NJW-RR 1241.
[109] See Klein 1991, 917, 919.   [110] See ibid., 921.   [111] On this see ibid., 923.
[112] See BGH, 4 October 1972, (1972) NJW 2300; OLG Schleswig, 12 January 1982, (1983) VersR 890.

liable, or on the contract for works and services (§ 631 BGB). To what extent recourse can be based on the contract obviously depends on the contract terms and the liability regime that the parties have agreed on. Recourse between two tortfeasors requires A to be liable for the damage under tort law as well. As set out below, A would be liable under the general tort law of § 823 para 1 BGB. Thus, both city B and A would be jointly liable (§ 830 BGB) and city B would have a recourse claim under § 426 para 1 BGB. In practice, one may assume that either city B or A would take out insurance to cover the damage.

The Netherlands

Assuming that the legal relationship between the city and the inhabitants is of a civil law nature and that this is a contract, there would probably not be liability if the city could prove that the non-performance of the contract was caused by an external cause against which the city could not defend itself (force majeure; Article 6:75 BW). However, perhaps one could argue that the security firm was the aide (auxiliary) of the city in the execution of contractual obligations vis-à-vis the inhabitants. If that reasoning is followed, the negligence of the aide would be ascribed to the city as debtor's fault in the execution of its contractual obligations (Article 6:76 BW). The result would then be that the city would be liable for the damage caused by non-performance.[113] As far as recourse between A and B is concerned, if A was at fault where B was not, it seems plausible that B can take recourse within the confines of Article 6:102 BW. Note, however, that the contract between A and B may explicitly or implicitly carry a different distribution of risks with it.

Poland

First of all, it should be observed that strict liability under Article 435 Civil Code will likely not be applicable here. This provision is formulated in the old-fashioned way; the accent being put on the natural forces (such as energy) that must set in operation the whole enterprise and not on the

---

[113] As far as delictual liability is concerned, it seems unlikely that the City could be held liable under Article 6:171 BW (liability for torts committed by independent contractors), given the restriction that the independent contractor must be considered to be part of the business operations of the client (here: the City). Moreover, it is debatable whether a City can be considered a professional business for the operation of Article 6:171 BW.

dangerousness of the activity as such. Thus, the water infrastructure for a city will probably fall out of the scope of Article 435 Civil Code beyond the damage to the environment. The basis for liability for other damage is hence fault.

In Case 4.3., company A is an independent contractor who renders services for B. Article 429 Civil Code provides that the person who entrusts an independent contractor with the performance of a task is liable for the damage he may negligently cause while doing so unless he refutes the presumption of *culpa in eligendo* in either of the following two ways provided: proof that B was not negligent in choosing the contractor or that B entrusted the performance of the transaction to a person, enterprise or institution which performs such transactions within the scope of their professional activity.[114] Hence, given the facts, B is likely to successfully raise the independent contractor defence.

The principal is still personally liable for any other negligence (e.g., negligent monitoring). In that case both the principal and the independent contractor are liable jointly and severally for damage according to Article 441 para 1 Civil Code. But no such inferences may be drawn from the above case scenario.

Even if we assumed that the infrastructure belongs to the sphere of imperium, i.e., acts of public authority, B is likely to escape liability, as there is no wrongfulness of conduct that can be imputed to B (Article 417 Civil Code). A's negligence facilitated the operation of the terrorist. This will be considered A's fault and the argument pointing to an intervening cause will be rejected.

Spain

To answer this question, one must make a distinction between matters of water safety and matters of security.[115] From the first point of view, B is not liable to the injured population of the city because the act of a third party – the terrorist in this case – amounts to force majeure and breaks the link of causation between the water consumption and the water supply. City B, as the one in charge of the quality and safety of the water

---

[114] See M Nesterowicz/E Bagińska 2003, 190–194.
[115] The waterworks of city B would probably be subject to the Act 8/2011 (28 April) on Protection of Critical Infrastructures (Royal Decree 704/2011, 20 May, contains the implementing regulation of the said Act). This Act does not regulate questions of third parties' liability.

supply, cannot be blamed for the intentional poisoning of the water by a third party. This is so even in the strict liability regime under which city B operates as a public body (Article 139 LRJPAC). Things might be different if B had failed to discover the poison in the water during the normal checks of water safety.

From the security point of view, the analysis begins with consideration of the fact that security is one of the public services provided, and the general rules on State liability establish that the public administration is liable for the normal or abnormal functioning of those services.[116] If the security service malfunctions, the question of liability is not difficult. One may think, for example, of the massive amount of case law regarding State liability for the harm caused by policemen. The malfunction of a fire brigade allowing the fire to reach another building nearby may be another example which shows that there can be State liability notwithstanding the fact that it was a third party who was liable for the initial damage.

If the security service causes harm – although it has worked properly – that will lead to liability, we are dealing with one of the cases in which harm is very close to the taking of private property by public authorities.

Things are a little bit more difficult if we think of cases in which a lack of vigilance is the act (or omission) at issue in one of the extremes of the link of causation. Legal writers are of the opinion that liability for omissions cannot be handled with the same strict liability system that generally applies to State liability.[117] The same has been argued in respect of the monitoring services provided by the public administration.[118] As one writer puts it, in those areas the public service does not create the risk, but rather to the contrary, it tries to prevent it and therefore there is no basis to impose a strict liability regime.[119] Additionally, it has been pointed out that if we increase the duty to monitor more and more activities, perhaps other rights and interests of the individual may be affected.[120]

---

[116] See a general presentation of this scenario Barcelona Llop 1988, 261. For a good exposition of the rules on damage caused by officers serving directly in the public administration, see Valriberas Sanz 1999, 139 ff. On damage caused by the use of fire arms, see Barcelona Llop 1988, 305 ff. As Casino Rubio 1998, 39 explains, there was a huge number of claims against police officers in the 1980s. For the reasons why, see ibid., 43 ff.

[117] Amongst many others see Gómez Puente 2002, 845.

[118] See Magide Herrero 1999, 374. Among private law legal writers, the same idea is presented by Carrasco 1999, 318. The idea is also invoked in case law; see STS, (3rd Chamber) 9 June 1998 (RJ 1998/5172), among some other judgments that can be seen in García Muñoz and J Carrasco Martín 2003.

[119] Rivero Ortega 2000, 224 and 225. Nevertheless, the case law does not always follow this line, even in the civil jurisdiction. See, for example, STS 22 November 1996 (RJ 8363).

[120] Bermejo 2005, 137 and 1998, 39, 53.

Taking these into account, it is not difficult to understand that in those areas the public administration strict liability regime does not apply. Therefore, State liability is only triggered by a malfunction of the public services, i.e., a public service that works beneath the relevant standard of conduct.[121] This has been assumed by contentious-administrative case law, which does not impose liability on the public administration for not preventing a crime, but has considered things the other way round when the public authorities had knowingly allowed a dangerous situation to continue.[122] The same outcome can be found in civil case law.[123] In a related way, in civil case law a defendant was held liable for not contracting a security service when it was compulsory to do so.[124]

Case 3 (4.3.) poses another problem that complicates the answer a bit more. Here the question at hand is how rules on State liability for security services coordinate with rules on public services performed by or in coordination with private enterprises. Public authorities are not liable for the harm caused by what in private law would be called an independent contractor. Only if public authorities are responsible for *culpa in eligendo* or *culpa in vigilando* can they be held liable for the harm caused by this kind of contractor. On the contrary, if the private enterprise or person is integrated in the public administration's structure, State liability will ensue pursuant to the general rules.

Following this reasoning, B would not be held liable for the harm caused by A's negligence if A can be seen as an independent contractor. The fact that A organises the security services with its own means and independently from B's instructions (*in proprium*) is the decisive point. Nevertheless, as has been repeatedly pointed out in this report, in the Spanish legal system there is another more flexible view of State liability that would allow imposing liability on B without much ado, simply as if State liability was a non-fault liability scheme similar to the social security

---

[121] Legal writers of administrative law would put it in other words. They would probably say that the damage suffered was not unlawful or that there is not a causal link between the service and the damage. See García Muñoz and Carrasco Martín 2003, who quote STS (3rd Chamber) 20 June 2000 (RJ 7082), among others.

[122] García Muñoz and Carrasco Martín 2003, 8 cite STS (3rd Chamber) 4 May 1999 (RJ 4911); STS (3rd Chamber) 20 February 1999 (RJ 3146).

[123] For example, in STS (1st Chamber) 20 December 2004 (RJ 8132), a person travelling by underground was murdered by criminals in a corridor where other crimes had previously been committed. The Barcelona Underground Company had to pay damages for allowing the dangerous situation to continue. In STS (1st Chamber) 2 October 1997 (RJ 6964), the owners of a disco were held liable for the damage suffered by a client because of the negligent behaviour of another client that was not prevented by the owners.

[124] This can be seen in STS (1st Chamber) 22 December 1999 (RJ 9206).

system. The victim's lawyers will probably explore this line of action in Spain. Remember also the subsidies that victims of terrorism can get from LRPIVT.

B can definitely take recourse against A for the negligent performance of the services contracted.[125] This would be on a contractual basis and with different scope depending on the harm that B has ultimately suffered in each case.

In Spain, with the French structure of the administrative law, there is a special contractual regime for the contracts made by the State. These contracts have special features (the so-called *factum principis*, for example) and are litigated under a special branch of the jurisdiction.[126] In Case 4.3., what is at stake is an administrative services contract as defined in Article 10 of the Act on Contracts in the Public Sector (TRLCSP).[127] This kind of contract may have a vast array of objects and is similar in structure to the civil contract of services.[128] Therefore, liability is triggered only if – as happens in Case 4.3. – A has acted negligently.[129]

Sweden

Operators of waterworks have specifically regulated duties under the Environmental Code (ch 11) to protect public and private interests. Ch 32 stipulates strict tort liability also for these waterworks enterprises, concerning personal injuries and property.[130] As earlier mentioned, this strict liability regime is not based on a notion of force majeure. Wilful contamination by third persons cannot be deemed as falling outside the protective scope of the strict liability of waterworks operators. Liability for third-party interventions in the causation of the damage is not excluded from

---

[125] Menéndez Sebastián 2009, 614; Parada 2012, 347.

[126] See a general description in ibid., 287 ff. The main differences between civil contracts and administrative contracts can be seen in García de Enterría and Fernández 2011, 730. Nevertheless, it has been pointed out that there are no substantial differences between these two kinds of contract. See Santamaría Pastor 2002, 182–183.

[127] For more information on this Article 10 TRLCSP, see Moreno Molina and Pleite Guadamillas 2012, 277 and 1217; see also García Gómez de Mercado et al. 2011, 794.

[128] See Annex II of TRLCSP, following Directive 2004/98/EC. Among legal writers, see Parada 2012, 346 for the said analogy. See García Gómez de Mercado et al. 2011, 796 for an explanation on how wide the object of a contract of services can be.

[129] This idea is clearly stated in civil case law deciding cases of private guards' liability. See STS 17 March 2011 (RJ 2883); STS 8 October 2001 (RJ 7548).

[130] The exemption on radiological contamination (ch 32 s 2) only refers to instances where the Nuclear Liability and Compensation Act is applicable, i.e. where liability for nuclear installations arises.

the strict liability. A finding of adequate causation is thus not necessarily excluded on that ground, even for serious contamination by third parties acting with intent.[131]

B, as the operator of the waterworks, has a contractual claim against A for damages due to its breach of contractual duties to protect B's facility from third-party attacks. Final liability will in practice be decided by both parties' respective insurance arrangements.

Besides B's tort liability, several other complex issues arise, including environmental liability for clean-up costs and the property owner's right to compensation for infringements of the constitutional right to property, resulting from public security and environmental protection measures which limit the property owner's use and access to his property.[132]

Question b: *Is A directly liable to the house-owner D who suffers property damage (35,000 euro) and severe health damage because of the contamination of the water?*

England and Wales

Yes, A would be directly liable in negligence to D for this harm. A duty would be owed on the basis that D is a reasonably foreseeable victim. Establishing breach and causation should be straightforward.

France

The *Cour de cassation* now recognises that breach of contract can be invoked as a tortious delict by third parties to whom such breach caused a loss.[133] A has thus committed a fault involving civil liability. The question that arises here is whether A's negligence can be considered directly linked to the injury suffered by D. Indeed, the terrorist act is a voluntary action that could be considered as breaking the causal chain. However, it is clear that A could have prevented this terrorist act according to the contract concluded with city B.

---

[131] Cf NJA 1981, 622 (liability of a municipality for contamination was not excluded on the basis of other enterprises discarding toxic agents into wells connected to the public sewage system).

[132] This is subject to reform by a Law Commission in order to define the scope of compensation for such incidents, *Dir 2012:59 Ersättning vid vissa särskilda fall av rådighetsinskränkningar.*

[133] Cass ass plén 6 October 2006, Bull civ 2006 no. 9.

Germany

German courts have held security personnel liable next to, for example, the operators of facilities or organisers of events, for damage caused to those that were meant to be protected. For example, lifeguards can be liable under tort law next to the operators of swimming pools. The lifeguards not only enter into a contract with the operator but also take on a tort law relevant duty of care towards the visitors of the swimming pool.[134] The same would seem to apply to the security personnel of the waterworks of city B.

A's liability is not excluded by the fact that the terrorist acted with intention to harm the citizens of city B. German courts have often held that, for example, the organiser of an event has the duty to ensure that third parties cannot cause damage to other spectators.[135] In fact, it was exactly the duty of A to prevent third parties from interfering with the water supply. Thus, it would seem that A could be directly liable to D under § 823 para 1 BGB.

The Netherlands

If A committed a wrongful act in the sense of Article 6:162 BW and the interests of D fall within the protected interests covered by the standard with which A should have reckoned (Article 6:163), then A is liable insofar as the damage suffered by D falls within the confines of Article 6:98 BW. This may depend on the nature of the property damage. The health damage as such seems to fall within the scope of the infringed standard of conduct.

Poland

Provided that D can establish A's fault, the main question will turn on adequate causation. If company A is in charge of the operation of the security of the waterworks, then any negligence that leads to damage suffered by end-users is causally linked with A's conduct. According to the prevailing view, a "normal consequence" of a fact means one which

---

[134] See, for example, BGH, 13 March 1962, (1962) NJW 959; BGH, 12 June 1990, (1990) NJW-RR 1245; *Kammergericht* (KG), 20 November 1998, (2000) NJW-RR 242.

[135] See, for example, OLG Frankfurt, 24 February 2011, (2011) *Monatsschrift des deutschen Rechts* (MDR) 725, with regard to a first league football match. See also Spindler 2004, 3146, with regard to the abuse by third parties of software failures.

typically occurs in the regular course of events; it is not required that it would always happen. The Supreme Court has explained the category of "normal consequences" in several judgments, using the objective criteria that flow from life experience and science. With some exceptional cases, the Court rejected the subjective factor related to the foreseeability of consequences, as predictability is not a category of causality but of fault.[136] Moreover, adequate causation may be both direct and indirect. The courts have held that there is a causal link between damage and an event if the event indirectly created the favourable conditions or facilitated another event or a sequence of events, the last of which became the direct cause of the damage. Thus, indirect causation is a multi-element causal chain, where there is a causal dependency between the parts of the chain and each part separately is subject to the causality test.[137] The answer to the question will ultimately belong to a court.

Spain

Based on Article 1902 CC, D can sue A and get damages both for the health and property damage, at least as far as it can be said that the harm suffered is adequately linked to A's negligence because it was foreseeable.

It is possible that D could explore the path offered by the TRLDCU to protect users from defective services. It is by no means clear whether it would be a plaintiff-friendly way or not. Note, in any case, the supporting role that the legislation on consumer protection has played in cases litigated under the objective view of Article 1902 CC.

Sweden

B's non-delegable duties towards the public cannot be transferred to A per se. A's negligence in relation to B does not transfer into a breach of duty to protect others, as well as a negligent breach for that matter. A is not part of the production process, unlike a producer in a product liability context. Any special "safety obligations" vis-à-vis a third person to a contract is thus questionable. A's duty to protect can naturally also

---

[136] SN judgment of 2 June 1956, 3 CR 515/56, OSNC 1/1957, at 24; SN judgment of 7 June 2001, III CKN 1536/00, LEX 52595, SN judgment of 14 March 2002, IV CKN 826/00, LEX 74400; SN judgment of 21 January 1946, C I 318/45, *Panstwo i Prawo* (PiP) 1946, no. 7, 114.

[137] SN judgment of 10 December 1952, C 584/52 PiP 1953, nos. 8–9, 366; SN judgment of 21 June 1960, 1 CR 592/59, OSNC 1962/III, at 84.

be construed in a wider sense, to include the general public. However, that still leaves issues of adequate causation. A is probably not liable in relation to D.

Question c: *Is A liable to State E who provides for disaster relief measures which amount to 18 billion euro?*

England and Wales

Given that this loss would be categorised as purely economic, A would not owe a duty of care to E to protect him from such harm, and so A could not therefore be liable in negligence.

France

A has committed negligence and may be liable towards third parties under Article 1382 *Code civil*. However, it appears here that the causal relationship is too indirect to justify A's liability towards State E. Indeed, not only terrorist action is interposed in the chain of causality, but also the decision of the State to grant aid, which is a free choice that breaks the causal chain.

Germany

The grounds for such liability can only be *negotiorum gestio* (§ 677 BGB). As in Case 4.2., State E could be regarded as acting as an agent for A who would otherwise be liable for the damage, or even greater damage, under § 823 para 1 BGB.

The Netherlands

This is a debatable issue. If one assumes that the standard of conduct with which A was obliged to comply aims to protect not only individual citizens from suffering death and personal injury but also to protect the State against damage of the kind it suffered, then clearly the answer is affirmative. The core question is whether A had to take the interests of the State into account when it acted negligently. Dutch case law does not take a clear stance on this issue. Moreover, the restrictive test of Article 6:98 BW would have to be applied: can the damage incurred by the State be reasonably considered to be the effect of A's negligence? Obviously, the issue with public authorities claiming on the basis of private law constructs is that there may be public law avenues for recoupment of such cost. In the absence of such avenues, the courts may infer that the legislature did not find recoupment of such public expenditure politically appropriate.[138] Note that Article 6:109 BW allows the court to attenuate any claim for compensation if the extent of the damages would be excessively burdensome on A.

Poland

State E is a competent authority that may take the necessary preventive and remedial measures by itself under PREP, which implements Directive 2004/35/EC. In accordance with the Directive, the State may recover the costs it has incurred in relation to the adoption of preventive or remedial measures from the operator. However, A is not an operator under those laws. B is the operator and is liable for the cost of the measures. The Polish act implementing the Directive does not provide for defences allowing the operator not to bear the prevention and remediation costs ("permit defence" and "state-of-the-art defence" – see Article 8.4 ELD). B, having paid E's costs, would have a recourse action against A.

Spain

The answer tends to be positive, as Article 1902 would also be open to the State E. Even assuming that the harm may be linked to A's negligence, a Spanish judge would probably limit the outcome on the basis offered by Article 1103 CC.

Sweden

A is not likely liable toward State E, at least not under the rules of tort law. General principles of tort law do, however, deem the injured person's preventive costs in limiting their injury compensable. State E will have to direct its claims to city B (or the State of city B).

4.4.   Case 4 – Border control

Company A is the security consultant of State B for border control security. A provided a comprehensive security concept for State B. It can be established that terrorist C of Case 4.3. slipped through the border-crossing

---

[138] Spier et al. 2012, 190 ff.

point X of State B on 1 October. This was only possible because A's security arrangements are seriously flawed.

Question a: *Is State B liable to the house-owner D of Case 4.3.?*

England and Wales

B could only be liable for proven negligence.

France

Ensuring security at borders and controlling passengers within airports are activities that can lead the State to be liable towards citizens if gross negligence is established.[139] In the present case, proving a gross negligence by the State appears to be difficult. It would be necessary to establish the existence of recent terrorist acts[140] which made the occurrence of an imminent terrorist attack probable and justified enhanced border control, even if it is not always sufficient.[141] D will also be compensated by the FGTI for his injury.

Moreover, even assuming that gross negligence by the State could be established in this case, the causal link between the negligence in border control and the terrorist attack appears to be too remote. Proving that the attack would not have occurred if the terrorist had not entered the territory is not sufficient to establish causation. The terrorist attack is an intentional act which breaks the causal chain.

Germany

The only possible grounds of liability would be § 839 BGB. Under this provision, if an official intentionally or negligently breaches the official duty incumbent upon him in relation to a third party, he must compensate the third party for damage arising from this. If the official is only

---

[139] CE 9 February 1979, *de La Villéon*, Rec CE 57, RD publ 1980.1759; CE 26 June 1985, *Mme Garagnon*, Rec.CE 209, D 1987, somm 379, obs H. Maisl, *Revue de droit public* (RD publ) 1986 927, Rev adm 1987, 38, obs J. Frayssinet, *Petites affiches* 1986, no. 87, 7, obs F. Moderne.

[140] *Cour administrative d'appel* (CAA) Marseille, 20 May 1999, *Min Intérieur c/ Caisse centrale de reassurance.*

[141] CAA Marseille, 4 March 1999, *Cie Assurances générales de France*, and 5 July 2001, *Cie Assurances générales de France.*

responsible because of negligence, then he may only be held liable if the injured person is not able to obtain compensation in another way. Here, a variety of problems arise. First of all, is border control an official duty in relation to each citizen? Second, did the relevant official acting for State B act negligently? Clearly, the negligence of A cannot be attributed to State B under § 839 BGB. One could, however, argue that the relevant official acting for State B should have been able to recognise serious flaws in a security concept and therefore has acted negligently. In contrast, the first hurdle is more difficult to overcome. Case law is not available. Legal doctrine and the courts distinguish between duties towards individual third persons and duties directed at the maintenance of public order. Case law on the fight against terrorism is not available but it would seem to fall into the second category,[142] and there seems to be consensus that the State can barely ever be held legally responsible for terrorist attacks.[143] Finally, State liability is subsidiary and only applies where the victim cannot obtain compensation in another way. This exception, however, is limited to enforceable claims.[144] Thus, although D would of course have a damages claim against the terrorist,[145] that latter claim would most likely be unenforceable.

The liability of State B would, however, also be subsidiary to A's liability (provided a claim against A is enforceable and not, for example, useless due to insolvency). This would require A to be liable for the damage. Since A has not caused the damage itself, this would only be possible if A had a duty to protect D's property; which it could only have assumed through the consulting contract. It seems, however, that this would not be the case. Neither did A assume responsibility for a certain source of risk nor for a certain group of people, as in the case of a lifeguard.[146] Responsibility for the public order and the protection of the population against terrorist attacks clearly remains with the State.

---

[142] See Melzer, Haslach and Socher 2005, 1361, 1367 on the question as to whether the State has the duty towards an individual to prevent a terrorist attack by shooting down a captured airplane.

[143] See Viezens 2007, 1494. A fairly far-reaching liability was accepted by the courts in the case of a strike of the – then public – flight security service which led to economic losses being sustained by travel agencies due to the cancellation of flights; see BGH (1977) NJW 1875. The BGH argued that it was one purpose of the flight security service to facilitate the smooth operation of flights at airports. Still, this connection seems to be more immediate than in the case of border controls.

[144] See, for example, BGH, 12 November 1992, (1993) NVwZ 1228.

[145] See also Melzer, Haslach and Socher 2005, 1364.   [146] See *supra*, Case 4.3., Question b.

The Netherlands

If State B itself committed a wrongful act in the sense of Article 6:162 BW and the interests of D fall within the protected interests covered by the standard with which A should have reckoned (Article 6:163), then A is liable insofar as the damage suffered by D falls within the confines of Article 6:98 BW. This may depend on the nature of the property damage. The health damage as such seems to fall within the scope of the infringed standard of conduct. As far as vicarious liability is concerned, it seems unlikely that the State would be liable for the tort committed by an independent contractor. States do not seem to fall within the remit of Article 6:171 BW (see above 4.1, question a). If, however, the employees of A were to be considered employees of the State B, then Article 6:170 BW would apply. This certainly is a possibility since vicarious liability under Article 6:170 BW is not restricted to employment contracts in the narrow sense. Thus, if A's employees are on secondment with B, B can be considered the "employer" for the purposes of Article 6:170 BW. This would mean that flaws in the security arrangements caused by negligence on the part of A's employees would lead to joint and several liability of both A and B.

Poland

If A's role is that of a security consultant, State B is solely liable for the decision regarding the implementation of the comprehensive security concept. However, with regard to D's claims, it is doubtful whether adequate causation will be established, especially having regard to the multiplicity of causes leading to the damage.

Spain

Following the general rules of State liability, B is liable to D notwithstanding the fact that the malfunction of the public service was caused by the flawed security arrangements provided by A.[147] To arrive at this outcome, it is crucial that A's services were "negligently performed" (it is

---

[147] Article 12.1. A.b) of the Organic Act of Security Forces and Bodies of the State (LO 2/1986, 13 March, *Ley de Fuerzas y Cuerpos de Seguridad*) provides that National Police forces are in charge of the control of the traffic of entrance and exit from the national territory. Art 12.1.B.d) provides that the Civil Guard forces are in charge of the guarding of roads, frontiers, coasts, ports, airports and other centres and premises.

doubtful whether "defectively performed" would suffice) and that terrorist C's crime was somehow foreseeable.

Sweden

State B has the general public responsibility for border control, even if that has been partly delegated to the airport operator and in turn to a security company. That also implies a shared tort law duty between the other actors in respect of airport safety, duties which however are non-delegable in tort law, due to the nature of the public law regulation. Additionally, State B has a positive obligation to protect persons and property (especially under the ECHR). The scope of a tort law duty to protect and prevent third persons from injuring the general public or specific persons has to be decided on these premises. In the present case, it is highly questionable whether the scope of this duty would extend to D.

Question b: *Can State B take recourse against company A?*

England and Wales

B could ask for A to be joined as co-defendant to any action in negligence brought. Alternatively, B could bring contribution proceedings under the Civil Liability (Contribution) Act 1978.

France

The State may, of course, sue A for breach of contract. But determining the loss may be difficult.

Germany

Since State B would most likely not be liable in the first place, there is no place for a recourse claim. Recourse under tort law between two jointly and severally liable tortfeasors would be superseded by the above-mentioned subsidiarity of State liability. To what extent recourse can be based on the contract obviously depends on the contract terms and the liability regime that the parties have agreed on.

The Netherlands

Recourse is possible, either on the basis of contract or on the basis of joint and several liability (Article 6:102 BW).

Poland

The recourse against A is highly unlikely if A is just an expert.

Spain

Yes, B can take recourse against A under the general rules of administrative contractual liability (explored in Question a). For cases in which a contractor prepares and executes the project to perform public works, the contractor's liability is limited to 50 per cent of the harm suffered by a third party and within the limit of five times the contract price.[148]

Sweden

B's recourse would be premised on A's non-contractual liability, based on a breach of duty to prevent D's harm and an adequate causal link between this negligence and D's harm. A primarily has a contractual duty to the airport operator and a public law obligation to the airport police authority to report risks and obey the directives of the police authority regarding airport security. The purpose of A's activity and A's authority is, according to public law regulations, to protect private property and persons including persons in public. However this does not necessarily transform into a tort law duty to prevent third persons suffering harm. The protective scope of A's negligence may thus not extend to the general public, but that can be subject to different opinions.

Question c: *What would the liability of State B be if company A was not a security consultant but rather the contractor who is obliged to service the video surveillance installation at the border crossing X and terrorist C slipped through the border control because of A's negligence?*

England and Wales

Both A and B's liability would remain as set out in the answers above. By analogy with *Bailey* v. *HSS Alarms* (*The Times*, 20 June 2000), A would owe a duty based on an assumption of responsibility in the circumstances, and it is likely that C would still be regarded as a foreseeable victim for the purposes of this duty. Granted, C will not have directly relied on this

---

[148] See Article 169.2 TRLCSP. Find more information in Menéndez Sebastián 2002, *passim*. That provision is the object of criticism among legal writers; see for example, Ahumada Ramos 2004, 531 and the literature quoted therein.

assumption of responsibility, but arguably direct reliance is not necessary where the harm is physical rather than purely financial.

France

A priori, the solution is not different from that to Question a.

Germany

There would be no difference to the solution under Question a since again § 839 BGB would require duties towards individual third persons as opposed to duties directed at the maintenance of public order; and a general duty to protect individuals from terrorism cannot be assumed.

The Netherlands

There is no particular difference. Naturally, the nature of the negligence is different but either case could lead to claims for negligence under Article 6:162 BW.

Poland

In this case, as the renderer of services A is an independent contractor. Article 429 Civil Code, discussed above, will apply. The possibility of raising independent contractor immunity as a defence is dependent on the determination of whether the direct tortfeasor is an independent contractor rather than a servant. In order to answer this question, one has to look at the scope of power of management and control over this person's activities.

Spain

As explained in Case 4.3. Question a, in principle the State is not liable for the harm caused by its independent contractors, unless the State itself has incorrectly chosen or monitored the contractor. Therefore, the outcome turns on whether it can be said that A is an independent contractor or whether it is integrated in the State structure as a servant and therefore its acts entail the liability of the principal. In this case A is in a very close position to guard C of Case 4.5. (see below), and State B would be liable for its negligence.

Sweden

The same reasoning in respect of B's liability as above would apply here. Any protective duties of B are of a non-delegable nature.

4.5.   Case 5 – Aeroplane crash

Company A is in charge of the security check at airport B. A's obligations are determined in the contract with airport B which inter alia provides that A shall only use specially trained and certified personnel. On Sunday 2 April, employee C, who lacks this special training, is in charge of baggage screening monitor 5 at gate 25 of airport B. When passenger D is passing through the monitor, employee C is chatting with another passenger and fails to detect that passenger D is carrying a box filled with highly inflammable chemicals in his hand baggage, hidden under a notebook. Passenger D gets on the flight F-676 of airline E. In full flight the chemicals become inflamed and a fire starts in the passenger cabin. After some minutes the crew can stop the fire and manage an emergency landing at airport F. Five passengers suffer severe gas poisoning, two of them die and three have severe lung injuries. The aeroplane is heavily damaged. The repair costs amount to 1.5 million euro. Air carrier E has to pay 100,000 euro for the emergency landing to airport F and the passengers of flight F-676 claim compensation for enduring fear of death and loss of profits.

Question a: *Is company A liable for these costs, if passenger D's behaviour resulted from mere carelessness?*

England and Wales

It is likely that A would be liable in negligence for any personal injuries suffered by the passengers, including any medically recognised psychiatric conditions and for any consequential financial losses. Liability would also extend to the costs of repairing the aeroplane (property damage) and the 100,000 euro emergency landing on the basis that this could be construed as a consequential financial loss. A's duty of care would be based on its assumption of responsibility to prevent the very kind of act that occurred in this case. Given that the harm was readily foreseeable as a consequence of taking highly flammable chemicals on board an aircraft, it does not matter that the fire was started carelessly rather than intentionally.

France

Here the problem is to determine the breach for which A could be blamed. If it is the case that the person employed by A had insufficient qualifications, then we must question the causal link between this fault and the consequences of the incident. In this case, the simple fact that C did not have sufficient qualifications seems hardly sufficient to be considered as the cause of the incident. Indeed, C probably could have made the same mistake even if trained. There is no evidence that the damage would not have occurred with qualified personnel.

However, it appears possible to blame A for letting a passenger pass the security check with inflammable chemicals. Here the question is whether A is bound by an "obligation of result" (*obligation de résultat*) not to let any passenger holding inflammable substances pass the security check. If the contract can be interpreted this way, then A has committed a breach of contract by letting passenger D pass the security check. A seems to be liable here because there is a direct causal link between the incident and the act of letting D pass through the barriers with inflammable materials.

Germany

The strict liability regime of the Air Traffic Act (LuftVG) does not apply to A but only to the owner of the aeroplane. As in Case 4.3. Question b, one may, however, assume that A has a duty under § 823 para 1 BGB to make sure that passengers are not harmed by dangerous substances once they have passed security control and entered the plane. Case law on the exact duties of the security personnel at airports does not seem to be available. The OLG Frankfurt, however, observed in passing, in a case on security checks in a football arena, that the usual security standards on airports far exceed those in football arenas (and would of course include metal detectors and the like).[149] Thus, it would seem that A could be held liable for the health damage that the three surviving passengers suffered. German law does not provide compensation for death as such.[150]

The other passengers have not been physically harmed, thus their fears would have to have reached the stage of damage to their health. Fear has sometimes been recognised as a ground for compensation although only

[149] See OLG Frankfurt, 24 February 2011, (2011) MDR 725.   [150] See Stahmer 2004.

if the fear was not unreasonable.[151] In those cases fear was, however, a consequence of a primary violation.[152] As a primary violation, the fear as such would have to amount to damage to health. Given the short period of time until the safe landing this seems highly unlikely. The pure economic loss of the passengers is not recoverable under § 823 para 1 BGB either.

E, however, would seem to be within the scope of A's duty to prevent harm and E suffered property damage to the aircraft of 1.5 million euro. The emergency landing fee is covered as consequential damage.

The Netherlands

First, it is a fact commonly known to passengers that they are not allowed to take inflammables on board and that D is probably liable himself as well. The intent or negligence of the passenger seems immaterial to the liability of A. A has breached the contract with B. The breach related to fundamental safety requirements and arguably increased the chances of inattentive work by C. Therefore, it seems plausible to argue that A acted wrongfully vis-à-vis those injured parties whose interests fall within the protected interests covered by the standard with which A should have reckoned (Article 6:163 BW). This would lead to A's liability insofar as the damage suffered falls within the confines of Article 6:98 BW. This may depend on the nature of the damage and the remoteness of the consequences. The death and personal injury fall well within the ambit of protection of the norm violated by A. So does the property damage suffered by the airline. Even the expenses incurred by E (the expenses of emergency landing rights and the compensation to passengers) may also fall within the ambit of protection. On balance, A is liable for these costs. Note, however, that Article 6:109 BW allows the court to attenuate any claim for compensation if the extent of the damages would be excessively burdensome on A.

Poland

A is liable for its employee C who should have been trained for the job. A's liability is based on the fault of the employee. The liability for A's fault

---

[151] For a case of unreasonable fear see *Amtsgericht* (District Court; AG) Düren, 13 October 1999, (2001) NJW 901.
[152] See, for example, BGH, 30 April 1996, (1996) NJW 2425.

rests on the airport B which contracted out the security checks because the operator of the airport performs tasks connected with security control in civil aviation (Article 186b s 1 Aviation Law). B's liability is based on Article 429 Civil Code, with possible independent contractor defence. Both A and B have very limited insurance coverage. D's terrorist attack or negligence or carelessness (unlawful interference) combined with A's negligence will not exculpate A from liability for negligence.

As concerns harm suffered by the passengers, the air-carrier (E) is responsible for any damage to persons or things suffered by passengers involved in an air accident under the Warsaw–Montreal system. For damages above SDR 100,000, E is liable unless it proves that the damage was not due to its negligence or other wrongful act or omission or due to the negligence or other wrongful act of its servants or agents (Article 21 para 2 of the Montreal Convention). Below this threshold, the air carrier cannot exclude or limit claims for compensation.

Spain

In Spain a legal entity called *Aeropuertos Españoles y Navegación Aérea* (AENA) is in charge of the airports of public interest.[153] AENA was a State body that recently has changed into a public corporation. In any case, when AENA's non-contractual liability is at stake, the strict liability regime of public authorities is applied (Article 139 LRJPAC).[154] AENA is the party in charge of aviation and airport security and is under a duty to cooperate with the different police forces that exist in Spain.[155] For their part, the police and a force called Civil Guards (*Guardia Civil*) are in charge of security matters in airports and at borders. As one legal writer put it: in any case security in airports is always a public service.[156]

Under the Spanish Act on Private Security (LSP) currently in force, only specially trained and certified personnel can be in charge of the monitoring of passengers. By contravening this, A is considered negligent and, if this lack of special training has a role in the aetiology of the case,

---

[153] See a monographic study in Gómez Puente 2006, 128 ff.
[154] See García de Enterría and Fernández 2011, 386 and 404; Ahumada Ramos 2004, 399 ff. (cf Article 144 LRJPAC).
[155] As explained by Arroyo Martínez 2006, 61 and Fernández-Piñeyro 2001, 111–174. See Article 82 of the Act 4/1990 as reformed by Act 62/2003 of 30 December.
[156] Arroyo Martínez 2006, 90.

A would incur liability.[157] Additionally, A would be subject to administrative sanctions.[158]

It must be highlighted that in Spain there is always at least one police officer (or *Guardia Civil*) participating in the passenger-monitoring tasks, and that he could have detected that A was employing non-certified personnel. In fact, under the LSP all private security guards are obliged to wear a uniform and a badge with their identification number. The lack of these is very easily detected, so the idea of some *culpa in vigilando* incurred by the State is plausible. This would entail State liability. As if that was not enough, there is another argument in support of State liability in this case. Although it may need additional analysis, it can probably be said that security guards operating in airports should not be deemed independent contractors but auxiliaries integrated in the public administration structure.[159] When the cooperation between the public administration and a private enterprise is organised in such a way that the private body acts under the control and under the orders of the public administration, this leads to imposing liability on the State in the same manner as if an authentic civil servant had acted.[160]

Were a case like this to be litigated in the Spanish legal system, the most probable scenario could be described as follows: operator E would be liable to pay damages to the F-676 flight passengers. Damages for personal injuries and death would not be problematic as a normal aeroplane accident is at stake.[161] Nevertheless, the final outcome would not be clear regarding the passengers' harm that consists of the fear of death and loss of profits. Although the general Spanish rules on non-pecuniary damage allow awarding damages for pure emotional shock, it is not clear

---

[157] Not having administrative permission does not suffice in order to be held liable in the event that one's conduct causes damage. A causal link between that conduct and the said damage is also necessary. This can be seen in Pantaleón 1993, and in some civil court decisions such as, for example, STS 8 October 2001 (RJ 7548) and STS 15 April 1985 (RJ 1764).

[158] Even A's personnel could be administratively sanctioned. On this, see *Manual del personal de la seguridad privada*, (CPD 2008) 66 ff.

[159] At least they were so as of 2009, when their work was integrated in the security department of AENA and under the authority of the police bodies which serve at airports. See González García 2008, 38, 39.

[160] See Carrillo Donaire 2000, 601 ff.

[161] Guerrero Lebrón 2005, 125 ff. In case law, personal injuries and death are compensated without any problem. See STS 17 December 1990 (RJ 10282), among others.

among legal writers whether or not these general rules apply to aeroplane accidents.[162] For its part, E – or the corresponding insurance company acting by subrogation – may sue A for the damage to the aeroplane and for the costs of the emergency landing.[163]

Sweden

To begin with, airline E is liable to the passenger for personal injuries in accordance with Regulation (EC) no. 2027/97 or the Montreal Convention.[164] E also suffers property damage (and damage consequential to that).

The airport operator bears the general responsibility for airport safety, including adequate security measures and staffing (together with the police authority). The security company A has a contractual duty to the airport operator for fulfilling the operator's requirements. Airline E has a contract with the airport operator, which also encompasses the provision of adequate safety on the airport and security checks of persons flying with the airline. This may be seen as a three-party relationship of a contractual chain: E – Airport – A. The general principle here is that each party holds their own contractual party liable for breaches of duties connected to the contract. The close-knit relation between the parties as regards the security service at hand, having regard to both mutual contractual clauses on liability, may result in the conclusion that a non-contractual claim would not be allowed either for E against A.

An exception to this principle may arise if A's conduct would amount to gross negligence, intent or breach of a special "security obligation". The notion of the last exception is ambiguous and has only been applied in a product liability context of chain contracts, where the negligence in producing a safety mechanism may put persons or property in serious

---

[162] See Álvarez Lata and Bustos Moreno 2008, 1430; Fernández Torres 2001, 282 or Guerrero Lebrón 2005, 146 ff. Regarding passenger D, it should be taken into account that contributory fault is applicable (Article 20 of the Convention for the Unification of Certain Rules for International Carriage by Air (Montreal, 28 May 1999; (2001) OJ L194/39)). On this, D. Lozano Romeral, "Transporte aéreo" in Menéndez (ed 2001, 132.

[163] On this kind of insurance, see Arroyo Martínez 2006, 245.

[164] The Swedish Act on Air Transport (*Lag* (2010:510) *om lufttransporter*) merely refers contractual liability issues to these two instruments.

danger. It is unclear whether the principle could be applied here to a security service.[165]

Question b: *Is A liable for these costs if passenger D acted with the intention to bring the aircraft down (in a terrorist attack)?*

England and Wales

Given that the security service being provided by A was supposed to protect against this very kind of act, it does not matter that the harm was caused intentionally by D.[166]

France

The question here is to determine whether the voluntary action of D breaks the causal chain of events. A's negligence made the terrorist attack possible, but one might ask whether "make possible" really means "caused". However, since A's mandate was precisely to prevent terrorist attacks, it could be argued that there is, in this case, a sufficiently direct causal link.

Germany

As mentioned in Case 4.3. Question b, harm caused by intentional acts of third persons does not necessarily exclude the liability of a person who has assumed responsibility for the safety of other persons. Case law on terrorist attacks is not available. One could argue that the prevention of terrorist attacks is one purpose of the security controls at airports and that the detection of dangerous materials such as those brought by D is one of the responsibilities of A. On the other hand, this view would increase A's risk to an extent that would make his business unviable. Here, one might also take into consideration that the legislator has regarded the airlines as the ones who should bear that risk, by imposing strict liability on them.

The Netherlands

See the answer to Question a above.

---

[165] Cf NJA 2007, 758; NJA 2009, 16.
[166] See *Reeves* v. *Commissioner of Police of the Metropolis* [2000] 1 AC 360.

Poland

See the answer to Question a above.

Spain

The use of non-certified personnel by A and the causal relevance of this fact in the aetiology of the damage would entail A's liability, as in Question a. In any case, note that the LRPIVT would be applicable.

Sweden

If E nevertheless is allowed a claim against A, based on a non-contractual duty to take preventive measures, Swedish tort law does not per se exclude liability based on the notion of *novus actus interveniens* – the intervention of a third person in the causation of a harm. As mentioned earlier, even intentional third-party interventions do not render the chain of causation inadequate. The primary issue here would instead be whether A's breach of duty of care increased the risk of harm to the injured person and whether a proper execution of security measures as required by the relevant standard of care would have considerably decreased the risk at hand.[167]

Question c: *Passenger D is a terrorist. The crew cannot exterminate the fire and the aircraft crashes into a residential area and causes disastrous damage to persons and property (3.5 billion euro). All the passengers and the crew are dead. Is A liable for the damage? Is the aircraft carrier E liable for the damage? Can E take recourse against A?*

England and Wales

A's duty of care would extend to such foreseeable third-party harm and so it is likely that A would be liable in negligence for the totality of the damages bill. E is strictly liable for such third-party liability harm under section 76(2) of the Civil Aviation Act 1982. However, in accordance with section 76(3), E is entitled to claim a full indemnity from A.

---

[167] Cf NJA 2013:20.

France

In France, the existence of a fund (FGTI) responsible for compensating victims of terrorism simplifies the victims' claims. Injuries are compensated by the fund, which is then subrogated into the rights of victims.

Today, passengers and third parties can obtain compensation from air carriers based on the same rules. There is a difference between international and domestic flights. If the flight was international, the Warsaw Convention of 12 October 1929 or the Montreal Convention of 28 May 1999 may be applied, depending on which one was ratified by the countries of departure and destination. If the Warsaw Convention is applicable, E is liable. E could try to prove that it had taken all reasonable measures to avoid the accident, but providing such proof will be hard since the crew did not manage to stop the fire. E could also try to show that such a terrorist act was a "force majeure" case but, again, this will be hard to establish since the box should have been discovered. The victims will be compensated but their compensation will be limited to SDR 16,000. They could be fully compensated if it is proven that the air carrier committed an inexcusable fault. However, since an inexcusable fault implies the awareness of the probability of harm and reckless acceptance of such a risk, the air carrier does not appear to have committed such a fault.[168]

If the Montreal Convention is applicable, E is strictly liable. The victims will be fully compensated for their portion of loss under SDR 113,100. However, the passengers may not be compensated for their portion of loss exceeding SDR 113,100 since the air carrier might claim that the accident is due to A's negligence or D's fault.

If the flight was domestic, the Code of Transports should be applied. If E is subject to Regulation (EC) no 1008/2008 of 24 September 2008 then the provisions of the Montreal Convention apply (see above). Otherwise, E is subject to Article L 6421–4 Code of Transports and to the provisions of the Warsaw Convention. In such case victims will be compensated within the limit of 114,336 euro per passenger.

The airline will reimburse the Fund for the amount corresponding to its liability. Whether the Fund then takes recourse against A for the portion of loss that has not been compensated depends on whether the airline may bring an action against A. Such an action cannot be based on the contract since neither the victims nor the airline have a contractual relationship

---

[168] Cass civ (1) 2 October 2007, no. 05–16.019, no. 04–13.004, Bull 2007, 612.

with A. However, A's tortious fault can be deduced from the breach since the breach caused damage to third parties. The difficulty is once again the establishment of causation. Is A's negligence in a sufficiently direct causal relationship to the injury suffered by the victims? It is possible here to argue that the terrorist attack has broken the causal chain of events. In other words, the causal link between D's negligence and the accident would be too remote.

Germany

A would only be liable for the damage if one could establish that A has assumed responsibility for all potential victims of an aircraft crash caused by terrorists using detectable substances. This would seem to go too far as it would mean that A would assume, jointly with E, tort law relevant liability for all risks connected with the aircraft. Although case law is not available, it would seem highly unlikely that a German court would find A liable for these grave consequences. Ultimately, prevention of and compensation for terrorist attacks are the responsibility of the State, and in practice a catastrophe such as the one described would most likely be dealt with by a special help fund for the victims.

E would be liable under the strict liability regime of § 33 LuftVG for the damage to persons and property in the residential area. No exception applies for terrorist attacks, or force majeure in general. The cap for E's liability under § 37 LuftVG depends on the set-off weight of the aeroplane and it is SDR 700 at the most (§ 37 para 1 with § 49b LuftVG).

Contractual recourse claims by E are unlikely since A and E do not have a contract. This would only be possible if A and B had a contract with protective effect on all aircraft operators starting from the airport.[169] The concept of a contract with protective effect on third parties, however, requires the number of those third parties to be limited,[170] which cannot be assumed given the vast number of flights departing from an airport every day. A recourse claim between two tortfeasors would require A to be liable for the damage under tort law, which seems highly unlikely.

The Netherlands

The liability of aircraft carrier E for damage to persons and objects on the ground is not covered by a specific regime. Therefore, the injured parties

---

[169] See *supra*, Case 1 Question d.   [170] See BGH, 7 November 1960, 33 BGHZ, 247.

would need to prove that the carrier committed an imputable wrongful act within the meaning of Article 6:162 BW. The case does not provide any clues in that direction, unless one argued that airport security checks are the responsibility of the carrier rather than the airport or border agency officials. Perhaps the carrier owes a duty to check baggage for chemicals towards his passengers but it is not clear whether this duty is extended to third parties; there is no apparent case law in this respect. If the facts are such that A was negligent in operating the baggage-checking procedure, it allowed untrained staff to work the belt and this negligence resulted in the employee not noticing the chemicals, then A is liable for the damage that ensued from this negligence. Possibly, one could argue that the consequences are extraordinary and that these cannot be ascribed to A (Article 6:98 BW). However, the whole point of baggage checks is to prevent enormous disasters – whether caused by terrorists or by inadvertent and negligent passengers – and there is no valid reason for excluding liability. To be fair, no security company will be able to bear the enormous financial burden of 3.5 billion euro. Presumably, it will have no insurance coverage extending to that amount. Thus, either A will go bankrupt or it may try to persuade the courts to apply the reduction clause of Article 6:109 BW.

Poland

According to aviation law, an operator of the aircraft is strictly liable to third parties for damage caused by the operation of the aircraft (Articles 206–207 Aviation Law).[171] Aviation Law refers to the Civil Code liability embraced in Article 435 Civil Code. This means that the exclusive fault of a third person can absolve the air-carrier from liability. Furthermore D's conduct should be proven to be the sole cause of the damage. E will probably bear the risk of compensating damage. Pursuant to Article 207 s 7 Aviation Law, all persons who were at fault are jointly and severally liable with the aircraft operator. A and B answer as multiple tortfeasors.[172]

As to the types of reparable damage, compensation for enduring fear of death and loss of profits is not likely to be awarded by Polish courts.

---

[171] SN judgment of 2 December 2003, III CK 430/03, OSP 2/2005, item 21.

[172] See Konert 2013, 82, 87, who suggests introducing some form of State liability for catastrophic damages arising from air terrorism (beyond any available insurance coverage).

The fear of death is not recognised as a separate head of damage and the latter type is not adequately causally linked with A's negligence. Lost profits may, however, be linked to the operation of the aircraft, so E may theoretically be held liable for lost profits (under the high probability standard of proof), but no case law can be provided to support such a conclusion in similar case scenarios.

E has recourse claims against B who answers for A, as well as against A. The recourse actions by E will be based on Article 441 paras 2 and 3 Civil Code.

Spain

Again, the most probable scenario in the Spanish legal system could be described as follows: in the two-tier liability system that derives from Regulation (EC) 2027/97 (as reformed by Regulation (EC) 889/2002), E is liable to the F-676 flight passengers for up to 100,000 SDR per person (Article 17.1 of the Montreal Convention). As the damage was caused by a terrorist attack, E's liability does not cover damages higher than that.[173] The Spanish Act of Aeronautical Navigation (LNA) does not provide whether a third-party act which causes the aeroplane accident can be relied on to exonerate the strict liability that the above-mentioned LNA imposes on operators. It has been said that the strict liability regime by its nature must cover even the accidents intentionally caused by third parties.[174] It should be pointed out that under the LNA-liability there are strict upper limits to the operator liability. Only if the victim proves the operator's negligence may those limits be exceeded. Under this aspect, the results are not so different from what happens with respect to damage sustained by passengers.

Sweden

Airline E is liable to its passengers and for personal injuries and property damage on the ground (based on strict liability, according to the 1922 Act on Liability for Damage Caused in the Course of Aviation). As mentioned under Question a, A's liability to E may perhaps be barred due to

---

[173] Under Article 4 Regulation 785/2004, E should be insured against terrorist attacks. On this see, Lozano Romeral 2001, 320.
[174] Álvarez Lata and Bustos Moreno 2008, 1413.

contractual considerations. A's liability to the persons on the ground –
and thus also E's right of recourse – raises difficult issues of the scope of
A's non-contractual duty to the public at large, beyond the contractual
duty in relation to A's contract party (probably the airport). A's non-
contractual liability is rather uncertain, but not very likely in the case at
hand.

5

Comparative analysis

MONIKA HINTEREGGER

5.1. Liability of operator of dangerous activities

5.1.1. Heads of liability

5.1.1.1. Fault-based liability

All operators of dangerous activities are liable to third parties under fault-based liability respectively negligence in common law (see 3.1.1.). In order to claim under fault-based liability the claimant must show that he suffered actionable damage as well as fault (respectively breach of duty in common law) and causation by the defendant. The Germanic jurisdictions (Germany, the Netherlands) require in addition that the defendant's behaviour was unlawful. The burden of proof lies in principle with the claimant, but courts may lighten the burden of proof according to the doctrine of *res ipsa loquitur* (common law) or the concept of prima facie evidence (civil law). Under certain conditions courts may have some flexibility to shift the burden of proof onto the defendant, for instance when damage is caused by a dangerous activity (Germany; Spain: theory of risk) or when it is seen to be reasonable and fair to do so (the Netherlands). Polish law provides for a presumption of fault in cases of vicarious liability concerning liability for the independent contractor, minors and incapable persons, and in France fault is assumed if a certain duty is imposed by a statute or by the courts. The defendant then can only escape liability in cases of force majeure or if he can show a ground of justification (e.g., self-defence).

The required standard of proof varies in the jurisdictions analysed. In England and Wales and the Netherlands the relevant standard of proof is the balance of probabilities. German, Spanish and Swedish law require that facts are established with high probability, while in Poland the required level of probability is close to certainty (beyond reasonable doubt).

The operator is liable for his own fault, but in all the jurisdictions also for the culpable behaviour of his agents. The rules on vicarious liability are, however, quite different (3.1.1.5.). Most jurisdictions follow a broad concept of vicarious liability and protect the employee also from recourse by the employer or direct third-party claims (England and Wales, France, Sweden, the Netherlands, Poland). Germany, however, restricts vicarious liability in non-contractual relationships. The employer is not liable for harm to third parties caused illegally by his agent if he proves that he exercised reasonable care when selecting the agent or managing the activity, or if the damage would have occurred even if this care had been exercised. Spanish law does not provide for vicarious liability in the strict sense, but holds employers nevertheless liable for damage caused by their employees by providing for a non-rebuttable presumption that the employer himself acted with fault.

Vicarious liability for an independent contractor who agrees with the principal to take over the whole responsibility for a certain activity is admissible in the Netherlands when the contractor's activity was actually, or at least in the perception of third parties, part of the client's business. Spanish law and Polish law require fault on behalf of the principal. Germany and Sweden do not accept vicarious liability for the independent contractor in extra-contractual liability. The independent contractor then assumes an independent duty in tort to protect third parties from harm caused by this activity or facility. This liability is fault-based and will not cover pure economic loss. All jurisdictions provide that contributory negligence of the claimant leads to a reduction of damages (3.1.1.4.).

5.1.1.2.   Strict liability

Operators of dangerous activities are very often, in addition to fault-based liability, subject to strict liability obligations. These may constitute general liability rules that provide for increased liability standards (see 3.1.3.1.), such as the rule in *Rylands* v. *Fletcher* in English law, the liability of the custodian of a thing according to Article 1384(1) French *Code civil* ("*responsabilité du fait des choses*"), the liability for the professional use or possession of dangerous substances according to Articles 6:175 Dutch BW et seq., or the broad liability for dangerous undertakings under Article 435 of the Polish Civil code. According to Article 435 of the Polish Civil code, the person who runs an undertaking set into motion by natural forces (steam, gas, electricity, liquid fuel etc.) is liable for any damage to persons and property caused through the operation of the enterprise or business. The operator is not liable in cases of force majeure, or if he proves that the damage was caused exclusively through the fault of the injured party or of a third party for whom he is not responsible. In Spains, courts tend to impose strict liability on the operator of abnormally dangerous goods or activities, although this is not explicitly provided by law. Germany and Sweden do not have such general strict liability rules but provide for a series of specific strict liability statutes.

All jurisdictions furthermore have special rules amounting to strict liability for damage caused to the neighbourhood by excessive polluting interference (England: private and public nuisance; France: "*troubles de voisinage*" etc.).

Most jurisdictions provide for strict liability rules for some specific activities, such as the operation of aeroplanes, GMOs, nuclear installations, medical products (pharmaceuticals) or environmental harm. These rules are partly provided by international conventions, such as the rules concerning the liability of the air carrier for damage caused to passengers (3.1.3.2.1.) or third-party liability for nuclear installations (3.1.3.2.3.) and partly on the national tort laws which are very incoherent in this regard. While all the analysed countries, with the exception of the Netherlands, provide for strict liability rules for harm caused to third persons by aeroplanes, this is not the case for the risks posed by genetically modified organisms (only Germany and Poland) or pharmaceuticals for which only Germany has a special strict liability regime (see 3.1.3.2.4.) Most of the countries analysed have special strict liability rules for activities that are dangerous for the environment (3.1.3.2.5.), which, however, differ a lot from each other.

5.2. Liability of security providers

5.2.1. Towards customers

Towards the client the security company is liable according to the **contract** concluded between the company and the client. The liability covers damages sustained by the client because of the fault of the security company, including fault of employees by way of vicarious liability, and comprises compensation for personal injury, property damage and pure economic loss.

The particulars of the liability of the security company are determined by the concrete contract. The parties are relatively free to shape the contents of the contract. It is evident that the security provider can only be liable, to the client (as well as to third parties), if he enters into a contractual obligation with the client. It is the contract which describes the tasks of the security company and the machinery the security company must use, and defines the security measures the company must provide. A company contracted to guard the premises of an industrial facility may, for instance, expressly stipulate that the security measures provided shall only prevent industrial espionage or shall only protect the client's personnel from personal injury. It must also be possible for the security provider to clarify that the stipulated security measures are not aimed at the prevention of damage caused by an act of sabotage or a terrorist attack.

As a specialist, the security provider must meet a high standard according to the special knowledge and abilities of a professional. He must inform the client of the available measures, devices and methods and must warn the client if he realises at the conclusion of the contract or later when fulfilling the contract that the stipulated security measures, devices or methods are inadequate or not sufficient for the stipulated task. If the contract clearly specifies the type of measure, device or method that must be provided by the security provider, then the client cannot claim that the security provider should have taken another measure or should have used another device or method when harm occurs. Liability of the security provider can then only be established for the failure to adequately inform and warn the client.

The contractual freedom also relates to stipulations for the contractual limitation of liability. They may thus limit the contractual liability of the security provider towards the client as well as the mutual-recourse obligations of both parties. The contractual freedom is rather broad and is only limited by national rules concerning the fairness of contractual clauses. According to these rules (see 3.5.2.), it would be rather problematic to limit fault-based liability for personal injury of the client (which can only play a role if he is a natural person) and his employees and to restrict the compensation of damage to property caused by gross negligence of the security provider. These restrictions, however, only apply for the direct liability of the security provider for such harm (damage to person and property) sustained by the client and his employees. They do not apply to other heads of damage (pure economic loss, environmental damage) and to the recourse obligation of the security provider for damage of third parties that were compensated by the client. Moreover, it must be considered that damage sustained by the client's employees will in many countries be compensated by workmen's compensation schemes.

5.2.2.   Towards third parties

5.2.2.1.   Fault-based liability

5.2.2.1.1.   Duty of care   The liability of the security company towards third parties is regulated by the rules of extra-contractual liability. There are two heads of liability available: fault-based liability (3.1.1.) and product liability (3.1.2.), if the harm was caused by a product in the sense of the EU Product Liability Directive which was put into circulation by the security company.

Fault-based liability always requires the breach of a standard of care. This standard of care is primarily defined by the contract the security provider concluded with the client. The wording and contents of the contract not only shape the potential liability towards the client, but also towards third parties. The contract is key in respect of the question to which persons the security provider owes a duty of care, whether only to the client and his employees or also to other persons who permanently or temporarily sojourn on the guarded premises, such as tenants, visitors or shoppers, or even to third parties outside the controlled premises.

If harm occurs, the victim who is part of this group is allowed in many countries to sue the security provider directly for damages. The relevant theories in this respect vary. It may be that courts allow the victim to rely on the contract between client and security provider to which is attributed a protective scope for the concrete victim (*Vertrag mit Schutzwirkung zu Gunsten Dritter*) or courts may conclude that the security provider assumed such responsibility for the concrete victim when he concluded the contract. As the duties of the security provider are specified by the contract, a third party will – like the client – not be able to base a liability claim on the fact that the security provider did not provide a certain service if the security provider is not contractually obliged to render this service (e.g., to provide video surveillance or to monitor incoming vehicles for explosives). In this case, the security provider will only be liable for the failure to adequately warn the client of the risk so that the client was therefore not able to take adequate measures to prevent the damage. As long as the security provider acts as an auxiliary of the client it is the client who is primarily responsible that third parties are not harmed by his activity. A broad liability for third parties, however, will apply if the security provider contractually takes over the responsibility from the client to provide for the security of a facility or a certain activity. In many countries this situation is described by the theory of the liability of the independent contractor.

In this regard it is important to note that the breach of a contractual duty towards the client does not automatically amount to tortious behaviour towards a third party. Most reporters indicated this quite clearly when they discussed Case 2 of Chapter 4. The reporter for England and Wales explained that English law recognises, according to the "*Caparo* test", only a duty of care towards the plaintiff if the damage was foreseeable and the requirements of proximity and, as a broad-policy consideration, the requirements of fairness, justice and reasonableness are met. In most civil law countries a comparable effect is generated by the criterion of unlawfulness. Only French law allows the third party to rely for the action in tort on the breach of the contractual duty between the security provider and the client, but French law requires a sufficiently direct link between the incurred damage and the behaviour of the tortfeasor and thus restricts the right to claim damages with reference to considerations of causality. These restrictions apply to all types of damage, but are quite essential for the compensability of pure economic loss sustained by third parties.

5.2.2.1.2.   Effect of regulations for the security provider on fault-based liability
Security enterprises are often engaged in areas that are heavily regulated by public law. This applies to the operation of nuclear installations and airports as well as to industrial plants for the production of pharmaceuticals, genetically modified organisms or hazardous material. These rules are addressed to the operators of these activities. Security enterprises are only indirectly affected by them.

Rules regulating the activity of the security industry itself are comparatively rare (see 3.2.2.). Such rules can influence the tort liability of the security provider. The liability of the security provider is mainly determined by fault-based liability. In fault-based liability public law rules governing the behaviour of the security provider can affect the determination of the required standard of care. Regulation by public law will usually increase the required standard of care and thus tighten the liability obligations of the security enterprise. For courts, the failure to comply with regulation is a strong indication that the defendant breached the required standard of care under tort liability. In several countries fault-based liability is aggravated in case of breach of a statutory rule with a protective scope (*Schutzgesetz*). Compliance with public law standards, however, does not necessarily exempt from liability. In all the jurisdictions analysed, courts usually rely on such rules but do not feel bound by them. Standards set by courts according to the circumstances of the case can thus surpass the standards set by public law.

5.2.2.2.   Product liability

If the damage is caused by a product that was put into circulation by the security company, liability is regulated according to the Product Liability Directive. Many reporters stress that national courts still apply specific national product liability rules derived from fault-based liability (England and Wales, France, Germany, the Netherlands).

Liability under the national laws implementing the Product Liability Directive is irrespective of fault. It does not include the compensation of pure economic loss and environmental damage if the environmental damage does not constitute personal injury or property damage. The national laws implementing the Directive[1] follow the rules of the Directive very closely, although some deviations gave rise to infringement proceedings before the European Court of Justice. All the countries analysed allow for the development risk defence as provided by Article 7(e) of the Directive, except for certain products (France: products derived from the human body; Germany: pharmaceuticals; Spain: medicines, food or foodstuffs for human consumption) and, except for Spain, include the recovery of non-pecuniary damages. Germany and Spain provide for liability caps in the case of death or personal injury (Germany: 85 million euro; Spain: 63,106,270.96 euro).

5.2.3.   Recourse of operator against security provider and vice versa

If indivisible damage is caused by two or several tortfeasors, although by independent and separate acts, it is the general rule in all jurisdictions that the tortfeasors are jointly and severally liable. As a consequence, each tortfeasor can be sued by the victim for the entire sum of compensation. The tortfeasor who compensated the victim then has a right of **recourse** against the other contributors (see 3.4.1.). The decisive criteria for the assessment of the shares of the contributors are quite different in the countries analysed. The apportionment may be carried out according

---

[1] France: Law no. 98–389 from 19 May 1998 which inserted the new section IV "*de la responsabilité du fait des produits défectueux*" (Article 1386–1 to 1386–18) into the *Code civil*; Germany: *Produkthaftungsgesetz*; Sweden: *Produktansvarslag* (1992:18); UK: Consumer Protection Act 1987; Poland: Article 449^1–449^{10} civil code; Spain: Law 23/1994 from 6 July 1994, "*de responsabilidad civil por los daños causados por productos defectuosos*" (LRPD) as revised by Royal Legislative Decree 1/2007 of 16 November 2007 "*por el que se aprueba el texto refundido de la Ley General para la Defensa de los Consumidores y Usuarios y otras leyes complementarias*" (TRLDCU).

to the seriousness of fault of each contributor, or simply per capita or according to the particular circumstances of the individual case.

The right of recourse applies to the client who compensated the victim for the loss incurred and vice versa to the security company if both client and security company are liable for the same damage. It must be borne in mind that the recourse between the client and the security company can be regulated by the **contract** concluded between both parties. It can be adjusted to the special circumstances of the situation and it is admissible that the client limits or completely renounces his right of recourse against the security provider.

5.3.   Liability for pure economic loss and environmental damage

In all jurisdictions fault-based liability covers damages for personal injury, harm to property and consequential economic loss. Compensation for **pure economic loss** is rather restricted and the rules for the compensation for **environmental damage** are rather complex and diverse in the various jurisdictions (see under 3.5.1.). In England and Wales, Germany and Sweden pure economic loss is only recoverable under exceptional circumstances. In the other countries (France, the Netherlands, Poland and Spain), which do not distinguish between pure economic loss and the other heads of damages in the first place, the compensability of pure economic loss is restricted by further considerations, such as the necessity for a sufficiently direct causal link (France, Spain), by the concept of adequacy (Poland) or by more general considerations (the Netherlands).

From the reporters' answers to Case 2 in Chapter 4 (defective safety programmable logic controller) it can be concluded that mistakes by the security provider in the exercise of the contractual duties towards the operator of the undertaking do not necessarily lead to liability for pure economic loss of third parties and for the prevention and remediation of environmental harm. In the answer to Case 2 the English reporter denied any liability of the operator of the chemical plant and of the security company for the cost of the relief measures of the fire brigade (C) and the water supplier (D) or for the lost profits of factory G. Liability of the operator of the chemical plant (under the rule in *Rylands*v. *Fletcher*) and of the security provider (under negligence) do not cover pure economic loss or environmental damage. Liability, thus, exists only with respect to the neighbour E, who suffers property damage and personal injury.

The French reporter came to the conclusion that the security provider would in any case only be liable for a small share of the losses. Direct liability of the security provider under general fault-based liability to third parties seemed rather doubtful to the French reporter, who discussed the responsibility of the security provider primarily under the aspect of contractual recourse of the operator of the chemical plant against the security provider. The recourse action requires under Article 1150 of the French *Code civil* foreseeability of the damage at the conclusion of the contract and, according to Article 1151 *Code civil*, a sufficiently direct link between the breach of the contractual duty and the loss. For the concrete case the French reporter doubted the existence of such sufficiently direct link.

The German reporter came to a similar conclusion as the English reporter. The operator of the chemical plant and the security provider are only liable to neighbour E who suffered property damage and personal injury. Available heads of liability for the operator of the chemical plant are the strict liability rules in § 1 UmwHG (environmental liability statute) and § 89(2) *Wasserhaushaltsgesetz* (Water Act; WHG). Both strict liability statutes (UmwHG, § 89 WHG) provide for an exemption in case of force majeure. There is no liability of the security provider either for the relief measures of the fire brigade C, the water supplier D or the loss sustained by company G, as the security provider is only liable according to fault-based liability under § 823 BGB which does not include compensation for pure economic loss and environmental damage. As fault-based liability only covers foreseeable damage, the German reporter is of the opinion that the security provider is not liable even if the computer program was especially designed for the prevention of pollution damage in case of natural disasters, if the earthquake was of an exceptional character (Case 2, Question b). The German reporter further discusses the question of whether defective software can be regarded as a product under the Product Liability Directive, which is unclear. This question was also raised by the Dutch and the Spanish reporter.

In Dutch law the operator of the chemical plant would be liable under Article 6:175 BW which provides for strict liability of the operator of dangerous substances. As in all the other countries, the security provider is only liable according to fault-based liability. Both heads of liability would cover the claims of the fire brigade C (given that it was not a public but a private entity), the water supplier D and neighbour E, but both subject to the restriction of Article 6:98 BW which gives courts considerable flexibility for the attribution of the different heads of damage to the tortfeasor. As it is thus in the discretion of the courts whether they award compensation of pure economic loss or not, the Dutch reporter seriously doubts whether the lost profits of company G will be compensable at all. The strict liability of the operator, moreover, underlies a series of defences according to Article 6:178 BW which includes, inter alia, damage resulting from armed conflict, civil war, revolt, riots, insurgence or mutiny, or damage caused by a natural event of an exceptional, unavoidable and irresistible nature, or by an intentional act of a third party.

In Spain the operator of the chemical plant B is liable according to the Spanish implementation law of the EU Environmental Liability Directive for costs of relief measures incurred by the fire brigade C and could claim for contractual recourse from the security provider A. This head of liability does not include the damage sustained by the water supplier D. The neighbour E and the company G could claim damages under general tort law (Articles 1902 and 1908 *Código civil*) which provides for aggravated liability in cases of environmental damage. The company G will only be able to claim the lost profits if the loss is certain and if there is a sufficiently close causal link. The security provider A would be directly liable to the water supplier D and the neighbour E under fault-based liability. According to the estimation of the Spanish reporter, no liability will apply to the operator and the security provider if the earthquake could be seen as an act of God and in case of a terrorist attack.

In Sweden the fire brigade C and the water supplier D cannot sue the operator B or the security provider A for the losses sustained, as public authorities are not entitled to claim such damages under general tort law. The operator B is only liable to neighbour E and company G under the strict liability regime of the Environmental Code (chapter 32 section 3), although, according to the estimation of the Swedish reporters, liability towards G may be rejected because of lack of adequate causation. The exceptional strength of the earthquake does not serve as a defence in Swedish tort law which does not provide for such defences outside the implementation acts of international liability conventions, such as the Paris Convention on nuclear liability. Chapter 10 section 19 of the Environmental Code, however, excludes the State's right to environmental clean-up costs in cases of exceptional natural disasters. With respect to acts of terror, liability under the Environmental Code may be declined pursuant to the notion that strict liability only covers the typical risk of the concrete strict liability regime. An act of terror, however, does not constitute a typical risk for an environmental liability statute. According to the Swedish reporters, the security provider A is not liable at all, as A infringed only a contractual duty towards the operator B and has no non-contractual duty towards third parties like the neighbour E.

The only reporter who held the operator of the chemical plant B and, by way of recourse, also the security provider A to be fully liable was the Polish reporter. The operator of the chemical plant would be liable under strict liability (Article 435 civil code; Environmental Protection Law) and, according to the estimation of the Polish reporter, the operator would in the concrete case not be able to invoke the defence of force majeure, either in the case of the exceptionally strong earthquake or the terrorist attack.

5.4.   Liability for damage caused by natural disaster or act of terror

5.4.1.   Case 2: Negligence and fault-based liability

The main head of liability for the security provider as regards third parties is the tort of negligence in the common law and fault-based liability in civil law countries. Both liability regimes require causation and the establishment of a breach of a duty of care. Under negligence (common law) and fault-based liability (civil law) the tortfeasor is only liable for harm that would not have occurred if the tortfeasor had not breached the duty of care. Neither the operator of a dangerous activity nor the security provider is liable for unforeseeable harm or harm that would not have been prevented by reasonable safety precautions. Both the operator and the security provider must meet an objective standard according to their special knowledge and abilities.

If the damage is caused by a natural disaster (Case 2: earthquake) or by an intentional act by a third party (Case 2: terrorist attack), the security provider will only be liable if he had a duty of care to prevent the occurrence of a specific type of damage in such a scenario. With respect to the client, the duty of care of the security provider will be specified by the contract. These contractual obligations govern the direct liability of the security provider for the damage sustained by the client himself and also in respect of the question if and to what extent the operator will be able to seek recourse from the security provider (for compensation rendered to third parties according to the heads of liability that are applicable to the operator). With respect to third parties, the question of whether the security provider owed them a duty of care or not must be assessed according to general tort law. For this assessment the contractual obligations of the security provider towards the client are very important, but not solely decisive.

Under strict liability such events (natural disaster, terrorist attack) are qualified in most countries[2] as a "force majeure" or "act of God" and may exonerate the person who is subject to the strict liability regime from liability. This, as most of the national reporters indicate in the answers to Case 2, will however only be the case if the event was of an external, unpredictable and irresistible character (French report) or, as defined by the German *Bundesgerichtshof*[3] as cited in the German report, if the event was "an external incident caused by natural forces or by third-party acts that cannot be foreseen and that cannot be avoided with reasonable cost and with utmost care and that also must not be accepted due to its frequent occurrence". This defence, however, applies not to the security provider, who usually is only under an obligation of fault-based liability, but to the operator of the activity which gives rise to strict liability. For the security provider it is only of importance for the recourse obligation towards the operator.

5.4.2.   Case 3: Public service undertaking

Case 3 of Chapter 4 explores the liability of the provider of security services in case of a terrorist attack against a public service (infrastructure) undertaking and the recourse option of the public service undertaking against the renderer of security services.

The question of whether an infrastructure undertaking (waterworks of city B) or the security provider of the waterworks A are liable for the poisoning of the water by a terrorist was answered very differently by the national reporters. In all the countries the water supplier is contractually liable to the consumers and, except in Sweden, the liability of the water supplier would require that the water supplier was at fault or vicariously liable for A.

Most reporters had serious doubts whether the security provider can be held directly liable by the victims of the attack. Only the reporter for England and Wales and the German reporter held A liable for the damage sustained by house-owner D. The Dutch reporter saw only liability for the personal injury of D, and the reporters from Spain, France, Poland and Sweden more or less rejected A's liability. In most countries there is no vicarious liability of the infrastructure undertaking for fault of the security provider who is regarded as an independent contractor either. Vicarious liability for the independent contractor is only recognised in German

---

[2] An exception is Sweden.   [3] See BGH, 23 October 1952, 7 BGHZ 338.

contract law and in the Netherlands. The Dutch reporter, however, like the Spanish reporter, came to the conclusion that water poisoning by a terrorist would be regarded as force majeure and the water supplier would thus not be contractually liable to the consumers. German law provides for special provisions for the public water supply and restricts compensation to personal injury and property damage. In France damage caused by terrorist acts is primarily borne by the FGTI. Only loss that is not covered by the Fund, namely property damage and pure economic loss, falls under the tort law system.

The only country where the water supplier would be fully liable under strict liability is Sweden. Liability is regulated by the Environmental Code and covers personal injury and property damage. The fact that the damage was caused by an intentional act by a third party (the terrorist) does not exclude liability, as the defence of force majeure is not provided in the Environmental Code. The water supplier will have a right of contractual recourse against the security provider A.

Another head of liability would be product liability of the waterworks, as water distributed by waterworks can certainly be regarded as a product in the sense of the Product Liability Directive. Product liability only covers damages for personal injury and property.

The liability of the security provider for the costs of **disaster relief measures taken by State E** was denied by most reporters, although with different reasoning. In England and Wales the decisive reason was that such costs are regarded as pure economic loss which is not covered by the tort of negligence. For the French reporter there was no sufficient causal relationship, as the decision of State E to grant aid is a free choice that breaks the causal chain. For the Dutch, Polish and Swedish reporters the security provider was not liable for such costs. According to the Spanish reporter, however, such costs are not excluded per se. Under the condition that fault of the security provider can be established, the liability of the security provider would also include such costs. German law would provide for a similar solution, although not under tort law but on the basis of *negotiorum gestio*.

5.4.3.   Case 4: Border control

The goal of Case 4 in Chapter 4 was to explore liability of the public authority for defaults of the renderer of security services and the recourse option of the public authority. For all reporters it was quite difficult to establish the liability of State B or the security provider as there is no case law on this. The reporters from four jurisdictions (France, Germany, Poland and Sweden) were of the opinion that State B would not be liable according to tort law for damage to a private person, caused by a terrorist who slipped through the border control and, consequently, there was no right of recourse against the renderer of the flawed security service. The reason was that the connection between the public duty of border control and the damage sustained is too loose. The French reporter discussed this notion with reference to the concept of causation, while the other reporters denied, or at least seriously doubted, that the public duty to control the border has the aim of protecting the individual citizen from a terrorist attack.

The other reporters came to the conclusion that there would be liability of the State if fault can be established and the damage was foreseeable (e.g., England and Wales, the Netherlands, Spain). All reports have in common that there is no difference between the security consultant and the contractor for the video surveillance installation at the border crossing, except for the fact that the latter might rather be regarded as an independent contractor for whom the State would not be vicariously liable (see the Polish and the Spanish report).

5.4.4.   Case 5: Aeroplane crash

Case 5 of Chapter 4 explores the liability of the renderer of airport security services in case of an aeroplane accident caused both by a careless passenger and a terrorist.

As outlined in 2.1.1.3.2., liability of the air carrier for damage caused to passengers is regulated by Regulation 889/02. The air carrier is obliged to compensate passengers for death and bodily injury for up to 113,100 SDR subject only to the defence of contributory fault of the victim. For damage exceeding this cap, the air carrier is liable according to fault-based liability with presumption of fault. The air carrier is exonerated if it proves that the damage was not due to the negligence or other wrongful act or omission of the carrier or its servants or agents, or that the damage was solely due to the negligence or other wrongful act or omission of a third party. Damage to persons other than passengers is regulated by national law.

The answers to Case 5 are much more straightforward than those to Cases 3 and 4. All the reporters except those from Sweden came to the conclusion that air carrier E can claim the costs of repairing the damaged aeroplane and the costs for the emergency landing from the security provider A under fault-based liability (civil law) or negligence (common law), if the security provider negligently failed to detect the highly inflammable chemicals in the hand baggage of the passenger. In England and Wales the tort of negligence would also cover the damage claims of the injured passengers. The security provider owes a duty of care towards both plaintiffs, airline E and the passengers, because of the assumption of responsibility to prevent exactly such damage. Even the fact that the fire was started by the intentional act of a third party, namely the terrorist, would not exonerate the security provider from liability under English law. The liability of the security provider extends also to claims of third parties who sustain personal injury and property damage, if the aeroplane crashes and the air carrier who is strictly liable for such damage under the Civil Aviation Act would have a right of full recourse against the security provider.

In France the main question for the liability of the security provider is the requirement of a direct causal link between the act and the damage. For the damaged aeroplane, the cost of the emergency landing and the harmed passengers, the French reporter affirmed liability, as the security provider was expressly in charge to prevent such damage, both in the case of the careless passenger and the terrorist. With respect to third parties harmed by an aeroplane crash caused by a terrorist, the causal link between the carelessness of the security provider and the damage, however, would be too remote. The French reporter hence denied direct liability of the security provider towards third parties and saw no room for an action of recourse by the liable airline against the security provider. If the damage was caused by a terrorist attack, the FGTI would compensate the claims for personal injury. The Fund can then seek recourse from the airline and the security provider as far as they are liable.

In German law the security provider would be liable under fault-based liability of § 823(1) BGB to the harmed passengers and to airline E in the case of the careless passenger. If the damage was caused by a terrorist the German reporter already hesitated to assume liability for the security provider as, according to tort law, it is the airline which is liable for damage to passengers. Liability for the aeroplane crash caused by a terrorist was frankly denied by the German reporter. Liability for such damage lies with the airline. Strict liability of the airline under § 33 Air Traffic Act (LuftVG) covers damage to persons and property up to a certain liability cap and there is no exception for terrorist attacks or force majeure in general. Airline E would have no recourse against the security provider, as there is no contract between the airline and the security provider, and the security provider is not liable for the damage.

In the Netherlands the security provider is liable under fault-based liability for the damage to the injured passengers and the damage incurred by the airline. Courts, however, may mitigate the compensation under Article 6:109 BW if the extent of the damages would be excessively burdensome for the security provider. In Dutch law the airline is not strictly liable for the damage caused to third parties by the aircraft. The Dutch reporters, however, assume that the security provider would be liable for the aeroplane crash caused by the terrorist. Again the reduction clause of Article 6:109 BW may be applied to reduce the liability burden.

In Poland the security provider would be liable under fault-based liability to the harmed passengers and to airline E when the damage was caused by the careless passenger, but not by a terrorist. The airline would have a right of recourse for damages paid to the passengers. For damage incurred by third parties the airline would be liable according to Articles 206–207 Aviation Law. If the damage is caused by a terrorist attack, liability is excluded and, hence, there is no recourse against the security provider.

In Spain, as in all the other countries, the security provider would be liable under fault-based liability for the damage incurred by airline E (damage to the aeroplane and the cost of the emergency landing), both in case of the careless passenger and the terrorist. For the damage sustained by the passengers liability lies with the airline. The airline is strictly liable for damage caused to third parties under the Act of Aeronautical Navigation (LNA) which does not provide for a defence when the damage was intentionally caused by a third party. The liability is limited in amount unless the operator of the aircraft acted with fault. The Spanish reporter saw also a good reason for State liability, as the security guards at airports act under the control and the orders of the public administration.

For the Swedish reporters it is the airport operator and the police authority that are responsible for airport safety. Airline E can thus claim for the damage sustained (cost of repairing the aeroplane and cost of the emergency landing) according to contractual liability from airport B who then may take contractual recourse against the security provider A. Extra-contractual liability of the security provider could only be assumed if A acted with gross negligence or intent or, quite speculatively, if A breached a non-contractual duty to prevent damage to E. If A can be held extra-contractually liable to E, which is rather uncertain, then A will also be liable for damage caused by a terrorist, as Swedish law does not per se exclude liability for an intentional act by a third party. In the scenario of the aeroplane crash caused by the terrorist, liability would lie with airline E according to the Act on Liability for Damage Caused in the Course of Aviation. Direct liability of the security provider to third parties would require that the security provider owes the general public an extra-contractual duty to prevent damage, which the Swedish reporters seriously doubt.

5.5. Conclusions

5.5.1. Liability of operators of dangerous activities

All operators of dangerous activities are liable to third parties under fault-based liability respectively negligence in common law.

In addition operators of dangerous activities are very often also subject to strict liability obligations. These are general liability rules with increased liability standards, such as the rule in *Rylandsv. Fletcher* in English law, the liability of the custodian of a thing according to Article 1384(1) French *Code civil* ("*responsabilité du fait des choses*"), liability for the professional use or possession of dangerous substances according to Articles 6:175 Dutch BW et seq., or liability for dangerous undertakings under Article 435 of the Polish Civil code. Germany and Sweden do not have such general strict liability rules but provide for a series of specific strict liability statutes. All jurisdictions furthermore have special rules amounting to strict liability for damage caused to the neighbourhood by excessive polluting interference (England: private and public nuisance; France: "*troubles de voisinage*" etc.).

Special strict liability regimes regulate third-party liability for aeroplanes, genetically modified organisms, nuclear installations, medical products (pharmaceuticals) and environmental harm.

5.5.2. Liability of security providers

5.5.2.1. Liability to customers

The security provider is liable to the client for **breach of the contract** concluded. As a specialist and professional, the security provider must meet a high standard according to the special knowledge and abilities of the profession. He must inform the client of the available security measures, devices and achievable security standards and must warn the client of the risks should the client not opt for the best available solution.

The same applies when the security provider takes note of this fact while performing the contract. If the contract specifies the type of measure, device or method that must be provided by the security provider, then the client cannot claim when harm occurs that the security provider should have taken another measure or should have used another device or method. Liability of the security provider can then only be established for the failure to adequately inform and warn the client.

The parties are free to shape the contents of the contract and can restrict the contractual liability of the security provider towards the client as well as the mutual recourse obligations of both parties. The contractual freedom is only limited by rules concerning the fairness of contractual clauses.

5.5.2.2.   Liability towards third parties

Towards third parties, the security provider is liable according to the rules of extra-contractual liability. There are two heads of liability available: fault-based liability and product liability, if the harm was caused by a product in the sense of the EU Product Liability Directive, which was produced and put into circulation by the security provider.

Fault-based liability requires the breach of a duty of care. The wording and contents of the contract shape the potential liability of the security provider towards third parties. The contract not only defines the duties of the security provider, but also circumscribes to which persons the security provider owes a duty of care. The victim who is part of the protected group may sue the security provider directly for damages. With respect to third parties too, the security provider can in principle only be obliged to fulfil his contractual obligations. He cannot be held liable by the client or any third party for the fact that the stipulated measure, device or security standard does not meet the highest standard provided by the industry. Liability can only then arise if the security provider, who knew or should have known that the security measures are inadequate, failed to inform the client of this fact in order to enable the client to take measures to prevent the damage. If the security provider, however, contractually agrees to provide for the security of a facility or an activity in a comprehensive and independent way, the security provider will also assume the liability in torts towards third parties. In many countries this situation is described by the theory of the liability of the **independent contractor**.

The breach of a contractual duty does not automatically amount to tortious behaviour towards a third party. All the seven jurisdictions that were examined provide for specific concepts to restrict the responsibility of the tortfeasor for harm that is not reasonably foreseeable or too remote. These restrictions play an important role for the liability of the security provider for damage caused by a natural disaster or by the intentional act of a third party. They apply to all types of damage, but are essential in respect of the compensability of pure economic loss sustained by third parties.

If the damage is caused by a product that was produced and put into circulation by the security provider, liability is regulated according to the rules of **product liability** set out by the Product Liability Directive. Liability under the national laws implementing the Product Liability Directive is irrespective of fault and covers compensation for damage caused by death and personal injury as well as damage to property intended for private use or consumption with a lower threshold of 500 euro. Liability does not cover the compensation of pure economic loss and environmental damage which does not constitute property damage. The decision whether liability includes the recovery of non-material damage (pain and suffering) is left to the Member States (Article 9 Product Liability Directive). Recovery for non-material damage under product liability is provided by all of the jurisdictions analysed except for Spain.

5.5.3.   Pure economic loss and environmental harm

In all jurisdictions fault-based liability covers damages for personal injury, harm to property and consequential-economic loss. Under extra-contractual liability, compensation for **pure economic loss** is rather restricted. In England and Wales, Germany and Sweden pure economic loss is only recoverable under exceptional circumstances. In the other countries (France, the Netherlands, Poland and Spain), which do not distinguish between pure economic loss and the other heads of damage in the first place, the compensability of pure economic loss is restricted by further considerations, such as the necessity of a sufficiently direct causal link (France, Spain) or by the concept of adequacy (Poland) or by more general considerations (the Netherlands).

The responsibility of the security provider will not usually extend to the compensation of **environmental damage** such as relief measures taken by a public entity, preventive measures by the public authority or remedial action, as the security provider is not liable according to the Environmental Liability Directive. The national rules for compensation of environmental damage are rather complex and diverse in the various jurisdictions.

5.5.4. Multiple causation and recourse

If both the operator of a dangerous activity and the security provider are liable for the same damage,[4] joint and several liability applies. Each tortfeasor can be sued by the victim for the entire sum of compensation and the tortfeasor who compensated the victim has a right of **recourse** against the other contributor. The right of recourse can be regulated in the contract concluded between the operator and the security provider and can be adjusted to the special circumstances of the situation.

5.5.5. Standard and burden of proof

The required **standard of proof** for the establishment of fault or causation varies in the jurisdictions analysed. In England and Wales and the Netherlands the relevant standard of proof is the balance of probabilities. In the other countries facts must be established with high probability or even with certainty which means that the court must be convinced beyond reasonable doubt.

All the jurisdictions provide that in extra-contractual liability the **burden of proof** lies with the claimant. For fault-based liability this applies to the proof of the damage sustained, fault and causation. Under product liability the injured person must prove damage, the defect in the product and the causal link between damage and defect. In all the countries analysed, courts have some discretion with respect to the establishment of fault and causation. Such discretion ranges from the doctrine of *res ipsa loquitur* or prima facie evidence for the proof of fault to complex strategies for the establishment of causation in cases of mere statistical evidence. Under certain circumstances the burden of proof may be shifted partly or entirely to the defendant. These strategies are often applied in medical malpractice or in environmental liability cases and have no specific relevance for the security industry.

---

[4] E.g., the client under a strict liability regime and the security provider under fault-based liability, or both under fault-based liability for the breach of a duty of care they owed to the victim.

All of the national legal systems analysed provide for special rules on **case management**, but none of the national legal systems analysed provides for a US-style class action.

5.5.6. Liability of operators or security providers for damage caused by natural disaster or act of terror

Fault-based liability requires the breach of a duty of care and the establishment of a causal link between the breach and the damage incurred. If the damage is caused by a natural disaster or by an intentional act of a third party, the operator of the activity or the security provider will only be liable if he had a duty of care to prevent the occurrence of such damage.

Operators of dangerous activities are often under an obligation of strict liability. In strict liability, however, such events (natural disaster, terrorist attack) are qualified in most countries as a "force majeure" or "act of God" and may exonerate the person who is subject to the strict liability regime from liability. This defence applies only to the operator and not to the security provider (who usually is only under an obligation of fault-based liability). For the security provider it is of indirect relevance, as there will be no recourse obligation towards the client, if his client is not liable.

For the security provider the main head of liability towards third parties is fault-based liability. With respect to the operator of the activity (his client), the duty of care of the security provider will be specified by the contract. These contractual obligations govern the direct liability of the security provider for the damage sustained by the client himself and also for the question of whether and to what extent the client will be able to seek recourse from the security provider for compensation rendered to third parties.

With respect to direct liability towards third parties, the question of whether the security provider owes them a duty of care or not must be assessed according to general tort law. For this assessment the contractual obligations of the security provider towards the client are very important. Liability can only be imputed to the security provider if his contractual duties implied the duty to prevent such damage. Even if the security provider assumed responsibility for the prevention of such damage in the contract, he may not be directly liable to third parties as the link between the carelessness of the security provider and the damage sustained may be assessed as too remote to trigger liability.

Damage caused by terrorist attacks is often compensated by the State. In France, Spain and the UK special compensation schemes for victims of terrorism have been established. While the British compensation scheme only grants compensation to victims of terrorism who cannot obtain compensation from other sources, the French and the Spanish compensation schemes provide for subrogation.

PART III

Assessment of liability for terrorism-related risk

6

Insurance of terrorism-related risks

MICHAEL FAURE AND NIELS PHILIPSEN

An important instrument to spread the risks of terrorism is insurance. Insurance may thus be an important instrument for both operators and the security industry to limit their risk exposure. This chapter will deal with the way in which insurance can act as a risk-spreading mechanism. It will first provide the legal and economic background to insurance, discuss conditions of insurability, explain the difference between first-party and third-party insurance and discuss techniques that are used in the insurance industry to remedy the so-called "moral hazard" risk (6.1.). Next, specific attention will be paid to catastrophe insurance and more particularly the insurance of man-made disasters. Some difficulties in the insurance of catastrophes will be sketched; in that respect attention will be paid to solutions that have been developed to deal with supply-side problems and demand-side problems, especially the emergence of so-called public–private partnerships in the insurance of (man-made) disasters (6.2.). It will be shown that those types of solutions have not only been employed for traditional man-made disasters, but also for the insurance of terrorism (6.3.). Other solutions that have been developed in the related field of natural disasters will be discussed in Chapter 8 of this book, which addresses alternative systems for redressing terrorism-related risks. Section 6.4. concludes.

6.1. Insurance: Legal and economic background

This section discusses the legal approach of insurance companies towards man-made risk (terrorism and large-scale industrial accidents with a chemical, biological, radiological, nuclear or explosive component) and natural disasters. The focus is on contractual features of liability policies, as well as case law pertaining to insurance claims due to man-made and natural disasters, including the position of insurers in these cases and the main reasoning that led to the outcome of the cases. Although the analysis centres on European cases and companies, a few other examples (the Bhopal disaster in 1984, the BP "Deepwater Horizon" oil spill in 2010) are briefly discussed.

Before discussing the way insurance manages risk, we first present a discussion of how insurance works and why it is desirable. This discussion is relevant to understanding risk management by insurers and the limits of insurance. Then, in the section on managing liability risks, we focus also on recent development in the area of insurance against the risks of terrorism.

Insurance is generally deemed desirable because it spreads risks. There are two type of risk-spreading: spreading over time (inter-temporal) and spreading over persons (inter-personal). Corporations are generally believed to be in a substantially better position than any single individual to spread risks broadly.[1]

6.1.1. Reducing risks

Insurance as an objective (or function) of civil liability has also been defended on grounds derived from insurance theory. In simple terms, insurance involves a choice to incur a small and certain loss (the premium) now in exchange for not being exposed to a larger, uncertain loss in the future. Like risk-spreading generally, insurance is attractive to risk-averse persons (and risk-averse societies). More precisely, insurance meets needs in society because it shifts risks from persons with inferior risk-bearing capabilities to persons with superior risk-bearing capabilities.

The theory of diminishing marginal utility of money can explain insurance only in terms of inter-temporal and inter-personal risk-spreading. However, insurance is a complicated mechanism for managing risk. In addition to risk-spreading, insurance has important risk-reducing effects. Its risk-reducing effects, according to Priest (1987), are likely to be far more significant than the risk-spreading effects. Insurance reduces risks in two ways: first, it reduces the underlying injury rate and, second, it reduces the effective cost of remaining injuries by lowering the magnitude of total risk. Since an insurance company aggregates many potential

---

[1] See Calabresi 1970, 47–55. As Priest has pointed out, under this theory an incidental social benefit of corporate-provided insurance is that it offers insurance coverage to consumers that would not otherwise obtain insurance. See Priest 1985.

losses incurred by the insured pool, the law of large numbers makes the total loss to the insurance company highly predictable, as a result of which the insurance company's reserves for anticipated losses is much smaller than the total of all reserves of individual risk bearers and, thus, losses ,can be dealt with more efficiently.[2] Insurance thus permits corporations to reduce or eliminate their reserves for anticipated losses so that their capital can be put to more efficient uses. In addition to risk aggregation, insurance employs risk segregation by defining risk pools and setting premiums according to the average level of risk brought to the pool. Both risk aggregation and risk segregation serve to reduce risk variance and, thus, insurance premiums. By segregating an individual into a risk pool with a sufficiently narrow range of exposures to risks, the insurance premium remains attractive to persons in the low end of the range.[3] This technique will keep the risk pool intact. Once the disparity between the insurance premium and the exposure of the low-risk pool members becomes too great, the risk pool will unravel.[4] Segregation reduces both pool risk and insurance cost and, accordingly, adverse selection (to be discussed below).

As noted above, insurance can help also to reduce the level of injuries actually suffered.[5] This effect flows directly from the risk-segregation function of insurance. Through the size of the premium charged, insurance informs decisions as to whether and how much to engage in the covered activity: high risks are charged a high premium and thus there is an incentive to scale down the activity. As a result of extremely high premiums, very high-risk individuals may not be able to contract insurance and may refrain from engaging in the pertinent activity, which may make the activity safer. In addition, to the extent that insurance companies possess superior knowledge about risk reduction and bring this expertise to bear in their relations with insureds, insurance can also play a direct role in risk reduction.[6] Thus, in addition to possible benefits through increasing utility, insurance may result in increased efficiency through reduced total risk.

---

[2] See Riegel, Miller and Williams Jr. 1976, 15–21; Marshall 1974.
[3] The more precisely risks are segregated, the more accurately premiums reflect the risk brought to the pool, the more broadly insurance is available in the society.
[4] See Priest 1987.
[5] Insurance's risk-reducing effect can be counteracted by the "moral hazard" arising from insurance coverage. This issue is discussed below.
[6] Insurance also provides a valuable function by monitoring the activities of the insured: see Freeman and Kunreuther 1997, 25.

6.1.2. Conditions of insurability

Not each and every risk[7] can be insured. To be insurable and for insurance to deliver the benefits discussed above, risks must meet certain prerequisites. The main requirements are the following. First, the risks to be insured must have a sufficiently probabilistic character. Insurability requires that risk is probabilistic either as to *whether* it will occur (e.g., a fire risk), or as to *when* it will occur (e.g., death). If there is no reliable information on whether or when, on average, damage occurs, insurability will be adversely affected. If the damage will likely or certainly occur, the aggregation advantages of pooling cannot be obtained. As a related matter, risks must be sufficiently predictable and quantifiable in monetary terms. If the risk posed by any given pool of policy holders cannot be predicted with a reasonable degree of confidence, insurance is impeded. If risks are entirely unpredictable in terms of probability and size of potential harm, they cannot be insured.[8] On the other hand, the magnitude of risks and size of potential harm do not have to be fully understood and quantifiable. Insurers can handle some degree of uncertainty in this regard but there are limits. If the risk to be insured is the risk of being held liable for damages, the applicable rules govern the size and scope of the risk. This, in turn, means that the law itself must be sufficiently certain and precise. One particular risk seriously undermining insurability is the risk of retroactive changes in the law increasing the scope of liability, as insurers have set their premiums and policy conditions not on the basis of such an expanded liability regime, but on the previous narrower regime. Thus, retroactive expansion of liability regimes, by definition, is uninsurable, since the relevant risk in this case is the risk of an unforeseeable court ruling, which is very uncertain and not quantifiable. Note also that where the time lag between the relevant occurrence and the damage increases (i.e. long-tail damage), informational and causal uncertainties increase, retroactive changes in liability law become more likely and the insurability of the risk decreases.

A further prerequisite is that the risks to be insured are statistically independent. Risks are statistically dependent if, when one insured suffers damage, the probability increases that another insured suffers damage; an example would be a nuclear war, where many insureds would suffer

---

[7] The term "risk" denotes a specifiable probability of loss. Uncertainty, on the other hand, involves an unspecifiable probability of loss.
[8] Faure and Hartlief 2003, 84–85.

damage at the same time. In insurance language, this risk is known as a "common factor", which is one of two major portfolio risks.[9] In the context of liability insurance, changes in the law present a common-factor risk.

A third requirement is that insurers must not be seriously restricted in managing and reducing threats to insurability. Two major threats are adverse selection and moral hazard. Adverse selection refers to the phenomenon that persons presenting higher than average (or median) risk are more likely to contract insurance than those presenting lower risk, while it is difficult or expensive for the insurer to distinguish between higher and lower risks. Adverse selection results from ineffective risk segregation.[10] Legal uncertainty may aggravate adverse selection.[11] Insurers can control adverse selection by defining their screening and selection procedures, including more sophisticated questionnaires, rejecting applicants presenting higher risks and applying more targeted policy conditions. Moral hazard increases risks for insurers in a different way: it causes insureds (and courts!) to act less carefully and to incur higher costs than they would have, had they not been insured. To control moral hazard, insurers employ instruments such as deductibles, co-insurance, caps, exclusions, premium differentiation, bonus/malus mechanisms and the like.

To understand the risk-spreading and risk-reduction functions of insurance, a sound understanding of the differences between two major types of insurance is required: first-party insurance and third-party or liability insurance. The differences between first- and third-party insurance arise from the fact that the pool of victims in a first-party context are the insureds themselves, while the victims in a liability context are third parties. In a first-party insurance context, insurers have a direct contractual relationship with the victims. In a third-party (liability) insurance context, however, insurers do not contract directly with the persons that may suffer the harm but with a party that under the law can be made to bear the losses incurred by the victims. This has serious implications for the extent to which insurers are able to control the threats to insurance discussed above, i.e. adverse selection and moral hazard. Many of the measures that first-party insurance policies incorporate to control these risks are not available to liability insurers. For instance, while in a first-party context an insurance company can reject potential victims who pose an increased risk (or charge them a higher premium), it cannot do

---

[9] The second major risk is known as pricing function. See Tanega 1996, 117.

[10] Priest 1987, 1548. On adverse selection, see Faure and Hartlief 2003, 109–112.

[11] See American Law Institute 1991, 86.

so with respect to the persons suffering the loss in a third-party context; the liability insurer can control only the pool of insureds, not the pool of victims. Compared to the first-party insurer, the liability insurer's ability to control adverse selection is significantly smaller, because it is more difficult and more expensive to assess risk only at the level of the insureds (not the victims) and achieve optimal risk segregation. Control of moral hazard is even more difficult, if not virtually impossible, for a liability insurer. To control moral hazard, first-party policies invariably provide for deductibles, co-insurance, caps, exclusions, premium differentiation, bonus/malus mechanisms and the like. Third-party liability insurers can use these instruments but only in relation to the insureds, not in relation to the victims, who create most of the moral hazard.

It is relevant to note that liability insurance, unlike first-party insurance, has regressive income effects. Regressive income effects result from a lack of differentiation in the "insurance premium" in the third-party context. The tort-law insurance premium, which is included in a product's or service's price, is the same for all consumers, although some, i.e. high earners, bring higher risk (e.g., with respect to the size of potential loss of income) to the insurance pool than the low-income earners and, thus, purchase more coverage for the same price.

Substantively, in light of the analysis set forth above, the risk-spreading objectives of liability rules are unpersuasive to the extent that they rely on insurance. Where liability is aimed at risk-spreading through insurance, the issue is whether the risk-reduction and risk-spreading functions discussed above should be pursued through third-party liability insurance or direct first-party insurance. A careful analysis of insurance mechanisms shows that the liability system is not an attractive way to spread risk, at least where liability is not justified on deterrence grounds.[12] In many ways, first-party insurance is a more efficient and otherwise more attractive alternative than third-party liability insurance.[13] As discussed above, disadvantages of third-party liability insurance, as compared to first-party insurance, include the lack of effective control over adverse selection and moral hazard, problems of excessive and retroactively expanding coverage, regressive income effects and the high administrative cost of this system. The problems of adverse selection and moral hazard become worse and

---

[12] Priest 1987; Priest 1991, 31–50. It has been argued that the deterrence incentives generated by liability in the real world (i.e. taking into account all other incentives and disincentives impacting an operator's decisions) are uncertain. See e.g., Bergkamp 2003, Chapter 5.

[13] Priest 1987.

more difficult to control when we move from fault to strict liability. In a first-party policy, premiums can be set in the function of the risk brought to the pool and the coverage offered; premiums for third-party liability insurance cannot be differentiated to the same extent and, accordingly, the price mechanism does not work optimally, as a result of which the total risk increases.[14] Compensation systems other than liability typically offer a much lower level of recovery for non-pecuniary losses than those available in liability suits.[15] Furthermore, victims may be in a better position than those causing the injury to diversify risk.[16] Risk-spreading may provide a justification for compensating and spreading losses, but it does not justify doing so through a liability rule.

6.1.3. Conclusions

Insurance can perform its useful risk-aggregation and risk-reducing functions only if the risks to be insured are sufficiently probabilistic and predictable, as well as statistically independent. Uncertainty regarding the scope and size of liability seriously undermines the insurability of liability risks.

In terms of first-party insurance versus liability insurance, in general, the former provides a much better ability to control the major threats to insurability, i.e. adverse selection and moral hazard. In other words, in terms of insurance efficiency, first-party insurance is superior to liability insurance.

There are issues around the insurability of catastrophic risks. Our analysis showed that liability for widespread damage, unlike e.g., product liability for personal injury caused by defective goods, does not necessarily spread risk; insurance does not function adequately in this context and does not produce risk-aggregation and risk-reduction benefits, unless it operates at a very large scale. Significant uncertainty regarding the scope and size of potential liability exposure undermines insurability. If no

---

[14] Epstein 1985, 645–669. Shavell has argued that regulation of liability coverage, requiring or forbidding insurance, may improve diluted incentives arising from judgment-proof problems or improve the possibility of escaping from liability when insurers are able to monitor insured behaviour. It remains unclear, however, how this ability should be assessed and whether government intervention in the insurance market should be preferred over the market in any situation. See Shavell 2000. Noting that it is much more expensive to insure victims through the legal system than directly by first-party insurance coverage, Shavell rejects the typical justification for mandatory liability coverage where it provides an implicit form of insurance protection for victims.

[15] Cane 1999, 405.   [16] Batsch 1998, 175.

reliable assessment of the monetary size of the potential liability exposure is possible, insurers cannot accurately predict risk. Monetary and time limits on potential liability exposure, generally, enhance insurability.

As discussed above, insurance works only if risks are insurable. Whether or not the risks of terrorism are insurable, is discussed below. We discuss first how insurance manages risks, given that risks are insurable. As noted above, insurers have to manage two types of risk: adverse selection and moral hazard. At the level of individual contracts, the focus is on managing the risks associated with moral hazard. In addition, insurers can manage their overall risk exposure generally through mechanisms such as pooling, reinsurance, etc., which is not discussed further because it is not relevant for the purposes of this book. The same is true for risk management through "claims-made" versus "loss occurrence" policies, which is not relevant here.

Insurers employ instruments such as deductibles, co-insurance, caps, exclusions, premium differentiation, bonus/malus mechanisms and the like, for managing risks.[17]

6.2.   Insurance of man-made disasters

When referring to man-made (technological) disasters, an important feature is that there is a tortfeasor who can be identified and be held liable. Hence, the main instrument to control man-made risk, also when it is catastrophic, is tort law. We are referring here, for example, to the operation of a nuclear plant, but also to risks emerging from petrochemical companies or offshore installations like the Deepwater Horizon.

---

[17] These concepts can be defined as follows. Deductibles: also called "own risk", i.e., the amount that the insured must bear before insurance kicks in. Co-insurance: under this arrangement, the insurance policy covers only a portion (typically expressed in a percentage of less than 100 per cent) of the damage, with the remainder being for the account of the insured. Caps: the upper financial limit of an insurance policy, i.e., the maximum amount that the insurer will pay out under the policy (per year, per event or otherwise). Exclusions: these are specific events, types of damage, causes of damages, or other aspects, that are excluded from insurance coverage and thus for the insured's account. Premium differentiation: charging different amounts of premiums to different insureds based on the nature and scope of insurance coverage provided and the risk that the insured brings to the risk pool. Bonus/malus mechanisms: such a scheme involves premium reductions for insureds with a good accident record (no or few claims) and premium increases for those with a bad record (many claims), and are intended to create incentives for damage- and claims-avoiding behaviour.

The insurance scheme that one would primarily look at in this situation is liability insurance. Liability insurance has two main functions. One function is that it protects risk-averse injurers from an exposure to liability. Insurance allows the shifting of the risk to the insurance company, thus increasing the expected utility of the insured injurer. In that sense insurance contributes to increasing social welfare. However, since (liability) insurance may create a moral hazard risk, the insurer needs to employ techniques to remedy this problem. The first solution is to perfectly monitor the behaviour of the insured injurer and adapt premium and other policy conditions accordingly. This will in practice be done via classification and differentiation of risks ex-ante and ex-post via experience-rating systems,[18] such as the well-known bonus-malus system.[19] In the ideal case the insurer will perfectly control the moral-hazard risk, as a result of which the insured injurer still has perfect incentives to take optimal care. However, under full insurance coverage his incentives for care no longer come from liability rules directly but from the control of moral hazard by the insurer.

Generally one would assume potential injurers to have a demand for disaster insurance coverage since even relatively large corporations may be averse against the risk of being exposed to catastrophic liability exposure. For smaller liability risks a willingness to pay the insurance premium may not necessarily emerge, especially when the injurer has alternative options like creating reserves or captives[20] that may provide protection against liability exposure in a cheaper way than insurance. However, for catastrophic risks even larger enterprises may have a demand for insurance.

Liability insurance may not only be beneficial from the perspective of the potential injurer. A serious problem that victims may face is insolvency of the liable injurer in case of damage of a catastrophic nature. In that case the damage could easily outweigh the personal wealth of the injurer, as a result of which the victims may not receive compensation.

In sum, both potential injurers and potential victims may have an interest in having liability insurance for man-made disasters. Insurance can protect risk-averse injurers against catastrophic liability risks; insurance can protect the victim against the potential insolvency of the injurer and

---

[18] Experience rating refers to adapting the premium to the behaviour of the insured.
[19] This is a system whereby an insured receives a reduction of premium (bonus) when during a particular period no accident was reported or a premium increase (malus) if the insured called on the insurance policy.
[20] These methods are in some cases referred to as "self insurance".

thus guarantee compensation.[21] However, there may be many reasons, as practice shows, why liability insurance for man-made disasters is not always available or not always used. Hence, to the extent that operators would have a demand for liability insurance and cannot obtain it, a market failure may arise; the same problem (emergence of a market failure) may equally arise to the extent that operators can externalise liability risks to society as a result of their insolvency which could be cured through compulsory liability insurance.

6.2.1.   Demand-side problems: the case for compulsory liability insurance

The fact that injurers may not take insurance coverage and thus remain insolvent is referred to in the economic literature as the so-called judgment proof problem.[22] If the injurer would be exposed to liability risks whereby the damage would be a lot higher than his personal wealth, an under-deterrence problem emerges. Especially under strict liability (which will often be introduced for these high-risk activities) injurers will consider the accident as one with a maximum damage equal to their personal wealth. As a result they will only take care to avoid accidents with a magnitude equal to their own wealth and not necessarily optimal care. Injurers would, from society's perspective, then be able to externalise harm, i.e. throw the harm on the shoulders of the victims or (if society compensates the victims instead of the injurer) of society at large. Economists have therefore argued that compulsory liability insurance should be introduced in cases where the potential loss caused by the disaster may exceed the injurer's assets.[23] In cases where the damage caused as a result of a disaster would outweigh the assets of an individual tortfeasor (which may often be the case), there is hence a strong economic argument to impose a duty on potential injurers to provide solvency guarantees (such as insurance) since otherwise they would be able to externalise risk. This potential of externalising harm to society may precisely be one of the reasons why liability insurance for disasters is not purchased as often as it should. Liability insurance after all creates costs for industry (paying the insurance premium) whereas injurers that can externalise harm to society can avoid those costs.

---

[21] Of course other legal issues would still have to be regulated, such as inter alia a direct right of action of the victim on the insurer and a guarantee that the insurance monies can actually be spent for victim compensation, for example in case of bankruptcy of the injurer after a disaster.

[22] See Shavell 1986.   [23] Kunreuther and Freeman 2001.

There are quite a few examples showing that in the absence of compulsory liability insurance injurers will often engage in externalisation of harm. For example, in some countries in the sector or marine oil pollution[24] it is common practice for a particular fleet of e.g., tankers to create a separate legal entity for each tanker. These are then constructed as so-called "single ship companies". As a result of the limited liability of corporations in case something goes wrong (like an oil pollution incident) the company has limited its risk to the assets within that particular company, which is basically only the ship that caused the marine pollution and will in practice often be worthless or even have a negative value.

Also in other cases there are examples of systematic underinsurance by industrial operators. For example in the Netherlands, following the explosion of a fireworks factory in Enschede on 13 May 2000 that caused 19 deaths and 150 injuries, it appeared that the operator of the factory only had purchased very limited insurance coverage.[25] A few months' later on New Year's Eve in 2000 yet another tragic accident took place in the Netherlands in a bar in Volendam, where as a result of a large fire many youngsters died and others were injured for life as a result of burning wounds. Again, the owner of the facility had only very limited insurance coverage.

This risk of externalisation of harm may hence explain to some extent underinsurance of catastrophic risks. Operators may prefer not to take insurance coverage for high amounts above their own assets for which they could anyway never be held liable in case of an accident because they would be insolvent. Some legal systems do have compulsory liability insurance for particular activities, but it is rather limited. For example, compulsory environmental liability insurance existed in Europe (before the implementation of the ELD) effectively only in Germany, Sweden and Spain.[26] Compulsory liability insurance for the risk of fire in public places such as nightclubs and restaurants exists in Belgium, but not in the Netherlands. This led a Belgian commentator to the conclusion that were the tragic fire to have taken place in a bar in Belgium on New Years' Eve 2000, victims would have been compensated largely through the compulsory liability regime.[27]

---

[24] Discussed in more detail above in Chapter 1.   [25] See Hartlief 2003, 58–59.
[26] For an overview of the German system see inter alia Richardson 2000, and for a description of the Swedish system see Faure and Grimeaud 2003, 189–192.
[27] Van Schoubroeck 2002.

6.2.2.   Supply-side problems

Insurers consider catastrophic risks as "difficult to predict".[28] This "insurer ambiguity" limits insurability;[29] insurers will add a risk premium and hence ask higher total premiums for catastrophic risks, which may not lead to a willingness to pay on the side of industry, as a result of which a market may not emerge. In other cases insurers may impose very strict conditions or exclusions which may reduce the availability of catastrophe liability insurance. Finally, the magnitude of the damage of a particular catastrophe may also outweigh the capacity of the private insurance market, even if the possibilities of co- and reinsurance are taken into account.[30]

In sum: insurers may (understandably), given the hard-to-predict nature of catastrophes, lacking statistics and the potentially high magnitude of the damage, be reluctant to provide large coverage for liability insurance for man-made disasters or may only do so at high premiums or with particular exclusions which may make the insurance unattractive.

6.2.3.   Government support needed?

If it is the catastrophic nature of the damage that restricts the possibilities of (re)insurance and financial markets to cover catastrophic risks, the government may intervene with a facilitative strategy to support the functioning of the private insurance market. This could take various forms. In some cases the government may act as insurer of last resort; in other cases the government could provide reinsurance in cases where capacity on the traditional reinsurance market is lacking.

6.2.3.1.   The case for public–private partnerships

In law, economics and legal scholarship criticisms have been formulated on the facilitative role of a government stimulating insurance markets.[31] Gron and Sykes argue that it would be unjust for the government to provide (re)insurance at a lower price than the market price.[32] This would give a wrong signal to the market as far as stimulating insurability is concerned. The authors prefer ad hoc solutions whereby compensation is provided to accident victims on an ex-post basis. This would avoid

---

[28] See Gollier 2005.   [29] See Kunreuther, Hogarth and Meszaros 1993.
[30] See Faure and Hartlief 2003, 88–94 and OECD 2005.
[31] See Trebilcock and Daniels 2006.
[32] See Gron and Sykes 2002 and Gron and Sykes 2003.

the situation that market participants are aware that the government will anyway guarantee compensation.

Also Dutch lawyers, Ammerlaan and Van Boom, have been critical of an intervention by the (Dutch) government to participate in reinsurance against terrorism. They argue that the premium that will be demanded is not a correct premium. Moreover, they argue that it should not be the task of the State to provide private insurance. Damage caused as a result of terrorism, so they hold, should be financed through the public purse.[33]

It is striking that most of this criticism is not addressed against the intervention of the government as such, but is based on the assumption that the government will not ask premiums that reflect market prices. It is a criticism shared by Levmore and Logue, who argue that such a regime (of acting as reinsurer of last resort) only has its desired effect of encouraging the purchase of commercially provided terrorism coverage when it involves a substantial subsidy.[34] They are sceptical of these types of interventions in the market (for terrorism insurance) arguing that, also without government intervention, "the market would likely have been able to provide the necessary coverage."[35]

Apparently, the arguments against government intervention are based on the assumption that the government will not ask competitive reinsurance premiums, hereby subsidising catastrophe insurance. Moreover, without this government support, insurance coverage could have probably developed anyway (at least for terrorism events). Those points can of course only be validated on the basis of empirical research.

The arguments in favour are not surprisingly the mirror image of the arguments against: assuming that capacity on the private insurance market is indeed severely falling behind, it can be assumed that without State intervention, insurance coverage for disasters would simply not have developed.[36] Reinsurance by the State can then be considered as an adequate method to resolve the uninsurability problem. A condition is of course that the government charges an actuarially fair premium for its intervention.[37] This type of government intervention has, moreover, the advantage that ex-post relief sponsored through the public purse can

[33] Ammerlaan and Van Boom 2003.
[34] Levmore and Logue 2003, 304 (arguing that otherwise disaster insurance would still not be "available").
[35] Levmore and Logue 2003, 311.
[36] This is a point strongly made by Kunreuther 1996, 180–183; Harrington 2000; as well as by Schwarze and Wagner 2004.
[37] Faure 2007, 358.

be avoided. Where the government acts as reinsurer, this at least has the advantage that a premium can be paid by those who actually cause or run the risk. It can thus facilitate market solutions, still provide incentives for prevention to potential victims and avoid negative redistribution. Thus a State intervention as reinsurer may avoid the "catastrophic responses to catastrophic risks".[38] This is further supported by the fact that in case of this type of government-provided reinsurance, the government has the capacity to diversify the risks over the entire population and to spread past losses to future generations, thus creating a form of cross-time diversification which the private market could not achieve.[39] On the other hand, they argue that, especially as far as terrorism is concerned, government participation in insurance programmes is crucial since the risk of terrorist attacks is partly in the government's control and the government can have more information on ongoing terrorist groups' activities through intelligence services.[40]

Although there is still some criticism on this intervention of government in providing reinsurance coverage, one can notice this type of government intervention in an increasing way, not only in the case of man-made disasters and terrorism but also in the case of natural disasters. However, the literature has indicated that this type of role of government as (re)insurer of catastrophic risks can only be considered efficient when particular conditions are met.[41] These conditions are inter alia the following:

- the intervention by government should not distort the normal functioning of the market;
- when government provides reinsurance risk-based premiums should be charged;
- the government intervention should be such that it stimulates the development of market solutions;
- freedom should be left with insurers to choose the statutory insurance; and
- the government intervention should in principle have a temporary character.

---

[38] Epstein 1996. See in this respect also Kunreuther and Pauly 2006, 113, who argue that this government's role in assisting the supply side allows avoiding the inefficiencies and inequities associated with disaster assistance.

[39] See Kunreuther and Michel-Kerjan 2004, 210.   [40] Kunreuther and Michel-Kerjan 2005.

[41] For a summary of those conditions see Bruggeman, Faure and Fiore 2010.

If these conditions are met it would be possible that government provides efficient reinsurance stimulating the supply of catastrophe insurance. However, as some of the actual cases of government intervention show, government intervention rarely fully complies completely with those conditions.

6.2.3.2. Government providing an additional layer

One example of government support foresees a role of the government to finance catastrophic damages through an additional risk layer, outside of the insurance market and on an ex-post level, above the injurers' own financing. Such a scheme aims at supplementing compensation from injurers (if needed) and thus at maximising the protection of victims in case the damage exceeds certain limits. In this case the role of the State is merely to guarantee an additional layer of compensation and it adds little as far as facilitating insurability is concerned. Examples are the cases of nuclear liability and marine pollution liability discussed above.

As we already made clear when discussing those international conventions, these models do not at all comply with an efficient government support to stimulate insurability. The goal of providing an additional risk layer is also not to stimulate insurability. The main problem is that the government does not charge any price for providing the additional funding; the intervention does not have a temporary character, market solutions are not stimulated by providing government intervention and the government intervention can in that sense largely be considered as distortive.[42]

In fact, the domains of nuclear power and marine oil pollution are the rare cases where specific statutory measures have been taken to deal with the insurability of liability for damage caused by man-made disasters. Some other cases also relate to civil aviation.[43] Before turning to the specific case of terrorism we will present two examples of how industry (supported by government) has dealt with particular catastrophic losses following from man-made disasters. We discuss a reinsurance arrangement with State intervention that has been created in Spain and we briefly discuss the Fukushima case.

---

[42] As we discussed in Chapter 1 this criticism mainly applies to the nuclear liability conventions since the additional funding there is provided as a State subsidy. However, in the case of marine oil pollution the additional funding is not paid by the liable ship-owner, but by the oil industry, hence still by a market participant (see above, 1.2.). In fact, in the marine oil pollution case there is in principle no government financing.

[43] Equally already discussed in Chapter 1.

6.2.3.3.   The *Consorcio de Compensación de Seguros*

The Spanish programme offers a good example of a government collecting a fee or premium in exchange for the provision of insurance coverage. The publicly administered disaster financing program "*Consorcio de Compensación de Seguros*" (CCS) was founded in 1954 as a corporation providing "extraordinary risks" insurance, namely coverage against natural disasters and risks with "social repercussions" (terrorism, riots, etc.).[44] The *Consorcio* in fact acts as a catastrophe insurer for certain types of insurance and perils in respect of Spanish risks, compensating losses and injuries arising from extraordinary events taking place in Spain and affecting risks located in Spain. It also covers personal damage for extraordinary events taking place abroad if the insured resides habitually in Spain.[45] This extraordinary risk coverage is a mandatory additional coverage added to fire and natural perils, motor and railway vehicles and other property damage policies. The extra CCS premium is automatically included in the base policy's premium and varies according to the type of policy offered, although it reflects the base rate charged on the primary policy. Until 1987, disaster insurance premiums were calculated as a percentage of property damage insurance premiums. However, since this meant that the premium income was influenced by events unrelated to disaster insurance, the CCS has set its own premium since 1987, which is not risk-related and equal for the entire country. The extra premium to a personal insurance policy amounts to 0.005 per mille, while that to a property insurance policy differs: 0.08 and 0.12 per mille of the total sum insured for houses and office buildings respectively; 0.18 per mille for businesses; 0.21 per mille for industrial risks; 3.5 euro for vehicle insurance; and between 0.28 and 1.63 per mille for infrastructure.[46]

CCS payments are subsidiary to payments made by the private insurance industry, and the *Consorcio* only pays if the risk was not covered by private insurance (e.g., for the poor who did not buy insurance) or if the private insurance company fails to pay due to insolvency. Typically, domestic insurers in Spain do not cover extraordinary risks but issue policy documentation clearly stating that such losses are not their responsibility but that of the *Consorcio*, to whom relevant claims should be addressed. Deductibles for property loss amount to 7 per cent of the amount of the indemnifiable damage.

---

[44] Over time, the activities of the CCS were extended beyond this core function.

[45] *Estatuto Legal del Consorcio* (Legal Statutes of the Consorcio), approved by Law 21/1990 dated 19th December.

[46] See www.consorseguros.es/web/guest/ad_re_er.

The legal nature of the CCS changed in December 1991, follow-ing Spain's accession to the European Community, from being a State monopoly institution to a public business institution attached to the Ministry of Economy and Finance. The CCS now has its own legal per-sonality, full capacity to act and its own assets independent from those of the State. In addition, given the peculiar characteristics of the *Consorcio*'s activity and especially given the high loss potential and the very nature of the *Consorcio* as a public organism, it is absolutely necessary for the *Consorcio* to count on an unlimited State guarantee. However, the set-ting up and appropriate financial management of its resources has always enabled it to face up to its claims obligations without having to make use of said guarantee since its inception over sixty years ago.

6.2.3.4.   The Fukushima case

We will briefly discuss the Fukushima case, not only because it is a large-scale and recent (March 2011) man-made disaster, but also because it follows a different structure from the compensation under the nuclear liability conventions discussed in Chapter 1. There are a few features of the insurance and reinsurance structure as well as the State intervention that make the Fukushima case interesting.[47]

Japan is not a member of the international nuclear liability conventions but has an Act on compensation for nuclear damage of 1961. Nuclear operators can still be held liable for the nuclear damage caused by a natural disaster such as an earthquake or volcanic eruption, but they can cover such losses through an indemnity agreement with the government. Since insurers usually exclude the damage caused by natural disasters from liability insurance policies, this kind of risk is covered by an indemnity agreement concluded with the government.[48] A major difference between the Japanese regime and the international regime is that in Japan the liability of the nuclear operator is unlimited. Although there is a minimum for the requirement of financial assistance that has to be provided by the operator, he is still liable for damage in access of that amount.[49] This indemnity agreement is hence a contract that the nuclear operator makes with the government with the view to cover damage which is not covered by liability insurance or other means of financial security. This is mostly

---

[47] A full discussion of the Fukushima case can inter alia be found in Weitzdörfer 2011; Faure and Liu 2012a and Faure and Liu 2012b.

[48] See Act on Indemnity Agreements for Compensation of Nuclear Damage, Act No. 148 of 1961, para 3.

[49] The Act on Compensation for Nuclear Damage, paras 6–7.

for damage caused by natural disasters. It is important that the operator has to pay the government an indemnity fee. The Japanese State hence intervenes in the compensation for the victims of a nuclear accident on the basis of an indemnity agreement for which the operator pays a fee to the State. However, if the damage is still higher than the amount of the indemnity agreement, the State could intervene under section 16 of the Act on compensation.[50] This State intervention then still takes place on the basis of a political decision.

Looking now at how compensation will take place in the Fukushima case the picture is slightly more complicated. According to the Act on Compensation, the nuclear operator faces unlimited strict liability and has the obligation to seek financial security up to 120 billion yen.[51] If the damage is caused by an earthquake or volcanic eruption, the government should indemnify losses up to the 120 billion yen minimum financial security requirement.[52] For damages exceeding this amount, the operator is still liable.

Beyond simply defining the scope of compensable damage, the question exists of how this compensation can be financed. Nuclear damage caused by a natural disaster is excluded from the insurance policy provided by JAEIP.[53] Thus, the insurance industry does not seem to be seriously impacted by this accident. The government may have to indemnify the losses up to 120 billion yen.[54] The remainder of the damage may still create a challenge to the financial capacity of TEPCO. According to the Act on compensation, if the operator's liability exceeds the amount of financial security and the government deems it necessary in order to attain the objectives of the Act, the government shall give aid to the operator.[55] However, whether and to what extent aid will be given depends on the government's decision. Because of the significant impact of the Fukushima

---

[50] Section 16 states: "[w]here nuclear damage occurs, the Government shall give a nuclear operator (except the nuclear operator of a foreign nuclear ship) such aid as is required for him to compensate the damage, when the actual amount which he should pay for the nuclear damage pursuant to Section 3 exceeds the financial security amount and when the government deems it necessary in order to attain the objectives of this act."

[51] Vásquez-Maignan 2012, p. 9.

[52] See *Fukushima – Compensation of Nuclear Damage after Great Earthquake in Japan*, *Enformable Nuclear News* (13 December 2011), http://enformable.com/2011/12/fukushima-compensation-of-nuclear-damage-after-great-earthquake-in-japan/.

[53] This is the insurer of the nuclear risk in Japan.

[54] Act on Compensation for Nuclear Damage § 3.

[55] Act on Compensation for Nuclear Damage § 16.

accident and the catastrophic nature of the damage, it will be difficult for TEPCO alone to provide full compensation.

To ensure a prompt compensation of the damage caused by the Fukushima accident, the government prepared a law to address compensation through the creation of a corporation in June 2011.[56] The Act to Establish the Nuclear Damage Compensation Facilitation Corporation was passed on August 3, 2011.[57] The Act has three aims: ensuring the prompt and proper nuclear damage compensation for affected people, stabilising the nuclear power station to prevent adverse effects on life and commerce in the surrounding area, and maintaining a stable supply of electricity.[58] To realise those aims, the Act establishes a Nuclear Damage Compensation Facilitation Corporation ("the Corporation") and a system of financing the compensation for damage.[59] The Corporation will receive contributions from nuclear operators to cover the costs of operation and reserve funds to prepare for compensation.[60] The victims still need to make a claim against the liable operator and the liable operator needs to make the payment to the victims. However, the Corporation can facilitate the compensation and "provide... necessary information and advice" to the affected people.[61] If the liable operator needs assistance, the Corporation can provide two forms: ordinary financial assistance, which can be given after a resolution of the management committee of the Corporation; and special financial assistance, which needs to be approved by the competent minister.[62] To obtain the special financial assistance, the Corporation and the operator need to formulate a special business plan.[63] Under this plan, the government will issue government bonds to the Corporation and the Corporation will grant the necessary funds to the nuclear operator.[64] The Corporation can also get government-backed support from financial institutions. After getting this support, the liable nuclear operator pays special contributions to the Corporation.[65] Other

---

[56] Japan's Parliament Approves TEPCO Compensation Plan, BBC NEWS (3 August 2011, 6:48 AM), www.bbc.co.uk/news/business-14383832; see Outline of the Bill of the Act to Establish Nuclear Damage Compensation Facilitation Corporation, Ministry of Economics, Trade and Industry, www.meti.go.jp/english/earthquake/nuclear/roadmap/pdf/20110614_damage_corporation_2.pdf (last visited 2 November 2012) (ereinafter Nuclear Damage Compensation Outline).

[57] See Outline of the Nuclear Damage Compensation Facilitation Corporation Act, Ministry of Economics, Trade and Industry (August 2011), available at www.meti.go.jp/english/earthquake/nuclear/roadmap/pdf/20111012_nuclear_damages_2.pdf (hereinafter METI Outline).

[58] Ibid.   [59] Ibid.   [60] Ibid.   [61] Ibid., 3.   [62] See METI Outline, 2.

[63] Ibid.   [64] Ibid., 2–3.   [65] Ibid.

non-affected nuclear operators also need to pay general contributions based on the principle of "mutual support".[66]

This Act established a mutual support "pooling system" to provide coverage for nuclear liability after the Fukushima accident.[67] Some scholars advocate pooling as a useful instrument to finance the compensation of catastrophic losses while preserving preventive incentives.[68] The mutual support system established in Japan has some characteristics different from the practice in other jurisdictions. In both Germany and the US, where resource pooling between nuclear operators has been established, pooling is done before accidents happen.[69] However, the ex-post system established in Japan cannot create incentives among operators to monitor each other. Unlike the American and German regimes, under the Japanese system the Corporation is not only financed by nuclear operators, but also by government compensation bonds and government-guaranteed bonds.[70] If those funds are financed without a market price, this system will look more like a bailout of TEPCO than a pooling system to prevent and compensate future damage.

This compensation scheme in Japan hence has a few interesting features. Though the Act on compensation does not set a cap on the potential liability of nuclear operators, the corporate structure only exposes them to risk up to the value of their assets.[71] In this situation, a financial guarantee is important to ensure efficient deterrence. In Japan, the required financial security is set at 120 billion yen.[72] This amount is provided through a combination of liability insurance, for which the operator will pay a premium, and an indemnity agreement with government, for which a fee will be paid as well.[73]

Compensation under this indemnity agreement is not a mere subsidy. However, the indemnity fee charged for government coverage is certainly not market-based. On the contrary, the fee is fixed and therefore not risk-related.[74] Moreover, though the operator remains liable beyond the insured amount of 120 billion yen (except when the incident would be qualified as a natural disaster of an exceptional character) the exposure to liability of the operator is de facto limited to its assets.[75] Beyond that amount, Japanese law provides that government may use its discretionary

---

[66] Ibid., 3.   [67] Nuclear Damage Compensation Outline, *supra* note 56.
[68] See Faure and Vanden Borre 2008, 222; Pelzer 2007, 51.   [69] See Pelzer 2007, 49.
[70] METI Outline, 1–2.   [71] See Ramseyer 2011, 3.   [72] Ibid., 8.
[73] See Act on Indemnity Agreements for Compensation of Nuclear Damage, §§ 2–4, 6.
[74] Ibid., § 6.   [75] See Ramseyer 2011, 17–18.

powers to "take measures", meaning that it will intervene to compensate victims. In that case a lack of full internalisation of the accident costs remains a problem.[76] This still raises the question to what extent a nuclear operator like TEPCO is fully liable for accident costs, and to what extent liability rules do provide adequate incentives for taking preventive measures with a view to cost internalisation.

As far as the financing is concerned, Japan's programme seems to do better than the international regime at compensating victims. As we have indicated above (5.2.), currently, of the total amount available under the international regime of 381 million euro, only 91 million euro consists of operator's liability, whereas the remaining 290 million euro consists of State aid.[77] In Japan this amount of 120 billion yen is in principle paid by the operator, either (in the general case) via liability insurance or, in case of uninsurable risks (more particularly damage resulting from earthquakes, tsunamis or volcanoes) via an indemnity agreement with government.[78] But the indemnity agreement is, unlike State aid in the international regime, not a subsidy since the operator has to pay a fee for the coverage provided by government via the indemnity agreement.

Of course one could question of whether the fee paid by the operator for the indemnity agreement is comparable to commercially risk-dependent premiums that would be charged on a commercial insurance market. One report shows that in 1998 the premium rate was set at an average of 7.9 per cent of the total amount of coverage,[79] which is substantially higher than the rate of indemnity fee (0.03 per cent or 0.015 per cent).[80] However, it should be borne in mind that, given the lack of actuarial data for nuclear accidents, commercial premiums are usually set higher than the actuarial premium. Thus the difference between the rate of indemnity fee and actuarial premium – a more accurate measure of risk – may not be that large. On the positive side, at least in Japan, some money is asked from the operator for the government indemnity, whereas in

---

[76] Act on Compensation for Nuclear Damage, §§ 16–17.

[77] Even after the entry into force of the modification protocol of 2004, only 700 million euro of the total amount of 1.5 billion euro would be operator's liability and a remaining 800 million euro would still be State aid. Yamori and Okada 2007 and accompanying text. See above 5.2.8.2. for the funding of nuclear liability in the international regime.

[78] See Ramseyer 2011 and the Act on Indemnity Agreements for Compensation of Nuclear Damage, §§ 2–4, 6 and accompanying text.

[79] Watabe 2006, 222.

[80] Order for the Execution of the Act on Indemnity Agreements for Compensation of Nuclear Damage, § 3.

the international regime the State aid is provided for free – functionally, a complete subsidy. Therefore less subsidy is given under the Japanese system. Moreover, unlike the international regime there is in Japan in principle unlimited liability of the operator beyond the amount of 120 billion yen,[81] for which the operator must seek either liability insurance or an indemnity agreement. Hence, the Japanese system has less of a subsidy effect than the international regime and thus better prospects of cost internalisation by the operator.

6.3.   Insurance of terrorism-related risk

In this section we will focus on the type of technological or man-made disaster that plays a crucial role in this book, being terrorism-related risks.[82] From an insurance perspective, terrorism has many features that make it look more like a natural disaster than like a "normal" man-made disaster: in case of terrorism, normal liability rules cannot be applied since the terrorist will usually not be identifiable or if he is, he will usually be insolvent. Moreover, remedies we suggested above with respect to liability for man-made disasters, such as compulsory liability insurance, do not work in the case of terrorists either. That is why in Chapter 8 some alternative systems for redressing terrorism-related risks will be addressed whereby also the examples from the insurance of natural disasters will be discussed.

Terrorism insurance has changed dramatically since 9/11. After that date insurance companies began massively cancelling terrorism coverage (usually on first-party insurance policies, but also related to airline insurance).[83] As a result of that cancellation, in many countries systems emerged where the State took the role as reinsurer of last resort. Public–private partnerships were created whereby terrorism coverage consisted of several layers with an intervention by insurers, reinsurers and government. The way in which terrorism insurance emerged in different countries is interesting, because it shows again how government can facilitate the functioning of the market mechanism and more particularly insurance. Of course we do not have the possibility to discuss all terrorism insurance schemes that emerged after 9/11. We have already referred to the CCS in Spain where the CCS provided terrorism cover until 31 October 2000,

---

[81] Weitzdörfer 2011, 70–71.
[82] This section draws heavily from Bruggeman, Faure and Heldt 2012.
[83] See Hartwig 2002.

after which the cover became available on the private market. Examples also exist inter alia in the United Kingdom, where reinsurance is provided through Pool Re.[84] We will now present the insurance schemes for terrorism in the US, France and the Netherlands.

The American Terrorism Risk Insurance Act of 2002 (TRIA) establishes a temporary programme of shared public and private compensation for insured losses resulting from foreign acts of terrorism in order to "protect consumers by addressing market disruptions and ensure the continued widespread availability and affordability" of terrorism insurance and to "allow for a transitional period for the private markets to stabilize, resume pricing of such insurance and build capacity to absorb any future losses".[85] TRIA creates a federal backstop for terrorism insurance, meaning that federal financial support is provided for payment of terrorism claims in the event of a fairly large terrorism incident. The programme is similar to reinsurance in that it provides reimbursement to insurers after they pay claims to a specified level (the deductible) and in that insurers retain a portion of the risk (a co-pay).[86] However, a difference with reinsurance is that insurers do not pay a premium to be eligible and the government does not establish any reserves. Instead, the costs of the TRIA programme are borne by the taxpayers with some or all of the costs subject to recoupment. In short, the Terrorism Risk Insurance Act of 2002 offers an illustration of the federal government providing coverage above a baseline risk that remains under the coverage of private insurers. The federal government temporarily assumes the role of excess liability insurer (i.e. reinsurer of last resort), providing a cap on the losses for which the private insurance industry remains responsible in the event of a terrorist attack.[87] The programme would initially exist for two years, with the expiration date set at 31 December 2005, but has been systematically extended ever since.

All insurers providing commercial[88] property or casualty insurance are required to participate in the programme as elaborated in the Terrorism

---

[84] See Huber and Amodu 2006.   [85] The TRIA act does not cover any of the 9/11 losses.
[86] Russell and Thomas 2008.   [87] Rabin and Bratis 2006, p. 325.
[88] TRIA only applies to commercial property and casualty insurance, which is defined to specifically include excess insurance, workers' compensation insurance, and during the first three years of the TRIA Programme, surety insurance. TRIA does not apply to personal insurance, such as homeowners', automobile or life insurance. Moreover, by law, the TRIA programme does not apply to: federal or private crop insurance; private mortgage insurance or title insurance; financial guarantee insurance offered by a monoline financial guarantee insurance corporation; insurance for medical malpractice; health or life insurance, including group life insurance; federal flood insurance; and reinsurance or retrocessional reinsurance.

Risk Insurance Act of 2002. The insurers must make terrorism insurance available to all policyholders, but are free to choose the applicable extra terrorism premium, which should not be excessive, inadequate or fairly discriminatory.

If a certified foreign act of terrorism causes losses in excess of $100 million, participating insurers must pay a certain amount in claims – a deductible – before federal governmental assistance can become available. This deductible is now set at 20 per cent of the insurer's directly earned premiums during the preceding year. Losses above the deductible will for 85 per cent be covered by the federal government, while the insurance industry contributes 15 per cent. An annual cap of $100 billion to all aggregate insured losses has been installed. In case the cap would be exceeded, Congress has the authority to decide who will pay and in what amounts: the Secretary shall determine the pro rata share of insured losses to be paid by each insurer that incurs insured losses under the programme. Insurers that meet the deductible will not be liable for losses in excess of this cap.

French primary insurers that offer fire insurance are required by law to also provide terrorism coverage. In practice, coverage against acts of terrorism was generally included in all standard insurance policies, which means that all private and commercial properties were generally covered against terrorism events. However, after the September 11th attacks, reinsurers cancelled their terrorism coverage and many primary insurers that could not obtain reinsurance chose to stop offering (especially commercial) property insurance to avoid the mandatory terrorism coverage. According to French insurance industry officials[89] the French government responded to this situation by, first, temporarily requiring the extension of all contracts and, second, beginning negotiations with the insurance industry to develop a more permanent solution. As a result, the "GAREAT" ("*Gestion de l'Assurance et de la Réassurance des Risques Attentats et Actes de Terrorisme*") reinsurance pool was created jointly by insurers, reinsurers and the *Caisse Centrale de Réassurance* (CCR) on 1 January 2002.[90] The idea is based on the existing administrative structures of the insurance associations and the natural catastrophe programme already in place in France. The goal of GAREAT is to cover acts and attacks of terrorism (including those involving the use of nuclear weapons) which cause damages on French territory (and assimilated territories).

---

[89] As interviewed by the United States Government Accountability Office. See GAO 2005, pp. 39–40.

[90] For all information on GAREAT, see: www.gareat.com/en, which includes the internal rules, co-reinsurance conventions, statutes, etc. of the pool programme.

Though GAREAT membership is not mandatory for insurance companies operating in France, insurers affiliated to FFSA (the national association of insurance companies) and GEMA (the main trade body for mutuals) automatically qualify as members of the pool. Upon subscription to GAREAT, each member is liable in proportion to the amount of the premiums ceded to the pool in respect of the subscription year.

The GAREAT programme is divided into two sections: the "Large Risks" section and the "Small and Medium-Sized Risks" section. The Large Risks section entails all contracts which fall within the scope of application of the GAREAT pool and whose sums insured for direct property damage, business interruption and construction, engineering and financial institution lines are in excess of 20 million euro. The pool's Large Risks section is in other words limited to commercial, professional and industrial risks where the sums insured are equal to or greater than 20 million euro. The Small and Medium-Sized Risks section, on the other hand, includes those contracts which fall within the scope of application of the GAREAT pool and whose total sums insured are less than 20 million euro. The Small and Medium-Sized Risks section will not be further discussed in the following section, since properties less than 20 million euro may be ceded to the pool on a voluntary basis.

Both sections are the subject of specific provisions and each section is divided into layers. GAREAT's structure (see Figure 7) may then briefly be described as follows:

(1) The first layer of the programme consists of co-reinsurance between the members of the pool. The losses to this layer are split between the members proportionally to their respective shares of the section in question.
(2) The next layers consist of reinsurance by professional reinsurers, who provide capacity in the form of Annual Aggregate Excess of Loss treaties. For the Large Risks section, the members of the pool may participate in these reinsurance layers. These layers are the subject of reinsurance treaties.
(3) The top layer consists of, for the Large Risks section, unlimited reinsurance granted by the CCR with a guarantee from the French State.[91] This layer is the subject of a reinsurance treaty with the CCR. The CCR receives for this purpose a premium from GAREAT.

---

[91] The scope of application of GAREAT is not exactly the same as that one of the top layer which is reinsured by CCR with the French State's guarantee. The scope of application of the CCR corresponds to that of Article L. 126–2 of the Insurance Code, which does

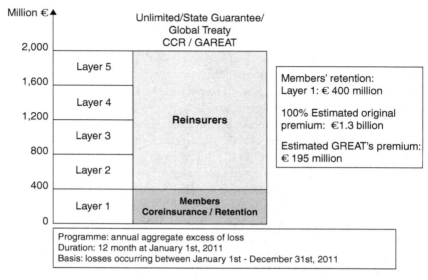

Figure 7   Structure of GAREAT

For the year 2012, the co-reinsurance layer has a limit of 400 million euro for the entirety of the losses. The second, third, fourth and fifth layers constitute the Annual Aggregate Excess of Loss reinsurance programme taken out by GAREAT on the international reinsurance market. The second to fifth layers are each limited to 400 million euro. The sixth layer constitutes the top layer where the CCR provides coverage (with an unlimited guarantee from the French State) in excess of a loss threshold of 2 billion euro.[92] The premiums paid to GAREAT are intended to cover: (1) the premiums paid to the members and reinsurers participating on the various reinsurance layers; (2) the premiums paid to CCR; and (3) GAREAT's operating expenses. The GAREAT premiums, paid by its members, are calculated independently of the terrorism insurance premiums these members charge under the contracts issued by them. With regard to

---

not include (or which excludes) a certain number of risks which are covered by GAREAT. Coverage for railway vehicles and coverage for business interruption following a shortage in supplies, for example, do not enjoy the CCR's unlimited coverage. The risks which do not fall within the scope of application of the top layer are co-reinsured by the members of the pool in the same conditions as those applicable to the first (co-reinsurance) layer.
[92] www.ccrif.org/partnerships/WFCP/Sessions/Day2/France_GAREAT_WFCP_Meeting_Oct_2011.pdf.

Table 8 *GAREAT rates*

Amount of total sums insured	GAREAT premium rate
Sum insured < € 6 mio (facultative session)	3%
€ 6 mio < sum insured < € 20 mio	6%
€ 20 mio < sum insured < € 50 mio	12%
€ 50 mio < sum insured	18%
Sum insured > € 750 mio	Quoted individually
Nuclear risks	24%
Exceptional risks (e.g., captives)	Special rating

the risks ceded to the Large Risks section, the GAREAT premiums are, in principle, calculated by multiplying the GAREAT premium rates, which vary according to the sums insured, by the total amount of the insurance premiums received by GAREAT. The premium to be paid to GAREAT is thus: GAREAT premium rate x premiums collected.

The GAREAT premium rates are indeed fixed by reference to the amount of the sums insured: Consequently, GAREAT earned in 2007 252 million euro in premiums on 105,000 policies.

The Dutch government and the Dutch Association of Insurers agreed to set up a dedicated reinsurance company, called the Dutch Terrorism Risk Reinsurance Company or "NHT" ("*Nederlandse Herverzekerings-maatschappij voor Terrorismeschaden*"), to cover insurance against terrorist acts in all classes of business.[93] This step represented an intervention measure to address a market failure following the limited supply of terrorism risk cover.

Since 1 July 2003,[94] more than 250 insurance companies (i.e. 93 per cent of all active Dutch insurers), together with the government and some reinsurance companies, participate in NHT. The participating insurance companies are deemed to cede all their terrorism exposure (irrespective of the category of insurance contract) to the NHT pool, which acts as a reinsurance company. The overall capacity of the terrorism-risk reinsurance pool is limited to 1 billion euro per calendar year. It was foreseen that

[93] See especially on the NHT: www.terrorismeverzekerd.nl; Ammerlaan and Van Boom 2003 and OECD 2005, 249–253.
[94] The NHT became operational on 1 July 2003. It has been periodically extended for additional periods, and is expected to be further extended as long as market conditions require.

this threshold of 1 billion euro would be gathered in three layers: the first 400 million euro will be reinsured by the participating primary insurers (even in case a particular insurer does not need to collect revenues from the NHT), while losses in excess of 400 million euro in the annual aggregate will be protected under a reinsurance market excess of loss programme valued at 300 million euro, with any shortfall taken up by the Dutch government, acting as a reinsurer of last resort, up to another 300 million euro. In the first layer applies, moreover, a so-called threshold deductible, meaning that all terrorism damage under the amount of 7.5 million euro belongs to the own risk of the insurers, although this clause has not been laid down in the official regulations. All in all, the solidarity principle among the insurance companies is an important aspect of the NHT – participation in the pooling construction is after all not mandatory, although the non-participants will be followed closely and critically by the supervisor PVK (*"Pensioen - en Verzekeringskamer"*). Further, in order to prevent that a large damage with one insured in one location would monopolise the total capacity of the NHT pool, a premier risk amount of maximum 75 million euro will be insured per location and per insured, for all participating insurance companies together, irrespective of the number of insurance contracts issued.

The Dutch government asks a premium for its reinsurance capacity which is chosen in such a way that it will price itself out of the market at the time insurability of the terrorism risk is restored. From the period of 1 July 2003 until 31 December 2003, the government asked a premium of 10 million euro (i.e. 20 million euro on a yearly basis).[95] A system of various portions is hereby operated, whereby the first part of coverage is relatively expensive: the first portion of 100 million euro demands the same premium as the second portion of 200 million euro. After all, an incentive is hereby incorporated in order to stimulate the recovery of commercial insurance: in case individual reinsurers would be capable to cover the risk, expectations are that they would offer this coverage against a lower premium. In case of recovery of the commercial insurability the government would indeed price itself out of the market. This point of departure seemed to have started to pay off since a commercial reinsurer declared itself willing to cover the first 100 million euro of governmental coverage (namely between 700 and 800 million euro), so that governmental

---

[95] Parliamentary Proceedings of the Second Chamber of Representatives 2002–2003, 28 668, No. 2, 23 June 2003.

intervention was decreased to 200 million euro.[96] Moreover, since 1 January 2006, the Dutch government only needs to guarantee 50 million euro in case the NHT compensates for more than 950 million euro.[97]

6.4. Conclusions

This chapter has presented theoretical and empirical insights in the approach insurers take with respect to man-made disasters and terrorism. It has shown that particular problems make it difficult to insure third-party liability for man-made disasters.

One problem is that demand for these types of insurances may be relatively limited, generally due to a preference of industry to externalise harm to society. That, of course, reduces incentives to seek insurance coverage for which premiums would have to be paid. The remedy suggested in the literature is to impose mandatory liability insurance. A few cases we presented from the Netherlands showed that this may be necessary. However, for a variety of reasons, one can notice a large reluctance on the side of policymakers to introduce mandatory guarantees.

The main problem in insurance of third-party liability for man-made disasters and terrorism may be related to supply-side problems which cause reluctance on the side of insurers to engage in the coverage of these types of risks. The highly correlated nature of catastrophic risks, the high capacity needed for these high damage events and lack of predictability and statistics all make man-made disasters and terrorism "difficult to insure". The answer to that problem, given not only in literature but also in practice, is a role for government to facilitate insurability in different capacities. It often takes the form of government acting as reinsurer of last resort.

Some examples, such as the case of the nuclear liability conventions show that government merely provides an additional layer of financing and, in fact, does not stimulate insurability. Case studies related to terrorism but also to Fukushima showed that there are examples where government can play a positive facilitative role in stimulating insurability of man-made disasters and terrorism. For example, the Spanish CCS charges a premium in exchange of the provision of insurance coverage,

---

[96] Parliamentary Proceedings of the Second Chamber of Representatives 2002–2003, 28 915, No. 5, 12 August 2003, 3.

[97] Parliamentary Proceedings of the Second Chamber of Representatives 2006–2007, 31 031 IXB, No. 1, 37.

and the same was the case for the indemnity agreement provided by the Japanese government for nuclear accidents. In some cases, like in the TRIA in the US, reinsurance is an outright subsidy, since insurers do not pay a premium for the State intervention provided. The NHT in the Netherlands, however, charges risk-based premiums and moreover creates strong incentives to create market solutions, since premiums are set in such a way that it becomes attractive for private (re)insurers to develop their own insurance products.

Of course, an important observation related to the preference for one solution or the other may be related to costs. On the one hand, one will have to take into account the potential costs that may arise in case no solution would exist, as shown e.g., by the case of the Netherlands, where operators succeeded in externalising harm. However, these costs of damage externalisation will have to be balanced against the potential costs of a mandatory regime. The problem with e.g., mandatory securities is that a mechanism such as insurance will always lead to costs that are higher than the objective value of the risk. After all, insurance also creates administrative costs (so-called loading) and insurers make a profit. Especially in cases where operators would not be risk-averse, e.g., because they would have substantial assets at their disposition and hence could self-insure, the additional costs of a mandatory regime may be substantial and should hence be taken into account.

The important lesson for the case of the security industry may be that the different schemes and examples we discussed show that even though there are substantial difficulties that insurers face in covering third-party liability for man-made disasters and terrorism, insurance techniques have been developed to mitigate those problems, as a result of which terrorism has become insurable again since most insurance companies first cancelled their policies after 9/11. Interestingly, government played a facilitative role in stimulating those insurance solutions which may be an interesting example for the security industry as well. Several examples also show that it is possible to construct this government intervention in such a way that it mimics market principles (e.g., by charging a risk-related premium) and hence stimulates the functioning of the insurance market, rather than distorting it (as was the case with the nuclear liability conventions discussed in Chapter 1).

7

Contracting for liability limitation

LUCAS BERGKAMP AND MICHAEL FAURE

It has been suggested[1] that the market for security services does not function well because security providers cannot negotiate and obtain adequate limitation of liability. Due to competition by small firms that are not concerned about their liability exposure, the larger firms are effectively forced to assume full liability under the law for damages caused by their malperformance. In addition, government agencies contract for security services in accordance with the legal provisions governing public procurement, and this process does not accommodate negotiations for limitation of liability of the security provider. Consequently, there could be a market failure as a result of which security firms are effectively forced to accept the complete lack of any liability limitations.

This chapter analyses this issue. The first part discusses practices in other sectors of industry that are exposed to analogous risks of potentially catastrophic damage to determine whether and, if so, to what extent they limit their liability exposure by contract or other risk management mechanisms. In the second part, we turn to risk mitigation strategies that are or could be employed by the economic actors in the security chain or by other operators exposed to terrorism-related risk. We assess the effectiveness of risk mitigation mechanisms in potentially reducing exposure of economic actors in the security chain and other operators to third-party liability. This analysis seeks to determine which of the mechanisms used in other sectors could effectively reduce exposure to liability for terrorism-related risk. To answer this question, the basic structure of the security industry and other relevant industries are compared with the basic structure of the industry sectors discussed in the first part. We attempt to identify potential restrictions on the possibility to contract for liability limitation and pay attention to public procurement for security products and services, which may not accommodate contracting for liability limitation. The last section presents our conclusions.

[1] Bergkamp, Faure, Hinteregger and Philipsen (eds.) 2013, 268.

7.1. Industry practices with respect to limitation of liability

7.1.1. Analysis of three specific sectors

In this section, the use of contractual protections (general terms and conditions, etc.) against unlimited liability vis-à-vis third parties in industry sectors other than the security industry is analysed. Practices in the following three sectors are reviewed:

- software, in particular cybersecurity software;
- pharmaceutical industry; and
- meteorological forecasting.

Risks and practices in each commercial sector will be analysed and presented in accordance with the following structure:

(1) Nature of potential exposure to risks of large-scale damage (including scope and historical exposure).
(2) Current industry practices to limit exposure contractually (liability limitation used in contracts; risk sharing and mutualisation pools; liability capping and exclusion schemes; and availability, prevalence and nature of any insurance contracts used).

The sectors of industry analysed in this chapter are exposed to potentially major liability for damages such as property damage, personal injury, including medical expenses and disability, pain and suffering (in some jurisdictions called "moral damage"), environmental damage and economic losses (also referred to as "lost profits"). In theory, each sector could be exposed to claims for each type of damage. Unsafe, defective or ineffective pharmaceutical products may result in a flood of claims for personal injury, which could lead to medical expenses, loss of income, pain and suffering, etc. Defective or ineffective security software could result in the unavailability of e-commerce websites, resulting in massive loss of income, or it could provide gateways for "hacking" into computer systems for managing critical infrastructure, such as nuclear power plants, which, in turn, could cause a nuclear accident with many casualties, massive property damage, environmental contamination and enormous loss of income. Likewise, incorrect meteorological reports could cause mischief for air, maritime and road traffic and result in accidents, personal injury, property damage, medical expenses and loss of income. Thus, in terms of the potential for exposure to massive liabilities, the pharmaceutical, software and meteorological industry may be in a position similar to the security industry and other operators exposed to terrorism-related risk. There may be significant differences, however, in terms of the probability of the risk of actual incidents and the risk of incurring liability therefore.

With respect to accidents leading to potential liability exposure, the level of regulation of an industry sector may play a role. Of the sectors analysed in this chapter, the pharmaceutical industry is the most heavily regulated, while the other sectors are regulated to a lesser extent. The level of regulation of the economic actors in the security chain would appear to be somewhere between the pharmaceutical industry and the other sectors, although the security-related industry is such a broad category that the level of regulation very much depends on the specific area. As discussed in Chapter 2, the level of regulation may have a positive or negative influence on liability exposure. Extensive regulation does not necessarily imply reduced liability exposure; regulation may have this effect if it is effective in reducing the actual risk of accidents. Conversely, it is also conceivable that onerous but ineffective regulatory standards could result in increased exposure, where plaintiffs can invoke non-compliance in support of claims based on negligence.

The actual risk of terrorism is a function of many variables, such as the political situation, the attractiveness of a target, the level of protection at the target, the sophistication and specialisation of the terrorists, etc.[2] The level of regulation is not likely to be an independent factor but more likely to reflect the actual or perceived risk of terrorism. If, in deciding where and when to attack, terrorists conduct a rational cost-benefit analysis, their decisions would be predictable. Past experience has shown that attacks targeting means of transportation (airlines, subways, etc.) are fairly common and tend to occur in large metropolitan centres (e.g., capital cities). Cyber-attacks, on the other hand, do not appear to have resulted in the kind of damage at which terrorists aim. Due to this and other factors, actual risk levels differ substantially from one sector to another.

Whether companies in a particular sector are able to negotiate contractual liability limitations and indemnification obligations is a function of the structure of the market, the main types of customers, their bargaining power, customs and other factors. There may be substantial differences between sectors of industry and between individual companies in this regard. For instance, small companies providing security services may

[2] Ibid., 189.

be willing to accept large liability exposure; large public entities that are purchasing security goods or services may be in a position to reject any limitation of liability, etc. The applicable law may also restrict the use of liability limitation; for example, the Unfair Contract Terms Directive[3] does not permit blanket liability limitations that unfairly bias contracts against consumers. While an exhaustive assessment of these factors is beyond the scope of this book, some observations on these issues are made in passing.

7.1.2.   Industry practices in other sectors

The actual liability exposure of companies in different sectors of industry varies due to factors such as the nature of their activities, the physical risk associated with such activities and, secondarily, the law and regulations applying to their activities, including the rules on liability. Another relevant factor is industry practice with respect to risk management. The relevance of these practices to operators and security providers exposed to terrorism-related risk is considered below. One of the primary considerations in attempting to draw useful parallels is the extent to which the mechanisms employed by the sectors of industry surveyed can be said to effectively limit liability within these sectors (i.e. software, pharmaceutical and meteorological industries).

To limit or exclude liability, the software industry has deployed contractual clauses set forth in an "End User Licensing Agreements" (EULA), also called "clickwrap agreements". These clauses effectively limit liability exposure and deter claims, but they are not enforceable in the European Union to the extent that they seek to limit consumers' choice of forum or court,[4] nor to the extent to which they seek to impose a limitation on liability for personal injury or death and any incidental or consequential damages arising therefrom under the Unfair Contract Terms Directive.[5] The Unfair Contract Terms Directive provides that "[a] contractual term which has not been individually negotiated shall be regarded as unfair if,

---

[3] Council Directive 93/13/EEC on unfair terms in consumer contracts [1993], OJ L095/29, (Unfair Contract Terms Directive).

[4] Ibid., Article 6 states: "Member States shall take the necessary measures to ensure that the consumer does not lose protection granted by this Directive by virtue of the choice of the law of a non-Member country as the law applicable to the contract if the latter has a close connection with the territory of a Member State."

[5] Ibid., Annex, sections 1(a) and (b).

contrary to the requirement of good faith, it causes a significant imbalance in the parties' rights and obligations arising under the contract, to the detriment of the consumer."[6]

Clickwrap agreements fall within the ambit of "not individually negotiated agreements", a term used in the following provision of the Unfair Contract Terms Directive: "A term shall always be regarded as not individually negotiated where it has been drafted in advance and the consumer has therefore not been able to influence the substance of the term, particularly in the context of pre-formulated standard contracts."[7] The Directive requires that such contracts do not contain terms that are "unfair" to the consumer. An illustrative list of terms considered unfair[8] includes those terms which have the object or effect of:

– excluding or limiting the legal liability of a seller or supplier in the event of the death of a consumer or personal injury to the latter resulting from an act or omission of that seller or supplier; . . .
– excluding or hindering the consumer's right to take legal action or exercise any other legal remedy.[9]

Many EULAs do not explicitly acknowledge that liability limitations may not apply in the EU. Some EULAs, however, acknowledge generally the non-universality of such limitations. For example, a cybersecurity firm's limited liability clause excluding "all damages whatsoever" is followed by an exception stating that "[b]ecause some States do not allow the exclusion or limitation of liability for consequential or incidental damages, the above limitation may not apply to you."

Where jurisdictions restrict the ability of EULAs to limit liability for personal injury and incidental or consequential damages, or to specify a specific court for claims, software companies are effectively forced to accept the liability exposure or avoid the jurisdiction altogether. The industry's current practices to limit exposure, however, to a large extent remain untested by the courts, and their actual legal effects are in many cases a matter of speculation. Moreover, where the insurance policies of software companies provide coverage for damages that are excluded by EULAs, there is a second layer of protection against potential future claims.

The question should be asked how it is possible that the software industry has been able to impose liability-limiting contracts on its customers

---

[6] Ibid., Article 3(1).   [7] Ibid., Article 3(2).   [8] Ibid., Annex 1.
[9] Ibid., Annex 1, para 1(a) and (q).

on an apparently large scale. In this regards, the software industry may be in a unique position. There are a number of reasons that may help explain this situation:

(1) Software cannot be held to any objective "safety" or "security" standards beyond the standard set by its manufacturer. Manifest manufacturing defects or design defects may render it obviously unusable and reasonable consumers expect that even well-functioning software contains some "bugs". It thus is hard to specify objectively what constitutes a failure of software, or lack of care in developing software, given the dynamic nature of the industry and the constantly evolving security threats to which it must respond. It is indicative that under the Product Liability Directive, which may or may not apply to software,[10] a producer cannot be held liable where he can demonstrate that "the state of scientific and technical knowledge at the time when he put the product into circulation was not such as to enable the existence of the defect to be detected."[11]

(2) The method of sale and delivery of software, which increasingly is done over the internet, allows for the utilisation of so-called "shrink" or clickwrap agreements. Linked to this is the respective bargaining power of both parties. Moreover, it is likely that the price of software would be dramatically different if software companies could not disclaim implied statutory warranties (like functionality and security) and limit the scope of their prospective liability. All firms in the software market are in the same position in this regard and all providers therefore include liability limitations in their EULAs, thereby normalising the use of these contractual terms and precluding consumers from acquiring these products without acquiescing to these terms.

(3) The position of contract software service providers may be different, however. With regard to the provision of bespoke security services for critical infrastructure, the generalised use of exoneration from liability is unlikely, since it would contradict the specific performance objectives agreed between the parties. Although, due to the sensitive nature of cybersecurity services for critical infrastructure, very little information is publicly available, security software providers may well have cyber liability insurance policies, which offer protection where direct liability limitation is not possible. Moreover,

---

[10] Stapleton 1994, 334.   [11] Unfair Contract Terms Directive, Article 7(e).

some of the most vulnerable industries are jointly operated with State agents, which may shield private contractors from sole liability, or bring them within the scope of sovereign immunity where available.

In Europe, the pharmaceutical industry, to a large extent, remains exposed to potential third-party liability claims. Strict regulation and pharmacovigilance procedures and the structure of the civil liability system (no class actions, etc.), however, may well work to reduce the number of claims against pharmaceutical companies. Note that regulation in the area of security does not necessarily produce the same effects. Unlike economic actors in the security chain, pharmaceutical companies have had a long history of facing claims and thus developed mechanisms to protect against such claims, without resorting to exoneration and other contractual liability limitations.

Again, the nature of the product concerned is key to understanding the industry's liability exposure. Pharmaceutical products are regarded as "inherently" risky; i.e., it is generally acknowledged that the products pose a certain degree of risk to the user and that the risks may well vary as a function of the disease to be treated and the physical condition or susceptibility of the user. The extent to which companies are exposed when it comes to such risks depends also on the Member State in question. Germany,for example, imposes strict liability for any risks that are not pre-identified and cause personal injury to the plaintiff.[12] Disclosure of the risks (specifically, the performance limits) of security products and services, by contrast, is often either impossible or undesirable. Although the public understands that these products and services cannot be effective against each and every attempted terrorist attack, the expectations are high. If and where security fails and terrorists are able to carry out their plans, the ensuing damage is not characterised as an "unfortunate side effect" in the same way as in the case of pharmaceutical products.

With regard to the general user who uses publicly available weather information, free of charge, the liability-limiting disclaimers employed by the meteorological industry, in general, are effective in limiting exposure. Alternatively, the meteorological industry can reduce its liability exposure by carefully describing the services rendered or the standard that applies to its forecast (e.g., forecasts are provided "as is", and may not be accurate, since they are based on predictions based on models). In cases in which such devices were not deployed by a company, however,

---

[12] German Pharmaceuticals Act (*Arzneimittelgesetz*, AMG).

the general standard of care (and, as a related matter, the public's under-standing of the unpredictability of the weather and the inherent limits of weather reports), the lack of foreseeability of harm in a specific case, the doctrine of risk assumption, the requisite proximate causal link between the weather report and the plaintiff's damage and the plaintiff's burden of proof would help to protect the company concerned against liability.

Although the same standards of liability apply to the economic actors in the security chain in the event of a terrorist attack, the results may well be different. The doctrine of risk assumption, for example, is highly dependent on the specific situation, and victims of a terrorist attack on an aeroplane may not be deemed to have accepted the risk of scanning equipment malfunction. The nature of the risk in the meteorological industry is a natural risk, independent of individual human activity, while the risk in the security industry is a risk arising from intentional human behaviour. This difference may well translate into a different level of exposure of economic actors in the security chain.

To be sure, there are areas and circumstances in which the meteorological industry remains vulnerable to liability exposure. Because the meteorological industry predicts event in the future, however, it can invoke the limits of available models and scientific processes to argue that incorrect reports are not the result of any fault or negligence. While the ever-evolving meteorological forecasting modelling may enhance the ability to predict, at the same time the weather itself may become less predictable. Moreover, accuracy is increasingly guaranteed by advertised services in the context of contractual relationships with particular customers.[13] In this sense, an analogy could be drawn with the security industry.

7.1.3. Relevance for the security industry

Each of the three commercial sectors surveyed above exhibits certain spe-cific characteristics that have influenced the nature of both its liability exposure and the instruments deployed to limit liability (and their effec-tiveness). The findings therefore cannot be generalised or extrapolated to the security industry, which operates in different markets and in different regulatory and economic contexts. In theory, however, the contractual mechanisms deployed in these three commercial sectors could be rele-vant to the economic actors in the security chain. Whether, in practice, contractual liability limitations can play a significant role is a function of

---

[13] Millington 1987, 238.

whether such limitations will be accepted by the business partners of the economic actors in the security chain, and to what extent such limitations are effective vis-à-vis third parties that have not agreed to them. This, in turn, is a function of market structure, relative bargaining power, specific laws and regulations, etc. (Similar reasoning applies also to the possible deployment of other instruments such as mutual risk pools, which are discussed in 8.2.) In theory, these arrangements could help, but whether, in fact, they can be established by and for the benefit of the economic actors in the security chain given the industry's specificities and the market structure, requires further analysis. Potentially relevant factors may be whether the industry's business partners are willing to accept liability limitations; whether there is sufficient standardisation across the industry to enable a general standard to be determined; whether the political and legal context in which the economic actors in the security chain operate would support liability limitations; which specific structures are most fitting to the industry; and whether other means, or a combination of them, could achieve the same effect in a more effective, cost-efficient or otherwise more desirable manner. In short, the analysis of industry practices in other commercial sectors provides useful insights into how liability risks can be managed. It demonstrates the respective strengths and weaknesses of each approach for the relevant industry and highlights the extent to which particular industry practices in this regard are a product of the particular needs and experiences of the industry in question.

In the security industry, however, there may be an additional complication that deserves attention. Contractual mechanisms may be difficult for the economic actors in the security chain to secure, to the extent contracts are awarded by public procurement based on contracts that are not negotiable. Public procurement is regulated extensively[14] to ensure fair opportunities and competition, but this law does not require that contractors assume full liability under the law. Of course, where a standard contract proposed by a purchaser does not provide liability limitations and a specific bidder insists on such limitations, its chances to be awarded the contract may be adversely affected (see further under 7.2.2., below). Sector-wide liability limitations and related mechanisms, in theory, would

---

[14] Directive 2014/24/EU of the European Parliament and of the Council of 26 February 2014 on public procurement and repealing Directive 2004/18/EC, OJ [2014] L 94/65 and Directive 2014/25/EU of the European Parliament and of the Council of 26 February 2014 on procurement by entities operating in the water, energy, transport and postal services sectors and repealing Directive 2004/17/EC , OJ [2014] L 94/243.

be an option, but they raise issues under competition law and there is as yet no evidence of any such attempt in the security industry. It remains to be seen whether and, if so, how specific tools could be relevant and workable for economic actors in the security chain in light of industry practice and market structure, procurement practices and the like.

7.2. Risk mitigation strategies

The analysis presented in previous sections suggests that, when compared to other sectors, security providers may be less capable of deploying risk mitigation measures to limit their liability. The reasons for their reduced ability to limit their liability include the following. First, economic actors in the security chain, in particular service providers, have argued that they have been unable to negotiate contractual limitations of their liability. Contractual liability limitations can involve (1) narrow descriptions of primary obligations and limited representations and warranties; (2) exoneration for certain types of damages, for all damage caused by negligence, or for other types of exposure; (3) liability limitations in the form of financial caps or similar mechanisms; (4) indemnities; and (5) hybrid provisions, combinations of or variations on the above. The customers of the economic actors in the security chain appear to have been able to impose their terms and conditions on their providers, which has resulted in a lack of contractual protection for the security providers.[15]

Second, as discussed, the customers of the security industry are often public or semi-public authorities, which buy products and services through a regulated and standardised public procurement process. This may mean that these customers impose their terms and conditions, which tend to favour them and that non-acceptance of such terms may disqualify the bidder. Where this is so, security providers must either accept unlimited liability or the risk of being excluded or disfavoured by purchasers. For economic and business reasons, companies may not want to forego this market and thus accept the terms offered.

Third, security providers may not have been able to contract adequate insurance at a reasonable price to cover the liability risks associated with terrorism-related risks. Where this is so, they are not insured or underinsured for the liability exposure associated with terrorist attacks.

Beyond these considerations, there are broader public policy issues associated with the civil liability exposure of the security providers. For

---

[15] Bergkamp, Faure, Hinteregger and Philipsen (eds.) 2013, 300.

instance, should we encourage innovation in security and if so, should we do so through liability limitations? In light of the differences between security providers and other economic actors, these policy questions deserve further consideration (see Chapter 11).

The position of the security industry in public procurement is not unique, and other sectors of industry that sell much of their output to governments may be in a similar position. Nevertheless, the issue requires further analysis, because security providers may be exposed to larger liability risks than other sectors and the lack of liability limitations may thus become a problem.

There is no reliable and representative research on the extent to which security providers are unable to negotiate limitations on their liability in contracts with the Member State's public authorities and governmental agencies in public procurement for security products and services. It has been reported, however, that Member State public authorities insist that security providers remain fully liable under the applicable law.[16] Because there are often one or more bidders willing to accept these conditions (in particular, smaller companies whose assets are much smaller than the potential liabilities), all other companies are effectively forced to go along or they must accept that their chance of being awarded the contract decrease significantly. In some cases, individual companies have decided not to participate in bidding because they are not willing to assume the liability risks.[17] It has been reported that companies willing to accept full liability exposure in the maritime security area are more likely to offer sub-standard products or services, or have limited assets.[18] If, due to their reluctance to accept unlimited liability risks, financially strong security providers offering high quality products and services were consistently losing business to financially weak providers offering sub-standard products and services, this would be a concern. In itself, this would not necessarily justify a legislative liability limitation, however. In lieu of a liability limitation, it could possibly provide an argument in favour of the regulation of security providers, or another measure targeting financially weak companies.[19] In the absence of problems of underdeterrence of financially weak companies and the "judgment-proof" problem,[20] if

---

[16] Ibid., 300.   [17] Ibid., 300.   [18] Ibid., 300.

[19] Such a measure could involve a solvency guarantee in order to avoid externalisation of insolvency risk.

[20] Shavell 1986. This problem arises where the amounts of potential liabilities exceed the assets of the potentially liable person, so that, to that extent, liability does not create any financial incentives to prevent harm.

and to the extent that security providers are "forced" to accept contracts that do not set any limits to their liability, such contract clauses could merely reflect the preferences of the Member State governments. Viewed in this light, any legislative intervention might have adverse consequences. Under these circumstances, the EU or a national legislature would have a hard time supporting contractual liability protection for the security industry, because that would appear to be diametrically opposed to the Member State governments' explicit preference for full liability exposure.

The practice of the Member State public authorities to refuse to grant liability limitations could be consistent with a well-functioning market, in which security providers decide whether to bid for a specific project according to the totality of the proposed transaction, including their liability exposure. There does not appear to be any documentary evidence of a structural problem that requires legislative intervention in the market. In the absence of such a problem, the market may simply be competitive in relation to the ability and willingness of providers to assume liability risks. In that case, a liability limitation would eliminate competition in this regard and thus encourage excessive risk-taking, which would result in higher risk levels.

7.3. Conclusions

The analysis presented in this chapter shows that security providers, unlike companies in other sectors such as software, may not be able to negotiate limitations on their liability in contracts with their customers. This appears to be true in particular where the government or public agencies purchase security services or products in a public procurement process governed by public procurement legislation.

Although no individual factor discussed above, such as the lack of contractual liability limitation or adequate insurance coverage, may place security providers in a unique position with respect to their liability exposure, it is possible that the combination of factors is unique to the economic actors in the security chain. For instance, software companies are potentially exposed to catastrophic liabilities, but they are able to limit their exposure by contract and to contract adequate insurance, while security providers are also exposed to catastrophic liabilities, but are unable to limit their exposure by contract and to contract adequate insurance. The combination of the exposure to large liabilities (even if it is based solely on fault) and the inability to limit such exposure by contract (and to obtain adequate insurance coverage, which, by definition, is subject to financial limits) might render security providers uniquely vulnerable to such liabilities. As noted, none of this means that liability exposure must therefore be directly limited, but it may mean that there is possibly exceptional liability exposure that may require policymakers' attention.

In addressing the liability of the security providers, it is important to consider not only the difficulties that they may face, but also the objectives of the liability system. Where liability exposure is excluded or limited, the realisation of these objectives may be impeded. Accordingly, there must be important policy reasons to justify an exclusion or limitation of liability, given the potentially negative effects of such a measure in terms of deterrence (prevention), risk allocation and loss-spreading. Moreover, there are differences between jurisdictions with respect to both liability exposure and the ability to deploy mitigation strategies; some of the arguments in favour of a liability limitation apply to the liability exposure of the US security industry and have not the same force in the European liability environment. In most EU Member States, specific direct compensation solutions have been worked out to cover damage resulting from terrorist activities. Indeed, a representative of a large reinsurer said that he was unaware of any problems with respect to the insurability of the liability exposure of the security industry in Europe.[21] This cautions against the adoption of any direct measures involving an exclusion or limitation of the liability of security providers. Measures such as direct State-provided compensation of damage caused by terrorists, of course, may result in a de facto limitation of their liability exposure.

---

[21] Bergkamp, Faure, Hinteregger and Philipsen (eds.) 2013, 306.

8

Alternative systems for redressing
terrorism-related risks

LUCAS BERGKAMP AND MICHAEL FAURE

This chapter turns to alternative systems for redressing terrorism-related risks. In the US, following the 9/11 attacks, specific legislation has been enacted to encourage security firms to develop and deploy new security technology, products and services. This legislation is called the US Safety Act. Under the Safety Act, protection against tort liability is available to qualifying companies. Section 8.1. sketches the key features of this legislation and asks whether this regime could be transplanted to Europe. Further, this chapter explores whether other alternative compensation mechanisms, more particularly direct compensation systems, might provide a solution. Insurance of natural disasters (8.2.), a victim compensation fund (8.3.) and government-provided compensation (8.4.) are discussed in turn. The final section (8.5.) presents some conclusions.

8.1. The US Safety Act

The Safety Act is the main legal instrument for producers of security-related products and services to limit third-party liability claims against them. It passed narrowly through the US Congress as part of the Homeland Security Act of 2002 ("HSA") to encourage innovation with respect to anti-terrorist security products and services after the September 11th attacks on the World Trade Center in New York City and other targets in the US.[1] The HSA also established the Department of Homeland Security ("DHS" or "the Department"), a Cabinet-level department within the US government, headed by the Secretary of Homeland Security ("the Secretary"), to administer the new legislation, including the Safety Act provisions. The rationale behind the Safety Act is that stimulating innovation and the development and deployment of anti-terrorist products and

---

[1] Safety Act Articles 861–865, 6 USC 441–444.

services is the best way to strengthen the US's front-line defence against terrorism.[2] Congress believed that this innovation was being stifled by risk and litigation management issues arising from the US product liability regime and the associated liability exposure of manufacturers and users of anti-terrorism products and services, potentially leading to crippling litigation as well as public relations and shareholder issues in the aftermath of a terrorist attack.[3] Congress also recognised that adequate and affordable insurance was either unavailable or far too costly to effectively mitigate liability for developers and providers of anti-terrorism products and services.[4] Additionally, government contractors had become increasingly unwilling to accept the potentially enterprise-threatening risk of developing and deploying anti-terrorism technologies and bidding for related contracts. This was limiting the pool of otherwise qualified bidders; reducing competition and limiting the range of cost-effective, best-value solutions for the buyer; and creating disincentives for investment in new technology.

Under the Act, an "act of terrorism" means "any act determined to have met the following requirements or such other requirements" as defined and specified by the Secretary:

– is unlawful;
– causes harm, including financial harm, to a person, property, or entity, in the United States, or in the case of a US-flagged carrier or vessel, in or outside the United States; and
– uses or attempts to use instrumentalities, weapons or other methods designed or intended to cause mass destruction, injury or other loss to citizens or institutions of the United States.[5]

DHS has broad discretion in determining whether to approve a product or service as a "qualified anti-terrorism technology" ("QATT") and, in

---

[2] See PL 107–296, House R. 107–609 (Part 1) at 118.
[3] Congressional Hearing Before the Subcommittee on Cybersecurity Infrastructure Protection, and Security Technologies of the Committee on Homeland Security House of Representatives, particularly the Statement of US Representative Daniel Lungren: "[l]egal precedents such as those emanating from the 9/11 attacks as well as those holding the Port Authority of New York and New Jersey liable for the 1993 World Trade Center attacks make it clear that civil litigation can intimidate the developers and users of security technologies and services after a terrorist event."
[4] Testimony by DHS Assistant Secretary Parney Albright, *Implementing the SAFETY Act: Advancing New Technologies for Homeland Security*, Hearing before the House Committee on Government Reform, 12, 17 October 2003.
[5] 6 CFR §25.2.

doing so, it must consider both technical and economic criteria which must include the following:

- Evidence of prior US Government use or demonstrated substantial utility and effectiveness;
- Availability of the technology for immediate deployment in public and private settings;
- Existence of extraordinarily large or extraordinarily unquantifiable potential third-party liability risk exposure to the Seller or other provider of the technology;
- Substantial likelihood that the technology will not be deployed unless Safety Act risk management protections are extended;
- Magnitude of risk exposure to the public if the technology is not deployed;
- Evaluation of scientific studies that can be feasibly conducted in order to assess the capability of the technology to substantially reduce risks of harm; and
- Evidence of the technology's effectiveness in facilitating the defence against acts of terrorism.[6]

The main tools employed by the US Safety Act to insulate certified security providers from third-party liability are examined below:

8.1.1.   Exclusive federal cause of action against sellers of QATT

The creation of a specific, federal cause of action confirms that the proper respondent in any civil claim is the manufacturer of a security product or the provider of a security service, which may mean that others in the supply chain, such as users, contractors, subcontractors, customers, vendors and suppliers, benefit from immunity from litigation in this regard. This is justified on the grounds that "[i]f the Seller of the Qualified Anti-Terrorism Technology at issue were not the only defendant, would-be plaintiffs could, in an effort to circumvent the statute, bring claims . . . against arguably less culpable persons."[7] This targeting of liability also creates confidence among suppliers and customers engaging in trade and contractual relations with producers and providers of QATTs.

---

[6] 6 USC § 442(b)(1)–(7).   [7] 71 Fed Reg at 33150.

8.1.2.   Exclusive jurisdiction in a federal district court

Before the passage of the Safety Act, terrorism-related liability lawsuits would likely have been brought in State courts, as a result of which defendants would not have had the benefit of significant liability protection. As DHS explains in the implementing regulations, federal suits under the Safety Act will nevertheless likely be decided in accordance with the law of the State where the attack occurred.[8]

8.1.3.   Limited relief

The Safety Act also limits the nature, type and scope of damages that plaintiffs may seek in bringing an action against a QATT supplier.[9] Condensing potential cases into a single cause of action restricted to the Federal Court allows the Act to ban the award of punitive damages in such cases.[10] The Act further limits liability by restricting the award of non-economic damages. While these damages are usually available to all plaintiffs in third-party liability claims in the US, the Safety Act stipulates that these damages may only be sought where the plaintiff has suffered an actual, physical injury. Plaintiffs who have not done so are precluded from seeking damages for pain and suffering, inconvenience, mental anguish, loss of enjoyment of life, loss of consortium, injury to reputation or any other non-pecuniary losses.[11] The total exposure of security providers is further limited by the collateral source compensation requirements, which reduce the respondent's liability where they have collected damages from other sources, including for example, from insurance.[12]

8.1.4.   Government contractor defence

The government contractor defence is an affirmative defence that immunises defendants from certain liability claims, thus providing a significant benefit to the seller of a QATT in a lawsuit. The defence is based on the principle that if a contractor works according to government-provided specifications, it is entitled to the government's privilege of immunity and should be protected by that immunity to the same extent that the government would be if it had performed the work itself. The Supreme Court applied this doctrine in *Boyle* v. *United Technologies Corp.*,[13] where

---

[8] 71 Fed Reg. at 33150.   [9] 6 USC §442(b)(1).   [10] 6 USC § 442(b)(1).
[11] 6 USC §442(b)(2)(A).   [12] 6 USC §442(c).
[13] *Boyle* v. *United Technologies Corp.*, 487 US 500, 512 (1988).

it concluded that holding contractors liable for damages resulting from
government contracts would subvert the sovereign immunity protections
of the federal government by causing the contractor to subvert its costs
back to the government. The Court said that it would apply the defence
to "shield ... contractors from tort liability for products manufactured
for the Government in accordance with Government specifications, if the
contractor warned the United States about any hazards known to the contractor but not to the Government".[14] Since this judgment, some federal
courts have applied the defence narrowly and refused to allow its use by
non-military contractors.[15] However, the Safety Act expressly extends this
defence not just to military procurements, but more broadly to companies
selling anti-terrorism technology or services to any customer, including
private entities. As a result, any seller of a certified technology cannot
be held liable for design defects or "failure to warn" claims, unless the
presumption of the defence is rebutted by evidence that the seller acted
fraudulently or with wilful misconduct. Once certified, the presumption
in favour of the government contractor defence applies in perpetuity to
all deployments of the product or service that occur on or after the effective date, as long as it was sold before the certification's expiration or
termination.

8.1.5.   Liability capped to the amount of insurance coverage

The Safety Act also limits liability by imposing a maximum liability ceiling. Following the approval of an application by the DHS, the security
provider will be furnished with the details of the level and amount of
insurance cover which he will be required to take out under the Act. This
amount, determined during the application process, is the maximum liability ceiling for any damages to be paid by a QATT provider found liable
after a terrorist incident.[16]

There are several prisms through which the effectiveness of the Act
may be assessed. First, one can consider the volume of applications that
the Department has approved: in Fiscal Year 2011, the DHS approved

---

[14] Ibid.
[15] See, e.g., *In re Hawaii* Fed Asbestos Cases, 960 F.2d 806 (9th Cir. 1992) (restricting
the federal government contractor defence to military contractors) and *Nielsen* v. *George
Diamond Vogel Paint Co.*, 892 F.2d 1450 (9th Cir. 1990) (restricting the federal government
contractor defence to military contractors providing military equipment).
[16] 6 USC § 443(c).

more than 40 per cent more applications than the previous year.[17] This
increase could be interpreted as an indication that the security industry
has warmly accepted the new regime. Second, one could consider the
impact that Safety Act designations and certifications have had on the
marketplace. Private companies have testified to the positive impact of
Safety Act benefits for them,[18] while the Federal Acquisition Regulations
were amended in 2007 to mandate that federal government agencies
consider whether their homeland security procurements are eligible for
Safety Act coverage.[19] The effectiveness of the Safety Act can also be
inferred from the broad scope of the products and services which have
been approved by the Department. To illustrate this with some specific
examples, successful applications include coverage to the comprehensive
internal security plan of a chemical company; a technology that provides
cybersecurity situational awareness and network security monitoring; and
even a process for the production of ammonium nitrate fertiliser to render it less detonable than standard fertiliser. Moreover, the widespread
use of the Safety Act Mark, which indicates that a product or service has
been properly vetted by the federal government and meets stringent criteria for effectiveness and usefulness, is another sign of the success of the
programme. DHS has not released any formal cost-benefit assessment of
the US Safety Act. Since these benefits have not been quantified, it is as
yet unclear how strong these incentives have been, or how many technologies and products would not have been introduced were it not for the
Safety Act.

Yet, the Safety Act has also created new challenges. One potential disadvantage is the risk of premature release and deployment of technology that
has not been sufficiently tested. However, this scenario is unlikely to arise
given that government must review technology before extending Safety
Act benefits to it. Another possible disadvantage is the unavailability of
compensation to plaintiffs that have been harmed by the products and

---

[17] S&T Directorate, FY2011 Year in Review at 47.
[18] Statement of Scott Boylan, Vice President and General Counsel, Morpho Detection, Inc.
    before the Congressional Committee on Homeland Security: "The transfer of Safety
    Act coverage ... was a pre-condition to closing when our company was sold by GE to
    Safran in 2009. This only serves to illustrate how important this coverage is to investment
    decisions." Statement of Craig A. Harvey, Chief Operations Officer and Executive Vice
    President, NVision Solutions, Inc: "By levelling the playing field and capping financial
    exposure The Safety Act encourages innovation. Without the Safety Act, our desire to
    bring [our anti-terrorism technology] to market may never have been realized."
[19] See 40 CFR Parts 50 and 52; and 48 CFR § 50.205–1(a).

services deployed by defendants that benefit from protection under the Safety Act. However, no such cases have arisen thus far. The Act has also been criticised because the liability protection it offers is conditional and not complete, while the insurance requirement ensures that compensation is available in appropriate cases. Another concern is the fact that the exclusive remedy provision directs all claims at the QATT producer, thus shielding other actors in the supply chain from liability. It is also unclear how effective the Safety Act would be if an act of terrorism were to occur outside the US, where an anti-terrorism product or service is deployed. While the DHS has stated that, in this case, the Safety Act would apply,[20] it has been argued that more should be done to strengthen protection similar to that afforded by the Act outside the US, or to encourage foreign nations to formally recognise its applicability to acts of terrorism occurring in their territory.[21]

The European liability landscape differs from the US system in several respects, which may have implications for both the necessity of a Safety Act-like regime and the way in which such a regime could be designed. This section attempts to identify the closest corresponding features of the EU legal tradition which would affect any replication of the Safety Act regime in the EU. To this end, the key features of the US Safety Act will be categorised as either (1) institutional; (2) procedural; or (3) substantive.

8.1.5.1. Institutional features

8.1.5.1.1. Central role of federal agency The entire process of pre-application review, consultation, application processing and approval is administered at a centralised level through a federal agency, staffed by experts and funded through the federal budget. No similar agency already exists in the EU. Therefore, an EU Safety Act would necessitate entrusting these duties either to an existing or a newly created agency, or the European Commission, which would have to swiftly amass expertise in security measures. Given the significant discretion involved in this process, the Commission would probably be the most appropriate actor to make these decisions. This is so because the long-established *Meroni* doctrine stipulates that delegating executive powers to an agency must involve powers which are clearly defined and must be exercised "subject to strict review

---

[20] The Homeland Security and Defense Business Council, *Why Robust Use of the SAFETY Act Is Critical to Homeland Security & How to Get There*, October 2008, 16.
[21] *Ibid.*

in light of objective criteria determined by the delegating authority".[22] Under this doctrine, broad powers similar to those currently vested in the US Secretary of the DHS could not be vested in an EU agency or network of agencies, but would have to be redefined so as to minimise the level of discretion afforded in the exercise. This would necessitate defining concepts such as "act of terrorism" and qualifying-product standards. If improperly defined, these definitions could undermine the entire purpose of the scheme, by, for example, allowing liability in cases where actions are deemed to fall outside the scope of an "act of terrorism". Another option would be the utilisation or creation of national agencies within the Member States, whose decisions would be valid across the EU, possibly through a mutual recognition mechanism.

8.1.5.1.2. Exclusive federal cause of action Another stumbling block is that there are no "federal" courts in the EU, except for the Court of Justice of the European Union (CJEU), which has limited jurisdiction and is currently not competent to hear any civil liability cases involving private parties as defendants. While, in theory, the CJEU's jurisdiction could be expanded to hear claims by private parties in relation to third-party liability covered by Safety Act-like legislation, this would constitute an unprecedented extension of the Court's jurisdiction, which would require substantial political will and an amendment of the European Treaties. Moreover, granting exclusive jurisdiction to the CJEU would deprive national courts of jurisdiction, which is currently uncharted terrain in the EU law context.

8.1.5.2. Procedural features

8.1.5.2.1. Review procedure While reviewing applications is familiar territory for the EU, the nature of the Safety Act review process is particularly stringent. Following a thorough internal review under the Safety Act, applications are further subjected to a peer-review evaluation process, during which each application is assessed against the criteria specified under the Act. This peer-review process depends on the availability of experts within the agency and other federally funded research and development centres and agencies. Transplanting this process into the EU may prove onerous or expensive, since an analogous agency or network of agencies would have to be created, or at least coordinated.

---

[22] Case 9/56 Meroni & Co, *Industrie Metallurische SpA v. High Authority* [1985] ECR 133, 152.

8.1.5.2.2. Publication of the decisions Decisions granting protection pursuant to the Safety Act could be published in the EU Official Journal, national official journals or a publicly accessible database (similar to the database established by the European Chemicals Agency). If decisions by national authorities are notified to the Commission, a central register could be created. The products and services that benefit from specific protection under the Safety Act should be clearly identified in the decisions and register.

8.1.5.2.3. Supervision of the use of the Safety Act mark If an EU Safety Act were to include a mark, supervision of the use of this mark could be performed by the Commission, the competent EU agency to be established and/or the Member States.

8.1.5.3.   Substantive features

1. The SAFETY Act limits liability exposure by (i) excluding punitive damages and prejudgment interest, (ii) excluding recovery for non-economic damages in the absence of physical injury; (iii) limiting recovery for non-economic damages in proportion to the defendant's liability for economic harm; and (iv) reducing recovery in a suit against the seller of the QATT by any amounts collected by the plaintiff from insurance or other collateral sources.

These methods of limiting liability are unprecedented in EU law. However, there does not seem to be any need to introduce these rules, since Member State civil liability regimes do not provide for punitive damages. Moreover, compensation for pain and suffering and moral damages tends not to be substantial, while collateral sources of compensation, such as insurance, significantly reduce the amount of compensation to be paid following civil lawsuits (and, thus, also the incentive to bring a lawsuit).

2. The US Safety Act authorises the Secretary to set a liability cap on the amount of liability insurance specified by the DHS based on the maximum amount of liability insurance reasonably available from private sources.

Although unusual, this rule is technically possible under EU law. Within the domain of national law, the amount of compensation awarded may be mitigated based on factors such as the insurance coverage limit of the defendant. However, this would entail agreement on pre-determined rules and definitions, which would raise boundary issues. Further, these rules would have to be standardised, so as to facilitate cooperation among Member State agencies and to ensure that the system is not vulnerable to charges of breach of competition law.

3. The Safety Act creates a rebuttable presumption of a "government contractor defence" in any product liability lawsuit.

The "government contractor defence" and the notions of sovereign and sovereign-derived contractor liability, are typically not found in the domestic laws of the Member States. Accordingly, no such concept could be included in EU law.

The transatlantic differences in the civil liability landscape highlighted above indicate that, while a Safety Act-like regime could be implemented in the EU, many issues would require specific attention and a high degree of legal innovation. While exploring uncharted legal terrain is certainly possible, there are a number of reasons why the EU may not want to look to the Safety Act regime as a source of inspiration. First, in the US, the Act has been criticised because it may extend protection even to those sellers who put anti-terrorism products on the market knowing that these products would provide inadequate protection against terrorist attacks.[23] Moreover, the US Safety Act does not provide a generalised exclusion of liability. Rather, designations are issued only for a reasonable period, no longer than thirty-six months. Additionally, the cap on liability to an insurable amount found in the Safety Act is arguably not necessary in the EU, since the security industry has as yet not experienced an insurability problem justifying similar regulatory action in Europe. Finally and crucially, the aforementioned transatlantic differences are indicative of the fact that the Safety Act was created to alleviate the effects of features specific to the US liability litigation environment. As a result, the Safety Act is not easily transplanted to a different jurisdiction. For example, imposing a liability cap equal to a maximum insurable amount assumes insurability problems for the security industry, while barring punitive damages and limiting the award of non-economic damages are necessary due to the high amounts awarded and the wider array of grounds for claiming damages in the US. These problems do not exist, or are not present to the same extent, in the European tort liability environment. Therefore, it remains doubtful whether a Safety Act-like regime would be a good regulatory choice for Europe.

---

[23] 149 US Cong Rec S46 (Jan 7, 2003).

8.2. Insurance of natural disasters

In this section we focus on the approach insurers take towards the coverage of large-scale natural disasters. At the outset, we should note that it has taken substantial experience and learning in several countries to arrive at an adequate coverage of natural disasters. The reasons are similar to the case of man-made disasters and terrorism: there are substantial problems both on the demand-side as well as on the supply-side that explain why these insurance regimes have not emerged on a large scale (with the exception of the countries where insurance has been made compulsory, such as in Belgium and France). We discuss the problems encountered and the solutions developed by insurers, as well as the facilitative strategies provided by government, which have played a significant role.

There is a big difference between natural disaster insurance and terrorism insurance, however. In the case of natural disasters, insurance provides first-party coverage, not tort law or third-party liability coverage. The reason, of course, is that natural disasters are typically "acts of God" or force majeure as a result of which no injurer can be identified that could be held liable. The only possibility to invoke third-party liability rules in case of a natural disaster may well be to focus on the public authorities. It has been argued that natural disasters are not necessarily beyond anybody's control, since most catastrophes are produced jointly by nature and humans.[24] Natural forces may create a flood, but what turns the flood into a disaster often is a human decision, for example, the decision of a government to provide permits for building in flood-prone areas. If such disasters occur, the public authority involved may be a possible liable party, if, for instance, it failed to take adequate preventive measures or to give adequate warnings.[25] The insurance solutions we discuss below, on the other hand, are so-called first-party insurance schemes, which involve potential victims contracting insurance to seek protection against the financial consequences of a natural disaster.

8.2.1. First-party insurance for natural disasters

First-party insurance is a system whereby insurance coverage is provided and compensation is awarded directly, by the insurer to the victim. It

---

[24] See Zeckhauser 1996, 113.
[25] See on the governmental responsibility after Hurricane Katrina Bier 2006 and Walter and Kettl 2006.

is thus the prospective victim itself who buys this type of insurance to cover possible future harm and corresponding damages. The underlying principle in first-party insurance is that the insurance company pays out once damage has occurred, provided that the particular damage is an insured risk covered by the insurance policy. Contrary to third-party insurance, payment to compensate damage is made by the insurance company irrespective of whether there is liability.[26]

Accordingly, insurance protection moves away from tort law and third-party insurance and towards victim-funded insurance coverage on a first-party basis. This trend is visible in the area of environmental damage, where insurance operates often as a form of first-party insurance.[27] There is a similar movement toward first-party insurance in the areas of medical malpractice[28] and traffic accidents.[29] Compared to third-party liability insurance, first-party insurance schemes offer some benefits. Indeed, Priest suggested that the shift towards first-party insurance would have been an appropriate remedy to the American insurance crisis that occurred in the 1980s.[30] Priest reasoned that:

> [I]n comparison to first-party insurance, third party tort law insurance provides coverage in excessive amounts, in a manner that substantially restricts risk segregation and at costs that far exceed the costs of first-party insurance. For both consumer and provider risk pools, these differences will increase the correlation of risks within existing pools and, as a consequence, increase the extent of adverse selection, leading to the breakdown of the pools.[31]

Other commentators, such as Bishop and Epstein, also favour first-party insurance.[32] Specifically, it has been argued that first-party insurance schemes operate at lower administrative costs,[33] and are better able to adapt premiums and policy conditions to specific risks.[34] These features enable superior risk differentiation in a first-party context, which is advantageous for both insurers and insured.[35] In the case of third-party insurance, the risks to be assessed are possible damages suffered by a third party not known at the time of contracting.[36] Lower administrative

---

[26] Faure and Hartlief 2003. See also on the difference between first-party and third-party insurance, *supra* 5.1.3.
[27] Faure 2002.   [28] Wendel 2004, 367 (showing Swedish system of patient insurance).
[29] Faure 2001, 177–179; Tunc 1996.   [30] Priest 1987, 1552.
[31] Ibid., 1552–1553.   [32] Bishop 1988; Epstein 1985; Epstein 1996.
[33] Indeed, there is no incentive to identify a liable tortfeasor and bring a liability claim; Epstein 1996.
[34] Perry 2004, 771–778.   [35] Bishop 1988, 246.   [36] Epstein 1985, 648–650.

costs under a first-party insurance policy result from the cost avoidance associated with liability claims and coverage limited to the risk of damage to a particular victim or a particular site.[37] It is therefore much easier for the insured to signal particular circumstances, which may influence the risk to the insurer.[38] These benefits largely explain the trend away from third-party insurance and toward first-party coverage.

First-party insurances can be divided into two main groups: (1) insurance that compensates for personal injuries; and (2) insurance that provides coverage for specific property damage.[39] Typically, the personal injury schemes do not vary coverage based on the source of the injury, i.e. whether or not the cause was a catastrophe.[40] Accordingly, it takes the form of generalised accident insurance coverage for the costs that a victim incurs as a result of an accident, such as lost income, coverage of (additional) medical expenses and in some cases even pain and suffering.[41] Most European countries cover a large chunk of personal injury expenses through a social security system.[42] Consequently, well-informed potential victims purchase additional or complimentary coverage according to their individual degree of risk aversion and corresponding need for insurance.[43]

The second type of first-party insurance schemes covers property damage, for example, fire insurance. In many countries, however, first-party insurance for property damage excludes damages caused by a natural disaster.[44] In the Netherlands, for example, property damage caused by flooding is excluded.

8.2.2.   Demand-side problems

Empirical evidence has demonstrated that even in those countries where disaster insurance is widely available (such as in the US and in Europe),

---

[37]   Bishop 1988, 249.   [38]   Ibid.

[39]   Medaglia et al. 1995, 829.   [40]   Ibid., 829–830.

[41]   This is more particularly the case in the French policy referred to as "*Garantie contre les accidents de la vie*". This new insurance policy provides broad first-party compensation against accidents and compensates as if tort law were applicable, thus including compensation for pain and suffering. See also The French GAV® Accident Compensation, SCOR Technical Newsl. (SCOR Group, Paris, France), Oct 2003, at 2, available at http://scor-front1.heb.fr .colt.net/www/fileadmin/uploads/publics/NTNV2003_05_en_tuknv05.pdf.

[42]   Miller 1982, 554–556.

[43]   This assumes that competitive insurance markets offer coverage.

[44]   The Demand for Flood Insurance: Statement before the Comm. On Banking, Housing, and Urban Affairs 2 (Oct 18, 2005) (Statement of Mark Browne, Gerard D. Stephens CPCU Chair in Risk Management and Insurance).

individuals tend not to buy sufficient amounts of it, resulting in dramatic cases of underinsurance. This came to light, for example, after the "flood of the century" of the river Elbe in Germany,[45] and in the US after the Katrina hurricane.[46] Several reasons have been suggested for this low demand for disaster insurance. First, as a result of cognitive limitations, low probability events such as natural disasters are systematically misjudged,[47] resulting in a "it will not happen to me" attitude.[48] Second, there is empirical evidence that people prefer uncertain losses rather than the certain loss incurred by paying the premium. Insurance is considered an investment. The problem with disaster insurance is that a potential victim (such as a house-owner) is confronted with the certain loss of a premium, whereas there is a low expectation of a return on the "investment" during a lifetime and hence a low demand.[49] Third, some literature indicates that ex-post government relief (i.e. provided after a disaster) may reduce incentives to purchase insurance coverage.[50]

8.2.3.   The case for comprehensive disaster insurance

Given the problems on the demand side, an efficient demand for insurance for natural disasters may not emerge. It therefore has been suggested repeatedly that a system of mandatory comprehensive insurance should be created.[51]

8.2.3.1.   Theory

In the liability context, the economic rationale behind compulsory insurance is the externality argument: in the absence of adequate insurance, insolvent injurers would externalise risk. As discussed in 6.2.1., that may be an argument in favour of compulsory liability insurance, but it is not an argument in the case of first-party insurance. One might argue, however, that uninsured (or inadequately insured) victims will call on public resources, such as the healthcare system, for help and thus also "externalise" the risk. Given that most European legal systems provide social security and coverage for healthcare through mandatory healthcare insurance, it is hard to see why that should be supplemented

---

[45] See for example Endres et al. 2003; Magnus 2006 and Schwarze and Wagner 2004.
[46] See Daniels, Kettl et al. 2006.   [47] See Slovic et al. 2000.
[48] Kunreuther 1996, 175.   [49] Slovic, Fischhoff et al. 1977.
[50] This is a point strongly made by Epstein 1996; and by Harrington 2000.
[51] Kunreuther 1968.

with an additional compulsory accident insurance. The same is true for the property damage that victims may suffer as a result of a disaster. While the absence of insurance may lead to calls from victims for government relief and possibly to political pressure for such relief (if the number of victims is large), there is no direct issue of externalisation of harm.

Another conventional economic argument in favour of compulsory insurance is based on information problems. This argument assumes that citizens would be willing to pay a premium to have the risk of large damages as a consequence of catastrophes removed from them, but simply do not purchase insurance because they lack information on the probability and magnitude of the risk and/or on the availability of insurance. This is some empirical basis for the argument that due to imperfect information, individuals are not fully informed of their own preferences.[52] Regulation would thus be the classic remedy for such an information deficiency.[53]

This would be an argument in favour of compulsory (first-party) insurance for property damage caused by natural disasters, where empirical evidence shows that victims greatly underestimate these risks and would demand insurance if they were well informed.[54] People might experience better life satisfaction or subjective well-being, if arrangements guaranteeing financial compensation after disasters could be made.[55] Support for a regulatory duty to insure against disasters, in addition to voluntary property insurance (as is the case in France), could also be drawn from behavioural experiments showing that where disaster insurance is sold along with insurance against likely losses (like property insurance) at a reasonable extra cost, this will result in more people taking out insurance against low-probability losses.[56] Thus, the argument goes, it is in society's best interest for people to insure themselves against unlikely calamities, and there are ways to provide such coverage efficiently.

On the other hand, there are drawbacks to such an insurance obligation. First, the limited empirical evidence available showed that it is not only the lack of information on risk that causes the low demand for insurance,

---

[52] Kaplow and Shavell 2001, 1332.
[53] See generally Schwartz and Wilde 1979.   [54] Kunreuther 1968.
[55] Frey and Stutzer 2002, and for a summary of recent research in this area, Frey and Stutzer 2004.
[56] See Slovic et al. 2000, 60–61 and 70–71. It has also been argued that compulsory insurance may help to improve hazard perception (Slovic, Kunreuther and White 2000, 25).

but rather "bounded rationality" linked to the idea that "it will not happen to me",[57] combined with unwillingness to pay a premium for an unlikely hazard. The question thus arises of whether forcing people to take out disaster coverage should not be considered as paternalistic.

Second, if, on the contrary, one assumes that potential victims are poorly informed as to their potential exposure to disasters and the benefits of first-party insurance, regulatory intervention should instead focus on mandatory disclosure of such information to potential victims, rather than mandatory coverage. Again, this is supported by behavioural experiments, which show that graphic presentations may – to some extent – increase the perceived risk of that hazard.[58]

Third, if a duty to purchase "disaster coverage" were to be introduced for all victims, those who do not run any risk may be at a disadvantage. Taking the example of flood insurance, a person living in a house close to a river may well need flood insurance, but someone living on the twentieth floor of an apartment building will likely not need it. A generalised duty to purchase insurance coverage would force all individuals to take insurance coverage, even if they run no risk at all. This would create inefficiencies and lead to cross-subsidies, whereby those who run no risk contribute to the coverage for those who benefit from the insurance coverage. A more efficient (and fairer) solution may therefore be to limit compulsory coverage (e.g., for flood risks) to those individuals who actually are exposed to the particular risk.

It has also been argued that compulsory insurance for disasters may be necessary to mitigate the risk of adverse selection, which results in only the "bad risks" purchasing insurance coverage. To make the risk insurable, "good risks" should also be covered and therefore insurance should be made compulsory.[59] Indeed, adverse selection is a crucial issue that merits attention in relation to the insurability of the disaster risk. A possible remedy against adverse selection is a narrow pooling of risks, which reduces the difference between "good" and "bad" risks.[60] This implies that making insurance mandatory is not necessary to ensure insurability of disaster risk. If it is required in a specific case, the obligation to buy

---

[57] Kunreuther 1996, 175.
[58] Slovic, Kunreuther and White 2000, 15; Slovic 2000, 70–71.
[59] This argument was, for instance, advanced in the Netherlands by the Dutch Insurers Association with respect to flood insurance. For details, see Faure and Hartlief 2002, 183–189.
[60] Schwarze and Wagner 2004.

insurance can be limited to those who are exposed to the risk.[61] Within the group that is exposed to risk (and need insurance), an adequate differentiation of risks and premiums, as a remedy to adverse selection, may well be possible.

Fourth, a duty to insure should be considered only if sufficient competition in the insurance market exists. If this is not the case, the introduction of a duty to insure creates dependency, as a result of which the (concentrated) insurance market could engage in quasi-monopoly pricing and determine unilaterally the conditions under which to sell coverage. Thus, in a monopolistic market, compulsory insurance will create inefficiencies,[62] and if mandatory coverage is introduced, sufficient room should therefore be left for competition. This means that premiums for disaster coverage should not be fixed by law but be the result of competition between insurers.

Fifth, some catastrophic risks may be so "new" that insurance markets have not yet developed insurance coverage. If a differentiated supply of insurance policies is unavailable, one might question of whether it makes sense to introduce mandatory insurance. The idea of mandatory disaster insurance has also been defended from the point of view that sentimental politicians are de facto unable to deny post-disaster aid.[63] Whether such inability exists, however, is an open question.

8.2.3.2.   Examples

A well-known example of mandatory first-party insurance is the French model, according to which all individuals who have taken out first-party property damage insurance policies have to pay a supplementary premium for mandatory coverage for natural disasters. Thus, France does not have a generalised duty to insure, but a compulsory complementary coverage on (voluntary) property damage contracts. However, property damage policies are widespread and all individuals who purchase such

---

[61] Priest 1996, 225–226.

[62] It has, for instance, in relation to environmental insurance, also been suggested that if one makes the availability of insurance coverage a prerequisite for the operation of an enterprise, insurance undertakings become de facto licensors of the industry. From a policy perspective, this may be particularly problematic if it happens on concentrated insurance markets (see Monti 2001, 65).

[63] Viscusi 2010, 142–148. "Saying that one will not support assistance after a future hurricane may, of course, be a form of hypothetical trash talk. It is a quite different matter to actually deny assistance once there are identified victims with their stories featured on the evening news." (146)

a policy have to pay for the additional coverage for natural disasters.[64] This system is apparently accepted in France, because the risk of cross-subsidisation may be small: France seems to be confronted with many types of natural disasters. This means that if one is, as inhabitant of an apartment on the twelfth floor, not exposed to the risk of flooding, one may be at risk from other natural disasters, such as earthquakes or heavy storms.[65]

Belgium has adopted a similar model. It has had a compensation fund for disasters since 1976. As a result of a legislative amendment in May 2003, a compulsory flood coverage has been introduced tied to (voluntary) property damage insurance contracts. The Belgian model appears to mimic the French system, but the difference is that this mandatory supplementary coverage applies only in specific risk areas. This avoids a negative redistribution, since those who are not exposed to the risk are not forced to take out coverage.[66] Recently, this system was changed again and Belgium now follows the French model of mandatory disaster coverage.[67] In Belgium, the disaster coverage applies to voluntary fire insurances.[68] In Italy and Germany, legislative initiatives for some form of mandatory coverage against damage caused by disasters are currently under discussion.[69]

In France, due to the explosion in Toulouse on 21 September 2001, a law was enacted in July 2003 that ensures that victims now also have additional compulsory coverage for damage caused by technological risks (such as the explosion in Toulouse). The rationale of this change, however, is unclear: mandatory coverage for technological disasters does not make much sense if a liable wrongdoer can be identified. Instead, the

[64] The supplementary coverage for disasters is financed through an additional premium of 12 per cent on all property damage insurance contracts. For a description and critical analysis of this French model, see Schwarze and Wagner 2004 and Lafay, Cannarsa and Moréteau 2006.

[65] The same point is made by Schwarze and Wagner 2004: if a number of previously distinct risks (flood, windstorms, and hail) is pooled, individual exposure to one or more of such risks would almost be guaranteed.

[66] Through the charging of exposure-related premiums "cross-subsidization" between various areas could be reduced (Schwarze and Wagner 2004).

[67] For a critical discussion of the Belgian system, also with a comparison to the Netherlands see Bruggeman 2011 and Faure, Bruggeman and Haritz 2010.

[68] Act of 17 September 2005, Moniteur Belge, 11 October 2005. It seemed impossible to pursue the idea of limiting the mandatory coverage given the high (political) costs of identifying the special "risk areas" where the duty to insure would apply.

[69] Faure 2006, 442–444.

introduction of solvency guarantees on the side of the wrongdoer, such as compulsory liability insurance, could have been examined.

8.2.4. Supply-side problems

In addition to questionable demand for catastrophe insurance, there are also problems on the supply side. A number of insurers exclude coverage for property damage caused by (natural) catastrophes based on alleged uninsurability of losses. The three principal reasons for this uninsurability are the fear of catastrophic losses, the uncertainty of the risk and the lack of insurance capacity.[70]

First, natural hazards normally affect a large area and, thus, are highly correlative. Past disasters indicate that a significant number of (in particular, non-geographically diverse) insurance companies became insolvent as a result of catastrophic losses caused by natural hazards. Consequently, property insurance became increasingly difficult to obtain in hazard-prone areas.

Second, the absence of historical data and the imperfect scientific knowledge contributes to the supply deficiencies of first-party catastrophe coverage.[71] However, this point needs to put into the perspective of new catastrophe modelling.[72] The lack of predictability regarding the probability of both an extreme event occurring and the outcomes of such an event, results in ambiguity. This ambiguity may lead to uninsurability of a specific type of catastrophic event or in a specific hazard-prone area.[73] Insurers, however, can take account of such uncertain probability of catastrophic damage by charging a so-called risk premium.[74] If they do, two problems still exist: (1) a higher insurance premium may decrease demand for insurance against catastrophic risks; and (2) insurance regulation may limit insurers' ability to charge higher premiums for catastrophic risks.[75] Regulated rates are a major problem in some countries and, in certain high-risk areas, may be the main obstacle to an effective voluntary insurance market for consumers.[76]

---

[70] Kunreuther 1996, 178–179; Gollier 2005, p. 28.   [71] Faure and Hartlief 2003.

[72] See generally, Hartington et al. (1997) (discussing scientific issues associated with catastrophes).

[73] Kunreuther, Hogarth and Meszaros 1993, p. 83; Kaplow and Shavell 2001.

[74] Kunreuther et al. 1995, p. 338. Doherty et al. recently found that, under one-year contracts, mean annual premiums are 25 per cent higher when the probability of the event is ambiguous than when it is given precisely. Under a 20-year contract, aversion to ambiguity is even stronger. See Doherty et al. 2008, 147. The source of the uncertainty does not affect the insurers, contrary to Cabantous' beliefs. Cabantous 2007, 220, 235.

[75] Faure and Hartlief 2003, 83, 86.   [76] Gollier 2005, 24.

Third, insurance companies need sufficient financial reserves to cover the particular catastrophic risk.[77] In many cases, however, and especially in relation to catastrophic events, the expected loss may exceed the capacity of the individual insurer.

Pooling between insurers may alleviate these issues, but in some cases leads to welfare losses due to cartel agreements that cause uninsurability of natural disasters. For example, in the Netherlands during the 1950s, the Dutch Insurers' Association issued a so-called "binding decision" on all of its members, prohibiting them from insuring flood and earthquake risks (the latter being a relatively small risk in the Netherlands with the exception of the area around Southern Limburg). Their argument was that these risks were technically not insurable, since flooding and earthquake risks were inherently uncertain and, hence, difficult to calculate. Moreover, these types of insurance would only be attractive to high-risk individuals (e.g., those living in flood-prone areas) and this would result in incurable adverse selection. As a consequence, the members of the Dutch Insurers' Association all refrained from covering these risks. While the arguments concerning the uninsurability are doubtful, the Association's binding decisions violated competition law. At the time, Commission Regulation 3932/92 of December 21, 1992[78] exempted, under certain conditions, cartel agreements in the insurance industry from the prohibition of Article 85(3) of the EC Treaty,[79] but this exemption was heavily criticised.[80] The Dutch binding decisions not to insure flood and earthquake risks, of course, limited supply and violated the conditions of Regulation 3932/92.[81] In a 1999 report to the European Parliament and to

---

[77] Doherty draws attention to the fact that the importance of capital as a requisite to secure an adequate rate of return is often not fully understood. The capital needed by an insurance firm to be able to cope with catastrophic losses must be high enough to cover (1) the expected claims costs and other expenses, and (2) the costs of allocating risk capital to underwrite this risk. See Doherty 2008, 149.

[78] 1992 OJ (L 398) 7–14.

[79] Pursuant to Article 85(3) of the EC Treaty (now replaced), agreements, decisions by associations of undertakings and concerted practices in the insurance sector which seek cooperation with respect to: (a) the establishment of common risk-premium tariffs based on collectively ascertained statistics or on the number of claims; (b) the establishment of standard policy conditions; (c) the common coverage of certain types of risks; or (d) the establishment of common rules on the testing and acceptance of security devices, shall not be prohibited as incompatible with the common market. EC Treaty Article 85 (as of 1985) (now article 81), available at http://ec.europa.eu/comm/competition/legislation/treaties/ec/art81_en.html (last visited October 2008).

[80] Faure and Van den Bergh 1995.

[81] It violated Preamble 8: Standard policy conditions may in particular not contain any systematic exclusion of specific types of risk without providing for the express possibility

the Council concerning the functioning of the exemption in Regulation No. 3932/92,[82] the Commission discusses these binding decisions and reports that, as a result of the questions asked by the Commission, the Dutch Association of Insurers decided to bring its binding decision in line with EU law by simply converting it into a non-binding recommendation, which left each insurer free to extend coverage to flood risks. This example demonstrates that a minimal supply of insurance coverage may well be the result of anti-competitive behaviour by insurers, who mutually agree not to cover particular catastrophic risks.

At a policy level, this demonstrates that a necessary condition of insuring catastrophic risks is a competitive insurance market that offers a wide variety of differentiated insurance policies and responds to the demand of the market. Instead of direct government intervention, government should guarantee an adequate competition policy with respect to insurance markets. Otherwise, uninsurability, as the Dutch example shows, may simply be the result of a cartel agreement.[83] As long as insurers are able to estimate the frequency and magnitude of potential catastrophic losses, catastrophic first-party insurance should be available. Due to problems of ambiguity, adverse selection, moral hazard and highly correlated losses, insurance companies may well want to charge a substantial risk premium that is not much lower than the expected loss. If this is the case, there may be little demand for coverage and the insurer may not want to invest the time and money necessary to develop the product. If, on the other hand, the insurer is convinced that there is sufficient demand, he will attempt to raise sufficient capacity to survive possible catastrophic losses.

8.2.5.   Government support

As in the case of man-made disasters and terrorism which we discussed in the previous section, a public policy that makes the government reinsurer

of including that cover by agreement and may not provide for the contractual relationship with the policyholder to be maintained for an excessive period or go beyond the initial object to the policy. This is without prejudice to obligations arising from Community or national law. 1992 OJ (L 398) 7–14.

[82] Report from the Commission to the Council and the European Parliament on the operation of Commission Regulation No. 3932/92 concerning the application of Article 81 (ex-Article 85), para 3 of the Treaty to certain categories of agreements, decisions and concerted practices in the field of insurance, COM 1999, 192 final.

[83] We do not argue, however, that competition necessarily provides better results than (State) monopolies. See Winand Emons 2001, 247–248 (empirical research showed that under specific circumstances, particularly when insurers are unable to differentiate risks adequately, a natural monopoly with one (State) insurer may provide better results than a competitive environment); see also Von Ungern-Sternberg 1996.

of last resort may cure some of the supply-side problems in the insurance of natural hazards.[84] Since the theoretical and policy considerations behind such facilitative strategies by government to stimulate insurability have been explained in the previous section,[85] a few examples of insurer approaches towards large-scale natural disasters with government support suffice.

8.2.5.1. CCR

To provide reinsurance back-up to the market, France established a publicly owned reinsurance company, the *Caisse Centrale de Réassurance* or "CCR".[86] Reinsurance is not compulsory and insurers are free to contract with other private reinsurance companies. Reinsurance with CCR, however, is particularly attractive in terms of premiums and scope of coverage: a State guarantee kicks in once CCR exhausts its resources. However, a CCR official noted that insurance companies must transfer half of their (natural) catastrophe risk to CCR in order to be covered under the State guarantee.[87] The French State thus intervenes as a reinsurer, or, more precisely, as a "*retrocessionaire*" of CCR. In exchange for this State guarantee, CCR pays a premium to the State (Article R. 431–16–2 Insurance Code).[88] The reinsurance programme is set up so that insurers manage policyholders' claims because they have the best claims-paying experience and expertise. Coverage from CCR takes effect after insureds have incurred a certain deductible.[89]

Insurance companies that decide to reinsure with CCR are offered two types of contracts: quota-share contracts and stop-loss contracts.[90] With a quota-share contract, the insurer cedes a certain proportion of the collected premiums to the reinsurer and the reinsurer undertakes, in return, to pay a corresponding portion of the losses. The reinsurer will

---

[84] Government acting as reinsurer of last resort, of course, can only deal with the supply-side problems of correlation, uncertainty and limited capacity, but not remedy the cartel agreement not to cover particular risks. In that case, competition policy should provide a remedy, as it did in the case of the Netherlands (even though there is still only limited flooding insurance available in the Netherlands).

[85] See *supra* 6.4.4.

[86] Decree No. 82–706 of 10 August 1982 on the Reinsurance Operations for the Natural Catastrophe Risks by the *Caisse Centrale de Réassurance*. Application of Article 4 of the Act No. 82–600 of 13 July 1982, JORF 11 August 1982. See for further details Bruggeman, Faure and Heldt (2012), pp. 185–241.

[87] GAO 2005, p. 33.   [88] Bidan 2001 and Bruggeman, Faure and Heldt (2012), p. 228.

[89] CCR's coverage for natural disasters is unlimited because of the State guarantee. The deductible under the CCR reinsurance contract represents the maximum amount that an insurer will have to bear in the course of a year, regardless of how many losses occur.

[90] Bruggeman, Faure and Heldt (2012), p. 228.

then be exposed in the same way as the insurer, since the latter has to cede a percentage of each of the policies in its portfolio to the reinsurer. The adverse selection risk is thereby avoided. Proportional cover varies between 40 per cent and 90 per cent. On the other hand, with a stop-loss contract, CCR covers all claims that exceed an agreed multiple of annual premium income. The insurer will then be protected against the risk of such excess claims. To avoid insurers buying their risk-sharing cover from private reinsurers and using CCR only for stop-loss cover, the two contracts were tied: stop-loss contracts were offered only to those insurance companies who also purchase quota-share contracts from CCR with a minimum participation of 40 per cent. It has been argued that the combination of these two types of reinsurance necessarily imply that CCR (and ultimately the taxpayer) will bear most of the cost if a large-scale disaster occurs.[91]

In the first twenty years of its existence, CCR never managed to accumulate any substantial level of reserves, despite the fact that the average claims/premium ratio of disaster insurance since its creation was only 60 per cent. Nevertheless, very few changes to the reinsurance scheme were made, although CCR reinsured mainly the bad risks[92] and excessively high compensation (24 per cent) was paid for claimed administrative costs.[93] In addition, the combined effects of changes in the market (mergers, freedom of services within Europe, etc.) and the deterioration of the claims figures made it increasingly unsuitable for just a single scheme to be offered. As a result, from 1 January 1997 onwards CCR introduced new reinsurance conditions which paid greater attention to the nature of each ceding company's portfolio and enabled insurers to retain a larger proportion of the risks.[94] Nevertheless, in 1999, CCR was on the verge of bankruptcy after it was called upon to make a major withdrawal from its reserves. Although no exceptionally large event occurred in 1999, two major events hit France: the flooding in the Aude department in the south

---

[91] Jametti and von Ungern-Sternberg 2004.

[92] von Ungern-Sternberg 2007, p. 160, at pp. 86–95. Since the insurers have a right, but not an obligation, to reinsure a share of their natural disaster risk with CCR, they have a strong incentive to lobby the government to set high premiums for natural disasters. It is then in the insurers' interest to reinsure only a small part of their risks and keep the rest of the premiums for themselves.

[93] The effective cost of disaster insurance for the private insurers were almost nil, since disaster insurance was simply added to already existing property insurance contracts. In comparison, Spain, which operates an identical system of premium collection, only charges a 5% commission for administrative costs.

[94] CCR 2007.

in November 1999 (insured losses of 240 million euro) and a flooding following the winter storms Lothar and Martin (insured losses of 240 million euro). A significant hurricane also occurred in the French Antilles the same year. At the same time, an unexpected peril new to the industry and to the scheme appeared in 1989 – namely subsidence – which eroded CCR's reserves over time. Consequently, the State guarantee was called into play. As a result, other amendments to the reinsurance scheme had to be made to adapt to the market situation and loss record by, inter alia, modifying underwriting conditions, changing deductibles (including in case the municipality does not have a PPRN),[95] recapitalising its reserves (the government injected 3 billion French francs, or 460 million euro), abolishing compensation for administrative costs, etc.[96] According to one scholar, these amendments to the CCR scheme were necessary to remedy flaws in the institutional setup.[97] Other experts, however, project a very positive outlook on the CCR.[98]

8.2.5.2. CEA

The California Earthquake Authority ("CEA") provides an example of a government stepping into the private insurance market and assuming the risk of a potential natural catastrophe.[99] The CEA is a publicly managed, privately funded organisation (without government backing) that was established in September 1996 after the Northridge earthquake in 1994, by the State of California. CEA sells California residential earthquake insurance policies through participating insurance companies to encourage Californians to reduce their financial risks of earthquake losses.

The State of California requires insurers doing business in the State to offer also earthquake coverage in homeowners' policies, either directly or through CEA. CEA is empowered to set premiums and to bear risks; a so-called "mini-policy" stipulates which classes of real estate losses are covered and which are not. Premiums must be set on an actuarial basis, but, in practice, CEA premiums are tempered so that the price differences between the regions are moderated. Also, CEA may purchase reinsurance, but it does not have access to public funds. As a result, CEA resources are

---

[95] The PPRN is the Plan for the Prevention of Foreseeable Natural Risks (*Plan de Prévention des Risques Naturels Prévisibles*) and is a specific plan that municipalities have to draw up concerning the prevention of catastrophic risks.

[96] Jametti and von Ungern-Sternberg 2004; Erhard-Cassegrain, Masse, et al. 2004; CCR 2007; Vallet 2005, pp. 293–301; Jametti and von Ungern-Sternberg 2006.

[97] von Ungern-Sternberg 2007.   [98] Moréteau and Cannarsa 2006, p. 102.

[99] Bruggeman, Faure and Heldt (2012), pp. 224–225.

adequate to compensate an event with a size no more than double the size of the Northridge earthquake; beyond that level, policyholders will receive only partial compensation.

Participation in the CEA programme is voluntary, so private insurance companies compete with CEA, although this competition is limited to low-risk locations. CEA charges considerable premiums and many homeowners find these too high relative to the coverage provided. Consequently, the percentage of Californians with earthquake coverage (through CEA or a private insurer) declined from 33 per cent in 1996 to 12 per cent in 2010.[100] CEA currently has a claims-paying capacity that exceeds $9 billion and writes 70 per cent of earthquake premiums. It provides deductibles of 10 or 15 per cent. These relatively high deductibles and the low amounts of compensation are subject to criticism.[101]

8.2.6. Conclusions

As in the case of insurance for man-made disasters,[102] insurance for large-scale natural disasters is also complicated by problems on the demand and supply side. Empirical evidence showed that notwithstanding large subsidies (for example, in the case of flooding insurance provided by the National Flood Insurance Plan in the US), insurance coverage for natural disasters is relatively low. Behavioural phenomena can explain why demand remains low. Mandatory coverage for natural disasters has been proposed to remedy this situation. France and Belgium have adopted this approach and it has been advocated in other European countries and in the US as well. This may be a way to guarantee large-scale coverage against natural disasters.

As in the case of man-made disasters and terrorism, problems on the supply side have been remedied through intervention of the government as reinsurer of last resort. Again, those interventions are not necessarily examples of efficient government strategies. For example, in the case of the CEA, the government steps in as primary insurer and thus competes with other insurers and suppresses supply. CCR in France does not stimulate the emergence of a market solution. Moreover, neither CEA nor CCR seem to have a temporary character.

---

[100] Residential and Commercial Earthquake Insurance Coverage Study, California Department of Insurance, available at: <http://www.insurance.ca.gov/0400-news/0200-studies-reports/0300-earthquake-study/index.cfm>.

[101] Bruggeman (2010), p. 460 and Bruggeman, Faure and Heldt (2012), pp. 224–225.

[102] Discussed in Chapter 6, more particularly in 6.2.

Many other examples exist of governments acting as reinsurer of last resort in the areas of natural disasters and terrorism. In Germany (like in most other European Member States), terrorism insurance is provided via a pool in which the government also participates, referred to as Extremus.[103] The model is always similar: after a first layer being provided by insurers and a second layer by reinsurers, a third layer (the amount of which depends on the specific Member State) will be provided by government. As discussed, although there may be advantages in those schemes (in particular, the ability to provide insurance coverage where market supply fails), there are disadvantages as well, which depend on the specific construction chosen. An important problem is that if government provides reinsurance without charging a price, this amounts to an outright subsidy that may provide perverse incentives to operators and will have the result that risks are not accurately reflected in prices. Moreover, to the extent that government provides the third layer of compensation for free, tax payers will end up having to pay for compensation to the benefit of victims. To that extent, one could argue that potential victims pay for their compensation themselves, not those who are creating the risk. However, in some Member States (like in the Netherlands), the third layer is not provided for free by government, but government charges a price which should provide incentives to market players to reduce the government intervention as much as possible. This has had the desirable effect of reducing government intervention in the third layer over time.[104] An important point to remember is the trend towards public–private partnerships, whereby government intervenes in a facilitative strategy to stimulate insurability of catastrophes, in particular in case of natural disasters.

8.3.   Victim compensation solutions

The concept of a victim compensation fund has been advocated as an alternative to traditional insurance and indeed a more efficient instrument in serving the goals of tort law. Based on the arguments discussed above, there is no reason why a compensation fund, as a general rule, would provide better protection against insolvency than private insurance markets. An insurer is probably better able to differentiate risks than a fund operator, since an insurer is specialised in risk differentiation and

---

[103] Bergkamp, Faure, Hinteregger and Philipsen (eds.) 2013, 301.
[104] For more detailed discussion of the advantages and disadvantages of the government acting as reinsurer of last resort, see Bruggeman, Faure and Heldt (2012), 185–241.

risk-spreading. Insurers use specific techniques to determine how much and in what way their insured contribute to the risk pool. Obviously, this works well only if the insurance markets are competitive. In the absence of competition in insurance markets, either the supply of insurance coverage could be too limited, or premiums could be excessively high. Under these circumstances, a compensation fund may be the preferred option.[105] But, as noted above, if insurance markets are competitive, insurers, compared to fund administrators, are generally better able to deal with classic insurance problems, such as moral hazard and adverse selection. Indeed, it is hard to see why a fund administrator would have better information on risks than an insurer.

No matter how a compensation system is organised, it is critically important that the incentives for prevention of damage remain adequate. Liability rules can have a preventive effect only if a duty to compensate is put on the person who controls the risk. This means that liability and a corresponding duty to compensate damage resulting from the risk, in principle, should be imposed on the person that actually created or contributed to the risk. To establish the right level of prevention incentives, the duty to compensate should be proportional to the extent to which the specific activity contributed to the risk. Typically, tort liability does exactly that and the duty to compensate is limited to the damage that the specific tortfeasor caused.[106] If a compensation fund takes the place of tort liability, it is important that this feature be mimicked and potential damage causers contribute proportional to the risk contributed. In insurance policies, this idea is reflected in risk differentiation which, as discussed above, means that bad risks pay a higher premium than good risks. Likewise, in any compensation fund programme, bad risks should contribute more to the funding than good risks. Through this differentiation, the contributors to the fund have proper incentives for prevention and reducing risk: bad risks will be financially punished and good risks will be rewarded.

These principles are important from both an efficiency perspective (incentives for prevention) and a fairness and justice perspective. If these principles are not followed, good risks would have to pay for and thus subsidise, bad risks. This negative redistribution will be perceived as unfair and should therefore be avoided; to be fair, a compensation fund should be financed by the persons that cause damage in proportion to the risk they

---

[105] Faure and Van den Bergh 1995, 65–85.
[106] An exception should be made for cases in which joint and several liability or channelling of liability is justified.

control. Differentiation of risks and the contributions due is possible only if the insurers and fund administrators possess the information necessary to assess the risks associated with a specific activity. A key element relevant to the choice between insurance and fund solutions therefore is who possesses or can acquire the best risk-related information.

If both insurance and compensation funds are available in principle, there is no reason to prefer a fund solution; *ceteris paribus*, insurance offered in a competitive market is more efficient. As discussed in Chapter 6, first-party solutions, such as funds, may be useful if no liable injurer can be identified, as in the case of natural disasters.[107] If, however, a liable injurer can be identified, either the operator or the security provider, a fund would not be desirable, if it does not pursue claims against a liable tortfeasor.

Because, as noted above, any compensation fund should be financed by potential damage causers (operators and/or security providers) in proportion to the risk they create, the French fund for compensation of victims of terrorism is problematic. It is not financed by operators or other potentially liable injurers, but through a tax on property insurance contracts paid by potential victims. Hence, in France, the potential victims themselves finance the fund and not the operators who control the risk. This is inconsistent with the principles of prevention and proportional funding discussed above.[108] The French model of a compensation fund therefore does not deserve to be considered as an option at the European level.

8.4. Government-provided compensation

8.4.1. Arguments in favour of government compensation

Although there are strong arguments against government-provided compensation, such schemes may have some positive aspects as well. A positive aspect of government intervention might be that the prospects of large-scale payments in the aftermath of a terrorism-related disaster might encourage the government to take efficient precautions (justified by cost-benefit analysis) before disasters strike.[109] For example, the government may build infrastructure to prevent damage resulting from security risks. Further, a terrorist attack can lead to serious disruption of society. Providing ex-post relief may help to restore public trust. Governments

---

[107] See *supra* 6.4.6.   [108] See *supra* 8.1.4.4.   [109] Levmore and Logue 2003, 310.

may also be able to implement strategies necessary to react to an attack. These public goods cannot be provided through private action and hence may require government intervention.

A related argument in favour of government intervention, the government has the capacity to diversify risks over the entire population and to spread past losses to future generations, thus creating a form of cross-time diversification and spreading. The market could not achieve such spreading. The argument could thus be made that in some situations the government is in a better position than the market to adapt to, or, in some cases, maybe even prevent, disasters.[110]

Further, the argument could be made that government, in principle, can compensate without predefined limits. If damages exceed current government budgets, as mentioned above, strategies for cross-diversification over time and spreading over future generations could be implemented.

8.4.2.   Arguments against government compensation

Notwithstanding these theoretical possibilities of government compensation, the arguments against such compensation are compelling. A strong argument against is that the government would effectively provide a subsidy to an industry. This argument has been advanced in relation to the international conventions on nuclear liability, pursuant to which the government provides compensation via the second and third layer. If the government provides compensation to victims, it provides a subsidy to the industry concerned, as a result of which this industry will be able to externalise the social costs of its activity.

Due to such subsidies, it is no longer the person causing the accident that has the burden of compensation, but society at large and ultimately the tax payer, which results in undesirable redistribution. Further, since operators do not have to bear the total external costs related to their activity, their level of prevention will be too low. Under these circumstances, liability rules cannot have their deterrent effect. The result may be increased accident rates and lower levels of safety. Further, since operators will invest less in safety measures and will be able to externalise part of the damage resulting from their activities, their relative prices will be too low. This market failure will result in higher activity levels and

---

[110] This argument has been made in relationship to terrorism by Kunreuther and Michel-Kerjan 2004.

overconsumptions of the goods or services produced. From a social welfare perspective, that would be an undesirable result.

8.4.3. Policy recommendation

On the basis of this analysis, we may conclude that direct compensation by government is not a preferred option to deal with terrorism-related risk and damage. That is not to say that there should be no role for government in the aftermath of a terrorist attack. Relief measures, coordination of disaster management and the like, are tasks that the government should undertake. If the government incurs cost in restoring damage caused (e.g. repair of destroyed infrastructure) or providing relief to victims, however, those costs should be recovered from the liable persons (either through the liability system or otherwise). Such cost recovery is consistent with sound economic principles of cost internalisation and the polluter-pays principle.

This chapter reviewed alternative systems for redressing terrorism-related risk, including their structure and their pros and cons. Such systems could serve as an alternative to or modification of traditional liability and third-party insurance. One such system is the US Safety Act, which is aimed at limiting liability associated with eligible security technology so as to encourage innovation. As discussed in this chapter, the US Safety Act, to a significant extent, is specific to the US liability context with features such as discovery and high punitive damages, which also adversely affect the insurability of third-party liability for terrorism-related risks. Since the European liability environment differs from the US situation and Europe, unlike the US, has never suffered a liability crisis, a Safety Act-like regime would not appear to be necessary in Europe.

Next, we reviewed government-mandated first-party insurance for natural disasters, which has been created in France and a few other countries. These programmes involve mandatory insurance contracted by victims and provide comprehensive coverage, even where data on the probability of adverse events is scarce. High coverage limits can be generated because the government acts as reinsurer of last resort. As this insurance model compels potential victims to take out insurance cover, it may be an option for natural disasters where tort liability plays no role. It is not an appropriate model, however, for terrorism-related risk, because it would reduce the incentives to prevent terrorist attacks. To keep prevention incentives intact, security firms and high-risk facility operators should be exposed to liability. On the other hand, the public–private partnership between government and insurers whereby government acts as a reinsurer of last resort is of interest and can be applied also with respect to terrorism-related risks. Importantly, such government involvement will result in high coverage limits for terrorism-related risk.

Finally, this chapter reviewed two alternatives to liability involving direct compensation by the government or pursuant to law. There are two main kinds of such alternatives: ex-ante, structured compensation funds and ex-post ad hoc victim compensation programmes. Such funds compensate victims out of public revenues or specific contributions. Depending on their design, major disadvantages of these programmes are that the government effectively provides subsidies to industry, or that the deterrent effect of liability is diminished if operators are not exposed to liability to the same extent. Consequently, these types of government-supported compensation mechanisms are not the ideal solutions for redressing damage arising from terrorism-related risks.

Is liability for terrorism-related risk enterprise-threatening?

LUCAS BERGKAMP AND NICOLAS HERBATSCHEK

9.1. Introduction

More than a decade after the 9/11 attacks on the World Trade Center in New York, a number of liability lawsuits against airlines, security contractors, airport operators and an aviation company are still pending before the US courts. This chapter explores whether unlimited liability for damages caused by a large-scale terrorist attack, such as 9/11, may pose a threat to enterprises in Europe, in particular operators of facilities that are high-risk targets of terrorism and security providers. An argument to this effect has been made by European security associations. Their argument was intended to prompt the European Commission to propose liability limitations for the benefit of security firms.[1]

An enterprise-threatening effect could arise from several potentially adverse effects. First, unlimited liability could discourage new potential entrants from entering the market for operating high-risk facilities or for the supply of security goods or services. Second, operators already active in these markets may be reluctant to develop, sell and deploy new security technologies for fear of exposure to liability suits in the wake of a terrorist attack. This potential threat may affect not only providers in the security industry but also operators of high-risk facilities, such as airports, train stations, nuclear power plants and industrial installations, which buy and apply security products and services.

This chapter comprises three sections. The first section (9.2.) discusses some well-publicised US court cases in which companies have been held liable for terrorism-related risk to illustrate the potential threat that might arise from such risk. The second section (9.3.) reviews the arguments in

---

[1] ASD and EOS, "European Union Third Party Liability Limitation – Executive Summary" www.eos-eu.com/files/Documents/Positions/third_party.pdf, accessed 6 December 2014. CoESS and ASSA-I, "A European Solution for Third Party Liability of the Aviation Security Services Providers", White Paper, June 2010.

favour of limiting liability for damages caused by terrorism. The final section (9.4.) concludes.

9.2.   Terrorist attacks and case law

In the aftermath of a terrorist attack, a number of economic actors could potentially be held liable for a failure to protect victims from the threat of terrorism. Once damage has occurred, plaintiff attorneys have incentives to develop liability theories that expose "deep pockets". Because terrorist attacks are unpredictable in terms of timing, target, method etc., the potentially liable companies vary and liability theories need to be adjusted to match the specific circumstances. Operators of facilities at which attacks occur and the security firms involved may be among the parties that are first in line to defend against the claims. As the potential damage caused by terrorists may be enormous, insurance coverage can be insufficient and security providers and facility operators may be uninsured above coverage limits. The nature and scale of the liability claims made against economic operators is illustrated below for a number of well-publicised terrorist attacks in the US.

9.2.1.   The September 11 attacks (9/11)

One of the most alarming terrorist attacks of the twenty-first century, on 11 September 2001, was a series of coordinated attacks on the World Trade Center and the Pentagon[2] using commercial aircraft. Specifically, four passenger airliners hijacked by the terrorist group al-Qaeda were flown into these buildings. The terrorist attacks killed almost 3,000 people and caused at least $10 billion in damages to property and infrastructure.[3] In the aftermath, a number of liability claims were made against the security companies and passenger airlines involved in these incidents. In the case of the plane crash into the World Trade Center, the claims alleged the failure of detection equipment, negligent omissions by security personnel and inadequate procedures to detect the hijackers' weapons, suspicious demeanours and false identification.[4] The claims against the air carrier were based on the propositions that (1) the cockpit doors were

---

[2] One of the flights, United Airlines Flight 93, crashed into a field near Shanksville, Pennsylvania, after some of its passengers decided to fight the hijackers. Wald 2004.
[3] www.iags.org/costof911.html, accessed 26 August 2014.
[4] Tomacik, Healy and Dawson 2013.

of insufficient strength to withstand hostile intrusion; (2) the hijackers were able to turn off the transponder; (3) there was no security system, such as password-protection, to prevent the hijackers from turning off the autopilot system or operating the flight controls; (4) there was no system to automatically notify the government or the airline that an unauthorised pilot was at the controls; (5) the flight management computer could be programmed to fly the aircraft to potential terrorist targets; (6) there was no video surveillance system to alert the pilots to the hijacking; and (7) there was no system to take over control of the aircraft and prevent terrorists from flying the aeroplane into the buildings.[5]

9.2.2. The Lockerbie bombing

The Lockerbie bombing is named after a Scottish town where, on 21 December 1988, a Pan American World Airways flight crashed after the detonation of a terrorist bomb on board the plane. The bombing killed all 259 people on the flight and eleven residents of Lockerbie, where the aircraft's wings and tanks landed before the crash. The incident also destroyed several houses in Lockerbie.[6] Following this devastating incident, Pan American was faced with a $300 million wrongful death lawsuit filed by more than 100 families of the flight victims.[7] The claims were based on its failure to detect the bomb in the luggage, and the fact that the luggage containing the bomb was loaded onto the plane even though it did not accompany a passenger on the flight. Aside from the reputational fallout from the incident, the financial setbacks resulting from these legal proceedings are seen to have contributed to the downturn leading to the collapse of Pan American, once the largest international air carrier in the world.[8]

9.2.3. The Korean Air Lines shootdown

In 1983, amid the tensions of the Cold War, the Soviets shot down a Korean Air Lines (KAL) passenger plane which inadvertently flew into Soviet airspace. A total of 269 passengers and crew were killed in the incident.[9] The KAL crew was cited for failure to properly navigate the plane so as to avoid intrusion into a hostile airspace. Claims against the airline itself were based on both security and navigation failures. The security

---

[5] Bergkamp, Faure, Hinteregger and Philipsen (eds.) 2013, 288.   [6] Whitney 1988.
[7] Treadwell 1992.   [8] Dallos and Gellene 1991.   [9] Haberman 1983.

failure was based on the argument that the protection of the aircraft from hostile attack depended on careful navigation, particularly in the case of this route which came so close to Russian airspace. The airline was sued in hundreds of claims before the courts in Washington D.C. (US) and paid several millions in settlement; a $50 million punitive damages award was reversed by the US Court of Appeals for the District of Columbia,[10] however and the Supreme Court ruled that plaintiffs were not entitled to claim for the recovery of "loss-of-society" damages.[11]

9.2.4.   World Trade Center bombing

Prior to 9/11, in 1993 the New York World Trade Center buildings suffered a terrorist bomb explosion that caused massive damage. The Port Authority, a government entity, was sued for hundreds of millions of dollars in damages and lost in the trial court[12] and the Court of Appeal.[13] Finally, the Authority avoided liability when the State of New York's highest court reversed the decision.[14] This reversal was based on the finding that the Port Authority could resort to the defence of governmental immunity, a defence which would not have been available to a non-governmental entity.

9.2.5.   School, theatre and mall shootings

The tragic shootings at Columbine,[15] Virginia Tech[16] and other schools have resulted in claims against school districts for inadequate security. Similarly, the Aurora Colorado theatre killings[17] and other shopping mall attacks have resulted in inadequate security claims against the security companies and property owners.

9.3.   Arguments in favour of limiting liability for terrorism-related risk in the EU

In the aftermath of a series of catastrophic terrorist attacks, economic factors that could potentially be held responsible for protecting victims

---

[10] "World in Brief; Washington, D.C.: Court Rejects Award in Fatal KAL Flight" 1991.
[11] Tatum 1997.
[12] CNN library, "1993 World Trade Center Bombing Fast Facts", http://edition.cnn.com/ 2013/11/05/us/1993-world-trade-center-bombing-fast-facts/ accessed 6 December 2014.
[13] Ibid.   [14] *In re* World Trade Ctr. Bombing Litigation, No. 217 (NY Sept 22, 2011).
[15] Brooke 1999.   [16] Hauser 2007.   [17] Frosch 2012.

from this threat have called for the limitation of terrorism-related liability, either through the complete exclusion of liability for incidents caused by terrorists, or through the establishment of a financial limit (cap) for liability, beyond which the government would intervene to make reparation. A number of factors can help to explain the position of these companies. The first is the nature of the threat itself. Terrorist attacks are not only unpredictable (in terms of timing, target, method, etc.), but they are also deliberate; terrorists intend to circumvent security systems and cause massive injury in an attempt to terrorise (punish and scare) the population of a certain country or area. Second, the potential damage can be enormous, since terrorist may kill or injure many persons, cause extensive property damage and derail entire economies. Simultaneously, operators and security providers may have had limited ability to mitigate liability risks through insurance; in the years following 9/11, insurance companies have been perceived to have stopped (or at least substantially reduced) coverage of terrorism-related risks.[18] It has been observed that where liability insurance covering damage caused by terrorist attacks is available, coverage limits are low compared to the potential size of damages awarded in successful liability suits.[19]

In the US, arguments in favour of limiting liability for terrorism-related risks have carried the day and resulted in liability protection being made available through the Safety Act.[20] The question is, however, whether, given the differences between the US and EU litigation environments, these arguments have the same force in the EU. Ro date, there has not been litigation in the EU on the same scale as the US litigation following 9/11, and despite the absence of any sound analysis of the liability risks of economic operators in the security chain in Europe, some have clamoured for EU intervention to limit their liability exposure in the event of terrorist attacks. Yet, as noted above, terrorist-related liability affects a wide range of economic actors involved at different stages of the security chain. Thus, any preferential treatment of a specific group of potentially liable persons raises the question of whether this groups presents a special case which necessitates a different approach, and how any such treatment would affect the position of other potentially liable parties that would not benefit from protection against terrorism-related liability. To assess the merits of this argument, this section will discuss the possible arguments with regard to the liability exposure of operators of high-risk facilities and security

---

[18] Makinen 2002.   [19] Ibid.
[20] For a discussion of the US Safety Act regime, please see 8.1.

providers (9.3.1.) and the risk mitigation strategies available to them, including those available to address problems associated with contracting for liability limitation and insurability problems (9.3.2.).

9.3.1.   The extent of liability exposure

A number of arguments could be made to support the proposition that the liability exposure of operators of high-risk facilities and security providers is greater than that of other industries. These arguments are addressed in turn below:

1: Terrorists are actively and intentionally employing their best efforts to "beat" security strategies, products and services, in an attempt to cause massive damage. If and when they succeed, they demonstrate incidentally that the design of these security systems can be improved. The risk posed by terrorists is therefore different from risks that are "passive" in relation to the products that are aimed at limiting them. For example, bacteria are not intentionally and actively trying to circumvent the effect of an antibiotic. The risk posed to security systems by terrorists is more akin to the risk that hackers and programmers of malware (such as computer viruses) pose to information technology systems.

This argument appears to be factually correct and has some intuitive appeal: clearly, operators of high-risk facilities are prime targets of terrorist attacks and they, as well as the firms that assist them in ensuring security, would likely be the first to be sued. At the same time, operators of high-risk facilities and security firms specialise in providing protection against security risks and have an increased duty of care when it comes to addressing the risks posed by terrorism. The standard of liability applicable to operators of high-risk facilities and security providers reflects the fact that they have a special, increased responsibility for ensuring security.

2: For security reasons, operators of high-risk facilities and security firms cannot (and are not permitted to) disclose the detection (or other) limits of security systems to the general public. The reason, of course, is that if they were to disclose the technical and other limits of their products, they would make it easier for terrorists to circumvent security measures and threaten security. (In this respect, a security product might be compared to a "placebo" in a medicinal experiment: it is only effective if the information that is provided about it is incomplete or even deliberately misleading, although a security system, of course, has a purpose independent of human perception.) However, so as to limit their potential liability exposure, they would have to provide accurate and complete information on their systems and products to any potential victims in advance of a terrorist attack. Not having provided this information could be construed as negligence or an informational defect, which could easily result in liability exposure.

This argument is correct, because it would be unacceptable (and potentially result in liability exposure), for an operator or security firm to disclose information about the limits of security systems that terrorist could use to circumvent such systems. The converse is not necessarily true, however: not informing the public of the limits of security systems might not be deemed to be negligent or otherwise unlawful or tortious behaviour. As discussed in Chapter 3, the assumption made in this argument that operators and security firms must disclose the limits of security systems and technologies to the general public so as to limit their liability exposure, is not true for the Member States surveyed.

3: The customers of the security industry, not the security providers themselves, decide which goods and services are procured to secure buildings, installations and people. Therefore, the type of equipment and the nature and level of the security services provided are within the control of the operators, not the security providers. It follows therefore that the security industry cannot be held liable for operators' preferences regarding the level of security provided within their premises. This argument is underscored by the fact that the preferences of the security industry's customers are not only determined by a desire to increase security, but also an appreciation of the anticipated costs and benefits of additional or more expensive equipment and services at the margin. For instance, in the case of airport security, better and more powerful screening equipment and services may come at a higher price and also increase waiting and clearance time at screening points. An airport may therefore rationally decide to purchase somewhat less powerful equipment and a lower level of service, not only to save money but also to reduce waiting and clearance time.

The first part of this argument helps security firms to escape from liability. It would appear to be entirely reasonable not to hold the security choices of operators of high-risk facilities against the security firms involved, and the analysis of the national laws of the Member States presented in Chapter 3 does not confirm that security firms are held liable for the choices made by their customers. On the other hand, security firms could reasonably be held to a standard that requires that they provide information about security options and their pros and cons, to their customers; whether and if so, under which conditions breach of this standard could result in security firms being exposed to liability for damage caused by terrorism is a separate question; if in a particular case the security firm had an obligation to inform the operator and it can be established that as a result of the firm's failure to inform the operator did not make the choice it would have made otherwise, liability based on breach of contract or negligence cannot be excluded. Even if security firms cannot be held liable for decisions made by their customers, the latter, of course, can be held liable for such decisions. It is conceivable that an operator of a high-risk facility breaches its duty of care vis-à-vis users of and visitors to the facility by not providing adequate security; this will likely be the case if the actual level of security at the facility falls below the level required by law and regulation. If there is no law or regulation that specifies the security measures that must be in place at a facility, however, deciding whether an operator met its duty involves an assessment of the trade-offs inherent to security decisions. The safest facility is one that is also highly ineffi-cient, unliveable and undesirable. Some concept of reasonableness (e.g., a reasonably careful operator, or the reasonable expectations of users) may play a role in making decisions in specific cases.

4: The aim of terrorists is generally to undermine a State or government, not a particular airport, airline, security firm or other facility concerned. The facility operators and security firms do not have any influence on the "attractiveness" of a target. Put differently, it is the government of a State, which, by changing its policy, can reduce the likelihood of a terrorist attack. Governments may therefore be the actor in the best position to take risk reduction measures or adopt adaptation strategies so as to limit terrorism-related risk.[21] Viewed in this light, the prevention of terrorism is a public good which should primarily be provided by the government and not by private citizens. Conversely, facility operators and security firms cannot do anything to reduce the "attractiveness" of a target; they can only reduce the chance that the target can be reached. Moreover, since all security strategies, products and services can be beaten, circumvented or rendered ineffective if enough resources are spent on the effort, there is only so much the security industry can do. In short, since the govern-ment is in the best position to reduce the costs of terrorist attacks, the government, not private parties, should be liable.

As a general rule, this argument has merit. Clearly, a State's foreign policy, e.g., military interventions in conflicts in other nations, may incite

---

[21] See Bruggeman, Faure and Heldt 2012, 205–206.

terrorist groups to attack targets in the intervening State. A government, of course, may have good reasons to send troops to another country and it may be willing to accept the increased risk of repercussions. On the other hand, the increased risk of terrorist attacks could be treated as a reason for facility operators and security firms to increase security to an appropriate level consistent with the threat. If they do so and a terrorist attack occurs despite enhanced security, there would be an issue if facility operators and security firms are exposed to liability on a no-fault basis. As discussed in Chapter 3, this is probably not the case. Facility operators and security firms are not exposed to liability, except where products are defective or some negligence has occurred.

5: Precisely because facility operators and security firms often intervene to assist government in fulfilling its task of providing security (i.e. the prevention of terrorism), the arguments advanced in the literature in favour of State immunity from liability[22] should be extended to these operators as well. Like public authorities, these firms should be considered "multi-task agencies" which balance various external costs against each other.[23] This balancing exercise may be extremely difficult. Even if the agency or firm performs the exercise with optimal care, it is possible that a court ex-post disagrees with the decision. Therefore, a higher threshold for liability of agencies and firms should be set. The rationale for public agencies is that, if the normal threshold for liability applies, fear of legal action may have a strong chilling effect on the agencies, because the agent does not internalise the precaution costs, i.e. the cost of not authorising (or restricting or prohibiting) activities or requiring excessive security measures.[24]

If the liability of public agencies is asymmetric, i.e. they are liable for authorising or permitting, but not for not authorising, restricting or prohibiting activities, there may be a problem, because agencies will err on the side of not authorising or permitting activities, or restricting or prohibiting them, resulting in a "chilling effect" on agencies' decisions. A solution would be to make their liability exposure "symmetric", either limited or unlimited. This rationale, however, does not apply to private entities, which do not authorise, permit or restrict anything; they make

---

[22] Bruno 2012, 431.   [23] De Geest 2012.

[24] See ibid. There is a risk that this chilling effect may arise if, for example, a public servant must decide whether a firm should be awarded a permit to carry out a risky activity that can cause substantial harm to third parties.

choices only for themselves. Their liability exposure is not asymmetric because they fully internalise the cost of the security measures they apply, as well as the cost of the lack thereof. Thus, this argument suggests that while it might be justified to limit the liability of public authorities for affirmative decisions (or to subject them to symmetric liability exposure), it does not follow that the liability of facility operators or security firms should be limited.

6: Neither facility operators nor security firms are necessarily free to determine how they design their security systems and which security products and services they use or provide. In some settings, such as airport security, facility operators must comply with specific security rules, which may even specify the equipment to be used and its degree of sensitivity. Exposure to civil liability, however, is based on the notion that, as a result of the financial incentives created by liability, operators and firms will take efficient prevention measures. To be able to take such measures, operators should be free to decide which measures to take. The fact that they are not free to do so is an argument in favour of a liability limitation, assuming the standard of liability is not sufficiently flexible to accommodate this level of complexity. In this vein, the national liability laws of some Member States[25] provide that where the government decides which security measures are to be used, liability for any damages caused by less than perfect security should be imposed on the State, not on the facility operators or security firm.

In principle, liability indeed presupposes that operators are free to decide what measures they take to prevent damage. It is possible, however, that liability serves merely as a sanction for not taking the preventive measures required by law and regulation. In this case, an operator is exposed to liability if its failure to take effective prevention causes damage. Conversely, if the operator has taken all measures required by law, it may or may not be exposed to liability, depending on national law (see Chapter 3). If the applicable law leaves an operator no freedom at all, no liability is imposed if an operator takes only the measures required by law. The analysis of the national liability systems presented in Chapter 3 does not reveal a potential problem with operators being held liable for events entirely beyond their control or for decisions made by others. As a general rule, the standard of liability pays due attention to legal and regulatory requirements.

---

[25] See Part II of this book.

9.3.2. Risk mitigation strategies

It could also be argued that when compared to other commercial sectors, the high-risk facility operators and security firms have a more limited ability to deploy risk mitigation measures to limit their liability. This would be so for several reasons, which are set forth above. In previous chapters of this book, these reasons have already been exposed. They are briefly repeated here and discussed in light of the question as to whether liability is enterprise-threatening.

1: As discussed in Chapter 7, security firms may be unable to obtain contractual limitation of their liability, in particular in public procurement. Contractual liability limitations can involve (1) narrow descriptions of primary obligations and limited representations and warranties, (2) exoneration for certain types of damages, for all damage caused by negligence, or for other types of exposure, (3) liability limitations in the form of caps (financial limits) or similar mechanisms, (4) indemnities and (5) hybrid provisions, combinations of or variations on the above. In other words, if this argument is factually correct, their customers, i.e. facility operators, have been able to impose their terms and conditions on the security industry, which would have resulted in a undesirable lack of contractual protection for security firms.

The main problem with this argument is that it suggests that the security industry's inability to obtain contractual protection against liability is an argument in favour of a liability limitation mandated by legislation. As discussed in Chapter 7, it is conceivable that this is simply the outcome of a well-functioning, efficient market and not the result of some market failure that requires government intervention. Further, if the liability of security firms is limited, but the liability of facility operators is not, this could result in a mere re-allocation of the duty to compensate damage caused by terrorist attacks from security firms to facility operators. It is not clear whether this serves a socially useful purpose; in theory, it could be socially useful if facility operators are structurally better positioned than security firms either to prevent or spread the risks associated with terrorist attacks[26] – there is no reason to believe that this is so.

It, of course, is possible to limit the liability of both security firms and facility operators, so that either would be liable for damage caused by terrorism only up to liability limits. Under such generalised liability limitations, facility operators and security firms may underinvest in security

---

[26] Calabresi 1970.

and safety measures. Thus, such limitations may have an adverse effect on the level of care and precaution and thus increase the risk of terrorism-related damage.[27] If it has been established that there is no adverse effect on the level of security and terrorism-related risk, liability limitations may still be undesirable if they adversely affect the spreading of risks.[28] This could be the case if facility operators and security firms have better risk-spreading capability than the victims of terrorist attacks; whether this is indeed the case requires complex analysis that should reflect the differences between first-party and third-party insurance. Thus brings us to the second argument.

2: Facility operators and security firms are not able to contract adequate insurance coverage at a reasonable price to cover the liability risks associated with terrorist acts. As a result, they are not insured for terrorism-related liability. Because they are not adequately insured, they should not be held liable for terrorist attacks, or be held liable only to the extent they are insured.

In the US, an exacerbating factor that increased the enterprise-threatening effect of terrorism-related liability was that, following the catastrophic events of 9/11, a number of insurers discontinued or limited insurance coverage for terrorist attacks.[29] This would have resulted in facility operators and security firms being unable to pass on terrorism-related risk to institutions with superior risk-bearing capabilities. In Europe, with its very different litigation environment, the market for terrorism insurance is not necessarily the same as the US market, however. There is reason to believe that the European insurers indeed offer more extensive coverage. A major reinsurer has indicated that facility operators and security firms have not been experiencing serious difficulty with regard to insurability.[30] Nonetheless, the market availability of insurance varies from one Member State to another. In some countries, such as Denmark and the UK, insurance covering terrorism-related risks appears to be widely available.[31] In other countries, in particular in Central and Eastern Europe, notably Slovenia, terrorism-related risk is often excluded from liability policies.[32]

As the risk that facility operators or security firms are held liable in relation to a terrorist attack is not substantial, it is not considered

---

[27] Shavell 1987; Shavell 2007; 139–182.   [28] Calabresi 1970.   [29] Makinen 2002.
[30] Bergkamp, Faure, Hinteregger and Philipsen (eds.) 2013, 301.
[31] Ibid., 302.   [32] Ibid.

uninsurable, although the damage could be extensive.[33] Of course, insurance coverage might be exhausted if a terrorist attack were to cause billions of euros of damage, as insurance coverage is always limited. This is true in general, however, in all commercial sectors and for all types of damage, and this argument therefore does not justify preferential treatment of high-risk facility operators and security firms.

Further, measures have been taken to make terrorism-related insurance more robust in Europe. The decision of some national insurers not to renew terrorism-related insurance beyond the expiration date of existing contracts led to the creation of public–private partnerships specifically designed to provide insurance for terrorist acts. In Germany, for example, after more than six months of discussion between representatives of the insurance industry and the German federal government, a public–private partnership called "Extremus" was established.[34] Extremus is a new insurance company that covers solely terrorism risk. It has proven to be an attractive option for airports, although some airports have decided not to purchase insurance cover every year; in some years, they prefer to run the risk of terrorist attacks, rather than pay the relatively high insurance premium. Large facilities, such as an airport, may have to pay an annual premium for terrorism-related risk of 1 million euro or more. Their preference not to purchase terrorism-specific insurance does not necessarily signal a problem, but may simply indicate that airports consider the risk of a terrorist attack relatively small. For an airport in, say, London, this may be different, because the United Kingdom might be more vulnerable to terrorism attacks.

Whether victims will sue facility operators, security firms or both depends on the circumstances of the case and the applicable national law. As a general rule, victims will be inclined to go after "deep pockets". Whether a defendant is a deep pocket is in part a function of whether the defendant is insured and, if so, what the conditions and limits of insurance are; e.g., damage caused by defective products falling within the scope of the EU Product Liability Directive may fall under product liability insurance (services, on the other hand, do not fall under product liability insurance). Information on the availability and limits of insurance coverage, however, is typically kept confidential and thus not available to victims. Insurance coverage is therefore not likely to be a significant factor in victims' decisions as to which potentially liable persons to sue. To maximise their chances of recovery, victims will have an incentive to sue

---

[33] Ibid., 301.   [34] Gas 2005.

facility operators, such as airports, security firms and the State, insofar as they have colourable claims against each of these.

3: There are also a number of broader public policy issues associated with the civil liability exposure of the facility operators and security firms. A main concern is the need to encourage innovation in the security chain. The liability threat discourages innovation in security technology and systems and the deployment of new technology and systems in practice. Consequently, as promising new technologies are delayed, liability has adverse effects on security. Liability limitation is therefore necessary to promote innovation.

The effect of liability on innovation is hard to gauge. To the extent that innovative security technology results in less damage due to terrorist attacks, facility operators have an incentive to deploy such technology, except if the cost of increased liability exposure outweighs the gains resulting from better security. This could be the case if, for instance, courts treat the deployment of the new technology concerned as negligence per se, as a result of which operators would effectively be exposed to strict liability.[35] Since this would not be the case if they stick to conventional technology, the introduction of innovative technology might result in increased liability exposure.[36] Whether in liability cases the courts are biased against novel risks, as opposed to known risks, is an empirical issue. The US evidence is mixed; at high levels of liability cost, however, liability seems to have a counterproductive effect.[37] In Europe, with its much less litigious environment, there is no reliable empirical evidence. At the level of theory, there would not appear to be a persuasive argument for assuming that liability discourages innovation in Europe.

9.4.   Conclusions

The argument that liability is enterprise-threatening is another way of saying that the liability of high-risk facility operators and security firms

---

[35] As Kip Viscuis explains, "The court's task of assessing innovative products often entails more problematic judgments than with assessments of existing technologies, so that the concern for safety with respect to innovations may in fact stymie such innovations. Novel products may be safer than existing products but may pose new kinds of risks. If there is a bias of product liability against novel risks, then there will be a disincentive with respect to product innovations". Kip Viscusi 2012, 24.

[36] In the US, it has been argued that liability has discouraged innovation in sectors of industry, such as automotive. See Hunziker and Jones (ed.) 1994.

[37] Kip Viscusi 2012, 28.

should be limited. Differential treatment of the high-risk facility operators and security firms for liability purposes could be justified only if it
could be shown that these firms are exposed to an excessive degree of liability, suffer from structural inability to deploy risk mitigation strategies
or underinvest in innovation due to the threat of liability. Below, each
argument in favour of limiting liability is reviewed and then the proposed
liability limitation is placed in a broader perspective.

First, it could be argued that high-risk facility operators and security
firms are highly exposed to liability, which is expanding in scope and
monetary amounts, as the 9/11 litigation demonstrates. As discussed
above, while there may be some truth to this in the US, there is no evidence
that this is also the case in Europe. Thus far, in Europe, there have been
few court cases in which high-risk facility operators or security firms have
been held liable for damages suffered by third parties due to terrorist
attacks. In addition, as the incidents invoked to support this claim are
typically US cases, account should be taken of the distinctively different
litigation environment in the US;[38] examples from this jurisdiction are
unlikely to be indicative of liability exposure in Europe. The analysis of the
national liability laws of the EU Member States presented in Chapter 3
does not suggest that the operators and security firms are exposed to
liability risks that are comparable to the risks in the US.

Second, to support a special liability regime for facility operators and
security firms, an argument can be made that these companies are different from other companies, because they are required to provide security
against terrorism, which is normally a government responsibility. Indeed,
in general, it is the government that assumes responsibility for public security and protection against terrorism through its monopoly over physical
force (for example, the military and the police force). The government,
however, may want private parties to perform certain security functions,
including security against terrorism. Asymmetrical liability of government agencies may cause adverse effects but does not justify a liability
limitation. Likewise, private entities cannot successfully argue that their
liability should be limited because they provide security to the public or
their customers.

Third, as noted above, there would not be sufficient liability insurance
coverage available to facility operators and security firms with respect to
terrorism-related risk. Again, this argument is based on the situation in
the US. While a specific monetary level of coverage may be insufficient in

---

[38] See 8.1.

the US, given the size of the potential damage awards, the same level may be adequate in the EU context. Further, there is no evidence that facility operators and security firms in the EU cannot obtain insurance coverage. Rather, the limited research we conducted suggests that, depending on the Member State involved, insurance against terrorism-related risks may be available, although it would be subject to a financial limit and to other exclusions, limits, obligations and conditions. Further, as an alternative to insurance, governments and insurers in some Member States have worked out public–private partnerships or compensation funds in order to provide cover for terrorism-related risk.

Third, operators and security firms would not be able to exclude or limit liability exposure for terrorism-related risk via contract. This is the argument that mitigation strategies are not available to these firms. The empirical evidence to support this argument is scant, however. As discussed above, as far as public procurement and government contracts are concerned, the difficulties experienced by security firms when negotiating liability limitations and indemnities may simply reflect the preferences of the Member State governments; a proposal to limit their liability would likely not be supported by these governments, because this would conflict with their policies in respect of public procurement of security goods and services. Moreover, as discussed in Chapter 7, operators and security firms can limit their liability exposure vis-à-vis third parties by contract, since the contractual standard plays a role in defining the standard of third-party liability.

Fourth, liability would have an adverse effect on the development and deployment of innovative security technology and systems. Although there is some US evidence that high liability costs have a negative effect on innovation, there is no such evidence for Europe with its much less litigious environment.

Thus, there are no persuasive arguments to support the proposition that unlimited liability for terrorism-related risk has an enterprise-threatening effect on enterprise within the EU. Even if not enterprise-threatening, liability for terrorism-related risk could have broader negative implications. In particular, high liability exposure could discourage economic operators from entering the market or expanding their services, but there is no evidence that confirms this speculation. Further, even though each individual argument discussed in this chapter may not place operators and security firms in a unique position with respect to liability exposure, it might be the case that, taken as a whole, the combination of these factors might be unique to high-risk facility operators or security firms.

For instance, similarly to these operators and firms, software companies are potentially exposed to catastrophic liabilities, but, unlike these firms, they are able to limit their exposure by contract. Therefore, the combination of the exposure to large liabilities (even where it is based solely on fault) and the inability to negotiate limits to such exposure by contract might render exposed facility operators and/or security firms uniquely vulnerable to catastrophic liabilities. That does not mean, however, that liability exposure must therefore be directly limited. It may simply mean that these companies are exposed to exceptional liabilities that require policymakers' attention.

10

Economic analysis of current liability for terrorism-related risk and alternatives

MICHAEL FAURE AND NIELS PHILIPSEN

In this chapter, the current liability regimes are examined from a law and economics perspective. The main focus is on the question of whether the liability regimes are structured in an efficient manner, i.e. whether they provide incentives for a minimisation of social costs.

We start by stressing the function and goals of tort law according to the economic analysis of law (10.1). Then, we draw some of the main lessons from liability for TRR under EU law (discussed in Chapter 2) and the liability for TRR under international law (discussed in Chapter 1). It is interesting to come back briefly to those two chapters (in 10.2. and 10.3., respectively) since some of the particular features of liability for TRR under EU law and international law can precisely be criticised from an economic perspective. This considers more particularly the channelling of liability and the financial caps, as well as the fact that compensation in some situations is not provided by operators but through public funds.

We then analyse options to limit liability in 10.4. from an economic perspective, focusing on options that fit within the current TRR liability regime, such as channelling and linking liability to regulation. From an economic perspective, a relevant question is whether operators are able to pay the compensation for which they are held liable. That is important not only from the perspective of compensation, but also – and especially – because insolvency may lead to under-deterrence. That may justify the question of whether mandatory financial security (which could also be observed in TRR liability under international law)[1] should be introduced (10.5.).

This chapter should be read in conjunction with Chapter 8, where alternative systems for redressing terrorism-related risks, more particularly victim compensation solutions, have been discussed. Section 10.6 concludes.

---

[1] See Chapter 1.

10.1.   Goals and functions of liability law

10.1.1.   Goals

There is a remarkable difference between the way in which traditional lawyers view the liability system and the way in which the goal of the liability system is viewed from an economic perspective. Traditional tort lawyers, at least in Europe but to some extent in the US as well, view the liability system as a system of compensating victims of accidents. In that perspective victim protection and more particularly ex-post compensation of victims is the main goal of accident law. The benchmark by which a liability system will be judged is then often whether or not it is able to grant this compensation.

In the economic analysis of accident law a different perspective is taken. Economists stress that the exposure to liability of a potential injurer will provide substantial incentives for accident prevention.[2] The central idea is that actors (mostly industrial operators, but also others) will react to a potential exposure to liability by taking optimal preventive measures. In this perspective the main goal of the liability system is not ex-post compensation, but rather ex-ante prevention. "Prevention is better than cure" is hence the guiding principle for the economic analysis of law. This starting point has two important consequences. First, if operators were not exposed to the financial consequences of their actions via a liability rule, their incentives for prevention would fail unless other legal rules (such as regulation) provided an alternative. Second, when an operator is ex-post (after the accident) appropriately exposed to liability (i.e. having to bear the costs of his action) this will provide an ex-ante incentive to take optimal care. From an economic perspective a liability system has an important social function in remedying market failures.[3]

At the end of the last century there have been fierce debates between economists and lawyers on the goals of tort law, and some attempts have also been made to reconcile the legal (corrective justice-based) approach with the economic (deterrence-based) approach.[4] Now, especially in the environmental arena, also the legal community and policymakers have become more and more convinced of the importance of liability rules

---

[2] A classic contribution in this respect is from Shavell 1980; see also Shavell 1987.

[3] See generally on the economic analysis of environmental liability and the role of tort law in that respect Bergkamp 2001, 67–119, De Smedt 2007, 28–64 and Wilde 2013, 138–148.

[4] See for example Schwartz 1997; Hinteregger 1994.

as an instrument of prevention.[5] One of the reasons for this change is the increasing empirical evidence that is available showing that at least industrial operators (as in the environmental field) respond to financial incentives provided through the liability regime.[6]

10.1.2.   Functions

In Chapter 8, the US Safety Act was already addressed. It is important to stress that there is an important difference between the use of tort law in the US and in Europe which should be discussed. This concerns the fact that most victims in western Europe, contrary to their American counterparts, do not have many incentives to bring a liability suit, since the social security system in many western European countries provides for a relatively wide coverage of many expenses that a victim incurs when an accident happens. Partially as a result of international conventions[7] and European directives, many countries have elaborated systems of compulsory first-party insurance covering medical expenses. In addition, lost income is often taken care of. Depending upon the legal system, this is usually mandatory if one is employed and on a voluntary basis for self-employed individuals. In some cases, even property losses are insured, depending upon the type of accident. A consequence of this relatively elaborate first-party insurance system is that a large part of the damage to the victim in European legal systems is already taken care of. Therefore, victims in Europe often do not have incentives to sue an injurer in tort. Their only incentive to use the tort system is for the part of the damage that was not taken care of via the first-party or social security insurance scheme. This may relate to property loss, or to the higher part of one's income which could not be compensated, but also to pain and suffering, for which first-party insurance is usually not available. In addition, the

---

[5] The preventive effect of liability rules was for example explicitly stressed in the so-called EU White Paper on Environmental Liability which preceded the European Environmental Liability Directive (EU Commission, White Paper on Environmental Liability, Brussels, 2000 (COM) 2000 66 final). See for a comment on this White Paper the contributions in Faure 2003.

[6] For an overview of empirical evidence concerning the effects of liability rules generally see Van Velthoven 2010, and for an overview of empirical evidence with respect to the deterrent effect of environmental liability rules see Faure 2012), 301–305.

[7] See in that respect e.g., the European Social Charter of 18 October 1961 and the ILO-Conventions No. 24 concerning sickness insurance for workers in industry and commerce and domestic servants, No. 25 concerning sickness insurance for agricultural workers and No. 102 concerning minimum standards of social security.

social insurance carriers could execute recourse against liable tortfeasors or their insurers.

As a consequence of this system, many victims in Europe do not use the tort system even if they could. This considers especially individuals with lower or average income who are compensated via social insurance schemes and who do not wish to use the tort system for pain and suffering. Indeed, for "*Existenzsicherung*", victims in European legal systems can call on social security and social insurance schemes. Furthermore, social insurance carriers de facto rarely use their right to exercise recourse, inter alia because exercising that right creates relatively high administrative costs.

The situation in the US is of course completely different where, in addition to Medicaid and Medicare and some workmen's compensation schemes, many tort victims cannot benefit to the same extent as in Europe from generalised social security schemes.[8] Hence, as a consequence victims in the US will (have to) use the tort system also to obtain compensation of their primary needs (medical expenses and lost income) whereas that is largely covered by social security and social insurance schemes in Europe. That hence creates fundamental differences between the need to call on tort law for victims in the US and in Europe. Whereas in the US using tort law for many victims is a matter of survival and receiving compensation of basic needs, in Europe, the tort system is rather a "luxury". That fundamental difference of course explains the fact that the exposure of (the security) industry in the US to liability suits is potentially much larger than in Europe.

We will now consider the goals of tort law from this economic perspective and critically analyse the liability for TRR under EU law (10.2.) and international law (10.3.).

10.2. Lessons from EU law

When first addressing the attribution of liability, it is striking that the ELD channels the liability exclusively to the operator, thus potentially limiting liability of other parties who could contribute to environmental harm. The system of allocation of liability in the PLD is more complex, in principle allocating liability to the manufacturer or importer, but also expanding to the supplier of a product if the first two are unknown. In

---

[8] See Faure and Hartlief 1996, 254–261. Even where victims benefit from certain social security benefits, the tort liability system provides strong incentives to initiate litigation.

case of auditor's liability,[9] joint and several liability is recommended not only for individual audit firms or accountants, but also for accounting networks who could (depending on the legal system) be held vicariously liable. Already this point shows how the attribution of liability can have an important bearing on the scope of liability of the security industry. A regime which would e.g., for airport-related security risks channel liability to air carriers and aircraft operators would thus exclude the liability of the security industry. A joint and several liability regime, to the contrary, would increase liability exposure of the security industry.

Also the scope of damages has an important bearing on liability exposure. This is not only the case for the (financial) limit on liability, but also for the heads of damages compensated. The ELD has no financial cap; the PLD does not have a financial limit either, but included the option for Member States to adopt a liability cap. Such an optional system is also provided for in the Recommendation concerning audit liability which basically provides three options to Member States if they wish to limit auditors' liability. The damages under the ELD are limited to damage to protected species, habitats, water damage and land damage, but traditional damage, such as damage to health and property, has been excluded. Also the damage covered in the ELD is limited to personal injury and damage to private property; other heads of damages are excluded. This may be an important issue since the literature, for example with respect to auditors' liability, held that especially economic losses and wrong assessment of damages were important reasons for a large liability exposure of auditors.[10]

The ELD has optional compliance with permit and state-of-the-art defences, whereas the PLD excludes liability for development risks, but provides Member States with the option to make producers nevertheless liable for development risks too. Whether it is desirable to hold the security industry liable for the development risk is an issue which will have to be discussed further, in the light of general goals of liability of the security industry. The question that will inter alia have to be addressed in that respect is to what extent liability for the development risk provides (additional) incentives to the security industry to invest in research and development.

An important aspect related to liability is whether it is covered by insurance. Especially when strict liability is introduced (such as in the ELD for Annex III activities and in the PLD for product defects) it is held

---

[9] Philipsen 2014.   [10] Ibid.

that it is important to provide a financial guarantee against the insolvency of operators. The ELD has no compulsory insurance requirement, but at least stimulates Member States to take measures to encourage the development of financial security instruments. The PLD completely lacks solvency guarantees. Interestingly, in some of the regulatory regimes discussed in this book, compulsory insurance was required, for example in the Machine Directive[11] and the Construction Products Regulation.[12] An interesting aspect of the Regulation on insurance requirements for air carriers and aircraft operators[13] is that in case of insurance market failure, the Commission may determine the appropriate measures to realise the obligation of providing insurance coverage. Here, the limits of the insurance market in providing security are recognised and the Commission sees an active role for itself in determining appropriate measures to realise the obligation of providing insurance coverage.

An important aspect bearing on the scope of liability is the relationship to regulation. We already mentioned that the existence of a regulatory regime could have an important influence on liability. Of course, compliance with regulation (such as REACH) may not automatically exclude liability, but compliance could lead to a presumption of products being not defective. We mentioned the example of EUDRALEX, which explicitly holds that regulated entities must not be subject to civil or administrative liability for unapproved use of medicinal products if such use is recommended or required by the authorities in response to particular public health risks. Also, compliance with the personal protective equipment may lead to an assumption of conformity with basic safety requirements, thus potentially reducing liability. Also the example of CE-marking directives, such as the Machinery Directive, is interesting: standards and certification could possibly result in a limitation of liability, and machinery especially designed and constructed for police purposes is excluded from the scope of the Machinery Directive.

It merits further analysis what this precisely means. One has to be careful with drawing from this the conclusion that safety regulation of the security industry would be needed. It depends on other factors, including

---

[11] Directive 2006/42/EC of the European Parliament and of the Council of 17 May 2006 on machinery, and amending Directive 95/16/EC [2006] OJ L 157/24.

[12] Regulation (EU) 305/2011 of the European Parliament and of the Council of 9 March 2011 laying down harmonised conditions for the marketing of construction products and repealing Council Directive 89/106/EEC [2011] OJ L 88/5.

[13] Regulation (EC) 785/2004 of the European Parliament and of the Council of 21 April 2004 on insurance requirements for air carriers and aircraft operators [2004] OJ L 138/1.

the contents and quality of the regulation. For example, there is criticism of REACH holding that it would provide limited incentives for innovation. Moreover, it is one thing to take into account compliance with regulation as a presumption of following the due care standard or assuming "safety" of a particular product; it is quite another to infer from compliance with regulation that the security industry could no longer be held liable. Hence, this relationship between regulation and liability still merits further analysis, also from the perspective of the economic analysis of law.

A final point, especially as far as potential EU action is concerned, is that one notices that the instruments analysed in Chapter 2 often provide various options for Member States. For example, the ELD leaves the important issue of the compliance with permit defence (which has a significant influence on the scope of liability) to Member States and the same is true for the PLD which, for example, allows Member States to reject the development risk defence. The Recommendation on auditors' liability even goes a step further by providing Member States three options of (financially) limiting auditors' liability. This way of regulating liability has the major advantage of providing a lot of flexibility and leaving it largely up to the Member State to determine the scope of liability, thus respecting the subsidiarity principle and having the benefits of flexibility and differentiation. However, for an industry branch where risks are typically transnational (as in the security industry) operators working in this transnational branch may wish to have a European-wide liability regime in order to create an EU-wide level playing field. This is again a trade-off that needs further attention.

Also it is important to stress that one particular issue which has an influence on the potential liability of the security industry is in fact not explicitly regulated in any of the EU legislation discussed in this chapter, being causation. This is a crucial issue since the security industry will normally never be considered itself a direct tortfeasor or injurer. The direct tortfeasor will often be a criminal organisation or terrorists who intentionally inflict harm on victims. The charge against the security industry may be that through its negligence it facilitated the terrorist activity that inflicted harm upon the victims. The extent to which one accepts liability of the security industry in that case is strongly related to the question of whether one considers the behaviour of the security industry (supposedly wrongful) as a cause of the damage suffered by the victims. Notions like the proximity of the cause, breaking the chain of causation and the remoteness of damage are hence crucial in that respect.

These issues are not dealt with explicitly in any of the EU legislation analysed in this chapter, but do have a crucial bearing on the scope of liability of the security industry.

10.3.   Lessons from international law

In Chapter 1, we analysed several international treaties regarding liability for damage. Based on that analysis, we concluded that the distinguishing features of these conventions, including exclusive channelling of liability and financial limits, reduce the incentives to invest in efficient prevention of damage. On this ground, we concluded that the model of these conventions is not appropriate for defining the scope of liability for damage resulting from terrorist attacks, because preventing such damage is generally more important than mitigating liability.

10.4.   Limiting liability

Channelling of liability basically means that only one party can be held liable, thus excluding the liability of other parties involved. Such channelling can be found in the liability regimes set forth in the international treaties described in Chapter 1. As the comparative overview made clear, many of the international treaties channel the liability to a particular party, such as a ship-owner (in the Civil Liability Convention and the HNS Convention) or the operator (in the nuclear liability conventions). The current channelling of liability is beneficial to the security industry, because it implies that it reduces the threat of liability from the security industry. However, the channelling is not perfect in all conventions. In some cases, it is not exclusive and other parties can still be held liable. This is for example the case in the Montreal Convention on international carriage by air.

Theoretically, one could envisage enlarging the channelling to an exclusive liability of operators (the customers of the security industry), thus preventing any liability of the security industry. However, also the channelling of liability, more particularly with respect to nuclear liability and marine oil pollution, has been criticised in the literature. The main problem is that when liability is exclusively channelled to one liable operator, this automatically excludes liability of all others who may also have contributed to the accident risk. If one believes that liability rules provide incentives for prevention, the disadvantage of channelling is that it removes the incentives for prevention from all parties other than the single operator to whom the liability is channelled.

The March 2011 Fukushima incident in Japan illustrates some of the undesirable consequences of channelling. The first reports on the Fukushima case made clear that the meltdown of the nuclear reactors may have been caused by the simple fact that the generators for the cooling system were located in the basement of the turbine buildings, which of course made them vulnerable to a tsunami.[14] The question could be asked whether this is the result of negligent action by the operator TEPCO or rather the result of bad design or engineering by General Electric. In the latter case, a channelling of the liability to the operator TEPCO would be problematic, since channelling would lead to an exclusion of liability of all other parties who may have contributed to the risk, in this particular case (at least potentially) General Electric. The Fukushima case suggests that channelling can be problematic in removing incentives for prevention from other parties who are able to limit or otherwise influence a risk.[15]

A similar argument can be formulated with respect to the liability of the security industry. In this respect it should not be forgotten that the security industry is contracted by its clients precisely to provide the security they expect and that third parties (the public at large) also rely on the security industry to do what they are paid for, i.e. provide security. Fully excluding their liability, by making customers exclusively liable, may therefore be undesirable.

As we made clear at the end of Chapter 2, many activities related to the security industry (although not necessarily the security industry itself) are subject to detailed safety regulation. Safety regulation can have an important influence on liability. Compliance with regulation does not automatically exclude liability, but compliance could lead to a presumption of a security-related product not being defective. For example, compliance with the Personal Protective Equipment Directive may lead to an assumption of conformity with basic safety requirements, thus potentially reducing liability of operators.

The question arises what lessons can be drawn from this relationship with regulation for the security industry. On the one hand, the suggestion could be made to issue additional detailed regulations with which the security industry should comply. However, the comparative analysis also made clear that failure to comply with regulation is in all jurisdictions a strong indication that the defendant breached the required standard of

---

[14] See Yoshiada 2011   [15] See Faure and Liu 2012b, 214.

care (common law) or acted unlawfully or negligently (civil law). Hence, it could be argued that the more regulation that is enacted,[16] the more the liability of the security industry could potentially be expanded or limited. Indeed, as was argued in Chapter 3, regulation in that sense constitutes a double-edged sword: to the extent that the security industry complies with the regulatory standards, compliance could constitute a presumption of not having acted unlawfully (although that is not certain and debated), but non-compliance, on the other hand, will likely be regarded as negligence per se. Compliance with safety regulation could generally increase care levels and thus reduce the accident risk, and in that way limit the exposure to liability of the security industry. However, more detailed rules in safety regulation also make it easier for victims to prove that a particular regulatory standard has been breached and, in that sense, the requirement of fault/negligence has been met. If the breach stands in a causal relationship with the damage of the victim, liability may be given.

Going a step further, one could argue that if detailed safety regulation were issued this would constitute more than just a presumption of lawfulness (which could be set aside if the court finds that the security provider nevertheless acted negligently). One could argue that compliance with safety standards, provided that those safety standards reflect optimal care levels, should exclude liability of the security provider. However, there are considerable problems with this option, both from a legal as well from an economic perspective.

From a **legal** perspective the problem would be that such a position would collide with the current principles of liability law and the tradition of the Member States. The mere fact that the operator complied with regulation is in most legal systems considered only a minimum and not a reason to exclude liability. This points at a second problem from a legal perspective: there is no legal system among those examined in this book that has a rule freeing an operator from liability if regulatory standards are complied with (see *supra* 3.2.). Introducing such a rule would hence constitute a deviation from traditions in national tort law.

There are also good **economic** reasons to reject a "regulatory compliance defence". If compliance with a regulatory standard or licence would automatically result in a release from liability, a potential injurer would have no incentive to invest more in care than is required by the regulation, even if additional care could still reduce the expected accident

---

[16] Several countries already provide for special rules concerning the licensing of security companies and the supervision of their activities.

costs efficiently.[17] A first reason to hold an injurer liable (if the other conditions for liability are met), although he has followed the regulatory standard, is that indeed this standard is often merely a minimum. A complete "regulatory compliance defence" prevents any incentive to take precaution in excess of the regulated standard.[18] Exposure to liability will give the potential injurer incentives to take all efficient precautions, even if this requires more than just following the regulation. This, by the way, holds both under negligence and strict liability. Since the regulatory standard cannot always take into account all efficient precautionary measures an injurer can take, testing the measures taken by the injurer even though the regulatory standard was followed will provide additional incentives. Allowing a regulatory compliance defence would also reduce the beneficial incentive effects of strict liability. Strict liability has the advantage that it provides the injurer with incentives to take all efficient measures to reduce the risk (prevention and activity level), even if regulatory requirements are followed. This outcome has been shown formally by Kolstad/Ulen/Johnson[19] and by Burrows.[20] They argue that a complete compliance defence prevents any precaution in excess of the regulated standard. If there is serious under-enforcement of standards, the role of liability as an incentive to take precautions remains important.

A second reason is that exposure to liability might be a good remedy for the unavoidable capturing and public choice effects that may play a role when regulations are adopted. If a regulation would always release from liability, an operator would have strong incentives to spend resources on securing a good regulation with easy conditions. That would then exclude any lawsuit for damages by a potential victim. Obviously, these capturing and public choice effects could be addressed also via direct tools. In this respect, one can think of the liability, even under criminal law, of regulatory authorities.[21] Liability of the regulatory authorities (and appropriate sanctions within administrative law) can provide incentives to civil servants to act efficiently when issuing regulations.[22] This, however, still requires tort law to take into account the fact that regulatory standards

---

[17] Shavell 1984, 365.
[18] Burrows 1999, 242. Later Schwartz added to the debate by discussing whether compliance with federal safety statutes should have a justificative effect in State tort cases; see Schwartz 2000.
[19] Kolstad, Ulen and Johnson 1990, 888–901.
[20] Burrows 1999, 227–244.   [21] Faure, Koopmans and Oudijk 1996.
[22] Note, however, that industry may argue against such a liability of the authorities, as this may entail the risk that authorities would be too reluctant in allowing emissions.

are not always set efficiently. If the optimal level of care is higher than the regulatory standard, liability will efficiently provide additional incentives.

Finally, tort law can also be seen as a "stopgap" for situations not dealt with by regulations. This makes clear that the exposure to liability notwithstanding the regulations and/or permit is an important guarantee that the plant operator will take efficient care.

10.5.   Mandatory financial security

One potential issue that we have not yet discussed is whether one should consider the introduction of mandatory financial security to be provided by the security industry to cover its potential liability exposure. Several arguments or criteria in favour of compulsory financial security are examined below.

One argument is related to information problems. These might arise in case the potential injurer cannot make an accurate assessment of the risk it is exposed to and/or the benefits of the purchase of insurance. An underestimation of the risk would in that case lead to the wrongful decision of the injurer not to purchase liability insurance. The legislature could remedy this information problem by introducing a general duty to insure. For example, this information problem is probably a valid argument to introduce a general duty to insure for motor vehicle owners, because the average driver of a car is likely to underestimate the benefits of insurance. If there were no information problem and the legislature nevertheless introduced a duty to insure, because this would be "in the best interest" of the insured, this would reflect mere paternalism.

If empirical evidence existed that the security industry would greatly underestimate the costs of damage it may cause and/or the probability that they would be held liable for this damage, this would then lead injurers to reserve too few resources to cover their potential liability. If these conditions are met and one can indeed assume that injurers underestimate the cost of damage, this information deficiency may be considered an argument in favour of compulsory insurance. But again, the policy argument based on information asymmetry relates merely to the fact that the injurer would underestimate the potential benefits of insurance. However, this argument does not seem very convincing in the case of the security industry where there is no proof of specific information deficiencies. The industry appears to be well aware of its exposure and suggests that insurance is either unavailable or priced at levels that make it prohibitive. This is also a possible problem; if few security companies seek insurance, it is harder for insurance providers to develop attractive products, because of problems relating to potential adverse selection and the lack of the benefits of the law of large numbers.

Another argument for introducing compulsory financial security would be the potential insolvency of an injurer. Insolvency may result in under-deterrence. If the expected damage exceeds the injurer's assets, the injurer will only have incentives to purchase insurance up to the amount of its own assets. It is indeed only exposed to the risk of losing its own assets in a liability suit. The judgement-proof problem may therefore lead to underinsurance and thus to under-deterrence. Jost has rightly pointed at the fact that in these circumstances of insolvency, compulsory insurance might provide an optimal outcome.[23] By introducing a duty to purchase insurance coverage for the amount of the expected loss, better results will be obtained than with insolvency whereby the magnitude of the loss exceeds the injurer's assets.[24] In the latter case, the injurer will indeed only consider the risk as one where he could at most lose his own assets and will set his standard of care accordingly. When it is, under a duty to insure, exposed to full liability, the insurer will obviously have incentives to control the behaviour of the insured. Via the traditional instruments for the control of moral hazard, the insurer can make sure that the injurer will take the necessary care to avoid an accident with the real magnitude of the loss. Thus, Jost and Skogh argue that compulsory insurance, provided that the moral hazard problem can be cured adequately, can provide better results than voluntary insurance under the judgement-proof problem. This is one of the reasons why, for instance, traffic liability compulsory insurance was introduced. Uninsured and insolvent drivers who have little money at stake which they may lose compared to the possible magnitude of accidents they may cause, may have little incentives to avoid an accident. Insurers might be better able to control this risk and could force the injurer to take care under the threat of shutting him out of the insurance. Thus, the insurer becomes a regulator of the insured activity.

Indeed, this economic argument shows that insolvency may cause injurers to externalise harm: they may be engaged in activities that may cause harm greatly exceeding their assets. Without financial provisions these costs would fall on society and would hence be externalised instead of internalised. Such an internalisation can be achieved if the insurer is able

---

[23] Jost 1996. A similar argument has recently been formulated by Polborn 1998, 141, 146. Skogh 2000 has also pointed out that compulsory insurance may save on transaction cost.
[24] See also Kunreuther and Freeman 2001, 316.

to control the behaviour of the insured. The insurer could set appropriate policy conditions and an adequate premium. This suggests that if the moral hazard problem can be cured adequately, insurance leads to higher deterrence than a situation without liability insurance and insolvency.

However, also this argument is not particularly convincing in the case of the security industry. In earlier chapters, we have repeatedly argued that as of yet (and probably in the future as well) the exposure of the security industry to liability risks is not of such a nature that this would be uninsurable, and that large insolvency risks are likely to emerge if companies are not negligent. Moreover, if one were to consider the introduction of mandatory financial security, the more logical step to take would be to impose mandatory financial security on operators, the clients of the security industry. As we have shown in Chapter 1 (dealing with the international treaties related to nuclear safety, civil aviation and environmental liability) many of those treaties do indeed impose compulsory financial security. Since we have argued also that it is more likely that liability will be focused on the operators who may be victims of particular security breaches (e.g., by terrorists), it is logical that a duty to obtain financial security is imposed upon those operators rather than on the security industry.

Since there is no convincing evidence yet of huge insolvency risks as a result of which the security industry may not be able to meet its liabilities towards third parties, imposing mandatory financial security upon the security industry would potentially only create huge administrative costs without compensating benefits.

10.6.   Conclusions

In this chapter we provided an economic analysis of current TRR liability. We first sketched that, from an economic perspective, the goal of tort law is not so much compensation, but rather efficient deterrence of accidents. We also explained that within the European context the function of tort law is usually different from in the US, where victims may need tort law for basic compensation of their losses.

We equally analysed the findings from Chapter 1 (international law) and Chapter 2 (EU law) from an economic perspective, pointing at the strengths and weaknesses of those regimes concerning liability for TRR. Whereas we argued that channelling liability protects the security industry by exclusively focusing liability on operators, at the same time we argued that this may lead to the undesirable effect of limiting the liability exposure of the security industry, thus potentially limiting its incentives for prevention. We equally pointed at the problematic aspect of e.g. nuclear liability conventions, which on the one hand strongly limit the liability exposure of operators but on the other hand provide public funds to compensate victims. As a result, neither operators nor the security industry is fully exposed to the true social costs of their activities, which does not correspond with the economic goals of tort law as they were sketched in 10.1.

We also sketched that, especially in the European regime which was central to Chapter 2, the standard of care to be followed by either operators or the security industry is often defined by safety regulation. Such safety regulation may, so we argued, under circumstances have either an expanding or limiting effect on private liability. However, from an economic perspective there is no reason to limit or exclude private liability of operators or the security industry merely because there would have been compliance with safety regulation. After all, the level of optimal care may be higher than the standard required by safety regulation.

Economic analysis has also pointed out that in case of a serious insolvency risk, under-deterrence may occur. If there were proof of such an insolvency risk, that may be a strong argument in favour of imposing mandatory solvency guarantees, such as compulsory insurance. Examples of that can be found in the international treaties that were discussed in Chapter 1. In many of those cases (nuclear accidents and marine oil pollution), the potential damage that an operator can cause could be substantially higher than his assets. In those cases, imposing mandatory financial guarantees (like insurance) upon operators is hence completely justified. However, we argued that the case may be different for the security industry itself. As long as there is no proof that the industry may not be able to meet its liabilities towards third parties, it may not be immediately necessary to introduce mandatory financial security since this obviously creates high costs as well.

An interesting question that we in fact already addressed in Chapter 8 is to what extent alternatives may be better able to deal with damage resulting from terrorism-related risks. We pointed at the possibility of introducing victim compensation solutions such as either victim compensation funds or government-provided compensation. Those have, so we argued in Chapter 8, negative effects on both the incentives of operators and the security industry to take preventive measures, and are from that perspective undesirable. However, an alternative may be the model of a mandatory first-party insurance scheme, as exists in France. To the extent that those victim compensation solutions exclude liability of either operators or the security industry, the disadvantage of those schemes is unavoidably that liability rules can no longer have their deterrent effect, and that there hence may be negative consequences as far as the incentives for prevention are concerned. This may result in an increase of the risk.

In this chapter, we looked at several devices limiting liability that are currently employed such as channelling of liability and linking liability to regulation. However, the analysis of TRR liability in international law equally made clear that many international conventions contain limits on liability which are, as we argued in Chapter 1, problematic from the perspective of providing incentives for prevention. This of course raises the question to what extent either operators or the security industry should at all be subject to direct liability limitations; which was the subject of analysis of Chapter 9.

11

Is there a role for the European Union?

LUCAS BERGKAMP AND NICOLAS HERBATSCHEK

In previous chapters, we analysed liability for terrorism-related risks faced by the security industry and operators of high-risk facilities. We discussed also whether these risks are enterprise-threatening and unique to the security industry and operators of high-risk facilities. Based on this analysis, we concluded that there is little evidence of any impending liability crisis due to terrorism-related risks, nor are there plausible arguments that such a crisis is to be expected. There have been no cases in which security providers or operators have been held liable for damages caused by terrorist attacks. There are no reported precedents of security providers being unable to provide goods or services due to excessive liability exposure. Subject to limited exceptions, potential liability under national law for terrorism-related damage requires negligence and is limited in terms of heads of damages to which liability attaches. Contractual liability limitations are generally enforceable and insurance may be available. These findings suggest that there is no urgent need for government intervention to limit liability exposure for terrorism-related risk.

The analysis does not necessarily suggest, however, that there is no problem at all. As noted above, like all other operators, security providers and operators of high-risk facilities may be exposed to liability where they are negligent, or where they breach their contractual obligations. Under the national laws of the Member States, liability based on negligence is generally financially unlimited. Although such liability requires breach of a duty of care or fault and applies not only to security providers but to all legal and natural persons, the large amounts of terrorism-related claims could easily bankrupt high-risk facility operators and security providers. The alleged lack of affordable insurance and the reluctance of the customers of the security industry to agree reasonable liability limitations would indirectly affect the industry's third-party liability exposure.

In this chapter, we review the role that the European Union could play to address these concerns. The first section discusses the authority of the European Union to adopt measures addressing the civil liability exposure of the security industry and operators of high-risk facilities to terrorism-related risks. The second section analyses the options available under EU law to reduce such exposure, including liability caps and victim compensation funds and whether any such measures would be justified. Our conclusions are summarised in the last section.

11.1.   Options to limit liability

In this section, we evaluate the various policy options open to the Commission. We point out where issues arise, what plausible policy responses may be available and what implications and consequences various policy options will have.

Policy options involving liability limitations and related instruments can be analysed with respect to contents (substance) and form. In relation to substance, policy responses can be grouped into seven main categories:

1. A fully fledged Safety Act-like regime;
2. Other liability limitations, notably a liability cap, exclusion of certain types of damage from the scope of liability or a regulatory compliance exception;
3. Initiatives addressing issues in the markets for security goods and services;
4. Initiatives aimed at the insurance market;
5. Initiatives aimed at informing the security industry and, as necessary, insurers, Member States and other stakeholders about issues relating to liability, insurance and contracting;
6. A procedural solution; and
7. Measures aimed at creating alternative compensation mechanisms.

In addition, there is, of course, the option to do nothing.

With respect to the form, for our purposes, three groups of EU measures can be distinguished:

1. Legislation (directive or regulation) to implement one or more of the possible policy options;
2. Non-binding policy measures, such as recommendations and communications; and
3. Other initiatives that are aimed at obtaining and disseminating sound and reliable information relevant to third-party liability exposure of the security industry, insurance and contracting.

Each of these main substantive categories and forms is briefly discussed below.

11.1.1.   Safety Act

A Safety Act, of course, would be in the form of binding legislation. For the reasons discussed, we do not see a need for an EU Safety Act. The EU liability environment is very different from the US liability environment and the reasons that necessitated the US Safety Act are not present in the EU. Any proposed EU Safety Act would have to meet the proportionality principle and the principle of equality, which is not self-evident.

If the EU decides to pursue a Safety Act, a EU-level agency would have to be designated to deal with the certification and designation of security products and services. Some features of the US Safety Act, such as the prohibition of punitive damages and litigation solely before federal courts, simply do not apply in Europe. The costs of operating an EU Safety Act regime would be substantial, while the benefits are less clear.

In light of the findings of Chapter 8, we believe that a Safety Act would be an exaggerated policy response to what appears to be a more limited problem.

11.1.2.   Other liability limitations

Instead of an EU Safety Act, other limitations of the liability of security providers and facility operators could be enacted. Possible options include a liability cap (i.e. a financial limit or ceiling), the exclusion of certain types of damage from the scope of liability (e.g., pure economic loss), or a regulatory compliance exception (e.g., if a product or service meets all applicable regulatory requirements).

These options have different pros and cons, but a common issue is the effect on incentives to prevent damage. If the EU decides to pursue a liability limitation, it should consider and mitigate, as necessary, the effect on prevention incentives. If a financial cap is set at an appropriately high level (e.g., up to insurance limits), little effect on incentives is to be expected; the lower the limit, the stronger the adverse effect on incentives may be, but this is also a function of regulatory and contractual standards. The exclusion of pure economic loss is also an option, but national laws are already quite reluctant to extend liability to include such losses in any event. A regulatory compliance exception or defence is an option that should be tied to a good programme of regulatory standard-setting and updating; if no guarantees exist for adequate and comprehensive standard-setting and updating, a regulatory compliance exception may not be a good idea.

Of course, the industry's concerns are not the only considerations relevant to possible liability limitations. Attention should also be paid to the objectives pursued by the liability system, inasmuch as fulfilment of these objectives may be compromised if liability is limited. Indeed, a liability limitation must be adequately justified, given the potentially negative effects of such a measure on the liability system's ability to effectively pursue deterrence, risk allocation and loss-spreading. As discussed in 9.1., some of the arguments invoked to support liability limitations fail to acknowledge that the European litigation environment differs considerably from the US system. Further, in most EU Member States specific solutions have been worked out to cover damage resulting from terrorist attacks, such as public–private partnerships and compensation funds. This cautions against the limitation of the liability of economic operators in the security chain.

As noted, a liability limitation may adversely affect the fulfilment of liability's objectives. From a law and economics perspective, a liability system is aimed at deterrence and prevention, as well as adequate risk allocation and loss-spreading. Adverse consequence of limiting the liability of the economic operators in the security chain may be that liability's objectives are not met to the same degree. Specifically, these effects could include the following:

1. A liability limitation for the benefit of economic operators in the security chain would imply that the preventive and deterrent effect of liability would be reduced. Exposure to liability has the desirable effect of providing security firms and high-risk facility operators with incentives to take preventive measures. If liability were limited, society might pay a price in terms of reduced investments in prevention. As discussed in Chapter 1 of this book, where international treaties provide for liability caps, they do so only in the context of strict liability, not fault liability.
2. Another consequence would be a change in risk allocation, which has further effects on insurance and activity levels. Being exposed to a lower level of liability, economic operators in the security chain would purchase less insurance to cover their liability (or spend less on other risk-spreading mechanisms), as a result of which their prices would be lower. From a law and economics perspective, the effect of a liability

limitation is comparable to a subsidy and could lead to market prices that do not reflect the full social costs of the activity. To the extent that demand increases at lower prices, this would result in increased activity levels and possibly also in an increase in damage.

3. From a distributional perspective, the consequence of a liability limitation would be that liability law's loss-spreading function is impeded. Consequently, victims would have to bear the losses that they cannot shift to economic operators, unless another loss-spreading mechanism is available. This, in turn, may result in a less efficient system of loss-spreading. Hence, the advantages of a possible liability limitation must be weighed against the disadvantages in terms of reduced prevention incentives and less efficient loss-spreading.

Additionally, in considering a liability limitation, the EU would first have to provide an accurate definition of group of beneficiaries of such a limitation and evaluate the effects for those that fall outside of this definition. Policy decisions would have to be made on issues such as whether both security service providers and suppliers of security products would be covered and which operators would benefit (e.g., how the concept of "high-risk" facility is defined). The specific features of the industry falling within the scope of the definition would have to be clearly identifiable. A similar debate arose during the drafting of the US Safety Act; this issue was addressed through a certification system, pursuant to which only those companies that have been certified enjoy protection under the US Safety Act.

If any liability limitation is deemed appropriate (which, as discussed, we doubt), it could be issued in the form of a non-binding policy measure. For instance, the EU might consider a recommendation an appropriate instrument to address liability limitations. There is precedent at the EU level for such a recommendation in the form of Recommendation 2008/437 on auditors' liability. A communication would be an alternative. We will discuss this option further below.

11.1.3.   *Initiatives addressing issues in the market for security goods and services*

As discussed in 7.3., it has been suggested that the inability of security firms to obtain contractual protection against liability for terrorism-related risk poses a problem. Many purchasers of security goods and services are public or quasi-public bodies that contract for security goods and services through open public procurement procedures. In such procurement procedures, there would be little or no room to negotiate reasonable liability limitations and indemnities. In comparison, in the software industry liability limitations are common practice and there is no evidence that this results in problems of under-deterrence.[1]

If indeed there is market failure in the markets for security goods and services, which could be due to issues such as concerted action by public authorities to disallow liability limitations and indemnities, the EU could play a role in facilitating more flexible procurement processes. Such EU action could involve open discussions between security authorities, operators of airports and other facilities and the security industry to discuss issues and identify and agree best practices. Once the nature and scope of the problems is understood, a Commission recommendation on contracting for security goods and services would be a possible option. Binding legislation, however, is not an option that can likely effectively and efficiently address this issue.

In the absence of strong evidence of enterprise-threatening risk, however, there is little justification for significant Commission-driven activities other than collecting and analysing documentary evidence of issues. In the absence of such facts and analysis, there is no basis for considering further measures.

11.1.4. Initiatives aimed at the insurance market

It has been asserted, as discussed in 9.3., that insurance for terrorism-related risks is either unavailable or unaffordable. Information provided by a European insurance association, however, suggests that the situation may differ significantly between EU Member States;[2] lack of affordable insurance may be an issue in some, but not all, Member States. Further analysis of the insurance market may be useful to get better insights into the nature of any issues that arise.

In addition, the EU could play a role in facilitating discussions between the insurance industry and the security industry. Such discussions could also be helpful in understanding and resolving any problems. Again, if there are issues in the insurance market, a Commission recommendation might be a suitable instrument to address these issues.

---

[1] See Chapter 8.   [2] Bergkamp, Faure, Hinteregger and Philipsen (eds.) 2013, 301.

11.1.5. A Commission recommendation or communication?

A Commission recommendation or communication could be considered to prevent potential problems from arising in the future, if and when a large-scale terrorist attack were to occur. Future problems cannot be entirely excluded because liability laws work with "open" standards (such as fault or negligence) that allow for potentially expansive interpretation and application. Note, however, that this issue extends beyond security providers to other sectors of industry that are exposed to liability for identical or similar "catastrophic" risks.

Any Commission action would likely be most effective once any issues surrounding insurance and public procurement have been documented and analysed.

Any such recommendation or communication could cover the following aspects:

- Explain the potential for an expansive interpretation and application of liability laws to cause problems for security providers and facility operators in the case of large scale damage arising from terrorist attacks.
- Set out various principles by which such liability can be kept within reasonable limits in future cases. These principles could include the following:
  - National liability laws recognise that security providers are not making the critical decisions about what equipment and services to use at facilities. A security provider is not liable on the grounds that not the best equipment and services were deployed.
  - Security providers and facility operators are not exposed to strict liability; a security firm or a facility operator is liable if it is at fault, acts negligently or provides a product that suffers from a manufacturing defect.
  - The standard of liability applying to security providers and facility operators is not the standard applying to laypersons, but a higher standard that is appropriate for professionals. This standard is not so high, however, that only the best firms can meet it; it is the expertise and skill of a reasonably experienced and skilled professional that is required.
  - Liability law takes due account of the security provider's contractual obligations and does not impose an independent standard of care in relation to third parties. If a security provider is held liable by a third party for terrorism-related damage, the agreement between

the security provider and the facility operator defines that scope of the security provider's obligations, including its obligations to accept liability. Liability limitations set forth in that agreement, in principle, also have effect vis-à-vis third parties, except, possibly, with respect to personal injury.

- Any alleged design defects are assessed in light of the agreement with the customer-operator.
- The fact that the security provider is unable to disclose the limits of security technology to the public does not result in liability exposure for failure to warn.
- The fact that binding rules may regulate the security industry (or its goods or services) and facility operators may mean that they can invoke a "mandatory order" defence, or benefit from a rebuttable assumption of having met the required due care standard.
- Liability for property damage and consequential and pure economic loss can be mitigated in light of all relevant facts, including insurance (both first and third party).

- Address any issues in the insurance market. Of course, the specifics can be set out only once these issues have been documented and analysed.
- Address any issues in the market for public procurement of security goods and services. Likewise, the specifics can be set out only once these issues have been documented and analysed.

11.2.   Procedural solutions

Terrorist attacks giving rise to claims in several Member States may be rarer than attacks giving rise to multiple claims chiefly within the same Member State, but both situations may occur in relation to terrorist attacks resulting in widespread damage. Where victims are based in more than one Member State, multiple claims could be filed against security industry providers and facility operators in several Member States. Consequently, defendants would be exposed to the substantial costs associated with defending multiple claims pending in multiple jurisdictions. To alleviate this burden, the EU could propose procedural solutions addressing the problem on an EU-wide basis. Such procedural solutions include central-isation of all claims in one Member State, or centralisation at the level of each Member State separately. If claims are centralised before one court, the aggregate cost of both plaintiffs and defendants would likely drop sub-stantially. Centralisation could be conceived as a right of defendants. In that case, a defendant that is being sued before multiple courts could seek

324   IS THERE A ROLE FOR THE EUROPEAN UNION?

to have all claims against it transferred to one court. A defendant could do so, for instance, to reduce cost or ensure consistency of adjudication; multiple judgments, of course, create a risk of inconsistency.

Proponents of a regime for centralising claims for the entire EU in one Member State need to consider how to deal with the differences in national laws and procedures, as well as how to address the difficulties associated with cross-border litigation. Depending on the incremental cost of cross-border litigation, it is conceivable that the cost savings associated with EU-wide centralisation would be less than the cost savings resulting from centralisation in each Member State separately. Centralisation at the Member State level avoids the complexities associated with differences between national laws. These complexities may be significant; for instance, a plaintiff may have a claim in one Member State but not in another Member State.

11.3. Victim compensation solutions

Compensation funds and similar measures to take the burden of liability off the security industry and facility operators do not appear to be indicated at this point. In general, such measures will have adverse effects on incentives to prevent damage and raise a host of other issues (who will fund, on what basis, rights of recourse, etc.). Limited alternative compensation mechanisms covering, for instance, pure economic loss or for losses in excess of any liability cap, could be considered however, if a need were to arise.

In any event, before the EU should even consider any such measures, it should explore other available policy options; if such options are not feasible, alternative compensation mechanisms might be considered. In designing any alternative compensation mechanisms, the EU should ensure that efficient prevention of damage remains a goal. Note, however, that this book has not found any significant need for such measures.

11.3.1.   Initiatives aimed at informing the security industry and, as necessary, insurers, Member States and other stakeholders about issues of liability (and, if necessary, insurance and contracting)

The Commission might consider initiatives aimed at disseminating accurate information about security providers' liability exposure under EU and national laws. Such initiatives could include information sessions, case studies, workshops, websites and the like.

Likewise, it is conceivable that Member State governments and judges, insurers and other stakeholders may have a need for reliable information about liability and any insurance and contracting issues. Again, the Commission could play a facilitating role here and promote the dissemination and exchange of accurate information, for example, about the situation in other Member States and "best practices".

11.4.   Prerequisites in institutional EU law

Possible measures to address terrorism-related risks vary from a mere recommendation to a fully fledged Safety Act regime. While a fully fledged Safety Act regime requires an institutional framework at EU level, other options raise more limited issues under EU law.

In this section, we review EU law prerequisites that must be met before the EU could consider whether to adopt such options to address the liability of the security industry and operators of high-risk facilities. The two main issues arise in relation to the EU's powers to legislate and general principles of EU law.

11.4.1.   EU competence

The EU does not have explicit authority to legislate in the area of national security, nor does it have explicit power to enact civil liability law. As Article 5 of the Treaty on the European Union (TEU) provides, the limits of EU's competences are governed by the principle of conferral, i.e. the EU has power only where such power is explicitly bestowed on it.[3] The Treaty on the Functioning of the EU (TFEU) defines three types of legislative powers ("competences") of the EU, as follows:

- **Exclusive competences under Article 3 of the TFEU**: these powers do not appear to be directly relevant to any possible measures.
- **Shared competences under Article 4 of the TFEU**: both the EU and the Member States are authorised to legislate in these areas, but the Member States may exercise their power only where the EU has not legislated. Article 4(2) lists as shared competences the "internal market" and "freedom, security and justice". Under Article 26 of the TFEU, the

---

[3]   Article 5(2) TEU provides: "Under the principle of conferral, the Union shall act only within the limits of the competences conferred upon it by the Member States in the Treaties to attain the objectives set out therein. Competences not conferred upon the Union in the Treaties remain with the Member States."

EU has the power to adopt "measures with the aim of establishing or ensuring the functioning of the internal market", which comprises "an area without internal frontiers in which the free movement of goods, persons, services and capital is ensured in accordance with the provisions of the Treaties".

- **Supporting competences under Article 6 of the TFEU:** the EU has the power to legislate only to support, coordinate or complement the Member States' policies. Consequently, it has no legislative power in these fields and may not interfere in the exercise of these competences reserved for Member States. These areas include health protection, industry and civil protection.

In addition, the EU has special competences in some areas (such as the coordination of economic and employment policies pursuant to Article 5 of the TFEU), but these are not directly relevant to civil liability legislation. Further, pursuant to the "flexibility clause" set forth in Article 352 of the TFEU, the EU can be authorised to act if necessary, but unanimity in the Council is required.

Under Article 4(2) TEU, national security remains the sole responsibility of each Member State. Further, Article 346 TFEU (ex Article 296 Treaty Establishing the European Community (TEC)), under (b), provides that

> any Member State may take such measures as it considers necessary for the protection of the essential interests of its security which are connected with the production of or trade in arms, munitions and war material; such measures shall not adversely affect the conditions of competition in the internal market regarding products which are not intended for specifically military purposes.

Pursuant to Article 73 TFEU, "it shall be open to Member States to organise between themselves and under their responsibility such forms of cooperation and coordination as they deem appropriate between the competent departments of their administrations responsible for safeguarding national security." Although not directly relevant to the issue of allocation of powers, Article 6 of the Charter provides that "everyone has the right to liberty and security of person."

Thus, national security policy is not a power of the EU. It should be noted, however, that legislation on third-party liability of security firms and facility operators is probably not national security policy. Like other policies and laws, such legislation may indirectly influence national security policy, but is likely not part thereof.

The EU does not have explicit powers to legislate on civil liability, but liability legislation may be covered by another EU competence. This raises the question of what the legal basis could be for EU legislation on liability of security providers and facility operators. A plausible legal basis for such legislative measures could be the EU's internal market powers. The internal market title of the TFEU gives the EU broad authority to adopt measures "with the aim of establishing or ensuring the functioning of the internal market, in accordance with the relevant provisions of the Treaties".[4] To this end, the "internal market shall comprise an area without internal frontiers in which the free movement of goods, persons, services and capital is ensured in accordance with the provisions of the Treaties". As discussed in Chapter 3, the issue of third-party liability for terrorism-related risk plays out somewhat differently in different Member States. To some degree, the nature and magnitude of the liability exposure varies based on the national law of the Member States. Differences in liability exposure could result in different competitive conditions and in barriers to trade in goods and services between the Member States. For instance, a security provider from a Member State where the liability exposure is low may be reluctant to sell products in a Member State where the liability exposure is high. This may be so, for instance, where a security provider does not have adequate insurance in place, because such insurance is not needed in his home country. Thus, differences in third-party liability exposure of security providers or facility operators may affect the movement of goods, persons and capital between the Member States. If differences in liability regimes between the Member States indeed affect the free movement of goods and services and frustrate the objective of establishing an internal market (which this book has not analysed), the EU has the power to take measures to address any such differences.

Thus, the first question that should be asked is whether the current differences between the Member States' national laws concerning liability of security providers could affect the free movement of goods and services. Any legislation based on the EU's internal market powers must meet the requirements for the exercise of such powers. Under those conditions, the EU could invoke its internal market powers to adopt legislation on civil liability of the security industry and facility operators, including legislation along the lines of the US Safety Act, subject to compliance with the Treaty and general principles of EU law.

---

[4] Article 26 TFEU (ex Article 14 TEC).

11.4.2.   General principles of EU law

In legislating, the EU must respect the relevant provisions of the Treaty and general principles of EU law.[5] For example, EU legislation should meet the subsidiarity and proportionality principles set forth in the TFEU. As Article 5 puts it, "[t]he use of Union competences is governed by the principles of subsidiarity and proportionality." Any EU legislation on civil liability, of course, would have to comply with these principles. Under the principle of subsidiarity, as Article 5(3) of the TEU provides, in areas which do not fall within its exclusive competence, the EU "shall act only if and in so far as the objectives of the proposed action cannot be sufficiently achieved by the Member States, either at central level or at regional and local level, but can rather, by reason of the scale or effects of the proposed action, be better achieved at Union level". This principle could be met if there is a problem in the internal market for security goods and services and such problem cannot be adequately addressed through only national measures. As discussed in Chapters 8 and 10, we found no evidence of any such problem. Only if differences between the Member States' national laws actually impede the working of the internal market could legislation on civil liability be justified on this ground.

Under the principle of proportionality, as Article 5(4) of the TEU provides, the content and form of EU action "shall not exceed what is necessary to achieve the objectives of the Treaties". In theory, legislation on civil liability could meet this requirement (note, however, that the analysis provided under Chapter 10 has not found any evidence of actual problems in relation to the security industry's and facility operators' liability exposure). The analysis, however, should be done on a case-by-case basis in light of a specific measure and specific facts. Obviously, a fully fledged Safety Act regime is more likely to raise issues in relation to proportionality than a Commission recommendation.

Likewise, EU measures should be consistent with other principles of EU law, such as the equality principle and legal certainty and legitimate expectations.[6] With respect to the latter, we can be brief: there is no generic reason why legislation on civil liability would raise issues of legal certainty and legitimate expectations. Of course, in a specific case such issues may arise, but that is not inherent to legislation on civil liability as such. The equality principle, on the other hand, is directly relevant to any possible legislation on civil liability. As legislation on civil liability, by

---

[5] Tridimas 2006.   [6] Craig 2012.

definition, provides some sort of liability limitation to a specific liability regime for the security industry and/or operators, the question arises why the security industry and/or facility operators should be singled out: why should not all companies benefit from this programme, or at least all companies that are exposed to potential catastrophic, large-scale damage? Under this principle, an objective justification is required for the differential treatment of the security industry.[7] Thus, the EU will have to provide an adequate objective justification to avoid a risk that measures limiting the civil liability of security firms and facility operators might be challenged successfully.

11.4.3. Conclusions

This book has not found any evidence of an impending liability crisis in the security industry. The assertions of "enterprise-threatening" liability exposure are not consistent with the liability standards under the laws of the seven Member States covered in this book. No urgent EU measures are therefore necessary. To prevent problems in future cases, a Commission recommendation or communication could be considered. Possible elements of such an instrument have been discussed in the preceding section. Given the complexity of national civil liability regimes, it may be helpful to launch initiatives aimed at enlightening the security industry, facility operators and, as necessary, insurers, Member States and other stakeholders about third-party liability exposure.

Perceived problems in the insurance market and in the market for public procurement of security goods and services may deserve further attention from policymakers, either at the EU or Member State levels.

---

[7] Cases 117/76 and 16/77 *Ruckdeschel* [1977] ECR 1753. Cases 103 and 145/77 *Royal Scholten-Honig* v. *Intervention Board for Agricultural Products* [1978] ECR 2037.

CONCLUSIONS

LUCAS BERGKAMP, MICHAEL FAURE,
MONIKA HINTEREGGER AND NIELS PHILIPSEN

In this book, we explored the civil liability of security firms and high-risk facility operators to third parties for damage caused by terrorism under European laws. Over the last several decades, Europe has suffered the consequences of multiple acts of terrorism. In response to the threats posed by terrorists, the European Union and nation States created counterterrorism strategies. As part of such policies, some countries established compensation funds to ensure that victims of terrorist attacks receive some relief. The 9/11 attacks marked the beginning of the "war on terror", a war that cannot be won definitively.[1] Beyond the massive direct and indirect damages, the 9/11 attacks raised the spectre of possible repeat strikes and even more deadly terrorist action. In this context, the role of civil liability in the fight against terrorism has been questioned.

International liability treaties do not specifically deal with liability for damage caused by terrorists. As discussed in Chapter 1, the international regimes governing liability for damage caused by aircraft and space objects, nuclear installations, oil and other hazardous substances channel liability exclusively to the operator of the relevant activities, to the exclusion of other parties involved such as security firms. Further, liability under these conventions is strict, but typically subject to a financial limit. Such a model, we found, is not ideal because it tends to reduce or eliminate prevention incentives for parties other than operators and for operators above the financial limit.

Likewise, European Union legislation has not specifically addressed liability for terrorism-related risk, although the EU did adopt legislation regarding the fight against terrorism. As discussed in Chapter 2, Member States may be liable under the *Francovich* doctrine if they act or fail to act in violation of EU law and, as a result, increase the chances of a terrorist attack. Of the potentially relevant EU legislative instruments, only the

---

[1] Smil 2012, 61.

ELD and PLD impose potential liability on private parties with respect to damage caused by terrorists. Interestingly, while the ELD provides a defence if the operator took "appropriate safety measures", the PLD imposes liability if a "defective" product causes harm and provides for a "state-of-the-art" defence; thus, both instruments reflect a fault element, which limits exposure in relation to damage caused by terrorists. Other EU regulatory regimes may indirectly affect liability exposure for terrorism-related risk, inasmuch as compliance with applicable safety standards may mitigate against liability and non-compliance may contribute to a finding of negligence or even constitute negligence per se. The EU rules regarding cross-border litigation, on the other hand, probably have only a small effect on actual liability exposure.

In the final analysis, liability for damage caused by terrorists is chiefly a function of national law. To understand in detail how this issue plays out, we surveyed and compared the relevant national liability laws of seven EU Member States and reported the result of this analysis in Chapters 3 to 5. Security firms and facility operators are exposed to liability under fault-based and product liability rules; strict liability rules play only a minor role. The liability exposure of security firms vis-à-vis both their customers and third parties is determined on the basis of the contract between the security provider and the customer. Fault-based liability requires the breach of a duty of care, the scope and substance of which, in turn, is determined by contract. Thus, a security provider is able to limit its liability exposure by detailing its obligations to provide security in the contract and complying with such obligations. Specifically, the facility operator may be liable vis-à-vis third parties under fault-based liability rules or under strict liability concepts if the activity is deemed "hazardous"; train stations are not usually considered as hazardous activities, but could be deemed hazardous, depending on whether the concept of hazard applies to the risk of a terrorist attack. Under fault-based liability rules, the facility operator may be liable if it chose a level of security that is too low for the facility involved (e.g., no scanning is conducted for semtex at an airport), or otherwise did not meet its duty of care. Where the facility operator provides services to a transportation service provider (e.g., an airport), like the security provider, the operator may define its obligations by contract and these obligations could also define its duty of care vis-à-vis third parties, such as the users of the facility (e.g., passengers and other persons). If the operator did not meet its obligations to provide security, it may be liable also vis-à-vis third parties. Whether a security firm or operator is liable depends also on the nature and proximity of the damage; pure economic loss sustained by third parties is often not compensable and some damage may be considered too remote. Under concepts of national law, the operator of an activity and the security provider may be jointly and severally liable. While the burden of proof lies with the claimant, the standard of proof varies between the Member States surveyed. Where special strict liability regimes apply, the fact that damage was caused by a terrorist attack is qualified as "force majeure" or "an act of God" in most countries and thus the operator or security provider will not be liable for the ensuing damage. Finally, in some countries, special compensation schemes for victims of terrorism have been established, which tend to effectively reduce the liability exposure of operators and security firms. All in all, this analysis does not suggest that operators and security firms are exposed to unlimited and uncontrollable third-party liability for damage caused by terrorists. On the contrary, national liability laws enable operators and security firms to avoid liability by demonstrating compliance with their duty of care, which can be defined by contract. Importantly, in none of the Member States surveyed have operators or security firms been held liable for damage caused by terrorists, and there are no signs of a liability crisis or an impending liability crisis.

Although the liability of operators and security firms is predicated chiefly on fault and contract, insurance can still play a useful role in managing such liability in an efficient manner, as discussed in Chapter 6. The main barriers to an effective insurance market, however, are the highly correlated nature of the risks concerned, the high insurance capacity required and the lack of sufficient historical data and predictability. These issues can be mitigated where the government accepts the role of reinsurer of last resort. As a result of such government back-up and sophisticated insurance techniques, terrorism-related risk has become insurable again after insurers reduced or cancelled coverage following the 9/11 attacks.

In addition to insurance, contractual liability limitations can help to mitigate liability exposure. The analysis presented in Chapter 7 demonstrated that security providers, unlike companies in other sectors such as software, may not be able to negotiate limitations on their liability in contracts with their customers, in particular where the government or public agencies purchase security services or products in a regulated public procurement process. The combination of exposure to large terrorism-related liabilities (even if based solely on fault) and the inability to limit such exposure by contract (and to obtain adequate insurance coverage, which, by definition, is subject to financial limits) might render security providers uniquely vulnerable to such liabilities. This does not mean, however, that their liability exposure must therefore be directly limited, but it may mean that there is possibly exceptional liability exposure that may require policymakers' attention. The advantages of a liability limitation must be weighed against its disadvantages, such as the potentially negative effects of such a measure on liability's objectives in terms of deterrence (prevention), risk allocation and loss-spreading.

Liability is one way to compensate damage caused by terrorism, but it is not the only way. Alternative systems that modify or exclude liability include the US Safety Act and victim compensation funds. These systems are reviewed in Chapter 8. In the US, the lawsuits following the 9/11 attacks had a chilling effect on some economic activities and resulted in significant reduction of the availability of insurance coverage for terrorism-related risk, including cancellation of insurance policies in some cases. These adverse consequences prompted US Congress to adopt the Terrorism Risk Insurance Act,[2] which requires that insurance companies offer coverage of business property and casualty losses,[3] as well as the Safety Act, which provides a mechanism for limiting the liability of the security industry and certain high-risk operators. The US Safety Act was specifically intended to stimulate innovation in security technology by mitigating the threat of civil liability. In Europe, the adoption of the US Safety Act and the continuing threat of terrorist attacks raised the question of whether the European Union should take action to limit civil liability for terrorism-related risks. Arguments have been made that the EU should adopt a regime like the US Safety Act, or at least a liability limitation for the benefit of the security industry. The liability litigation environment in Europe, however, is different from the litigation environment in the US, in terms of both procedure and substantive law. For instance, discovery does not exist in Europe and punitive damages are basically non-existent. Further, national social security regimes and specific terrorism funds and public–private partnerships in the European Union provide monetary compensation to victims, which reduces the need to rely on the liability system for purposes of compensating damage caused by terrorist attacks. Thus, even if there is a good case for the Safety Act in the US, it does not follow that there is a case for an EU Safety Act.

An alternative that limits liability exposure in a different way is government-mandated first-party insurance, which is also discussed in Chapter 8. Such programmes have been established for natural disasters

---

[2] Pub. Law 107–297, 116 Stat. 2322.
[3] The act excludes losses due to nuclear, biological or chemical attacks, however. 2004, 172.

in France and a few other countries. They typically involve mandatory insurance contracted by victims and provide comprehensive coverage. Although possibly useful to address natural disasters, this model is not appropriate for terrorism-related risk, because it would reduce the incentives to prevent terrorist attacks. Further, ex-ante, structured compensation funds and ex-post ad hoc victim compensation programmes, which compensate victims out of public revenues or specific contributions, effectively provide subsidies to industry, or diminish the deterrent effect of liability if operators are no longer exposed to liability to the same extent. Consequently, these types of government-supported compensation mechanisms are not the ideal solutions for redressing damage arising from terrorism-related risks.

Liability for terrorism-related risk might have to be limited on the ground that unlimited liability would be enterprise-threatening. Differential treatment of high-risk facility operators and security firms for liability purposes could be justified if it could be shown that these firms are exposed to an excessive degree of liability, suffer from structural inability to deploy risk mitigation strategies, or underinvest in innovation due to the threat of liability. Each of these arguments have been reviewed in Chapter 9. None of them, however, was found to be persuasive. There is some US evidence that unlimited liability would have an adverse effect on the development and deployment of innovative security technology and systems, but the situation in Europe with its much less litigious environment is quite different. We concluded that there are no persuasive arguments to support the proposition that unlimited liability for terrorism-related risk has an enterprise-threatening effect on enterprise within the EU.

To better understand the findings of our analysis thus far, we also conducted an economic analysis of liability for terrorism-related risk. In Chapter 10, the results of that analysis were presented. This analysis identified the inefficiencies associated with the current international and EU liability regimes for other kinds of damage. With respect to alternatives to liability, the analysis suggested that a reduction in prevention incentives that may be associated with such alternatives could result in increased terrorism-related risk. It also showed that in case of a serious insolvency risk, under-deterrence may occur under a conventional liability rule. If there were proof of such an insolvency risk, that may be an argument in favour of imposing mandatory solvency guarantees, such as compulsory insurance. However, as long as there is no proof that the industry may not be able to meet its liabilities towards third parties, there may not be an urgent reason to introduce mandatory financial security, given the substantial costs associated with such a measure.

In light of the preceding analysis, the question can now be answered whether there is a role for the EU with respect to third-party liability for terrorism-related risk and if so, what that role should be. As discussed in Chapter 11, perceived problems in the insurance market and in the market for public procurement of security goods and services may deserve further attention from policymakers, either at the EU or Member State levels. Our analysis focused on the alleged lack of affordable insurance coverage for terrorism-related risk and the impossibility of limiting liability by contract, in particular in the context of public procurement. Despite claims that terrorism-related insurance is generally unavailable, the reality appears to be more complicated; while there are well-developed markets in some Member States, coverage availability may be limited in other Member States. Further, if and to the extent that security and other firms are "forced" to accept contracts that do not provide for any limits on their liability, these contract clauses could be viewed as merely reflecting the preferences of the contracting parties; there is no reason to believe that this would reflect some "market failure". Accordingly, it is hard to see why the EU should take action. Even if the argument that the EU should act prevails, as a matter of fact the EU would likely not support liability protection for the benefit of security firms and other economic operators, given the Member State governments' preferences for full liability exposure.

Despite suggestions to the contrary, evidence of an impending liability crisis in the security industry is absent. The assertions of potentially "enterprise-threatening" liability exposure are not consistent with the liability standards under the laws of the seven Member States covered in this book. Thus far, facility operators and security firms have not been held liable for damage caused by terrorist attacks in Europe. No urgent EU measures are therefore necessary. In light of the complexity of national civil liability regimes, it may be helpful to launch initiatives aimed at enlightening the security industry, facility operators and, as necessary, insurers, Member States and other stakeholders about third-party liability exposure and ways to mitigate liability for terrorism-related risk.

Although security firms and high-risk facility operators in Europe are not exposed to potentially enterprise-threatening liability for terrorism-related risk, under the laws of the Member States surveyed in this book they could be held liable for damage caused by their negligent acts or omissions or by defective products, including where such damage results from terrorist acts. In principle, subject to legal provisions regarding mitigation and the like, such liability is unlimited and thus could bankrupt a liable entity. Further, negligence and duty of care are flexible and open-ended concepts that are subject to interpretation and construction in a particular case by judges ex-post facto. It thus is conceivable that these concepts are construed in ways that effectively create strict liability for damages caused by terrorists, despite the fact that, as noted, we have not seen evidence of such extensive interpretations in national case law.

Even though such liability exposure in theory exists, it does not follow that liability should therefore be limited. Where liability is limited or even eliminated, the liability system is hindered in achieving its objectives, i.e. deterrence, risk allocation and loss-spreading. An unavoidable consequence of limiting the liability of security firms and other operators is that their incentives to invest in security may be reduced, as a result of which the preventive effect of liability would be reduced. This, in turn, might mean an increased rate of terrorist attacks or increased magnitude of harm. In addition, under a liability limitation regime, security firms and facility operators would contract less insurance or other financial guarantees to cover their liability. As a result, relative prices would be too low and over-consumption would ensue. Finally, from a distributional perspective, the consequence of a liability limitation or exclusion would be that liability's loss-spreading function would be affected and some losses would lie with the victims of a terrorist attack (unless some other loss-spreading mechanisms were established). In short, the benefits of a liability limitation should be weighed against the costs in terms of reduced prevention incentives and the related distributional consequences.

The analysis presented in this book allows us to conclude that although the case for a liability limitation is weak, civil liability for terrorism-related risk is an issue that requires the attention of policymakers, including the EU. As there is no evidence of an impending liability crisis threatening the continued existence of security firms and operators of high-risk facil-ities, policymakers should take time to analyse the issues, in particular any malfunctioning of the markets for terrorism-related insurance and public procurement of security services. Policymakers might anticipate possible future problems that could arise from expansive judicial con-struction of liability standards and consider guidance on how liability rules, in particular negligence, should be applied to cases involving dam-age caused by terrorist attacks. To prevent such problems from emerging, a Commission recommendation or communication, along the lines of the recommendation concerning the limitation of the civil liability of auditors,[4] would appear to be an adequate instrument. Possible elements of such an instrument are discussed in Chapter 11. In developing policy on this issue, the government should keep in mind that its primary responsibility is to prevent terrorist attacks from occurring, and liability for damage caused by such attacks can contribute to accomplishing this objective.

---

[4] Commission Recommendation of 5 June 2008 concerning the limitation of the civil liability of statutory auditors and audit firms (notified under document number C(2008) 2274), OJ L 162/39.

BIBLIOGRAPHY

F.J. Ahumada Ramos, *La Responsabilidad Patrimonial de las Administraciones Públicas* (Thomson-Aranzadi, 2004), 531.

N. Álvarez Lata, 'Responsabilidad Civil por Daños al Medio Ambiente' in F. Reglero (ed.), *Tratado de Responsabilidad Civil III* (Thomson-Aranzadi, 2008), 59.

N. Álvarez Lata and Y. Bustos Moreno, 'Responsabilidad Civil en el Ámbito del Transporte y la Navegación Aérea' in F. Reglero (ed.), *Tratado de Responsabilidad Civil II* (Thomson-Aranzadi, 2008), 1430.

American Law Institute, *Reporters' Study: Enterprise Responsibility for Personal Injury* (American Law Institute, 1991), vol. I, 86.

K. Ammerlaan and W.H. Van Boom, 'De Nederlandse Herverzekeringsmaatschappij voor Terrorismeschaden en de rol van de overheid bij het vergoeden van terreurschade', *Nederlands Juristenblad*, 45/46 (2003) 2330–2339.

I. Arroyo Martínez, *Curso de Derecho aéreo* (Thomson-Civitas, 2006).

ASD and EOS, 'European Union Third Party Liability Limitation – Executive Summary', www.eos-eu.com/files/Documents/Positions/third_party.pdf.

A. Azagra Malo, *La Tragedia del Amianto y el Derecho Español* (Atelier, 2007).

A. Azparren, 'Artículos 128–149' in S. Cámara Lapuente (ed.), *Comentarios a las Normas de Protección de los Consumidores* (Colex, 2011), 1196.

J. Barcelona Llop, *El Régimen Jurídico de la Policía de Seguridad* (IVAP, 1988), 261.

E. Batsch, *Liability for Environmental Damages: Incentives for Precaution and Risk Allocation* (Mohr Siebeck, 1998), 175.

D. Bello Janeiro (ed.), *La Responsabilidad Patrimonial de las Administraciones Públicas* (Reus, 1999), 318.

L. Bergkamp, *Liability and Environment. Private and Public Law Aspects of Civil Liability for Environmental Harm in an International Context* (Kluwer Law International, 2001).

European Community Law for the New Economy (Intersentia, 2003).

'European Court Clarifies Application of "Polluter Pays Principle" and Causation', *Journal for European Environmental and Planning Law* (2010), 355.

L. Bergkamp, M. Faure, M. Hinteregger and N. Philipsen (eds.), *Study Evaluating the Status Quo and the Legal Implications of Third Party Liability for the European Security Industry* (Maastricht University, Metro, 2013): http://ec.europa.eu/enterprise/policies/security/files/final-report-tpl-11_10_2013_en.pdf.

L. Bergkamp and B. Goldsmith (eds.), *The EU Environmental Liability Directive: A Commentary* (Oxford University Press, 2013).

R. Bercovitz and J. Salas (eds.), *Comentarios a la Ley General para la Defensa de los Consumidores y Usuarios* (Civitas, 1992), 715.

J. Bermejo Vera, 'La Administración Inspectora', *Revista de Administración Pública* (RAP), 147 (1998) 39, 53.

   Derecho Administrativo: Parte Especial (Civitas, 2005), 137.

V. Bier, 'Hurricane Katrina as a bureaucratic nightmare', in R.J. Daniels, D.F. Kettle and H. Kunreuther (eds.), *On Risk and Disaster. Lessons from Hurricane Katrina* (University of Pennsylvania Press, 2006), 243–254.

W. Bishop, 'The Contract-Tort Boundary and the Economics of Insurance', *Journal of Legal Studies*, 12 (1983) 241–266.

P. Blanchard, 'Responsibility for Environmental Damage under Nuclear and Environmental Instruments: a Legal Benchmarking', *J. Energy & Nat. Resources L.*, 18 (2000) 233–253, 236.

J. Brooke, 'Terror in Littleton: The Overview; 2 Students in Colorado School Said to Gun Down as Many as 23 and Kill Themselves in a Siege', *New York Times*, 21 April 1999.

V. Bruggeman, *Compensating Catastrophe Victims: A Comparative Law and Economics Approach* (Kluwer Law International, 2010).

V. Bruggeman, M. Faure and K. Fiore, 'The Government as Reinsurer of Catastrophic Risks?' *Geneva Papers on Risk and Insurance Theory*, 35 (2010 369–390.

V. Bruggeman, M. Faure and T. Heldt, 'Insurance Against Catastrophe: Government Stimulation of Insurance Markets for Catastrophic Events?' *Duke Environmental Law & Policy Forum*, XXIII (2012) (1), 185–241.

V. Bruggeman, M. Faure and M. Haritz, 'Remodelling Reparation: Changes in the Compensation of Victims of Natural Catastrophes in Belgium and the Netherlands', *Disasters*, 35 (2011) 766–788.

J.R. Bruno, 'Immunity for "Discretionary" Functions: A Proposal to Amend the Federal Tort Claims Act', *Harvard Journal on Legislation*, 49 (2012) 431.

O. Bures, *EU Counterterrorism Policy: A Paper Tiger?* (Ashgate, 2011).

P. Burrows, 'Combining Regulation and Liability for the Control of External Costs', *International Review of Law and Economics*, 19 (1999) 227–242.

G. Calabresi, *The Costs of Accidents: A Legal and Economic Analysis* (Yale University Press, 1970).

P. Cane, *Attiyah's Accidents, Compensation and the Law* (Buttersworth, 6th edn, 1999), 405.

A. Carrasco, 'Artículos 1104–1107' in M. Albaladejo (ed.), *Comentarios al Código Civil y Compilaciones Forales XVI-1* (Edersa, 1989), 680.

   'Responsabilidad de la Administración y medio ambiente' in D. Bello Janeiro (ed.), *La Responsabilidad Patrimonial de las Administraciones Públicas* (Reus, 1999).

'El Régimen Civil de la Responsabilidad por Inmisiones Ambientales Preexistentes a la Ley' in B. Lozano Cutanda (ed.), *Comentarios a la Ley de Responsabilidad Medioambiental* (Thomson-Aranzadi, 2008), 158.

J.A. Carrillo Donaire, *El Derecho de la Seguridad y de la Calidad Industrial* (Marcial Pons, 2000), 601 ff.

M. Casino Rubio, *Responsabilidad Civil de la Administración y Delito* (Marcial Pons, 1998), 39.

W. Chao, *Pollution from the Carriage of Oil by Sea: Liability and Compensation* (Kluwer Law International, 1996).

CNN library, '1993 World Trade Center Bombing Fast Facts', edition.cnn.com/ 2013/11/05/us/1993-world-trade-center-bombing-fast-facts/.

CoESS and ASSA-I, 'A European Solution for Third Party Liability of the Aviation Security Services Providers', White Paper, June 2010.

Congressional Hearing Before the Subcommittee on Cybersecurity Infrastructure Protection, and Security Technologies of the Committee on Homeland Security House of Representatives, 26 May 2011.

Council of the European Union, 'The European Union Counter-Terrorism Strategy', (14469/4/05 REV 4), Brussels 30 November 2005.

P. Craig, *EU Administrative Law* (Oxford University Press, 2nd edn, 2012).

D.E.J. Currie, 'The Problems and Gaps in the Nuclear Liability Conventions and an Analysis of how an Actual Claim would be brought under the Current Existing Treaty Regime in the Event of a Nuclear Accident', *Denver Journal of International Law and Policy*, 35 (2008) 85–127.

R.E. Dallos and D. Gellene, 'Pan Am, a 50-Year Leader in Aviation, Goes Bankrupt: Economy: Carrier Cites Fuel Costs, Downturn and Flight 103 Bombing. It Says Travelers Will Not Be Affected', *Los Angeles Times*, 9 January 1991.

R.J. Daniels, D.F. Kettl et al., *On Risk and Disaster: Lessons from Hurricane Katrina* (University of Pennsylvania Press, 2006).

G. De Geest, 'Who Should Be Immune from Tort Liability?', *Journal of Legal Studies*, 41 (June 2012)2.

P. del Olmo, 'Tort and Regulatory law in Spain' in W.H. van Boom et al. (eds.), *Tort and Regulatory Law* (Springer, 2007), 260.

Department of Energy and Climate Change, 'Compensating Victims of Nuclear Accidents', 24 January 2011, www.gov.uk/government/consultations/ compensating-victims-of-nuclear-accidents.

K. De Smedt, *Environmental Liability in a Federal System. A Law and Economics Analysis* (Intersentia, 2007).

L. Díez-Picazo, *Fundamentos de Derecho Civil Patrimonial II* (Civitas, 2012).
Fundamentos de Derecho Civil Patrimonial V (Civitas, 2012).

G. Domenech Pascual, '¿Por qué la Administración Nunca Ejerce la Acción de Regreso Contra el Personal a su Servicio?', *Indret*, 2 (2008) 5.

W. Dubis in E. Gniewek (ed.), *Kodeks cywilny. Komentarz* (CH Beck, 2008), 770.

T. Dybowski in Z. Radwanski (ed.), *System prawa cywilnego* (Wyd PAN, 1981), vol. III, part 1, 288.

W. Emons, 'Imperfect Tests and Natural Insurance Monopolies', *Journal of Industrial Economics*, 49 (2001) 247–248.

A. Endres, C. Ohl and B. Rundshagen, 'Land Unter!, Ein insitutionenökonomischer Zwischenruf', *List Forum für Wirtschafts- und Finanzpolitik*, 29 (2003) 284–294.

R.A. Epstein, 'Products Liability as an Insurance Market', *Journal of Legal Studies*, 14 (1985) 645–669.

'Catastropic Responses to Catastrophic Risks', *Journal of Risk and Uncertainty*, 12 (1996) 287–308.

European Commission, 'Report from the Commission to the European Parliament and the Council on the Implementation of Council Framework Decision 2008/919/JHA of 28 November 2008 amending Framework Decision 2002/475/JHA on combating terrorism'.

European Environmental Liability Directive (EU Commission, White Paper on Environmental Liability, Brussels, 2000 (COM) 2000 66 final).

M. Faure, 'Tort Liability in France: An Introductory Economic Analysis', in B. Deffains et al. (eds.), *Law and Economics in Civil Law Countries* (JAI, 2001), 169–179.

'Environmental Damage Insurance in the Netherlands', *Environmental Liability*, 10 (2002) 31–37.

(ed.), *Deterrence, Insurability and Compensation in Environmental Liability. Future Developments in the European Union* (Springer, 2003).

'Comparative and Policy Conclusions', in Faure, M. and Hartlief, T. (eds.), *Financial Compensation for Victims of Catastrophes. A Comparative Legal Approach* (Springer, 2006), 389–452.

'Financial Compensation for Victims of Catastrophes: A Law and Economics Perspective', *Law & Policy*, 29(3) (2007) 339–367, 358.

'Effectiveness of Environmental Law: What Does the Evidence Tell us?', *William & Mary Environmental Law and Policy Review*, 36 (2012) 2, 293–336.

M. Faure and D. Grimeaud, 'Financial Assurance Issues of Environmental Liability' in M. Faure, *Deterrence, Insurability and Compensation in Environmental Liability. Future Developments in the European Union* (Springer, 2003), 189–192.

M. Faure and T. Hartlief, 'Towards an Expanding Enterprise Liability in Europe? How to Analyse the Scope of Liability of Industrial Operators and their Insurers', *Maastricht Journal of European and Comparative Law*, (1996) 235–270.

Nieuwe risico's en vragen van aansprakelijkheid en verzekering (Kluwer, 2002).

(eds.), *Insurance and Expanding Systemic Risks, Policy Issues in Insurance, No. 5* (OECD, 2003).

M. Faure, I. Koopmans and J. Oudijk, 'Imposing Criminal Liability on Government Officials under Environmental Law: A Legal and Economic Analysis', *Loyola of Los Angeles International Comparative Law Journal*, (1996) 529–569.

M.G. Faure and J. Liu, 'Compensating for Nuclear Accidents in Japan: the Fukushima Case', *TGMA*, 26(2) (2012a) 74–84.

'The Tsunami of March 2011 and the Subsequent Nuclear Incident at Fukushima: Who Compensates the Victims?', *William & Mary Environmental Law and Policy Review*, 37 (2012b) 1, 129–218.

M. Faure and R. Van den Bergh, 'Restrictions of Competition on Insurance Markets and the Applicability of EC anti-trust law', *Kyklos*, 48 (1995) 65–85.

M. Faure and T. Van den Borre, 'Compensating Nuclear Damage: A Comparative Economic Analysis of the US and International Liability Schemes', *William & Mary Environmental Law & Policy Review*, 33 (2008) 219–232, 220–232.

F. Fernández-Piñeyro, 'La Administración Aeronáutica' in A. Menéndez (ed.), *Régimen Jurídico del Transporte Aéreo* (Civitas, 2001), 111–174.

I. Fernández Torres, 'El Transporte Aéreo en la Jurisprudencia Civil y Mercantil' in A, Menéndez (ed.), *Régimen Jurídico del Transporte Aéreo* (Civitas, 2001), 282.

U. Foerste, 'Die Produkthaftung für Druckwerke', *Neue Juristische Wochenschrift* (NJW), (1991), 1433, 1438.

Fondazione Rosselli, *Analysis of the Economic Impact of the Development Risk Clause as provided by Directive 85/374/EEC on Liability for Defective Products* (2004).

G. Franßen and H. Blatt, 'Ersatzansprüche aus Geschäftsführung ohne Auftrag beim Feuerwehreinsatz', *Neue Juristische Wochenschrift* (NJW), (2012) 1031, 1031.

P.K. Freeman and H. Kunreuther, *Managing Environmental Risk Through Insurance* (Kluwer, 1997), 25.

Happiness and Economics (Princeton University Press, 2002).

B.S. Frey and A.W. Stutzer, 'Happiness Research: State and Prospects', Working Paper, Institute for Empirical Research in Economics, University of Zurich, 2004.

D. Frosch, 'Gunman Kills 12 in Colorado, Reviving Gun Debate', *New York Times*, 20 July 2012.

B. Gas, 'Extremus – The German Terrorism Insurance Solution', *Etudes et Dossiers* 298 (The Geneva Association, 2005), 13–1.

E. García de Enterría and T.R. Fernández, *Curso de Derecho Administrativo II* (Thomson-Civitas 2011), 730.

F García Gómez de Mercado et al., *Manual de Contratación del Sector Público* (Comares, 2011), 794.

O. García Muñoz and J. Carrasco Martín, 'Deberes de vigilancia y prevención de la Administración de conductas ilícitas y prohibición de regreso', 2 (2003) *Indret* 9.

P. Giliker, *Vicarious Liability in Tort: A Comparative Perspective* (Cambridge University Press, 2010), 32 f.

H. Gluver and D. Olsen (eds.), *Ship Collision Analysis* (Balkema, 1998).

C. Gollier, 'Some Aspects of the Economics of Catastrophe Risk Insurance' in OECD, *Catastrophic Risks and Insurance* (OECD, 2005), 13–30.

F. Gómez Pomar, 'Ámbito de Protección de la Responsabilidad de Producto' in P. Salvador and F. Gómez Pomar (eds.), *Tratado de Responsabilidad Civil del Fabricante* (Thomson-Civitas, 2008), 668–669.

M. Gómez Puente, *Derecho Administrativo Aeronáutico* (Iustel, 2006), 128 ff. *La Inactividad de la Administración* (Aranzadi, 2002), 845.

GAO, *Catastrophe Risk. U.S. and European Approaches to Insure Natural Catastrophe and Terrorism Risks*, GAO-05-199, Washington D.C., United States General Accountability Office: 74 (2005).

M.J. Guerrero Lebrón, *La Responsabilidad Contractual del Porteador Aéreo en el Transporte de Pasajeros* (Tirantlo Blanch, 2005), 125 ff.

E. González García, 'La Vigilancia Privada en la Seguridad de los Entornos Aeroportuarios', *Seguritecnia*, 345 (2008) 38, 39.

A. Gron and A.O. Sykes, 'A Role for Government?', *Regulation*, 25(4) (2002) 44–51.
'Terrorism and Insurance Markets: A Role for the Government as Insurer?' *Indiana Law Review*, 36 (2003) 447–463.

J. Guerrero Zaplana, *La Responsabilidad Medioambiental en España* (La Ley, 2010), 62.

D.-K. Günther and F. Borbe, 'Kostenersatz der Feuerwehr am Beispiel der Sachversicherung', *Versicherungsrecht* (VersR), (2012), 1197, 1197 ff.

C. Haberman, 'Korean Jetliner with 269 Aboard Missing Near Soviet Pacific Island', *New York Times*, 1 September 1983.

S.E. Harrington, 'Rethinking Disaster Policy', *Regulation*, 23(1) (2000) 40–46.

T. Hartlief, 'De Meerwaarde van het Aansprakelijkheidsrecht' in T. Hartlief and S. Klosse (eds.), *Einde van het Aansprakelijkheidsrecht?* (Boom Juridisch euitgevers, 2003), 58–59.

R.P. Hartwig, 'The Impact of the September 11 attacks on the American Insurance Industry' in P.M. Liedtke and C. Courbage (eds.), *Insurance and September 11 – One year after: Impact, Lessons and Unresolved Issues* (The Geneva Association, 2002), 10–42.

C. Hauser, 'Virginia Tech Shooting Leaves 33 Dead', *New York Times*, 16 April 2007.

J. Hellner and M. Radetzki, *Skadeståndsrätt*, (NorstedtsJuridik, 2010), 177, 341.

M.G. Hinteregger, *Grundfragen der Umwelthaftung* (Manz, 1994).

M. Hinteregger and S. Kissich, 'The Paris Convention 2004 – A New Nuclear Liability System for Europe', *Environmental Liability* 3 (2004) 116.

M. Huber and T. Amodu, 'United Kingdom' in M. Faure and T. Hartlief (eds.), *Financial Compensation for Victims of Catastrophes: A Comparative Legal Approach* (Springer, 2006), 261–301.

J.R. Hunziker and T.O. Jones (eds.), *Product Liability and Innovation: Managing Risk in an Uncertain Environment* (DC National Academy Press, 1994).

Institute for the Analysis of Global Security, www.iags.org/costof911.html.iopcf; www.iopcfund.org/intro.htm.

M. Jagielska and G. Żmij, 'Tort and Regulatory Law in Poland' in W.H. Van Boom, M. Lukas and C. Kissling (eds.), *Tort Law and Regulatory Law* (Springer, 2007), 224 ff.

P.J. Jost, 'Limited Liability and the Requirement to Purchase Insurance', *International Review of Law and Economics*, (1996) 259–276.

M Kaliński, *Szkoda na mieniu i jej naprawienie* (CH Beck, 2008), 276 ff.

L. Kaplow and S. Shavell, 'Fairness versus Welfare', *Harvard Law Review*, 114 (2001) 967–1388.

W. Katner, *Ochrona własności nieruchomości przed naruszeniami pośrednimi* (Wyd Prawnicze, 1982), 130.

D. Keohane, 'The EU and Counter-terrorism', Centre for European Reform, Working Paper, May 2005, 3.

W. Kip Viscusi, 'Does Product Liability Law Make Us Safer?', *Regulation*, Cato Institute, 2012.

W. Klein, 'Die Haftung von Versorgungsunternehmen nach dem Produkthaftungsgesetz', *Betriebs-Berater* (BB), (1991), 917, 919.

B.A. Koch (ed.), *Damage Caused by Genetically Modified Organisms* (De Gruyter, 2010).

C.D. Kolstad, T.S. Ulen and G.V. Johnson, 'Ex post Liability for Harm vs. Ex ante Safety Regulation: Substitutes or Compliments?' *American Economic Review*, 80 (1990) 888–901.

A. Konert, 'Terroryzm lotniczy – problematyka kompensacji szkód', *Państwo i Prawo* (PiP), 3 (2013) 82, 87.

H. Kunreuther, 'The Case for Comprehensive Disaster Insurance', *Journal of Law and Economics*, 11 (1968) 133–163.

'Ambiguity and Underwriter Decision Processes', *Journal of Economic Behaviour and Organisation*, 26 (1995) 337.

'Mitigating Disaster Losses through Insurance', *Journal of Risk and Uncertainty*, 12 (1996) 171–187.

H. Kunreuther and P. Freeman, 'Insurability, Environmental Risks and the Law' in A. Heyes, (ed.), *The Law and Economics of the Environment* (Edward Elgar, 2001), 304–316.

H. Kunreuther, R. Hogarth and J. Meszaros, 'Insurer Ambiguity and Market Failure', *Journal of Risk and Uncertainty*, 7 (1993) 71–87.

H. Kunreuther and E. Michel-Kerjan, 'Challenges for Terrorism Risk Insurance in the United States', *Journal of Economic Perspectives*, 18(4) (2004) 201–214.

Insurability of (Mega-) Terrorism Risk: Challenges and Perspectives. Terrorism Risk Insurance in OECD Countries (OECD Publishing, 2005), vol. 9, 107–148.

H. Kunreuther and M. Pauly, 'Rules rather than Discretion: Lessons from Hurricane Katrina', *Journal of Risk and Uncertainty*, 33 (2006) 101–116, 113.

F. Lafay, M. Cannarsa and O. Moréteau, 'France', in M. Faure and T. Hartlief (eds.), *Financial Compensation for Victims of Catastrophes: A Comparative Legal Approach* (Springer, 2006), 81–118.

V. Lamm, 'The Protocol Amending the 1963 Vienna Convention', in OECD, *International Nuclear Law in the Post-Chernobyl Period* (OECD, 2006).

E. Łętowska, *Prawo umów konsumenckich* (CH Beck, 2nd edn, 2002), 123.

S. Levmore and K.D. Logue, 'Insuring against Terrorism and Crime', *Law & Economics Working Papers Archive: 2003–2009*, Paper 14.

B. Lewaszkiewicz-Petrykowska, *Odpowiedzialność cywilna prowadzącego przedsiębiorstwo wprawiane w ruch przy pomocy sił przyrody (art 435 kc)* (Wyd Prawnicze, 1967), 130.

E. Llamas Pombo, 'Artículos 1094–1110' in A. Domínguez Luelmo (ed.), *Comentarios al Código Civil* (Lex Nova, 2010), 1218.

Lovells, *Product Liability in the European Union, A Report for the European Commission* (Lovells, 2003).

M. Magide Herrero, 'El criterio de imputación de la responsabilidad in vigilando a la Administración; especial referencia a la responsabilidad de la Administración en su actividad de supervisión de sectores económicos' in J.L. Martínez López-Muñiz and A. Calonge Velázquez (eds.), *La Responsabilidad Patrimonial de las Administraciones Públicas. III Coloquio Hispano-Luso de Derecho Administrativo* (Marcial Pons, 1999).

U. Magnus, 'Germany' in M. Faure and T. Hartlief (eds.), *Compensation for Victims of Catastrophes: a Comparative Legal Approach* (Springer, 2006), 119–144.

U. Magnus and P. Mankowski, *Brussels I Regulation* (Sellier European Law Publishers, 2007).

G. Makinen, 'The Economic Effects of 9/11: A Retrospective Assessment', *Congressional Research Service* (27 September 2002), CRS–4.

Manual del Personal de la Seguridad Privada (CPD, 2008), 66 ff.

J.M. Marshall, 'Insurance Theory; Reserves v. Mutuality', *Economic Inquiry*, 12 (1974) 476–492.

M. Martín-Casals, 'La Modernización del Drecho de la Responsabilidad Extracontractual' in Asociación de Profesores de Derecho Civil, *Cuestiones Actuales en Materia de Responsabilidad Civil* (Editum, 2011), 15.

M. Martín-Casals and J. Ribot, 'Compensation for Pure Economic Loss under Spanish Law' in W.H. van Boom et al. (eds.), *Pure Economic Loss* (Springer, 2004-a).

'Liability for Acts of Terrorism under Spanish Law' in B. Koch (ed.), *Terrorism, Tort Law and Insurance* (Springer, 2004-b), 97–98.

M. Martín-Casals and J. Solé Feliu, 'The Development of Product Liability in Spain' in S. Whittaker, *The Development of Product Liability* (Cambridge University Press, 2010), 2050.

'Veinte Problemas en la Aplicación de la LRPD', *Práctica de Derecho de Daños*, 9 (2003) 23.

'¿Refundir o Legislar?', *Revista de Derecho Privado* (RDP), 92 (2008) 379, 98–99.

'Artículos 1902–1910' in A. Domínguez-Luelmo (ed.), *Comentarios al Código Civil* (Lex Nova, 2010), 2055.

J.L. Martínez López-Muñiz and A. Calonge Velázquez (eds.), *La Responsabilidad Patrimonial de las Administraciones Públicas. III Coloquio Hispano-Luso de Derecho Administrativo* (Marcial Pons, 1999), 374.

D. Maśniak, *Ubezpieczenia ekologiczne* (Zakamycze, 2003), 99 ff.

E. Medaglia et al., 'The Concurrent Cause, Theory: Inapplicable to Environmental Liability Coverage Disputes', *Tort and Insurance Law Journal*, 30 (1995) 823–829.

K. Meier and A. Wehlau, 'Produzentenhaftung des Softwareherstellers', *Computer und Recht* (CR), 95 (1990) 95 ff.

W. Melzer, C. Haslach and O. Socher, 'Der Schadensausgleich nach dem Luftsicher-heitsgesetz', *Neue Zeitschrift für Verwaltungsrecht* (NVwZ), (2005) 1361, 1367.

E.M. Menéndez Sebastián, *El Contrato de Consultoría y Asistencia* (Civitas, 2002). *Los Contratos de Servicios del Sector Público* (Thomson Civitas, 2009), 614.

O. Meyer and H. Harland, 'Haftung für softwarebezogene Fehlfunktionen technischer Geräte am Beispiel von Fahrerassistenzsystemen', *Computer und Recht* (CR), (2007) 689, 694.

A. Miller, 'Should Insurance Pay Compensation for Pain and Suffering?', *International and Comparative Law Quarterly*, 31 (1982) 550–556.

D. Millington, 'Weather, Forecasting and the "Limitless Seas"', LQR, (1987) 238.

A.M. Morales Moreno, *Incumplimiento del Contrato y Lucro Cesante* (Civitas-Thomson-Reuters, 2010), 61.

J.A. Moreno Molina and F. Pleite Guadamillas, *Texto Refundido de la Ley de Contratos del Sector Público: Estudio Sistemático* (La Ley, 2012), 277 and 1217.

A. Monti, 'Environmental Risk: A Comparative Law and Economics Approach to Liability and Insurance', *European Review of Private Law*, 9 (2001) 51–79.

M. Nesterowicz and E. Bagińska, 'Liability for Damage Caused by Others under Polish law' in J. Spier (ed.), *Unification of Tort Law: Liability for Damage Caused by Others* (Kluwer Law International, 2003).

OECD, *Catastrophic Risks and Insurance* (OECD, 2005).

E. Orteu Berrocal, 'Ámbito de Aplicación de la Ley' in B. Lozano Cutanda (ed.), *Comentarios a la Ley de Responsabilidad Medioambiental* (Thomson-Aranzadi, 2008), 165, 192.

M. Nesterowicz in J. Winiarz (ed.), *Kodeks cywilny z komentarzem, I* (Wyd Prawnicze, 1988), 428.

F. Pantaleón, 'Artículo 1902' in C. Paz-Ares et al. (eds.), *Comentario del Código Civil* (Civitas, 1993), 1987.

R Parada, *Derecho Administrativo I* (Marcial Pons, 2012), 347.

M.A. Parra Lucán, 'Responsabilidad Civil por Productos Defectuosos' in F. Reglero (ed.), *Tratado de Responsabilidad Civil II* (Thomson-Aranzadi, 2008), 587–592.

La Protección del Consumidor Frente a los Daños (Reus, 2011), 309.

M. Pasquau, 'Daños causados por productos' in M. Rebollo Puig and M. Izquierdo Carrasco (eds.), *La Defensa de los Consumidores y Usuarios* (Iustel, 2011) 1838.

N. Pelzer, *Begrenzte und Unbegrenzte Haftung im Deutschen Atomrecht* (Nomos, 1982), 51.

'Concepts of Nuclear Liability Revisited: A Post-Chernobyl Assessment of the Paris and the Vienna Conventions' in P. Cameron, L. Hancher and W. Kühn (eds.), *Nuclear Energy Law After Chernobyl* (Graham and Trotman, 1988), 97.

'"International Pooling of Operators" Funds: An Option to Increase the Amount of Financial Security to Cover Nuclear Liability?' *Nuclear Law Bulletin*, 79 (2007) 37–55.

R. Perry, 'Relational Economic Loss: An Integrated Economic Justification for the Exclusionary Role', *Rutgers Law Review*, 56 (2004) 711–778.

F. Pertíñez, 'Disposiciones Communes en Material de Responsabilidad' in M. Rebollo Puig and M. Izquierdo Carrasco (eds.), *La Defensa de los Consumidores y Usuarios* (Iustel, 2011), 1826.

N.J. Philipsen, 'Limiting Auditors' Liability: The Case For (and Against) EU Intervention', *Geneva Papers on Risk and Insurance*, 39 (2014) 585–597.

M. Polborn, 'Mandatory Insurance and the Judgement-Proof Problem', *International Review of Law and Economics* (1998), 141.

A.M. Polinsky and S. Shavell, *Handbook of Law and Economics* (Elsevier, 2004), 139–182.

R.A. Posner, *Catastrophe: Risk and Response* (Oxford University Press, 2004), 172.

G.L. Priest, 'The Invention of Enterprise Liability: A Critical History of the Intellectual Foundations of Modern Tort Law', *Journal of Legal Studies*, 14 (1985) 461–527.

'The Current Insurance Crisis and Modern Tort Law', *Yale Law Journal*, (1987) 1521–1590.

'The Government, the Market and the Problem of Catastrophic Loss', *Journal of Risk and Uncertainty* 12 (1996) 219–237.

'The Modern Expansion of Tort Liability: Its Sources, its Effects, and its Reform', *Journal of Economic Perspectives*, 5 (1991) 31–50.

R.L. Rabin and S.A. Bratis, 'United States' in M. Faure and T. Hartlief (eds.), *Financial Compensation for Victims of Catastrophes. A Comparative Legal Approach* (Springer, 2006), 303–360.

J.M. Ramseyer, 'Why Power Companies build Nuclear Reactors on Fault Lines: The Case of Japan', Harvard John M. Olin Centre for Law, Economics and Business, Disc. Paper No. 698, 2011 and *Theoretical Inquiries in L.*, 31 (2011).

B.J. Richardson, 'Financial Institutions for Sustainability', *Environmental Liability*, 2 (2000) 52–64.

R. Riegel, J.S. Miller and C.A. Williams Jr., *Insurance Principles and Practices – Property and Liability* (Prentice Hall, 6th edn, 1976), 15–21.

R. Rivero Ortega, *El Estado Vigilante* (Tecnos, 2000), 224, 225.

A. Ruda, 'Comentario a STS 31 mayo 2007', *Cuadernos Civitas de Jurisprudencia Civil* (CCJC), 76 (2007) 153.

El Daño Ecológico Puro (Thomson-Aranzadi, 2008), 374.

M. Ruffert, 'Verantwortung und Haftung für Umweltschäden', *Neue Zeitschrift für Verwaltungsrecht* (NVwZ), (2010) 1177, 1178.

C. Runte and H. Potinecke, 'Software und GPSG', *Computer und Recht* (CR), (2004) 725, 725 ff.

T. Russell and J.E. Thomas, 'Government Support for the Terrorism Insurance Industry: Where Do We Go From Here?', Research Symposium on Insurance Markets and Regulation, Searle Center on Law, Regulation, and Economic Growth, Northwestern University (2008).

Science and Technology Directorate, *FY 2011 Year in Review* (US Department of Homeland Security), 47.

M. Safjan in K. Pietrzykowski (ed.), *Kodeks cywilny. Komentarz* (CH Beck, 2005), 1233.

P. Salvador and S. Ramos, 'Defectos de Producto' in P. Salvador and F. Gómez Pomar (eds.), *Tratado de Responsabilidad Civil del Fabricante* (Thomson-Civitas, 2008), 139.

P. Sands and J. Peel (with A. Fabra and R. MacKenzie), *Principles of International Environmental Law* (Cambridge University Press, 3rd edn, 2012).

J.A. Santamaría Pastor, *Principios de Derecho Administrativo II* (Centro de Estudios Ramón Areces, 2002), 182–183.

M.J. Santos Morón, 'Acerca de la Tutela Civil del Medio Ambiente: Algunas Reflexiones Críticas' in A. Cabanillas et al. (eds.), *Estudios Homenaje al Profesor Díez-Picazo* (Civitas, 2003), vol. II, 3027.

A. Schwartz, 'Statutory Interpretation, Capture, and Tort Law: The Regulatory Compliance Defense', *American Law and Economics Review* (ALER), (2000) 1–57.

A. Schwartz and L. Wilde, 'Intervening in Markets on the Basis of Imperfect Information: A Legal and Economic Analysis', *University of Pennsylvania Law Review*, 127 (1979) 630–682.

G. Schwartz, 'Mixed Theories of Tort Law: Affirming both Deterrence and Corrective Justice', *Texas Law Review*, 95 (1997) 1801–1834.

J.A. Schwartz, 'Great Expectations: Where do we Stand with the International
Nuclear Liability Conventions?' in N. Pelzer (ed.), *European Nuclear Liability
Law in a Process of Change* (Nomos, 2009), 43–67.

R. Schwarze and G. Wagner, 'In the Aftermath of Dresden. New Directions in
German Flood Insurance', *Geneva Papers on Risk and Insurance*, 29(2) (2004)
154–168.

S. Shavell, 'Strict Liability versus Negligence', *Journal of Legal Studies*, (1980) 1–25.
'Liability for Harm versus Regulation of Safety', *Journal of Legal Studies*, (1984)
357–374.
Economic Analysis of Accident Law (Harvard University Press), 1987.
'The Judgment Proof Problem', *International Review of Law and Economics*, 6(1)
(02/1986) 45–58.
'On the Social Function and the Regulation of Liability Insurance', *Geneva Papers
of Risk and Insurance*, 25 (2) (2000) 166–179.
'Liability for Accidents' in M. Polinsky and S. Shavell (eds.), *Handbook of Law
and Economics* (Elsevier, 2007), vol. 2.

J. Sirvent, *La Acción Subrogatoria* (BOE, 1997).

J. Skoczylas, 'Odpowiedzialność cywilna na podstawie ustawy – prawo ochrony
środowiska', *Przegląd Sądowy* (PS), 4 (2003) 68.

G. Skogh, 'Mandatory Insurance: Transaction Costs Analysis of Insurance' in
B. Bouckaert and G. De Geest (eds.), *Encyclopedia of Law and Economics*
(Edward Elgar, 2000), 521–537.

P. Slovic, B. Fischhoff et al., 'Preference for Insuring Against Probable Small Losses:
Insurance Implications', *The Journal of Risk and Insurance*, 44 (1977) 237–
258.

P. Slovic, H. Kunreuther and G. White, 'Decision Processes, Rationality and Adjust-
ment to Natural Hazards' in P. Slovic (ed.), *The Perception of Risk* (Earthscan,
2000), 1–31.

V. Smil, *Global Catastrophes: The Next Fifty Years* (MIT Press, 2012), 61.

A. Soler, *La Valoración del Daño en el Contrato de Compraventa* (Aranzadi, 1998),
156 ff.

J. Spier et al., *Verbintenissen uit de Wet en Schadevergoeding* (Kluwer, 2012), 190 ff.

G. Spindler, 'IT-Sicherheit und Produkthaftung – Sicherheitslücken, Pflichten der
Hersteller und Softwarenutzer', *Neue Juristische Wochenschrift* (NJW), (2004)
3145, 3146.
'IT-Sicherheit – Rechtliche Defizite und rechtspolitische Alternativen', *Multi
Media und Recht* (MMR), (2008).

G. Spindler and L. Klöhn, 'Fehlerhafte Informationen und Software – Die
Auswirkungen der Schuld- und Schadensrechtsreform', *Versicherungsrecht*
(VersR), (2003) 410.

N. Stahmer, *Entschädigung von Nichtvermögensschäden bei Tötung* (Dr. Kovacz, 2004).

J. Stapleton, *Product Liability* (Cambridge University Press, 1994), 334.

A. Szpunar, *Odszkodowanie za szkodę majątkową. Szkoda na mieniu i osobie* (Branta, 1998), 118, 119.

J. Taeger, 'Produkt- und Produzentenhaftung bei Schäden durch fehlerhafte Computerprogramme', *Computer und Recht* (CR), (1996) 257, 261.

J. Tanega, 'Implications of Environmental Liability on the Insurance Industry', *Journal of Environmental Law*, 8(1) (1996) 115–138, 117.

B.S. Tatum, 'Exclusivity of the Warsaw Convention's Cause of Action: The U.S. Supreme Court Removes Some of the Expansive Views Foundations in Zicherman v. Korean Air Lines Co., Ltd.', *Ga. J. Int'l & Comp. L.*, 26 (1997) 537.

C. Thole, 'Die Geschäftsführung ohne Auftrag auf dem Rückzug – Das Ende des "auch fremden" Geschäfts?' *Neue Juristische Wochenschrift* (NJW), (2010) 1243, 1243 ff.

A. Toffoli, J.M. Lefèvre et al., 'Towards the Identification of Warning Criteria: Analysis of a Ship Accident Database', *Applied Ocean Research*, 27(6) (2005) 281–291.

T. Tomacik, W. Healy, C. Dawson, *A Case Study of: Mass Tort Litigation: Litigating the 9/11 Disaster* (ABA, 2013).

TOVALOP, *International Legal Materials*, 8 (1969) 497–501.

M.J. Trebilcock and R.J. Daniels, 'Rationales and Instruments for Government Intervention in Natural Disasters' in R.J. Daniels, D.F. Kettl and H. Kunreuther (eds.), *On Risk and Disaster – Lessons from Hurricane Katrina* (University of Pennsylvania Press, 2006), 89–107.

D. Treadwell, 'Pan Am Guilty of 'Willful Misconduct: Verdict: Jury finds airline, now defunct, to be negligent in the Lockerbie bombing that claimed 270 lives. Victims' families can now seek further damages', *Los Angeles Times*, 11 July 1992.

T. Tridimas, *The General Principles of EU Law* (Oxford University Press, 2nd edn, 2006).

A. Tunc, 'The loi badinter. Ten years of experience', *Maastricht Journal of European and Comparative Law*, 4 (1996) 3.

UN Economic Commission for Europe, www.unece.org/env/civil-liability/welcome.html.

UN Environmental Policy, www.unece.org/env/welcome.html.

UN Treaty Collection, https://treaties.un.org/.

A. Valriberas Sanz, *Cuerpo Nacional de Policía y Sistema Policial Español* (Marcial Pons, 1999), 139 ff.

C. Van Schoubroeck, 'Objectieve Aansprakelijkheid en Verzekeringsplicht bij Schade door Rampen. Een Belgische Case-Study' in A. Akkermans and E.

Brans (eds.), *Aansprakelijkheidheid en Schadeverhaal bij Rampen* (Ars Aequi Libri, 2002), 145–171.

B. Van Velthoven, 'Empirics of Tort' in M. Faure (ed.), *Tort Law and Economics* (Edward Elgar, 2010), 453–498.

T. Vanden Borre, 'Nuclear Liability: An Anachronism in EU Energy Policy?' in M.M. RoggenKamp and U. Hammer (eds.), *European Energy Law Report VII* (Intersentia, 2010), 192.

R. Vandermeeren, *Responsabilité des Services de Police, Répertoire de la Responsabilité de la Puissance Publique* (Dalloz, 2005).

X. Vásquez-Maignan, *Liability and Compensation for Nuclear Damage* (OECD Nuclear Energy Agency 26, 2012), available at www.aec.gov.tw/www/info/files/energy_news_01142.pdf.

A. Verheij, 'Shifts in Governance: Oil Pollution' in M. Faure and A. Verheij (eds.), *Shifts in Compensation for Environmental Damage* (Springer, 2007), 133–195.

L. Viezens, 'Katastrophenschutzrecht – Grundlagen und Perspektiven', *Versicherungsrecht* (VersR), (2007) 1494.

K.W. Viscusi, 'The Hold-up Problem: Why it is Urgent to Rethink the Economics of Disaster Insurance Protection', in E. Michel-Kerjan and P. Slovic (eds.), *The Irrational Economist: Making Decisions in a Dangerous World* (Public Affairs Books, 2010), 142–148.

T. Von Ungern-Sternberg, 'The Limits of Competition: Housing Insurance in Switzerland', *European Economic Review*, 40 (1996) 1111.

G. Wagner, 'De gemeinschaftsrechtliche Umwelthaftung aus der Sicht der Zivilrecht' in R. Hendler and P. Marburger (eds.), *Umwelthaftung nach neuem EG-Recht* (Berlin, 2005).

'§ 823' in F.-J. Säcker and R. Rixecker (eds.), *Münchener Kommentar zum Bürgerlichen Gesetzbuch* (CH Beck, 5th edn, 2009), vol. 5, no. 13.

M.L. Wald, 'Details Emerge on Flight 93', *New York Times*, 22 July 2004.

J. Walter and D. Kettle, 'The Katrina Breakdown', in R. Daniels, F. Kettle and H. Kunreuther. (eds.), *On Risk and Disaster. Lessons from Hurricane Katrina* (University of Pennsylvania Press, 1983), 255–261.

H. Wang, 'Shifts in Governance in the International Regime of Marine Oil Pollution Compensation: A Legal History Perspective', in M. Faure and A. Verheij (eds.), *Shifts in Compensation for Environmental Damage* (Springer, 2007), 212–219.

A. Watabe, 'An Economic Analysis of Nuclear Accidents in Japan', in G.V. Liu (ed.), *Perspectives on International State and Local Economics* (Nova Science Publishers, 2006), 209–234.

J. Weitzdörfer, 'Die Haftung für Nuklearschäden nach japanischem Atomrecht – Rechtsprobleme der Reaktorkatastrophe von Fukushima I', *Journal of Japanese Law*, 31 (2011) 61–115.

L. Wendel, 'Compensation in the Swedish Healthcare Sector', in J. Dute et al. (eds.), *No Fault Compensation in the Healthcare Sector* (Springer, 2004), 367.

P.E. Wenneras, 'Permit Defences in Environmental Liability Regimes – Subsidizing Environmental Damage in the EC?', *Yearbook of European Environmental Law* (Oxford University Press, 2004), vol. 4.

C.R. Whitney, 'Jetliners Carrying 258 to U.S. Crashes in Scottish Town', *New York Times*, 22 December 1988.

M. Wilde, *Civil Liability for Environmental Damage. Comparative Analysis of Law and Policy in Europe and the US* (Kluwer Law International, 2nd edn, 2013).

N. Yamori and T. Okada, 'The Japanese Insurance Market and Companies: Recent Trends' in J.D. Cummins and B. Venard (eds.), *Handbook of International Insurance: Between Global Dynamics and Local Contingincies* (Springer, 2007).

R. Yoshiada, 'GE Plan Followed with Inflexibility', *The Japan Times*, 14 July 2011.

M. Yzquierdo, 'Responsabilidad civil por accidentes de trabajo' in F. Reglero (ed.), *Tratado de responsabilidad civil III* (Thomson-Aranzadi, 2008) 804 ff.

R. Zeckhauser, 'The Economics of Catastrophes', *Journal of Risk and Uncertainty*, 12 (1996) 113–140, 113.

K.A. Zscherpe and H. Lutz, 'Geräte- und Produktsicherheitsgesetz: Anwendbarkeit auf Hard- und Software', *Kommunikation und Recht* (K&R), (2005) 499, 499 ff.

Statutory materials

P.L. 107–296, House R. 107–609 (Part 1) at 118.

Parliamentary Proceedings of the Second Chamber of Representatives, 2002–03 and 2006–07.

Plan for the Prevention of Foreseeable Natural Risks (*Plan de Prévention des Risques Naturels Prévisibles*).

Report from the Commission to the Council and the European Parliament on the operation of Commission Regulation No 3932/92.

Residential and Commercial Earthquake Insurance Coverage Study, California Department of Insurance, www.insurance.ca.gov/0400-news/0200-studies-reports/0300-earthquake-study/index.cfm.

Stationery Office, 'The Victims of Overseas Terrorism Compensation Scheme 2012' (Gov.uk, 27 November 2012), www.official-documents.gov.uk/document/other/9780108512124/9780108512124.asp.

Statute of the Consortium for Insurance Compensation (*Estatuto Legal del Consorcio de Compensación de Seguros*, ECCS). www.ccrif.org/partnerships/WFCP/Sessions/Day2/France_GAREAT_WFCP_Meeting_Oct_2011.pdf.

www.elmundo.es/documentos/2004/03/espana/atentados11m/hechos.html.

www.gareat.com/gareat/rtaccueil.nsf/documentation?Openpage.

www.iags.org/costof911.html www.nytimes.com/interactive/2011/09/08/us/sept-11-reckoning/cost-graphic.html?_r=0

www.oecd-nea.org/law/legislation/sweden.pdf

www.terrorismeverzekerd.nl

www.theguardian.com/uk/july7

Fukushima – 'Compensation of Nuclear Damage after Great Earthquake in Japan', *Enformable Nuclear News*, 13 December 2011, http://enformable.com/2011/12/fukushima-compensation-of-nuclear-damage-after-great-earthquake-in-japan/.

'Japan's Parliament Approves TEPCO Compensation Plan', BBC News, 3 August 2011, www.bbc.co.uk/news/business-14383832.

Min Alimentation, Agriculture et Pêche, req no 337062, *AJDA* 2011.1985, obs Grand.

Outline of the Bill of the Act to Establish Nuclear Damage Compensation Facilitation Corporation, Ministry of Economics, Trade and Industry, www.meti.go.jp/english/earthquake/nuclear/roadmap/pdf/20110614_damage_corporation_2.pdf.

Outline of the Nuclear Damage Compensation Facilitation Corporation Act, Ministry of Economics, Trade and Industry (August 2011), www.meti.go.jp/english/earthquake/nuclear/roadmap/pdf/20111012_nuclear_damages_2.pdf.

The Demand for Flood Insurance: Statement before the Comm. On Banking, Housing, and Urban Affairs 2 (Oct 18, 2005) (Statement of Mark Browne, Gerard D. Stephens CPCU Chair in Risk Management and Insurance).

The French GAV® Accident Compensation, SCOR Technical Newsl (SCOR Group, Paris, France), Oct 2003, at 2, www.scor.com/en/www/fileadmin/uploads/publics/NTNV2003_05_en_tuknv05.pdf.

The Homeland Security and Defense Business Council, 'Why Robust Use of the SAFETY Act Is Critical to Homeland Security & How to Get There', The Homeland Security and Defense Business Council, October 2008, 16.

Testimony by DHS Assistant Secretary Parney Albright, 'Implementing the SAFETY Act: Advancing New Technologies for Homeland Security', Hearing before the House Committee on Government Reform, 12.

'World in Brief; Washington, D.C.: Court Rejects Award in Fatal KAL Flight', *Los Angeles Times*, 8 May 1991.

Conventions and protocols

1952 Rome Convention.

1978 Protocol.

Brussels Complementary Convention.

Brussels Convention on the Liability of Operators of Nuclear Ships.

Bunker Convention.

Civil Liability Protocol and Compensation for Damage Caused by the Transboundary Effects of Industrial Accidents on Transboundary Waters to the 1992
Convention on the Protection and Use of Transboundary Watercourses and
International Lakes and to the 1992 Convention on the Transboundary Effects
of Industrial Accidents.

CLC Convention.

Convention for the Unification of Certain Rules Relating to International Carriage
by Air (Warsaw, 12 October 1929).

Convention on Supplementary Compensation for Nuclear Damage.

Convention on the Liability of Operators of Nuclear Ships.

Convention on the Transboundary Effects of Industrial Accidents.

Convention Supplementary to the Paris Convention on Third Party Liability in the
Field of Nuclear Energy.

European Social Charter of 18 October 1961.

Fund Convention 1971.

HNS Convention.

ILO-Conventions No. 24.

International Convention on Civil Liability for Oil Pollution Damage.

Joint Protocol relating to the Application of the Vienna Convention and the Paris
Convention.

Liability Convention.

Montreal Convention.

Paris Convention on Third Party Liability in the Field of Nuclear Energy.

Treaty on Principles Governing the Activities of States in the Exploration and Use
of Outer Space, including the Moon and Other Celestial Bodies.

Vienna Convention on Civil Liability for Nuclear Damage.

European legislation

Article 81, EC Treaty.

Commission Recommendation of 5 June 2008 concerning the limitation of the civil
liability of statutory auditors and audit firms (C(2008) 2274), OJ 2008, No.
L162, 21 June 2008, 39.

Commission Regulation (EEC) No 3932/92 of 21 December 1992 on the application
of Article 85(3) of the Treaty to certain categories of agreements, decisions and
concerted practices in the insurance sector, OJ 1992, No. L398, 31 December
1992, 7.

Compensation Directive.

Council Directive 93/13/EEC on unfair terms in consumer contracts, OJ 1993, No.
L95, 21 April 1993, 29 (Unfair Contract Terms Directive).

Council Framework Decision.

Council Regulation (EC) 1206/2001 on cooperation between the courts of the Member States in the taking of evidence in civil or commercial matters, OJ 2001, No. L174, 27 June 2001, 1.

Council Regulation (EC) 44/2001 on the jurisdiction and the recognition and enforcement of judgments in civil and commercial matters, OJ 2001, No. L12, 16 January 2001, 1.

Directive 2004/35/CE of the European Parliament and of the Council on environmental liability with regard to the prevention and remedying of environmental damage, OJ 2004, No. L143, 30 April 2004, 56.

Directive 2008/52/EC on certain aspects of mediation in civil and commercial matters, OJ 2008, No. L136, 24 May 2008, 3.

Directive 2012/18/EU of the European Parliament and of the Council on the control of major-accident hazards involving dangerous substances, amending and subsequently repealing Council Directive 96/82/EC, OJ 2012, No. L197, 24 July 2012, 1.

Regulation (EC) 1393/2007 on the service in the Member States of judicial and extrajudicial documents in civil of commercial matters (service of documents), and repealing Council Regulation (EC) 1348/2000, OJ 2007, No. L324, 10 December 2007, 79.

Regulation (EC) 592/2008 of the European Parliament and of the Council of 17 June 2008 on the law applicable to contractual obligations (Rome I), OJ 2008, No. 177, 4 July 2008, 6 (Rome I Regulation).

Regulation (EC) 864/2007 of the European Parliament and of the Council of 11 July 2007 on the law applicable to non-contractual obligations (Rome II), OJ 2007, No. L199, 31 July 2007, 40 (Rome II Regulation).

INDEX

differentiation, 214, 217, 268, 278, 306
  premium, 213, 214, 216
  risk, 263, 277–279
direct causal links, 109, 149, 173, 178,
    192, 199, 203
direct liability, 148, 188, 192, 195, 199,
    201, 205
  limitations, 244, 315
direct tortfeasors, 139, 147, 171, 306
Directive 2004/80/EC relating to
    compensation to crime victims,
    62–63
  implications for liability for
    terrorism-related risk, 63
  summary of regime, 62
disaster insurance, 217, 224, 264–269,
    274
disaster relief measures, 164, 197
disaster risk, 267
disasters, 209, 216, 217–220, 221, 223,
    230, 262, 265–267, 269–270
  exceptional natural, 52, 142, 194
  large-scale natural, 262, 273, 276
  technological, 61, 104, 112, 269
  and terrorism, 222, 237–238, 262,
    272, 276
discretion, 59, 77, 107, 109, 118, 143,
    204, 253, 258–259
disturbances, 94, 109, 116, 150
diversification, cross-time, 222,
    280
duties, 88, 125, 161–162, 163, 167,
    169–171, 267–268, 278,
    311–313
  of care, 88–89, 91, 179, 189–190,
    195, 199, 202, 205, 331–332
    breach and fault, 89
    towards third parties, 189–190
  general, 88, 171, 311
  non-contractual, 142, 179, 183, 194,
    200
  non-delegable, 91, 163
  to provide financial security, 55
  regulatory, 105, 266
  statutory, 87–88, 105, 108, 115

earthquakes, 129–130, 131–132,
    134–136, 141, 142–144,

    150–151, 193–195, 225–226,
    271
  strong/heavy, 128, 136, 145, 195
ECJ (European Court of Justice), *see*
    CJEU
ecological damage, 11, 12, 15, 29, 39,
    50, 131–132
economic actors, 239–241, 245,
    246–249, 250, 284, 287
economic analysis of liability for
    terrorism-related risk, 300–315
economic losses, 36, 121, 132, 150, 154,
    240, 304
  compensability of pure, 108–109,
    190, 192, 203
  consequential, 108, 172, 192
economic operators, 284, 287, 298,
    319–320, 335
economic perspective, 7, 55, 300–301,
    303, 309, 313–314, 319
effectiveness, 48, 58, 239, 246, 254,
    256–257
efficient prevention of damage, 307,
    324
ELD (Environmental Liability
    Directive), 6, 57–58, 63–68, 82,
    105, 165, 203, 304–306, 331
  causation, 66–67
  exclusions and defences, 64–66
  implications for terrorism-related
    risk, 67–68
  summary of regime, 63–64
emergencies, 128, 136, 172–174, 177,
    198–199, 200
empirical evidence, 264–266, 276, 296,
    298, 302, 311
employees, 64–65, 89–90, 145–148,
    168, 172, 174, 182, 186, 187–189
employers, 89–90, 145–148, 168, 186
employment, 13, 18, 89–90, 148
  contracts, 147, 168
End User Licensing Agreements
    (EULAs), 242–243
enforcement, 6, 57, 78, 84
England and Wales, 85, 91–92, 97,
    106–107, 118–119, 149–150,
    169–170, 185, 196–197
  aeroplane accidents, 172, 178, 179

basis of liability, 37–38
financial security and compensation
    mechanism, 42
jurisdictional issues, 42–43
liable persons, 38–39
limitation of liability, 39–42
summary of regime, 36–37
International Convention on the
    Establishment of an
    International Fund for
    Compensation for Oil Pollution
    Damage, *see* Fund Convention
International Fund for Compensation
    for Oil Pollution Damage, 28, 51
international law, 6, 11, 34, 50, 300,
    303, 313, 315
    lessons from, 307
    liability for terrorism-related risks,
    11–55
international nuclear liability
    conventions, 225
international reinsurance market, 234
intervention, state, 26, 52, 55, 221–222,
    223, 225–226, 238
irresistibility, 134, 143–144, 194
insurance, liability, *see* liability
    insurance

Japan
    Fukushima, 20, 223, 225–230, 237,
    308
    Nuclear Damage Compensation
    Facilitation Corporation, 227
juridical persons, 49–50
jurisdiction, 6, 27, 34, 36, 42–43,
    78–80, 84, 85, 100, 259
    exclusive, 27, 42, 78, 100, 255, 259

knowledge, 18, 31, 38, 40, 50, 73, 93, 97
    special, 89, 188, 195, 201
    technical, 60, 66, 72, 73, 244
Korean Air Lines shootdown, 285–286

labour relations, 90, 148
landing, 172, 177, 198–199, 200
large liability exposure, 242, 304
large-scale natural disasters, 262, 273,
    276

large-scale terrorist attacks, 283,
    322
launching States, 48–50, 52–53
legal persons, 46, 63
legal systems, 113, 148, 183, 205, 219,
    302–304, 309
    victims in European, 302–303
legal writers, 120, 158, 175–177
legislation, 21–22, 26, 29, 57, 59,
    82–84, 252, 326–328, 330
legitimate expectations, 328
liability
    absolute, 21, 48, 50
    apportionment of, 67, 107, 118, 135,
    191
    attribution of, *see* attribution of
    liability
    basis of, *see* basis of liability
    burden of, 33, 90, 147, 200, 324
    caps, 13–14, 17–18, 39–40, 93,
    96–97, 100–102, 111, 260–261,
    317–319
    higher, 18, 100–101
    in cases of force majeure, 92, 185
    catastrophic, 217, 250, 299
    congruence with coverage, 100
    for damage, 4, 7, 15, 57, 97, 102, 183,
    330–331, 337
    caused by natural disaster or act of
    terror, 195–201, 205–206
    pure economic loss and
    environmental damage, 7,
    192–195
    deterrent effect of, 280, 282, 315,
    319, 334
    direct, *see* direct liability
    environmental, *see* environmental
    liability
    EU product, 189, 202
    exclusion of, 38, 110, 308
    exposure, 56–57, 82–84, 241–243,
    245–246, 248–251, 297–299,
    309–311, 327–328, 331–332
    extra-contractual, 87, 91, 186, 189,
    200, 202, 203–204
    fault-based, *see* fault-based liability
    heads of, 87, 95, 114, 185, 189,
    193–194, 195, 197, 202

Books in the series

Necessity, Proportionality and the Use of Force by States
Judith Gardam

International Legal Argument in the Permanent Court of International Justice: The Rise of the International Judiciary
Ole Spiermann

Great Powers and Outlaw States: Unequal Sovereigns in the International Legal Order
Gerry Simpson

Local Remedies in International Law
C.F. Amerasinghe

Reading Humanitarian Intervention:Human Rights and the Use of Force in International Law
Anne Orford

Conflict of Norms in Public International Law: How WTO Law Relates to Other Rules of International Law
Joost Pauwelyn

Transboundary Damage in International Law
Hanqin Xue

European Criminal Procedures
Edited by Mireille Delmas-Marty and John Spencer

The Accountability of Armed Opposition Groups in International Law
Liesbeth Zegveld

Sharing Transboundary Resources: International Law and Optimal Resource Use
Eyal Benvenisti

International Human Rights and Humanitarian Law
René Provost

Remedies Against International Organisations
Karel Wellens

Diversity and Self-Determination in International Law
Karen Knop

The Law of Internal Armed Conflict
Lindsay Moir

International Commercial Arbitration and African States: Practice, Participation and Institutional Development
Amazu A. Asouzu

The Enforceability of Promises in European Contract Law
James Gordley

International Law in Antiquity
David J. Bederman

Money Laundering: A New International Law Enforcement Model
Guy Stessens

Good Faith in European Contract Law
Reinhard Zimmermann and Simon Whittaker

On Civil Procedure
J. Jolowicz

Trusts: A Comparative Study
Maurizio Lupoi

The Right to Property in Commonwealth Constitutions
Tom Allen

International Organizations Before National Courts
August Reinisch

The Changing International Law of High Seas Fisheries
Francisco Orrego Vicuña

Trade and the Environment: A Comparative Study of EC and US Law
Damien Geradin

Unjust Enrichment: A Study of Private Law and Public Values
Hanoch Dagan

Religious Liberty and International Law in Europe
Malcolm D. Evans

Ethics and Authority in International Law
Alfred P. Rubin

Sovereignty Over Natural Resources: Balancing Rights and Duties
Nico Schrijver

The Polar Regions and the Development of International Law
Donald R. Rothwell

Fragmentation and the International Relations of Micro-States: Self-determination and Statehood
Jorri Duursma

Principles of the Institutional Law of International Organizations
C.F. Amerasinghe

CPSIA information can be obtained
at www.ICGtesting.com
Printed in the USA
LVHW052224070119
603029LV00021B/268

9 781107 496552